To Teach, to Delight, and to Move:

Theological Education in a Post-Christian World

To Teach, to Delight, and to Move:

Theological Education in a Post-Christian World

Edited by

David S. Cunningham

Cascade Books
A division of *Wipf & Stock Publishers*
199 West 8th Avenue, Suite 3 • Eugene OR 97401

Cascade Books
A division of Wipf and Stock Publishers
199 W 8th Ave, Suite 3
Eugene, OR 97401

To Teach, To Delight, and To Move
Theological Education in a Post-Christian World
Edited by David S. Cunningham
Copyright©2004 by David S. Cunningham
ISBN: 1-59244-986-7
Publication date 10/30/2004.

A revised version of chapter 5 was published as "Teaching as Confessing: Redeeming a Theological Trope for Pedagogy," *Teaching Theology and Religion* 2/3 (October 1999): 143-53

To the memory of

Donald Harrisville Juel

colleague and friend

whose joyful love of biblical texts
and commitment to theological education
taught, moved, and delighted us
across the years

this volume is dedicated
in gratitude and with thanksgiving

Table of Contents

Foreword • L. Gregory Jones   ix

Introduction: Re-Visioning Theological Education   1

Part One: Theological Education as Faithful Persuasion

1. The Classical Rhetorical Tradition and Theological Education • David S. Cunningham, Don H. Compier, and James L. Boyce   13

2. Beyond the Classical Paradigm: Contemporary Rhetorical Analysis and Theological Education • Janet L. Weathers   35

3. Rhetoric, Postmodernism, and Theological Education: What Has Vincennes to do with Athens *or* Jerusalem? • A. K. M. Adam   61

Part Two: The Tasks of Theological Education

4. Theology as Communication: Revelation, Faith, and the Church as Ongoing Dialogues • Bradford E. Hinze   85

5. Theology as Confession: Redeeming a Theological Trope for Pedagogy • Stephen H. Webb   109

6. Theology as Discernment: Truth, Power, and Authority • Wes Avram   127

7. Theology as Testimony: Rhetoric, Public Theology, and Education for Ministry • Don H. Compier   149

Part Three: Re-Visioning the Theological Encyclopedia

8. Rhetoric and Practical Theology: Toward a New Paradigm •
   Richard R. Osmer   171

9. Rhetoric and the Word of God: Treasure in Earthen Vessels •
   James L. Boyce   201

10. Rhetoric and Historical Theology: Gregory the Theologian •
    Frederick W. Norris   223

11. Rhetoric and Christian Doctrine: Trinity and Teaching •
    David S. Cunningham   243

12. Rhetoric and Proclamation: A Relational Paradigm •
    Susan Karen Hedahl   267

Conclusion: Theory in Practice

A Rhetorical Approach to Theological Education: Assessing
an Attempt at Re-Visioning a Curriculum •
Donald Juel and Patrick Keifert   281

Bibliography: Rhetorical Resources for Theological Education   297

List of Contributors   305

Index of Names   309

Index of Subjects   315

Foreword

L. Gregory Jones
Dean, Duke University Divinity School

What are the purposes of theological education? What and who are its primary constituencies? What are the appropriate structures and contexts in which theological education ought to occur? What patterns of thinking and what kind of character do theological educators hope graduates will exhibit? What kinds of courses need to be required, and in what sequence, to cultivate those patterns of thinking and that character? How does theological education need to be changed and re-thought in order more adequately to fulfill its mission?

Such questions have been at the heart of an extended series of conversations about theological education over the past two decades. These conversations were initiated by an increasingly widespread sense that the "four-fold" structure of modern theological education, a curriculum organized around divisions of Bible, History, Theology, and Ministry, was not working effectively. As the conversations developed, it became apparent that the sense of what was broken was more widely shared than either diagnoses of what caused the brokenness or prognoses for the appropriate remedies.

Hence, despite vigorous discussion and debate throughout the 1980s and 1990s about the nature and purpose of theological education and despite substantively developed and creative proposals for transformative (and sometimes radical) change, comparatively little actually has changed in theological education. So Edward Farley, whose 1983 landmark book

Theologia: The Fragmentation and Unity of Theological Education was widely hailed as launching these conversations, published an article in *The Christian Century* at the end of the 1990s asking why there had been so little change.

Part of the problem is, to be sure, that it is difficult to effect change in any large-scale enterprise, especially an educational system that had taken root over two centuries and that involves tenured faculty where turnover in leadership is comparatively slow. Part of the difficulty is also that there are implicit (and sometimes explicit) disagreements among theological educators about the *telos* of this education. To take but one example, do seminaries exist primarily to educate persons for ordained ministry, or for some other or more comprehensive purpose?

Most determinatively, I would suggest that such change is difficult because each of the questions identified in the first paragraph have complicated histories that involve intellectual judgments and arguments, theological and ecclesial commitments and controversies, institutional configurations and power structures, as well as pragmatic considerations of what is desirable and feasible in particular local circumstances.

Yet there is also exciting ferment that can bring renewal, but perhaps not in the ways the earlier conversations anticipated. This ferment is evident because, positively, there have been broader intellectual, ecclesial, and cultural developments that are encouraging fresh thinking and even retrievals of received wisdom about patterns of education and formation. Yet the ferment is also evident because, negatively, theological educators are increasingly compelled to self-examination by questions and criticisms that are coming both from within the churches to which they are connected and from other academic structures that no longer assume the importance or even the relevance of theological education.

In such a time and in the midst of the contemporary contexts of North American theological education, where is hope to be found? In many places, and not least among people who are willing to work hard to examine cherished assumptions, retrieve insights from the past, rethink conventional disciplinary boundaries, and explore new and renewed ways of connecting things that are often left fragmented — theory and practice; church, academy, and world; reason, emotion, and action; education, formation, and service. Or, to take up one of the central themes of this book, *logos*, *ēthos*, and *pathos*.

In short, hope can be found in books such as this, books that emerge out of extended conversation among talented and committed scholars who share enough in common to make their conversation fruitful, yet who have enough differences to make that conversation necessary. These authors share a conviction that what they call "the classical rhetorical tradition and its twentieth-century successors" provide insights that can illumine our contemporary predicament, offer wisdom from previous eras of Christian faith and its modes of theological education, and enliven our imagination for concrete, constructive change in the future. Yet the authors, who come from different academic disciplines, ecclesial bodies, and specific institutional contexts, also have diverse angles of vision that invite readers to enter the conversation.

The essays in this book provide an opportunity to reorient our thinking precisely because they first disorient us. They challenge received assumptions about modern structures of theological education as well as the intellectual assumptions that underlie those structures. They disorient us by showing how differently education, including theological education, has been understood and practiced in other eras. And they create a constructive disorientation by pointing out the various thickets of the complicated histories that have shaped us and the ways we think about fundamental questions.

In so doing, they also commend a particular way, or set of ways, of thinking about theological education, what the concluding essay calls "a rhetorical approach." Yet it may not be immediately obvious to readers what such an approach would entail. There are at least two ways of thinking about what might be involved here. The first might be called a "minimalist" understanding, a sense that classical rhetoric (and its twentieth-century successors) provides a lens for seeing aspects of theological education in fresh ways and thus for imagining some creative and constructive change. So, for example, it is not insignificant that Augustine remained a rhetor and drew on the rhetorical tradition in his theological reflection, after his conversion to Christianity.

The second might be called a "maximalist" understanding, a conviction that classical rhetoric (and its twentieth-century successors) provides the normative means by which we ought to understand the task of theology as well as theological education. On this view, the rhetorical tradition ought to be the fundamental and normative approach to knowledge and reality, and thus rhetoric should be *the* central organizing approach for theological education.

The essays in this book do not fit neatly into either of these understandings, and the authors seem to fall along various places of the spectrum between a minimalist and a maximalist approach. But that is indeed part of the attraction of the book, so long as we recognize that there is not a single way of understanding the significance of rhetoric for theological education. That is, even those who might dissent from the stronger intellectual accounts of rhetoric as a mode of knowing (in relation to, for example, classical logic), still ought to be able to glean insights of how rhetorical approaches and analyses can illumine important themes that theological education needs to address.

In that sense, then, this is an important book precisely because it does not presume any one method — or even any one proposal — for how theological education ought to be changed. Rather, it offers insightful essays, themselves well-written and with an ear for persuasion, about important matters to which theological educators ought to attend. Indeed, engaging this book can help to reframe the fundamental questions that we ask and debate within the churches — as well as within theological education.

To take but one example: rhetorical analyses ought to press us to rethink how we discuss issues of formation (whether, spiritual, moral, or — even less often discussed — intellectual) and education. We tend to start with a presumption that there are two enterprises here: education, which is fundamentally rational and about conveying information, and formation, which covers that which is non-rational. But rhetorical analyses, including this book, ought to press us to recognize that education is intrinsically formative (for good or for ill), and formation is intrinsically educational. This is not a problem peculiar to theological education, for as Julie Reuben has shown in her book *The Making of the Modern University: Intellectual Transformation and the Marginalization of Morality* (Chicago: University of Chicago Press, 1996), the modern research university has typically marginalized moral formation for exactly the same reasons. But theological education, precisely because of the centrality of spiritual and moral formation to our task, could lead the way toward a rethinking of the categories and a reframing of the questions.

Rhetorical analysis in general, and the essays in this book in particular, are important means for reframing our questions as well as pressing us toward constructive change. As one who remains skeptical of the "maximalist" understanding of rhetoric's significance for theology and theological education, I nonetheless am absolutely convinced that rhetoric offers a significant way to address the challenges and opportunities of theological education in contemporary North America. If we truly want to envision transformation and implement life-giving change in theological education, the essays in this book are a crucial part of that conversation. Their authors have much to teach us; conversing with them is a delight; and they can move us to new patterns of thought and action. We are in their debt.

Introduction: Re-Visioning Theological Education

David S. Cunningham

Theological education has been a topic of concern for the church, and for the academy, from the earliest days of the Christian era. The new faith had particular beliefs and practices that differentiated it both from Judaism and from the Hellenistic mystery cults. How were new converts to be taught the faith? In addition, Christianity understood itself as "good news" that should be offered to all people. How were potential leaders to understand it rightly, so that they could proclaim it to the widest possible audience? The faith was to spread very quickly into parts of the world that differed markedly from one another. How could the education of Christians be attentive to local customs and cultures, while maintaining some sense of unity?

These questions have been with Christianity from its origins, and they continue to demand our attention in the present day. Throughout the church's long history, Christians have employed a wide variety of models for the education of one another and of their leaders; in one era, monastic orders took the lead, while in another time and place, popular itinerant preaching was the most common way to catechize and to inspire. No single model has dominated in all times and all places.

Indeed, the model of theological education that holds the most sway in the present era — the one employed by most seminaries and divinity schools in Europe and North America today — is actually relatively new. It began to take shape with the founding of the University of Berlin, the first "modern" university. At that time, the question of the moment was: what role should the university play in the preparation of Church leaders?

Unsurprisingly, the dominant models for modern theological education mirrored the dominant curricular models of the modern university.[1]

But as we are all aware, the "modern" era has begun to display certain stresses and strains. We no longer have the degree of confidence that we once had in achieving a neutral, "objective" accounting of all phenomena. We are increasingly aware of the role of the observer in every interpretive process. We know that modern claims about "rationality" were often heavily invested with assumptions about race, gender, social class, sexual orientation, and so many other particularities. As we look back on these claims now, from our present perspective, we find their pretensions to universality incredibly parochial and often rather silly. A century of world war, genocide, oppression, and degradation has put a stop to all but the most rose-tinted claims about the ever-upward progress of the human race.

Although the modern era was not always particularly kind to Christianity, it did usually assume the ongoing presence and dominance of the Christian faith; it assumed that Christendom would continue to be present, at least as a vestige of its former glory, into the foreseeable future. Not all people would be believers, but most could be expected to have learned a good deal about the Christian faith, almost by osmosis. Now, as the modern era comes to an end, so must this assumption (which was, in any case, usually somewhat overstated). No longer can we expect everyone to be aware of even the most basic outlines of a faith and a worldview that was, at one time, an integral part of European culture. We have entered a post-Christian era.

Our increasing awareness of these various symptoms of "the end of modernity" has put similar strains on the models of theological education that were forged during the modern era. The coherent systems of thought, modeled on the newly-emerging social sciences and believed to provide an "objective" basis for theological education, are no longer serviceable. The supposedly all-encompassing canons of much "enlightenment rationality" are regularly interrogated by new perspectives and shown to be narrow and exclusive. All theological education, indeed all catechesis, must begin at a more and more basic stage — unable to rely on the cultural transmission of the faith. All over the world, church leaders and academic theologians are

---

[1]For a thorough discussion of these developments, see David H. Kelsey, *Between Athens and Berlin: The Theological Education Debate* (Grand Rapids, Mich.: William B. Eerdmans, 1993).

searching for ways to meet these challenges and to re-envision theological education for a postmodern, post-Christian era.

This book offers one such attempt at re-visioning theological education. Its contributors teach in seminaries and church-related colleges across the United States, in a variety of denominational settings: Christian Church, Community of Christ, Disciples of Christ, Episcopalian, Lutheran, Presbyterian, and Roman Catholic. Taken together, these authors have amassed literally hundreds of years of teaching and research in the service of the church and the academy. And they have all discovered new insights for the future of theological education in what might appear, at first glance, to be an unlikely source: namely, the classical rhetorical tradition and its twentieth-century successors.

The sources of these contributors' interest in rhetoric are widely varied. Some of them have professional training in the discipline, either at the undergraduate or the Ph.D. level; others have made it the methodological center of a dissertation or other book-length research project in theology; still others have been employing it as an educational tool for decades in their own pedagogical practices. But despite the different ways in which the contributors have developed their interests in rhetoric, they are alike in one important respect: they have been able to see beyond the common tendency to malign rhetoric as "mere ornamentation" or "deceptive speech." Instead, they have come to see it as it was seen by its greatest theoreticians and practitioners: namely, as a set of communicative tools for educating, pleasing, and moving the will of any given audience. Saint Augustine believed that the chief goals of Christian theology, like those of rhetoric, should be "to teach, to delight, and to move."[2] And the contributors to this volume are united in their conviction that these must also be the goals of theological education in a post-Christian era.

We have all spent some significant time investigating the recent renaissance of scholarly interest in the classical rhetorical tradition, and in concomitant developments in argumentation theory, narrative rationality, and postmodern philosophy. We believe that these conversations can generate a perspective on theological education that can integrate Christianity's traditional roots with the new challenges that have appeared at the end of modernity. In order to attend to both these elements, any new theological vision will need to be fully aware of the diversity of

[2]*De doctrina Christiana* IV.27[74].

Christianity, but at the same time, it must also maintain a sense of the identity of the whole.

In the early 1990s, a series of conversations and scholarly projects were begun under the general heading of "The Bible and Theological Education." These conversations, funded by the Lilly Endowment, Inc., led to a number of specific projects in research and teaching. One group chose to examine the recent flurry of interest in the classical rhetorical tradition, and particularly the recent (even more recent) theological appropriation of that tradition. To this end, a group of scholars who had shared an ongoing interest in this area began to gather, approximately twice a year, in order to present their research, to plan joint projects, and to establish common ground for conversation. Although the precise composition of the group varied over time, nearly all of the contributors to the present volume were in attendance at nearly all of the meetings. Eventually, we were able to write essays that we believed could contribute productively to a volume such as this, intended to describe the benefits of a rhetorical approach to theological education. Because the essays in this volume grew out of a long-term conversation, the reader will discover a considerable level of coherence among the chapters. Indeed, it might be best to think of this book as a jointly-authored work, attempting to present an integrated vision for the future of theological education.

At the same time, we have made no attempt to offer a "blueprint" for curriculum revision, nor have we recommended specific policies that seminaries should adopt in order to implement the approach that we are attempting to sketch here. Every seminary or divinity school is different, and each one will have particular goals and constraints that would make it impossible to devise a plan in which "one size fits all." Instead, we think of this book as an attempt to draw other theological educators into the conversation that we have been having amongst ourselves for the past several years.

Such a conversation, we believe, is long overdue; moreover, it is the only real way that change is likely to come about. It has been remarked that "the real curriculum of any educational institution is the conversation that the students and the faculty have amongst themselves." If that claim is true, then the best way to re-orient theological education for a post-Christian era is to encourage seminary faculties and student bodies to enter into such a conversation. We have attempted to provide one model for doing so in the pages that follow.

Part One of the volume, "Theological Education as Faithful Persuasion," seeks to outline the basic elements of a rhetorical approach to theological education. It does so in three steps, covering the history of the rhetorical tradition in more-or-less chronological fashion. Its three constituent chapters focus on the pre-modern, modern, and postmodern eras, respectively.

The opening chapter is jointly authored by three of the volume's contributors, each of whom wrote from his special area of interest. Entitled "The Classical Rhetorical Tradition and Theological Education," it introduces readers to ancient rhetoric and provides a general perspective on its historical sojourn. This chapter introduces many of the key concepts and assumptions that will be at work throughout the volume, and it offers some preliminary suggestions as to how the rhetorical tradition might help address some of the issues now facing theological educators.

In Chapter 2, Janet Weathers, formerly of Princeton Theological Seminary, helps us to move "Beyond the Classical Paradigm." Her essay employs the work of several important twentieth-century rhetorical theorists — including Chaïm Perelman, Lucie Olbrechts-Tyteca, Stephen Toulmin, and Walter Fisher — in order to demonstrate why Cartesian forms of rationality have had such a grip on our collective imaginations. She then shows how the rhetorical paradigm can help us fashion new forms of rationality that are more suited to our present postmodern condition. She explains how this alternative perspective can help the Church come to terms with its traditional investment in informal hierarchies, particularly those for which it can offer no compelling theological justification. This in turn leads her to explore the broader implications of such a reassessment for the practice of theological education.

We cast the net yet more widely in chapter 3 and take note of how the contemporary appropriation of rhetoric and rhetorical theory opens out into the more general category of the *postmodern*. We are fortunate to have, among the contributors to this volume, a leading theoretician and practitioner of postmodern biblical criticism, who — unlike most writers in this category — can present its nuances with clarity and without jargon. The writer is A. K. M. Adam, Professor of New Testament at Seabury-Western Theological Seminary. Professor Adam offers an exposition of Jean-François Lyotard's critique of modernity, describing its resonances with the rhetorical tradition and showing how it can help us call into question some fossilized assumptions surrounding theology and theological education. In the final part of the chapter, he provides an example of what one aspect of theological education might look like, were it to take seriously the critique of the modern project that is embodied in both rhetorical theory and postmodern philosophy. His proposal is for a new approach to "biblical theology" — a practice that he believes can integrate some of the more fragmented segments of current theological education.

By offering a concrete proposal, this chapter leads us naturally into Part Two of the book, entitled "Christian Theology as Practical Reasoning: The Tasks of Theological Education." Here, we examine some of the specific skills and abilities that we believe seminaries and theological schools should be seeking to engender in their students — abilities that the rhetorical tradition can help to generate. In this part of the book, we approach these questions, *not* through the standard lens of the "theological encyclopedia," but rather, by examining four tasks of theological education that cut across all the subdisciplines as they are presently constituted. These four tasks are: communication, confession, discernment, and testimony. All four tasks are addressed, in one way or another, by all four chapters in Part Two; but at the same time, each chapter concentrates most of its attention on one of these four tasks.

Chapter 4, "Theology as Communication: Revelation, Faith, and the Church as Ongoing Dialogues," is written by Bradford E. Hinze, Associate Professor of Theology at Marquette University. This chapter begins with the insight that "dialogue and communication constitute the very identity and practice of Christianity." The theological categories of revelation, faith, and the Church are understood to be acts of God's self-communication; but they also require a communicative response on the part of human beings. Professor Hinze explores these "dialogical" activities through the classical rhetorical categories of *logos*, *ēthos*, and *pathos*, demonstrating in each case that the most fundamental categories of Christian theology are themselves best understood in rhetorical terms.

Chapter 5, "Theology as Confession: Redeeming a Theological Trope for Pedagogy," is authored by Stephen H. Webb, Professor of Religion and Philosophy at Wabash College. Professor Webb investigates the theological practice of confession, not so much as a discrete ecclesial practice, but as a dialogical mode of conversation that is appropriate in the classroom. He suggests that we have been led astray by some of the political and cultural assumptions of modernity, which have discouraged both teachers and students from adopting a confessional stance in the classroom. We are taught to be objective, critical, and neutral, whereas theological conversation — like the rhetorical tradition — naturally expects a close-knit interrelationship among speaker, audience, and argument. Building on the argument of his recent book, *Taking Religion to School* (Grand Rapids, Mich.: Brazos Press, 2000), Professor Webb encourages us to redeem the theological trope of confession as a means to improve pedagogy within theological education (and education more broadly).

Chapter 6, "Theology as Discernment: Truth, Power, and Authority in Rhetorical Theology," is written by Wes Avram, Assistant Professor of Homiletics at Yale Divinity School. Professor Avram begins with an extended narrative that illustrates the differing sensibilities about certain central theological issues that can be evoked by a rhetorical approach to theology. He then demonstrates how three standard theological concerns are refigured by a rhetorical approach: *truth* is understood through the category of *testimony; power* must be reconfigured in terms of *discernment*, and issues of *authority* are best understood through the lens of *rhetorical positioning*, relying on a decentered (but not vacated) account of the self. At the end of his essay, Professor Avram outlines a number of important implications of this approach for theological education.

This second part of the book concludes with chapter 7, "Rhetoric as Testimony: Public Theology, Rhetoric, and Education for Ministry." Here, Don H. Compier, Dean of Community of Christ Seminary, Graceland University, explores the role of theological education in helping leaders address a wider public. The obstacles here are significant, in that theology often runs the risk of either retreating from all broader conversations, or collapsing itself and its categories into those of the wider public. Professor Compier suggests that the rhetorical tradition provides us with a vocabulary and an approach to practical reasoning that can offer other alternatives. His essay emphasizes the importance of training future Christian leaders to speak to a wider audience, particularly in our postmodern, post-Christian context.

In Part Three of the book, we attend to the very concrete and practical question of how the standard theological subdisciplines might be revised and reconfigured through attention to rhetorical categories. For a very long time, the task of theological education has been structured according to a four-fold pattern, along the lines delineated by the academic guild: biblical, historical, doctrinal, and practical theology. There are, of course, some very sensible reasons for such a division. Nevertheless, given that the standard theological encyclopedia was developed under particularly modern (and largely anti-rhetorical) influences, it will behoove us, at the end of modernity, to submit it to some fairly severe scrutiny. The essays in this part of the book attempt to do precisely that.

We sound a central key-note by beginning with the subdiscipline that usually appears last in the list: practical theology. We do so not in order to reconfigure all theological study as matters of "practical" concern, but rather, to raise some questions about how the subdiscipline of practical theology has traditionally been defined. In a particularly thorough essay, Richard Osmer, Professor of Practical Theology at Princeton Theological Seminary, offers a historical and theological account of the forces shaping this subdiscipline of theological study. He demonstrates why it is so important that we break down the traditional theory-practice distinction and rediscover how these categories cut across all the theological subdisciplines. His chapter offers the outline of a new paradigm for thinking about the theological encyclopedia, and concludes with a re-examination of the proper place of those activities that have traditionally been subsumed under the heading of "practical theology."

We then turn to the Bible. Chapter 9 is entitled "Rhetoric and the Word of God: Treasure in Earthen Vessels," and is written by James L. Boyce, Professor of New Testament at Luther Seminary. Professor Boyce demonstrates why the texts of the Bible lend themselves to a rhetorical analysis. He also observes that the current flurry of interest in "rhetorical criticism," because it typically restricts the scope of "rhetoric" to matters of arrangement and style, has not produced particularly helpful results. This chapter employs a much broader knowledge of the rhetorical tradition in order to map out some of the possible benefits of an approach to biblical theology that is "rhetorical" in a much more thoroughgoing way. Because rhetoric is able to take account of both the "earthen vessel" of religious language, and the "treasure" to which this language refers, it provides a more adequate model for thinking through the relationship between the biblical text and the faith that the text is meant to inspire.

In the realm of historical theology, we learn about the deleterious consequences of the fact that, at least in the modern age, "Rhetoric lost." This two-word sentence opens chapter 10, "Rhetoric and Historical Theology: Gregory the Theologian." Here, Professor Frederick Norris of the Emmanuel School of Religion presents the overwhelming significance of rhetorical categories for the Greek fathers, and helps us to understand why this perspective has received less and less attention in the modern age. The example of Gregory of Nazianzus demonstrates both the influence of rhetoric and its extraordinary effectiveness as a tool for framing theological claims. By displaying for us the extraordinary vitality of Gregory's theological rhetoric, Professor Norris not only helps us rethink how we teach Church history and historical theology; he also demonstrates just how persuasive a theological argument can be, if it is constructed by a leader who is trained in rhetoric as well as theology.

This chapter leads us naturally to the broader doctrinal claims of the Christian faith. In chapter 11, "Rhetoric and Christian Doctrine: Trinity and Teaching," I have employed my training and research work in both classical rhetoric and in trinitarian theology in order to describe the parallels between the two enterprises. Drawing on my book *These Three Are One: The Practice of Trinitarian Theology* (Oxford: Blackwell, 1998), I develop an analogy between the triadic structure of the classical rhetorical tradition and the doctrinal claims surrounding the Triune God. I conclude with some suggestions about the ways in which this analysis might affect how we teach theology in the seminary context.

Finally, in chapter 12, we turn to the all-important discipline of preaching. Here, Susan Karen Hedahl, Professor of Homiletics at Lutheran Theological Seminary at Gettysburg, presents an essay on "Rhetoric and Proclamation: A Relational Paradigm for the New Millennium." In the first part of the chapter, she sets out the basic features of a "rhetorical homiletics": a perspective on Christian proclamation that takes the insights of the rhetorical tradition into account. By examining the essential features of both the rhetoric and the homiletical traditions, she is able to demonstrate their confluences — as well as the places where they are in tension with each other. In the second half of the chapter, Professor Hedahl sketches the outlines of a "rhetoric of relationality," in which all elements of the rhetorical situation are allowed to play a role in the event of Christian proclamation.

The book concludes with a description of how some elements of a rhetorical approach to theological education have played a role in the curriculum revision process at a particular seminary. The conclusion is written by Don Juel and Patrick Keifert, respectively Professors of New Testament and of Systematic Theology, both of whom were, at the time described in this account, teaching at (what was then known as) Luther

Northwestern Theological Seminary.[3] This narrative account of the process by which rhetorical categories were introduced into a process of curriculum revision will help readers to envision how some of the theoretical material elaborated throughout the present volume might actually take shape in practice. This concluding account also provides some hints about possible pitfalls, as well as obvious advantages, of helping a seminary faculty think through the process of re-visioning theological education.

Over the past several years, the contributors to this volume have worked together, argued with one another, presented our research, and prayed together. We have often sat down to break bread together, and we have enjoyed one another's company. For these good gifts, we would like to express our heartfelt thanks: first, to the program officers of the Lilly Endowment, Inc., for their confidence in our work; second, to our various institutions, for administrative support that often went well beyond normal faculty expectations; and finally, to the many friends, family members, and colleagues who have supported us in our work. Thanks also to David Root, Jim Tedrick, and everyone at Cascade Books for their diligence in bringing this project to final fruition.

We are, of course, delighted that our work is being published; but at the same time, we are saddened to see our lengthy collaboration come to an end. During the past several years, we have become good friends; and our friendships have helped to make this volume what it is. One of our friends has now parted from our midst and dwells with the saints above; it is to his memory that this volume is dedicated.

Over the past several years, we have been involved in precisely the kind of enterprise that we advocate here: the fostering of a community of mutual persuasion, in which we have attempted "to teach, to delight, and to move" one another toward a more integrated vision of theological education. We believe that we have succeeded in this task — at least among ourselves. We now invite you, our readers, to enter into this conversation with us, and to persuade and be persuaded toward this same end. Perhaps in the process, a new network of mutual friendships will develop. And perhaps we will all learn how we might teach, delight, and move our students — and one another — toward a more integral vision of the Christian faith, as we seek to form leaders for the future of the Church.

---

[3] It is now known as Luther Seminary, and Professor Juel later moved to Princeton Theological Seminary.

PART ONE

THEOLOGICAL EDUCATION AS FAITHFUL PERSUASION

Chapter 1

The Classical Rhetorical Tradition and Christian Theology

David S. Cunningham, Don H. Compier, and James L. Boyce[1]

As noted in the Introduction, the contributors to this volume came together because they shared two interests: they cared greatly about theological education, and they thought that its future scope and direction might profit from an encounter with the classical rhetorical tradition. As in the case of any tradition, the issues arising from classical rhetoric are multifaceted and occasionally contested; the tradition itself has many diverse layers, and we will be unable to explore all of them here. In addition, the classical rhetorical tradition is now, once again, a *living* tradition: it continues to undergo new developments as it encounters other modes of thought and is practiced in diverse environments. This means that any "description" of the tradition will be perspectival and temporary — like a journalist's account of a sporting event that is still in progress. We can say

---

[1]Material for this chapter was drawn, with revisions, from the following sources: David S. Cunningham, *Faithful Persuasion: In Aid of a Rhetoric of Christian Theology* (Notre Dame, Ind.: University of Notre Dame Press, 1991), chap. 1; Don H. Compier, *What Is Rhetorical Theology? Textual Practice and Public Discourse* (Harrisburg, Pa.: Trinity Press International, 1999); David S. Cunningham, "Rhetoric," in *A Handbook of Postmodern Biblical Interpretation*, ed. A. K. M. Adam (St. Louis: Chalice Press, 2000), 220–26; and an unpublished manuscript by James L. Boyce.

something about how we got where we are and how things look at the moment; but we must also recognize that change and continued development are a necessary part of any tradition.

Rhetoric is a highly contested term. It is often used pejoratively, referring either to empty speech ("mere rhetoric") or to outright deception. The standard historical accounts of rhetoric usually take pains to repudiate various negative definitions of the term, including: (1) rhetoric as flowery, excessively ornamental language; (2) rhetoric as "mere" appearance, as opposed to some other, more objective measure of reality; (3) rhetoric as concerned exclusively with style and delivery; and (4) rhetoric as another name for all human communication, regardless of its form.[2] While the fourth definition is troublesome because of its breadth, the other three clearly seek to *restrict* the scope of rhetoric to a range much smaller than it has enjoyed throughout much of its effective-history. In the classical tradition, rhetoric referred broadly to the art of persuasion — primarily in speaking but also in writing.

In chapters 2 and 3, two of our contributors will present much more detailed accounts of the modern and postmodern appropriation of the classical rhetorical tradition. In the present chapter, we concentrate on the historical roots of classical rhetoric — attempting to clarify its origins, trace its history, and offer some initial pointers concerning its usefulness.[3] The specific details of rhetoric's usefulness for theological education will be addressed in parts two and three of this book; in the present chapter, we

---

[2]See James L. Golden, Goodwin F. Berquist, and William E. Coleman, *The Rhetoric of Western Thought*, 2nd ed. (Dubuque, Iowa: Kendall/Hunt, 1978), 3.

[3]There are numerous treatments or introductions to classical rhetorical theory and practice. Among the most helpful and easily available are a number of works by George A. Kennedy: *Classical Rhetoric and Its Christian and Secular Tradition from Ancient to Modern Times* (Chapel Hill: University of North Carolina Press, 1980), as well as his three-part history: *The Art of Persuasion in Greece; The Art of Rhetoric in the Roman World;* and *Greek Rhetoric under Christian Emperors* (Princeton: Princeton University Press, 1963, 1972, and 1983). Kennedy is also the author of *New Testament Interpretation Through Rhetorical Criticism* (Chapel Hill: University of North Carolina Press, 1984). See also Renato Barilli, *Rhetoric*, trans. Giuliana Menozzi, Theory and History of Literature, vol. 63 (Minneapolis: University of Minnesota Press, 1989) and Brian Vickers, *In Defense of Rhetoric* (New York: Oxford University Press; Oxford: Clarendon Press, 1988).

will limit ourselves to some concluding remarks on the confluences of theology and rhetoric, and a few passing comments about the classical tradition's potential to help us re-vision theological education.

The Significance of Ancient Greek Rhetoric

Discussions of the classical rhetorical tradition typically begin in ancient Greece, where the word *rhētorikē* first emerges. In this section, we will begin with a close examination of the claims of the ancient Sophists, the critique of rhetoric in Plato, and the supreme importance of Aristotle's treatise on rhetoric. We will then examine the continuing significance of the ancient Greek tradition for some of the philosophical concerns that have dominated the modern and postmodern eras.

The Emergence of Rhetoric

In ancient Greece, the Sophists introduced rhetoric as a means of communication that might compete with epic poetry in moving the audience to adopt particular attitudes and to take certain actions. They apparently claimed to practice rhetoric as a political art (*politikē technē*),[4] which could teach excellence in the *polis*. They emphasized that, in politics (and in many fields of inquiry), widely varying opinions can justifiably be held; agonistic structures are therefore a standard feature of life. Judgments in such matters are made on the basis, not of incontrovertible evidence, but of probability (*eikos*) or opinion (*doxa*).[5] For the Sophists, these terms did not connote unreliability and uncertainty, as we might assume today; they suggested instead that something was apparent, almost obvious. Unencumbered by modernist claims to universally objective certainty, the Sophists believed that probability and verisimilitude were the best one

---

[4] Plato *Protag.* 315c.

[5] *Doxa* is related to *dokei moi*, which might be translated as "it seems to me." (Compare the use of *edoxen* in Acts 15:28: "it has seemed good to the Holy Spirit and to us.") Similarly, *eikos* is closely related to *eika*, which is the word that Socrates frequently uses to begin his statements in the Platonic dialogues (often translated "it seems" — to me, or, to us). See the clarifying comments by Lawrence W. Rosenfield, "An Autopsy of the Rhetorical Tradition," in *The Prospect of Rhetoric: Report of the National Development Project*, ed. Lloyd F. Bitzer and Edwin Black (Englewood Cliffs, N.J.: Prentice Hall, 1971), 65.

could expect to achieve. Common opinion was considered reliable because of its broad, general appeal among those with whom one is likely to converse.

The later rhetorical tradition judged the Sophists harshly — not so much because of their techniques (as is sometimes assumed), but because of their lack of concern for the *moral* assumptions and implications of persuasive discourse. They recognized that communication is facilitated by what binds a community together, but they showed little interest in offering accounts of the proper moral and political *norms* of such communities. Their amoralism generated many of the negative connotations of "sophistic" speech and, by association, lent a pejorative sense to *rhetoric* as well. Writers such as Isocrates attempted to emphasize that the orator must also be a person of good character; but such efforts were drowned by the more general critique of rhetoric, particularly in Plato.

Plato argued that rhetoric is suspect, since it relies upon the opinion of the many and is committed to the *particularity* and *fragility* of truth. Rather than relying on "mere" opinion, Plato sought true knowledge or science (*epistēmē*) — a knowledge attainable only through philosophy. Rhetoric, in contrast, was merely a knack or a routine, comparable to cookery.[6] Of course, according to the more general definition of rhetoric as "the art of persuasion," Plato himself was *very good at it*. Certainly, he succeeded in persuading generations of philosophers, politicians, and educators that his view was the truth; the very success of his argumentative strategies underscores his rhetorical prowess. Moreover, we often read Plato through the objectifying lenses of modernity; perhaps his epistemological commitments are not as foundationalist as they are assumed to be. In the *Phaedrus*, for example, Plato seemed to contemplate a "true philosophical rhetoric" that could lead to truth.[7] Nevertheless, the notion of a rhetoric that could be true — and could be known to be true in some timeless and universal sense (i.e., true in the strong sense that Plato is assumed to be using the word) — would be useless for reasoning about the practical

---

[6] Plato *Gorg.* 463a.

[7] See Jane V. Curran, "The Rhetorical Technique of Plato's *Phaedrus*," *Philosophy and Rhetoric* 19/1 (1986): 66–72; James S. Murray, "Disputation, Deception, and Dialectic: Plato on the True Rhetoric (*Phaedrus* 261–66)," *Philosophy and Rhetoric* 21/4 (1988): 280.

affairs with which most people are concerned. Why? Because if the truth could be known for certain and agreed on by all parties, disputation would be unnecessary. Moreover, many writers argued that no one could ever achieve the kind of certainty that Plato sought. Isocrates, for example, believed that, "in pursuing such knowledge, the 'disputers' pursue a phantom and their results are useless to the community."[8]

The dispute between Plato and the Sophists might be understood another way — namely, that they were pursuing different ends. While Plato was willing to sacrifice "usefulness" for truth, the Sophists were willing to sacrifice "certainty" for progress. This difference can be clarified by Aristotle's division of all inquiry into two categories: analytic and dialectic. Analytic method operates from an agreed-upon set of first principles and can claim finality for its results; but because the principles actually "determine" the results (in some sense), its claims cannot be novel. Dialectic, on the other hand, begins not with first principles but with common opinion (*endoxa*) — that is, with whatever most people consider to be the case. Because common opinion is often wrong and never univocal, dialectic cannot claim absolute finality for its results; nevertheless, its ambiguity makes it able to achieve genuinely new (nontautological) insights.[9]

In the ancient world, these two approaches were not hierarchically ordered; their difference was to be found in their applications. An analytic method is needed when one must be able to demonstrate a clear congruence between a particular outcome and its first principles (as in physics, metaphysics, and logic); but dialectic is more appropriate when first principles are in dispute, or when the goal is to achieve new insight (as in politics, ethics, and poetics). In these terms, rhetoric is a thoroughly *dialectical* enterprise; is most useful for those matters which "could be otherwise." Indeed, Aristotle says that "rhetoric is the counterpart

---

[8]Rosemary Radford Ruether, *Gregory of Nazianzus: Rhetor and Philosopher* (Oxford: Clarendon Press, 1969), 3.

[9]On the significance of this distinction, see William M. A. Grimaldi, S.J., *Aristotle, Rhetoric I: A Commentary* (New York: Fordham University Press, 1980) and Larry Arnhart, *Aristotle on Political Reasoning: A Commentary on the Rhetoric* (DeKalb: Northern Illinois University Press, 1981).

[*antistrophē*] of dialectic."[10] This allusion to the role of the divided chorus in Greek tragedy suggests something of equal importance and purpose but moving in the opposite direction. Like dialectic, rhetoric begins with "common opinion" (*endoxa*),[11] which is malleable and highly specific to place and time, and so cannot be universalized or even generalized. Thus rhetoric cannot guarantee tautological finality. What would be the use of deliberating about something which could never be otherwise? "Nothing would be gained by it."[12]

But although similar to dialectic, rhetoric is not identical with it; the two enterprises, like *strophē* and *antistrophē*, move in opposite directions. Dialectic is most appropriate for purely *theoretical* inquiry; but when the discussion turns to *practical* matters — especially in the realms of politics and ethics — the faculty of dialectic is insufficient. Dialectic may move a person's intellect, but it does not necessarily bring about fundamental changes in a person's attitudes and actions. People are induced to such thoroughgoing changes not by dialectical arguments but by rhetorical ones; for only rhetorical arguments are able to attend to the concrete specificity of speaker, audience, and argument.

According to Aristotle, rhetoric is a "faculty" (*dunamis*) — a capacity, an ability, a way of organizing and making sense of the practical exigencies of the world. More specifically, rhetoric is defined as "the faculty of discovering, in the particular case, the available means of persuasion."[13] This involves the discovery and actual construction of arguments that will be appropriate in a given situation. It treats *pathos*, which is concerned with the emotions and tendencies that can be expected of an audience; *ēthos*, which is concerned with the character of the speaker; and *logos*, which deals with the arguments themselves. In sum, rhetoric encouraged comparative judgments about the effectiveness of particular arguments in moving audiences to action in contingent matters (matters that "might be otherwise").

---

[10] Aristotle *Rh.* 1354a1.

[11] Aristotle *Rh.* 1355a14–18; cf. *Top.* 100a18–21; *Soph. El.* 183a37–183b1.

[12] Aristotle *Rh.* 1357a7.

[13] Aristotle *Rh.* 1355b25–26.

The Lasting Influence of Aristotle

Aristotle's *Rhetoric* is still the basic text for a good understanding of classical rhetoric. Even those modern treatments which have sometimes been styled as a "new rhetoric" or the "new criticism"[14] can be understood as restatements or refinements of basic principles laid out by Aristotle.

> Aristotle brought to the subject an extraordinary eye for what really went on in the rhetorical practice of his day, and an unflagging interest in the relationship between the various objectives that a particular speech might have and the means necessary to achieve those objectives. He was perhaps also the first to discover that logic and rhetoric were not two different modes of argument, that the enthymeme (a syllogism with an implicit major premise) was a major element in public rhetoric, even though it was generally used to establish a probability and not a certainty.[15]

Most aspects of rhetoric, as presented in the classical handbooks and taught in the schools, are present already in outline in Aristotle's *Rhetoric*.

At the same time, Aristotle's "treatise" on rhetoric probably comes to us as notes made of his lectures by his students, and the work is not always straightforward. It was inevitable that Aristotle's somewhat *ad hoc* presentation would later be codified and systematized.

One of the later forms of systematization was the division of rhetoric into five parts, mirroring the stages observed in the development of a particular oration or text from conception to delivery. Traditionally, the five parts of rhetoric were: the invention and/or discovery of various means of persuasion (*inventio*); the arrangement of these arguments into an effective

---

[14]To be noted for example are the works of Chaïm Perelman *The Realm of Rhetoric*, trans. William Kluback (Notre Dame, Ind.: University of Notre Dame Press, 1982); with L. Olbrechts-Tyteca, *The New Rhetoric: A Treatise on Argumentation*, trans. John Wilkinson and Purcell Weaver (Notre Dame, Ind.: Notre Dame University Press, 1969); and "Rhetoric and Philosophy," *Philosophy and Rhetoric* 1 (1968): 15–24. See also the work of Kenneth Burke, including *Counter-Statement* (Berkeley: University of California Press, 1968); *A Rhetoric of Motives* (Berkeley: University of California Press, 19690; *The Rhetoric of Religion: Studies in Logology* (Berkeley: University of California Press, 1970); and "Methodological Repression and/or Strategies of Containment," *Critical Inquiry* 5 (1978): 401–16.

[15]William J. Brandt, *The Rhetoric of Argumentation* (Indianapolis and New York: Bobbs-Merrill Company Inc., 1970), 7.

whole (*dispositio*); the elements of style, including word choice and word order (*elocutio*); the preparation for the delivery of the speech, which usually included its memorization (*memoria*); and finally, its appropriate delivery through voice and gesture (*pronunciatio*).[16] This fivefold division tends to place more emphasis on the outward appearance of the speech than on the development of the argument (which is more or less exhausted by the first part, *inventio*).

In some ways, the first of these five divisions — "Invention" — is of most importance to us in this volume; the second and third divisions (arrangement and style) will also receive some attention. The fourth and fifth divisions are specific to an oral presentation; and while we will also be discussing the importance of spoken communication, we are aware that much of the ongoing theological "conversation" is carried on by writing. In both speech and writing, matters of arrangement and style (the second and third divisions of rhetoric) are obviously important; but they are primarily matters of technique, and can sometimes contribute to rhetoric's "bad reputation" by emphasizing form over content (though one might well want to dispute that distinction in any case). But the first of the five divisions (invention) is a necessary part of spoken and written communication, and its importance remains — whether or not the speaker or writer puts a great deal of energy into matters of style.

In the classical tradition, "invention" meant at least two things: first, an analysis of the particular case in order to pinpoint the issue to be argued; and second, the search for specific arguments or "means of persuasion" in support of that analysis. Of importance here are the forms of logical argumentation on which rhetors rely, and the common "topics" that they employ (such as possibility, fact, degree, or quality). Important, too, was the way in which the particular occasion shaped the discourse.[17] The whole

---

[16] For a simple description, see George A. Kennedy, *New Testament Interpretation*, 13-14. For a more complex examination, see Kennedy's history of rhetoric (cited above), or Josef Martin, *Antike Rhetorik: Technik und Methode*, Handbuch der Altertumswissenschaft (Munich: C. H. Beck'sche Verlagsbuchhandlung, 1974), which uses the fivefold division to structure its entire contents.

[17] Aristotle identified the three types of oratory according to the three possible occasions: deliberative, for public assemblies; judicial or forensic, for the law courts; and epideictic, for public ceremonies when the issue was to offer praise or blame, or to call forth or reaffirm communal values or opinions.

process of invention had to remain mindful of the sorts of judgment or responses that the discourse ultimately sought to engender.

According to Aristotle, every rhetorical or persuasive situation involves the triad of speaker (or writer), the audience, and a discourse. Relating to these three elements, though not corresponding with them exactly, are the three means of persuasion: *ēthos*, *pathos*, and *logos*. These two triads have become a hallmark of the classical rhetorical tradition, and many of the contributors to this volume will mention them and engage with them in their essays. Ethos means "character," and ethical proofs depend on those qualities in the speaker or writer which bring about a favorable impression and dispose and audience to accept the arguments of the discourse. *Pathos* means "emotion"; the word refers primarily to the emotions of the audience, which influence the way in which an argument is heard or effective. Of course, the emotions of the speaker can have an impact as well; and, as Aristotle emphasizes, certain kinds of argument are more amenable to emotional appeals than are others. *Logos*, which in this context might be translated "word(s)" or "language" or "argument," refers to the linguistic construction of the argument within the discourse.

The second part of traditional classical rhetorical theory, arrangement, dealt with the effective ordering of the arguments presented by invention into a unified and persuasive whole. Observation and experience taught the Greek rhetoricians that certain arrangements were naturally more effective than others, and there is much about the task of arrangement that simply represents the common sense and practical wisdom of tradition. Aristotle could say that, in its simplest form, arrangement implies two parts: stating the subject of the discourse, and then proving it. Of course, he had rather more to say on the subject, as did other ancient rhetoricians (both in their theories and in their practice). At least four divisions are present in most persuasive writing or speaking: an introduction, a statement of the case, the proof or arguments, and a conclusion.

The fullest conventional order and structure, from which modification could be made to meet the situation, reached some agreement in the handbooks. The typical speech begins with an introduction, the *proem* or *exordium*, which seeks to obtain the audience's attention or goodwill or sympathy toward the speaker. Next come the *narration*, which lays out the situation and any pertinent background information, and the *proposition* or thesis, which the speaker seeks to prove. It is often effective to divide the thesis through *partition* into headings to be treated separately. The heart of the discourse is the *proof* or presentation of the argument, followed by *refutation* of opposing views. At points of the argument the speaker may include a *digression*, in which relevant circumstances or motivation might be discussed. Finally comes the *epilogue* or conclusion, which summarizes the argument and seeks to dispose the audience to the action or judgment intended by the discourse.[18]

The third part of rhetoric, style, has traditionally reflected some of the best and worst aspects of classical rhetoric. In book three of the *Rhetoric*, Aristotle identified excellences of style in the virtues of "clarity" and "propriety," as understood with reference to the situation and the audience. Aristotle also led the way in consideration of the effects of figures of speech and thought, prose rhythm, and types of sentence structure. As one of the tools of persuasion, style, with its various devices, supplemented the investigation into "what to speak" (invention) by supplying the speaker with "how to speak" — with all due attention to the nature of language as a persuasive medium. These aspects of style were especially elaborated in the Hellenistic age; and at its worst, in periods of the decay of oratory, as well as in its reflection in many modern uses of classical rhetoric, style could even usurp the goal of oratory to persuade and become a matter of mannerisms for their own sake and of empty or gratuitous ornamentation or brilliant display.

One of Aristotle's supreme contributions in his *Rhetoric* lay in his gift of keen observation of what was rhetorically effective, along with his ability to describe what he saw. In the later handbook traditions, these observations tended to be codified into "rules" for good oratory. In the classical tradition, the descriptive and the prescriptive elements of rhetoric always stand in tension with one another. In the same way, the observed needs of persuasion for any particular occasion always stand in tension with the generalized normative prescriptions of the handbooks. Rhetoric thus always involves practical wisdom — paying at least as close attention to the text as to the handbooks, in order to be open to the particularities of each case. At the same time, attention to the handbooks can often train the eye or the ear to see or hear something that would otherwise pass unnoticed.

Perhaps the most valuable contribution of Aristotle — and one which needs to be kept at the forefront when examining his ongoing influence —

---

[18]George A. Kennedy *New Testament Interpretation*, 23–24.

is his sense of the rhetorical enterprise as a comprehensive unity. At every moment in the process of persuasion — from conceptualization through delivery — are present the necessary components of speaker or author, the audience or hearer, and the speech or discourse. Aristotle reminds us of the simultaneous presence of all these elements, and their ability to work together to bring about change and action.

Rhetoric had a profound impact in the Hellenistic era, and particularly in the Roman era; here, it eventually developed into a more codified and formal system. Quintilian would come to define rhetoric as *bene dicendi scientia* — a specialized knowledge about speaking well.[19] Thus, we now turn from the significance of Aristotle and ancient Greece to the importance of ancient Rome.

The Tradition of Roman Oratory

For some fifteen centuries, most Christian writers knew Aristotle secondhand, if at all. The attention that they did give him focused more upon his analytical treatises and much less on dialectical treatises such as the *Rhetoric*. Hence, most of the influence of rhetoric on Christianity was mediated through the Roman rhetoricians, who provided the basis for most of the distinctively Christian appropriation of rhetoric. We turn first to the history of Roman rhetoric, focusing on its two best-known exponents.

Cicero and Quintilian

Here, we will rely primarily on the treatises of Marcus Tullius Cicero (106–43 B.C.) and Marcus Fabius Quintilian (40–95 A.D.). Of course these Roman orators and educators respectfully followed the precepts of Aristotle; but they greatly developed the tradition bequeathed by the great peripatetic philosopher, applying and refining his rhetorical principles through specific public and pedagogical practice.[20]

In his early treatise, *De Inventione*, Cicero defined rhetoric in these terms: "we will classify oratorical ability as a part of political science. The

---

[19]Quintilian *Inst. Orat.* 2.15.34–38.

[20]Even George Kennedy, a great defender of Aristotle's primacy, admits that the seminal *On Rhetoric* is not a finished and polished treatise. See the preface to his translation of *Aristotle On Rhetoric: A Theory of Civic Discourse* (Oxford: Oxford University Press, 1991), xi.

function of eloquence seems to be to speak in a manner suited to persuade an audience, the end is to persuade by speech."[21] Consequently Cicero considered rhetoric to be the most useful virtue for the maintenance of healthy human societies. Cicero recognized that it could, of course, be misused by unscrupulous persons, as Plato had argued; he therefore insisted that rhetorical study must be accompanied by training in philosophical ethics and moral conduct, "which is the highest and most honourable of pursuits." Wisdom and eloquence go hand in hand, for "wisdom without eloquence does too little for the good of states, but . . . eloquence without wisdom is generally highly disadvantageous and never helpful."[22] Cicero even speculates that a wise man's discovery of the principles of persuasion transformed the animal-like, violent condition of primitive humanity into peaceful social existence. While reason determined the necessary antecedents of political science, without eloquence people would never have agreed to voluntarily adopt the arrangements of civil life.[23]

If oratory thereby receives credit for laying the foundations of social concord, its continual cultivation also "renders life safe . . . and even agreeable." Through activity in the law courts and legislative debates the rhetor prevents evil persons from inflicting private or public harm on the citizenry. Provided that it be ever accompanied by wisdom, eloquence will bestow innumerable benefits on every state.[24] What could therefore be more disastrous for the commonwealth than to neglect this art because some have abused it, or to separate its cultivation from the pursuit of philosophy?

Having established the glorious nature and necessity of rhetoric, the Roman orators then offer considerable technical detail about how one might achieve the end of their noble vocation, namely persuasion. Matters such as the types of rhetorical situations (judicial, deliberative, or epideictic), the

---

[21] In *Cicero: De Inventione. De Optimo Genere Oratorum. Topica. The Loeb Classical Library*, trans. H. M. Hubbell (Cambirdge: Harvard University Press, 1949), I.v.6 (p. 15). In classical texts, "the political" refers to action on behalf of the welfare of the *polis*, so that it has a wider range of reference than our English adjective.

[22] Cicero *De Inv.* I.i.1 (pp. 3, 5).

[23] Cicero *De Inv.* I.ii.2–3 (p. 7).

[24] Cicero *De Inv.*, I.iv.5 (p. 13).

stages of rhetorical composition (invention, disposition, etc.), modes of persuasion (logical, ethical, and emotional), and specific persuasive techniques (matters of style, figures of speech, rhythm, etc.) are certainly important, for attention to these details enables successful acts of public persuasion to occur. At the very least effective orators (including theologians!) must know how to write and speak with skill and elegance. But discussion of these specific points need not detain us here, since these can be explored at length in more comprehensive treatments that are readily available.[25]

For the purposes of this chapter, however, it is important to grasp the cardinal principle of Roman rhetorical art, namely what Cicero exalted under the name of *decorum*. In *Orator* he defines the rhetor's lodestar as follows:

> The eloquence of orators has always been controlled by the good sense of the audience, since all who desire to win approval have regard for the goodwill of their auditors, and shape and adapt themselves completely according to this and to their opinion and approval.[26]

The task of rhetoric, therefore, always remains essentially the same: "to determine what is appropriate" and to "consider propriety."[27] This will depend on the nature of the subject and on the character of both the speaker and the listeners. Only the wise can perform the necessary and most difficult act of discernment. Consequently rhetoric does not consist of a body of principles that could be memorized. Cicero always resisted excessively schematic presentations of his subject.[28] Rhetorical performance

---

[25]See, for instance, George A. Kennedy, *Classical Rhetoric and Its Christian and Secular Tradition*; Brian Vickers, *In Defense of Rhetoric*; and Kenneth Burke, *A Rhetoric of Motives*, especially pp. 49–78.

[26] In *Cicero: Brutus. Orator. The Loeb Classical Library*, trans. H.M. Hubbell (Cambridge: Harvard University Press, 1962), viii.24, p. 323.

[27]*Cicero: Brutus. Orator*, xxi.70 (pp. 357–59).

[28]See especially *De Oratore*, in *De Oratore. De Fato. Paradoxa Stoicurm. Partitiones Oratoriae*, 2 vols., trans. H. Rackham and E.W. Sutton (Cambridge: Harvard University Press, 1959–1960). Here I use the English edition by J.S. Watson, *Cicero*

is an art, a practical skill acquired through much practice and exercise of judgment. By the same token, we see that once again virtue and eloquence are intimately wedded in Roman rhetorical vision.[29]

The public character of rhetoric, then, cannot be established once and for all in some general fashion. Its practitioners must time and again exercise influence in the polis through specific persuasive performances. Their success depends upon their ability to have a clear sense of the audience being addressed. Envisioning who the listeners will be — determining as well as possible their character, inclination, and tastes — the skilled orator will discover, organize, and stylistically embellish arguments tailored to this concrete group on this unique occasion.

This type of public activity required a special mode of training. In fact, much space in Roman oratorical treatises is devoted to the elaboration of a pedagogical program. Cicero strongly believed that the capable rhetor must acquire knowledge in virtually all subjects, since one never knew what specific cases might require. In *De Oratore* he considered "eloquence to be the offspring of the accomplishments of the most learned."[30] He refused to accept disciplinary specializations, especially the separation of philosophy and rhetoric.[31] Faced with the charge, repeated often over the centuries, that in this way one sets an impossibly high standard for potential speakers, Cicero insists in *Orator* that although he is presenting an ideal rhetor, "such a one as perhaps has never existed,"[32] sound pedagogy requires instilling a striving after the highest exemplar so that all will achieve the very best skill within their ability.

---

on *Oratory and Orators* (Carbondale and Edwardsville: Southern Illinois University Press, 1970).

[29]Compare Victoria Kahn's discussion of the way that the ethical notion of prudence became identified with the rhetorical principle of decorum during the Renaissance; *Rhetoric, Prudence and Skepticism in the Renaissance* (Ithaca, N.Y.: Cornell University Press, 1985).

[30]Cicero *De Oratore* I.ii (p. 7).

[31]Cicero *De Oratore*, III.xvi (pp. 208–209).

[32]Cicero *De Oratore*, ii.7 (p. 311).

Rhetoric, then, becomes nothing less that a full-blown educational theory and practice aimed at equipping and forming youths for responsible citizenship—what the Germans would later call *Bildung*.[33] Quintilian's *Institutio Oratoria* ("Education of the Orator") would serve as the unrivaled classic in this area for at least fifteen centuries.[34] The curriculum laid out for prospective public speakers was formidable indeed: civil law, history, literature, all areas of philosophy, the sciences, and of course the principles of rhetoric, accompanied by frequent practice in declamation.[35] Nothing that might assist the achievement of persuasion could be neglected, and every human endeavor would benefit from the grace supplied by rhetorical expression. Still, it appears that hermeneutics played a particularly key role in rhetorical education, for by determining how previous authors addressed their audiences one learned by example. Much of classroom time, then, was occupied by what we would call case studies. Through much practice a student might acquire a well developed sense of decorum and have the judgment to perform successfully in ever new situations.[36]

The Roman tradition that we have here presented in outline may well require some updating, but we are convinced that, in general terms, it can contribute significantly to a perspective and a set of practical resources most useful for Christian theology and theological education.

---

[33]On this notion, which becomes synonymous with "culture," see Hans-Georg Gadamer's *Truth and Method*, trans. Garrett Barden and John Cumming (New York: Crossroad, 1988), 10–19.

[34] I use the translation by J.S. Watson, *Quintilian's Institutes of Oratory: Or, Education of an Orator*, 2 vols. (London: George Bell and Sons, 1875–76). For the Latin text, consult *The Institutio Oratoria of Quintilian*, 4 vols., trans. H.E. Butler (Cambridge: Harvard University Press, 1959–1963). On the importance of this work see, for instance, Kennedy, 100–102.

[35]For a brief statement of the requirements, see *De Oratore* I.xxxiv (p. 44).

[36]Victoria Kahn, "Humanism and the Resistance to Theory," in Walter Jost and Michael Hyde, eds., *Rhetoric and Hermeneutics in Our Time: A Reader* (New Haven, Conn.: Yale University Press, 1997), 149–70; and Kathy Eden, *Hermeneutics and the Rhetorical Tradition: Chapters in the Ancient Legacy and its Humanist Reception* (New Haven, Conn.: Yale University Press, 1997).

The Continuing Influence of Roman Rhetoric

The first thing that deserves mention concerning the influence of Roman rhetoric is its longevity. Certainly, the medieval period witnesses a certain degree of development and further systematization of rhetoric; but the ancient Roman writers remain the font and origin of the tradition, always remaining an important cornerstone of any further developments. When Peter Ramus delivered his rationalistic attacks against rhetoric in the sixteenth century, the primary objects of his scorn were still Cicero and Quintilian.[37]

Roman rhetorical theory and practice was particularly adaptable to an era dominated by a broadly unified empire. The Romans had written under a more unified and singular conception of the *polis* than had Aristotle, who was a aware of just how greatly matters differed from one Greek city-state to another. The Roman political order, which assumed that there was only one *polis* that really mattered, helped to sustain a similar Christian assumption of that era — even if, for Christians, the true *polis* was the *civitas Dei* rather than the *civitas terrena*.

But these are no longer the political assumptions that dominate the current landscape, and so any appropriation of the tradition of Roman oratory must take a slightly different shape. One of most important aspects of the Romans' work is its ability to direct our attention to the public nature of argument, and to help us recognize the multiplicity of audiences that we are always addressing. The Roman orators help us in the development of a *political* rhetoric, not so much in the narrow sense of "party politics," but in the broader sense of the *polis* as a community of discourse.

This argument is not affected by the claim that the political stances of the classical orators make their discourse inherently suspect. Cicero undoubtedly represented the landed elite, and Quintilian served as a tutor at the imperial court. But there is no obvious reason why the rhetorical precepts they developed cannot be used just as well to argue against their generally reactionary social positions.[38]

---

[37]See Peter Ramus, *Arguments in Rhetoric Against Quintilian*, trans. Carole Newlands, with an Introduction by James J. Murphy (DeKalb: Northern Illinois University Press, 1986).

[38]See Neal Wood, *Cicero's Social and Political Thought* (Berkeley: University of California Press, 1988), and George Kennedy, *Quintilian* (New York: Twayne

Perhaps a more serious matter involves the marked preference Roman oratory displays for judicial rhetoric. Cicero, after all, distinguished himself as a masterful trial lawyer, which imbued his rhetorical approach with an indelible combative tenor.[39] Whether, and to what extent, this agonistic approach can be of use to us today must be one of our topics of inquiry in the present volume. Similarly, epideictic rhetoric may be of use as theological educators seek to "delight" their listeners; but when employed by itself, the language of encomium and diatribe tends to be seen as "mere entertainment." Exclusive use of epideictic rhetoric can thereby undermine the seriousness of the message that we seek to convey. It may well be that deliberative rhetoric will need to receive more of our attention than has been the case for most theological appropriations of rhetoric thus far.[40]

The Effective-History of Classical Rhetoric

Before bringing this chapter to a close, we need to note some of the specific influences that classical rhetoric has already had on Christian life and thought. Some of this influence has been quite direct; in other cases, rhetoric has influenced Christian theology's conversation-partners and has thus made an impact by means of a more indirect route. Because many of these influences will be mentioned in passing in the chapters that follow, it may be well worth our time to take note of them here.

The New Testament writers clearly manifest rhetorical influences — employing commonplaces and tropes, and attending to the specificity of their audiences ("I have become all things to all people," says Paul, "that I might by all means save some": 1 Corinthians 9:22). The Fathers knew the art of persuasion, as did their opponents; Origen, in his *Contra Celsum*, demonstrates both. The great fourth-century writers employed tropes and argumentative forms that had been well rehearsed in the schools; obvious

---

Publishers, 1969). One example of what I consider excessive suspicion of classical oratory is presented by David Jasper, *Rhetoric, Power, and Community* (Louisville, Ky.: Westminster/John Knox Press, 1993).

[39]Burke speaks of rhetoric's "agonistic" character. See his *A Rhetoric of Motives*, 52.

[40]For more on this point, see Don Compier's essay on "Theology as Testimony," chapter 7 of the present volume.

examples include the Cappadocians (particularly Gregory of Nazianzus[41]), John Chrysostom, and Augustine, whose *De doctrina Christiana* counsels the appropriation of rhetorical techniques in the service of the Gospel.

Christians recognized that their mission ("Go therefore and make disciples of all nations": Matthew 28:19) required them to speak and write persuasively; hence, rhetoric was a natural ally. It helped preachers and theologians to assess audiences, to weigh alternative argumentative forms, and to speak and write with clarity, grace, and wit. Like advocates in the lawcourts and Roman senators, Christians sought to *move* their audiences — asking them not just to *think* differently, but to *act* differently (indeed, to reorder their entire lives). Such appeals are the natural subject-matter of rhetoric, which is thus closely linked with moral philosophy; Aristotle's *Rhetoric* parallels his *Nicomachean Ethics*, while Cicero and Quintilian understood rhetoric as formative for the character of the citizen-orator.

The art of rhetoric thus shaped Christian preaching and polemic from the very beginning; and its influence continued to be felt into the medieval and reformation eras. Although its significance waned with the rise of other approaches to argument (such as 'text and commentary' and scholastic disputation), it significantly shaped the work of writers such as Bonaventure, Luther, and Calvin. Rhetoric flourished in the late medieval and early Renaissance eras (especially in Italy); here, Leonardo Bruni (1360–1442), Lorenzo Valla (1407–1457), and Giambattista Vico (1668–1744) are extremely important.[42] Enlightenment rationalism renewed the attacks of Plato, dismissing rhetoric as excessively focused on contingent matters and on the emotions (and thus likely to lead to deception and error).

Critiques of rationalism gave new life to rhetorical theory. John Henry Newman (1801–1890) argued that persuasion takes place not through the intellect alone, but also by the movement of the affects and the will — and not through sheer deduction, but through the "cumulation of probabilities." Newman's *Essay in Aid of a Grammar of Assent* is an important post-Enlightenment retrieval of classical rhetorical insights. Friedrich Nietzsche

---

[41]See the essay on Gregory by Frederick Norris in chapter 10.

[42]On this point, see the work of Ernesto Grassi, e.g., *Rhetoric as Philosophy: The Humanist Tradition* (University Park: Pennsylvania State University Press, 1980); "Humanistic Rhetorical Philosophizing: Giovanni Pontano's Theory of the Unity of Poetry, Rhetoric, and History," *Philosophy and Rhetoric* 17/3 (1984): 136–55.

(1844–1900) lectured briefly on classical rhetoric, but is better known as a master of its practice in deconstructing various universalizing pretensions (including those of much Enlightenment theology). In the twentieth century, rhetoric re-entered the academy, especially in the United States, in departments of English, Speech, and Communication Studies. The emphasis is not so much on rhetoric as a technique, but as an epistemological process — a new way of knowing.[43] Recent influential theorists of rhetoric include, among many others, Kenneth Burke,[44] Chaïm Perelman,[45] Wayne C. Booth,[46]

---

[43]The literature here is vast. See the work of William Grimaldi, already cited, as well as the following three notes. See also Paolo Valesio, *Novantiqua: Rhetorics as a Contemporary Theory*, Advances in Semiotics, ed. Thomas A. Sebeok (Bloomington: Indiana University Press, 1980) and Calvin O. Schrag, *Communicative Praxis and the Space of Subjectivity* (Bloomington: Indiana University Press, 1986). The phrase "rhetoric as epistemic" originated in an article by Robert L. Scott, "On Viewing Rhetoric as Epistemic," *Central States Speech Journal* 18 (February 1967): 9–17.

[44]Important works include the already-cited *A Rhetoric of Motives* and *The Rhetoric of Religion: Studies in Logology*; and "Methodological Repression and/or Strategies of Containment." See also *Language as Symbolic Action: Essays on Life, Literature, and Method* (Berkeley: University of California Press, 1966) and *The Philosophy of Literary Form*, 3rd ed. (Berkeley: University of California Press, 1973).

[45]We have cited his comprehensive study, jointly with Lucie Olbrechts-Tyteca, *The New Rhetoric: A Treatise on Argumentation*; see also *The Realm of Rhetoric*, trans. William Kluback (Notre Dame, Ind.: University of Notre Dame Press, 1982) and "Rhetoric and Philosophy," *Philosophy and Rhetoric* 1 (1968): 15–24. For evaluation of his work, see Ray D. Dearin, "Chaïm Perelman's Theory of Rhetoric," Ph. D. Dissertation, University of Illinois, 1970; and William Kluback and Mortimer Becker, "The Significance of Chaïm Perelman's Philosophy of Rhetoric," *Revue Internationale de Philosophie* 33 (1979): 33–46. For more on Perelman, Kenneth Burke, and many other twentieth-century appropriations of the classical tradition, see the following chapter of the present volume, by Janet Weathers.

[46]See especially *Modern Dogma and the Rhetoric of Assent* (Chicago: University of Chicago Press, 1974) and *The Company We Keep: An Ethics of Fiction* (Berkeley: University of California Press, 1988); also *The Rhetoric of Fiction*, 2nd. ed. (Chicago: University of Chicago Press, 1982) and *Critical Understanding: The Powers and Limits of Pluralism* (Chicago: University of Chicago Press, 1979).

Walter Ong,[47] and Brian Vickers, whose magisterial treatment of the subject, *In Defense of Rhetoric*, has already been cited.

Also of considerable significance is the study of rhetoric as formative for various Christian thinkers (including their interpretation of the Bible). Tertullian, Gregory Nazianzen, John Chrysostom, and Augustine have received book-length treatment, as have Calvin, Newman, and Karl Barth. Most recently, rhetoric has been promoted as a methodological framework for Christian theology, based on the claim that theology does not rely on universally-recognized first principles (as do, for example, logic and lower-order mathematics). Moreover, many objects of theological study are not empirical and cannot be verified to the satisfaction of all parties. Hence, theology bears fewer similarities to analytical enterprises (such as logic) than it does to such endeavors as politics, law, and even poetry.

Postmodern appropriations of the term *rhetoric* have been, not surprisingly, many and various. For some writers, the descriptions of rhetoric mentioned at the outset of this article and regularly dismissed (rhetoric as flowery, ornamental language, or as "mere appearance") have been taken up in a positive vein and celebrated as an overcoming of the classical paradigm. Celebrations of the ironic play and carnivalesque playfulness of language, in writers from Derrida to Baudrillard, are good examples of this approach. These writers are often charged with some of the same criticisms that met the ancient Sophists; the challenge is always to articulate the moral basis of their claims. In this respect, the work of Lévinas and some of the more recent work of Derrida is an important corrective.

Other postmodern interpreters have focused on rhetoric's critical and/or deconstructive potential. Nietzsche is a guiding figure here, and the later work of Michel Foucault is an obvious contemporary representative, examining how particular forms of language (e.g., "madness" or "crime") have been employed to organize, marginalize, and institutionalize. In this genre, one might include studies organized under the general rubric of "the rhetoric of inquiry," which is interested in "how scholars communicate among themselves and with people outside the academy" and "investigates

---

[47]See, among many works, *Ramus, Method, and the Decay of Dialogue* (1958; reprint, Cambridge: Harvard University Press, 1983) and the essays in *Interfaces of the Word: Studies in the Evolution of Consciousness and Culture* (Ithaca, N.Y.: Cornell University Press, 1977).

the interaction of communication with inquiry."[48] Here also one might cite Stanley Fish's observation of the following sign that rhetoric is once again becoming a key category: "in discipline after discipline there is evidence of what has been called the interpretive turn, the realization (at least for those it seizes) that the givens of any field of activity — including the facts it commands, the procedures it trusts in, and the values it expresses and extends — are socially and politically constructed."[49]

Still others argue that a postmodern appropriation of rhetoric will help to move scholars out of their ivory towers and into direct political engagement. Here, the work of Terry Eagleton and Frank Lentricchia is particularly powerful. These writers have directly addressed the concern that rhetoric might become an amoral enterprise by putting it in the service of particular political ends. The particular *polis* will differ for different writers; for some, it is the nation-state, but for others, the academy itself (or some other entity) may be understood as a coherent political structure within which specific rhetorical engagement must take place.

Each of these three perspectives is reflected in various theological appropriations of rhetoric in the postmodern era. One can point to advocates of various "rhetorical theologies," whether ironic and playful,[50] critical,[51] or political.[52] A hybrid of the last two categories is an approach

---

[48]John S. Nelson, Alan Megill, and Donald N. McCloskey, eds., *The Rhetoric of the Human Sciences: Language and Argument in Scholarship and Public Affairs* (Madison: University of Wisconsin Press, 1987), ix.

[49]Stanley Fish, "Rhetoric," in *Doing What Comes Naturally: Change, Rhetoric, and the Practice of Theory in Literary and Legal Studies* (Durham, N.C.: Duke University Press, 1989), 485.

[50]For example, Jasper, *Rhetoric, Power, and Community*; also Mark C. Taylor, *Erring: A Postmodern A/Theology* (Chicago: University of Chicago Press, 1984).

[51]E.g., David Klemm, "The Rhetoric of Theological Argument," in Nelson, Megill, and McCloskey, eds., *The Rhetoric of the Human Sciences*, 276–97; also Stephen H. Webb, *Re-Figuring Theology: The Rhetoric of Karl Barth* (Albany: State University of New York Press, 1991).

[52]For example, Compier, *What is Rhetorical Theology?*; also, Rebecca S. Chopp, *The Power to Speak: Feminism, Language, God* (New York: Crossroad, 1989).

that understands the Church as the *polis* (or at least as one of them) within which persuasion should take place.[53] Needless to say, most writers move among these categories rather freely. Like so much else in the postmodern world, the appropriation of the language of rhetoric is still very much contested.

Rhetoric's adaptability is attested by its use both as a critical tool in deconstructing theological edifices, and as a means of setting the traditional claims of the faith in a brighter and more convincing light. As Aristotle and Augustine both emphasized, the art of rhetoric is itself indifferent; its value depends on the ends to which it is employed. Whatever their theological position, Christians throughout history have sought to persuade their audiences, and rhetoric has helped them do so. Indeed, in describing the goals of theology, St. Augustine adopted a commonplace from Roman rhetoric: "to teach, to delight, and to move."[54]

---

[53]For example, Cunningham, *Faithful Persuasion*; see also the work of David Tracy, e.g. *The Analogical Imagination: Christian Theology and the Culture of Pluralism* (New York: Crossroad, 1981).

[54]Augustine *De doct. Chr.* IV.27[74].

Chapter 2

Beyond the Classical Paradigm:
Contemporary Rhetorical Analysis
and Theological Education

Janet L. Weathers

During the last few decades, Enlightenment confidence in objectivity has eroded significantly. Scholars in all disciplines are more aware of the ways in which the subjective knowledge and experience of observers influence what we observe and how we interpret reality. No longer confident that we can secure certain knowledge through the application of objective analysis, we must accept the reality of contingent knowledge. As scholars engaged in theological education, we are wrestling with the implications of contingent knowledge and the contribution rhetoric can make to our understanding of and approach to the theological disciplines, the processes of theological education, and the practices of the church.

My contribution to this conversation involves exploring three of the most important developments in contemporary rhetoric: the emphasis on practical reasoning as developed by Perelman and Olbrechts-Tyteca, and by Stephen Toulmin; Kenneth Burke's radical shift toward conceiving of rhetoric as an ontological process rooted in natural language; and the expanded conceptuality of human rationality proposed by Walter R. Fisher. I am interested in ways an interdisciplinary conversation among theological disciplines and rhetoric will increase our awareness and enhance our understanding of the diverse practices of the intentional and unintentional, verbal and nonverbal, oral and written communication events that constitute theological scholarship, theological education, and the formal and informal practices of the church.

As indicated in the preceding chapter, classical rhetoric focuses on oral and written messages in which there is a clear intention to persuade. Primary attention is given to the content of the discourse, that is, the efficacy of the rhetorical strategies chosen by a particular speaker in light of the content of the presentation and the particular audience for whom it was intended. Aristotle defined rhetoric as the faculty of discovering the available means of persuasion in a particular situation. He identified three interdependent means of persuasion: *ēthos*, the credibility of the speaker, *pathos*, the emotions of the audience relative to the subject under discussion, and *logos*, the logic of the argument itself. Great orators may not be able to analyze and name the technical aspects of their rhetorical effectiveness. Rhetoricians, however, have the technical competence to identify the available means of persuasion in a given context and identify the dynamic interplay of elements in a communication event that help to explain why some orators are able to teach, to delight, and to move an audience in a given situation, while other orators fall flat — in spite of their equal or even greater knowledge of matters relative to the communication event.

Skilled rhetoricians have a deep understanding of people and of communication dynamics. This knowledge can be used constructively and for the benefit of others, or it can be used in self-serving, destructive ways. Those who have knowledge of rhetoric, and the communication competence to employ that knowledge effectively, are in possession of a two-edged sword. This has led to both the valuing of rhetoric and the condemnation of the discipline.

From its inception, rhetoric always had its detractors. Nevertheless, it was considered one of the classical disciplines in ancient Greece. Its status diminished significantly, however, with the ushering in of the Enlightenment, which led scholars to value objectivity and emphasize scientific and technical knowledge. Rhetoric — with its focus on contingent knowledge — was simultaneously demoted to being mere stylistics. The popular insult, "it's just rhetoric," reveals the low regard many have for what historically was one of the great classical disciplines studied by all who wished to be considered educated.

As the twentieth century came to a close, it was increasingly clear that the ground beneath our faith in objectivity had given way. As postmodern proclamations shattered one ledge after another, scholars scrambled to find secure footing and began to discover the contribution rhetoric could make to their efforts.

Calvin Schrag, a philosopher who acknowledges the important contribution rhetoric can make to philosophy, notes that the deconstructive critique of philosophy aims at philosophy "understood as a special body of knowledge, a formalized epistemological discipline programmed to represent reality."[1] Schrag calls for moving through the first deconstructive critique of authority claims and foundationalist thinking to the second deconstructive move, which embodies the "posture of hermeneutical recovery or retrieval." For Schrag, this move from epistemology to hermeneutics brings philosophy into the *"hermeneutical space of communicative praxis,* textured *as an amalgam of discourse and action.* Hermeneutics as the performance of interpretation is at work wherever there is speech and action, and this speech and action is at once an understanding and an expression of meaning through which both self and world are disclosed."[2] This particular understanding of philosophy clearly intersects the concerns of rhetoric.

As scholars in diverse disciplines begin to recognize that confidence in foundationalism and objectivism cannot be sustained, the rhetorical dimension of all scholarly and scientific discourse becomes apparent. This is reflected in a growing literature devoted to identifying the rhetorical underpinnings of different disciplines.[3] Such work has reinvigorated the

---

[1] Calvin O. Schrag, "Rhetoric Resituated at the End of Philosophy," *Quarterly Journal of Speech,* 71 (1985): 166.

[2] Schrag, "Rhetoric Resituated," 170.

[3] See, for example, D. N. McCloskey, *The Rhetoric of Economics* (Madison: University of Wisconsin Press, 1985; the rhetorical base of psychology is explored in C. Bazerman, *Shaping Written Knowledge* (Madison: University of Wisconsin Press, 1988) and in D. Leary, *Metaphors in the History of Psychology* (Cambridge: Cambridge University Press, 1990); studies of rhetoric in the human sciences in general are found in Herbert W. Simons, ed. *Rhetoric in the Human Sciences* (London: Sage, 1989), and Simons, *Case Studies in the Rhetoric of the Human Sciences* (Chicago: University of Chicago Press, 1990); a rhetorical approach to social psychology is offered by Michael Billig, *Arguing and Thinking,* 2nd ed. (New York: University of Cambridge Press, 1996).

study of rhetoric and the valuing of rhetorical scholarship, both within the communication discipline and within academia as a whole.

Extensions of Classical Rhetoric

Scholars from many disciplines, including theology and biblical studies, are exploring the contemporary relevance of classical rhetoric, as well as twentieth-century developments in the areas of practical reasoning and theories of argumentation. Many of the other essays in this volume highlight the contributions of classical rhetoric. In the twentieth century, there are several significant extensions and modifications of classical rhetoric that hold great promise for scholars and educators in the theological disciplines. I will focus on three of these developments as represented in the work of Chaïm Perelman, Lucie Olbrechts-Tyteca, Stephen Toulmin, Kenneth Burke, and Walter R. Fisher.

The first development is the focus on practical reasoning as represented by the seminal work of Chaïm Perelman and Lucie Olbrechts-Tyteca.[4] In *The New Rhetoric*, the authors offer detailed insight into the rhetorical dimension of all practical reasoning. They argue that no special privilege can be given to claims for an absolute standard for truth. Whatever claim to truth one makes, the case must be argued before a public audience in order for the claim to have any actual significance as part of social reality.

Perelman and Olbrechts-Tyteca's perspective does not *necessarily* entail the conclusion that there is no truth. Their point is that human beings have no way of inducing others to assent to their understanding of absolute truth without making an argument for their perspective, an argument that will, undoubtedly, be countered by those who claim knowledge of a contradictory truth for which they assert an absolute claim. Even if one believes there are philosophically defensible arguments for claiming that truth exists, and I support such a claim, Perelman's point still stands. We can never know for sure how partial and erroneous our understanding of "truth" is.

This perspective has implications for all truth claims, including those associated with religious faith. If Perelman and Olbrechts-Tyteca are right, we must argue the relative merit of our understanding and share with

---

[4] Chaim Perelman and L. Olbrechts-Tyteca, *The New Rhetoric: A Treatise on Argumentation*, trans. J. Wilkinson and P. Weaver (Notre Dame: University of Notre Dame Press, 1969).

others the evidence we have for our convictions, if we hope to influence others to join us in our view of God, humanity, creation, and the meaning of life.

Acknowledging the relativity of all truth claims makes many theological educators nervous. It seems a short step from the ledge of relativity to the slippery slope of radical relativism that characterizes every truth claim as equally valid. The fact that no perspective can be definitively proven to be true does not mean, however, that we must accept a radical subjectivism in which all perspectives are held to be of equal value.[5] If all claims to absolute truth must be argued in order to gain adherents within a constructed social reality, we are faced with the task of developing criteria in terms of which we will evaluate alternative truth claims. Perelman and Olbrechts-Tyteca argue for drawing our evaluative criteria from the values that are inevitably embedded in knowledge claims. Once the values entailed in competing knowledge claims are identified, we can evaluate the relative merit of competing positions.

To test the merit of any argument, Perelman and Olbrechts-Tyteca ask the question, "to whom would the values entailed by this argument appeal?" The argument with greatest merit is the one that would be compelling to an audience that embodies the virtues to the greatest extent possible.[6] Obviously there will be no universal agreement on the nature and scope of those virtues; nevertheless, this perspective helps us to articulate explicit criteria in terms of which we can compare the relative

---

[5] This point is developed in a very helpful and clear way by Richard J. Bernstein in *Beyond Objectivism and Relativism: Science, Hermeneutics, and Praxis* (Philadelphia: University of Pennsylvania Press, 1983).

[6] Current dialogical views of communication influenced by the Russian philosopher Mikhail Bakhtin emphasize the ways in which speakers help to construct the audience in the process of communicating with them and offering them ways of understanding themselves that may transform their self-understanding and self-identity so that they become the kind of audience that finds the speaker's rhetoric compelling. This perspective has significant implications for helping us think about the communication events of preaching and teaching in the church. See, for example, Leslie A. Baxter and Barbara M. Montgomery, *Relating: Dialogues and Dialectics* (New York: Guilford, 1996).

merit of competing arguments.[7] When we uncover the virtues that are embodied in a given argument (the virtues may be embodied consciously or unconsciously as far as those creating the argument are concerned), we can assess whether they are virtues we want to affirm and embody in our lives and our communities of faith.

As Perelman and Olbrechts-Tyteca make clear, rhetoric does not offer simple answers to the complexities of competing truth claims in our world. What it does offer are ways of helping us to be more conscious, thoughtful, and competent in assessing and responding to the diverse truth claims that vie for our adherence.

Stephen Toulmin is a contemporary scholar who has contributed significantly to our understanding of practical reasoning and informal logic.[8] Whereas Perelman and Olbrechts-Tyteca emphasize the audience as central to the evaluation of an argument, Toulmin provides ways of analyzing an argument's implicit and explicit structure. The soundness of an argument, Toulmin explains, can be evaluated in terms of the argument's anatomy: the data provided in the argument, the warrant for moving from data to a conclusion, the backing for the warrant, and the presentation of any reservations. With these components in mind, we can compare with precision the arguments in scholarly articles and books that support competing views, the arguments embedded in sermons, or the arguments presented for adjudicating issues within a denomination. As we look closely at the data a speaker or author uses, the warrant used for moving from the data to a conclusion, the backing for the warrant, and the presentation of any reservations, we have a basis for engaging our practical reasoning in deciding which perspective is the most sound. This process will not necessarily lead all the people in a given group to the same conclusion, but it will help them to understand where there is agreement and at what point their perspectives diverge.

---

[7] On this point, see especially the work of Aristotle on the virtues (in the *Nicomachean Ethics*), and the Christian appropriation of that tradition in Augustine, Thomas Aquinas, and contemporary theological ethics, e.g., Stanley Hauerwas and Charles Pinches, *Christians Among the Virtues: Theological Conversations with Ancient and Modern Ethics* (Notre Dame, Ind.: University of Notre Dame Press, 1997).

[8] See for example, Stephen Toulmin, *The Uses of Argument* (London: Cambridge University Press, 1958); Stephen Toulmin, Richard Rieke, and Allan Janik, *An Introduction to Reasoning* (New York: Macmillan, 1979).

Although Toulmin is particularly well known for his focus on the structure of arguments, he demonstrates a broader view of the contribution of rhetoric to the discipline of philosophy in *Cosmopolis*, in which he focuses on the philosopher Descartes. Toulmin's analysis of the philosophy of Descartes provides an engaging example of how we might teach theology in order to help pastors and scholars understand the rhetorical dimension of all theological thought.

The Dominance of Cartesian Rationalism

Toulmin approaches his analysis with a rhetorical question: Why was Descartes's rationalist program so well received? Descartes believed human beings could discover a rational method of establishing the certainty of foundational truth claims. To determine why Descartes's commitment to foundational truth was compelling, it is not sufficient to analyze the structure of Descartes's argument, although the careful logic of his argument is a factor. Toulmin claims that scholars writing about the development of philosophical thought without taking into account the issues that emerge from a rhetorical perspective, have reached erroneous conclusions. According to Toulmin, the philosophies of Descartes and other seventeenth-century scholars were not

> arbitrary creations of lonely individuals in separate ivory towers, as the orthodox texts in the history of philosophy suggest. The standard picture of Descartes's philosophical development as the unfolding of a pure *esprit* untouched by the historical events of his time, so graphically presented in the *Grande Encyclopedie*, gives way to what is surely a more lifelike and flattering alternative: that of a young intellectual whose reflections opened up for people in his generation a real hope of *reasoning* their way out of political and theological chaos, at a time when no one else saw anything to do but continuing fighting an interminable war.[9]

Critical events in Descartes's life expose the unrelenting pressures that forged his commitment to finding a rational method for establishing certain knowledge and created an audience ready to embrace his new perspective. The young Descartes lived in France during the reign of Henry of Navarre who became King Henry IV in 1589. The Treaty of Augsburg in 1555

---

[9] Stephen Toulmin, *Cosmopolis: The Hidden Agenda of Modernity* (Chicago: University of Chicago, 1990), 70.

authorized each ruler in Central Europe to impose the ruler's chosen religion on the subjects in his or her territory. While this approach worked in many countries, it was not a satisfactory solution in France. Living under a succession of Catholic monarchs from the family of Francis I during most of the sixteenth century, France had a strong sense of national identity and national loyalty. Catholics believed that French unity was dependent on the principle of one king, one law, one religion.

When, after a quick series of deaths and assassinations, Henry IV became king, France found itself with a Protestant monarch. Challenges to his authority, particularly in Paris, led Henry to renounce Protestantism and become a Catholic in 1593. This move helped Henry to consolidate his power, a power that he used to protect the rights of Protestant Huguenots. He called for a bold approach in which religious plurality would be accepted. He challenged the notion that national unity necessarily required the imposition of one religion on subjects. He believed both Catholic and Protestant subjects could be loyal to him and to France. The 1598 Edict of Nantes regularized the status of Protestant citizens. Henry IV's commitment to plurality was extremely rare among monarchs. Only in Poland's constitution of 1555 could one find another country that guaranteed religious tolerance (in this case, of Protestants).

Henry found support for his commitment to pluralism in the climate of intellectual freedom that characterized Renaissance humanists such as his trusted friend, Montaigne, himself a Catholic. Montaigne wrote freely about his experiences of life and his attitudes. Although he showed little evidence of struggling with the theological correctness or goodness of his actions, he was not anti-religious. Montaigne was a skeptic, but Toulmin claims that Montaigne, like his friend Henry IV, was not a "negative dogmatist."[10] That is, his skepticism did not take the hard line of rejecting anything that cannot be proven with certainty. Montaigne argued in "Apology" that "unless some one thing is found of which we are *completely* certain, we can be certain about nothing."[11] His own position was that there was nothing about which we could be completely certain.

Montaigne's commitment to intellectual freedom is reflected in Henry IV's commitment to toleration of religious plurality. Henry reasoned that

---

[10] Toulmin, *Cosmopolis*, 50.

[11] Toulmin, *Cosmopolis*, 42.

if, as a result of thoughtful reading and reflection, a Frenchman felt persuaded to join a Protestant movement, that need not imply that the person could not simultaneously retain loyalty to the nation of France and to the king. The courageous experiment ended in 1610 when Henry was assassinated. Following a custom of the time, Henry had promised that at his death his heart would be enshrined at a Jesuit academy that was located on one of his family properties. After his murder, with the country in shock, the heart was delivered in a silver chalice to the school with great solemnity. One of the young students at the academy was René Descartes. Perhaps because the Jesuits were under suspicion in the murder of Henry, the Jesuits emphasized their respect for him with a series of annual celebrations in his memory. The significance of his murder was kept alive in the students' minds.

Following his years in the academy, Descartes became immersed in another life-defining historical event: the Thirty Years' War. It ended only two years before his death. During the first 12 years of the war, Descartes took every opportunity to observe the war firsthand. Conflicting religious truth claims that could not be resolved with certainty fueled chaos and mayhem.[12]

It was in this chaotic and destructive maelstrom that Descartes sought to conceive some basis for certainty that would answer Montaigne's challenge. By approaching Descartes's work with rhetorical questions in mind, Toulmin contextualizes Descartes's move to epistemology and natural philosophy. The seemingly uncontrollable violence that raged for thirty years — with religious doctrine used sincerely or as political cover to fuel the conflicts — created an audience that found Descartes's philosophical perspective compelling. Descartes's philosophy was not an arbitrary creation dreamed up by a man out of touch with the real world. Fifty years earlier, at the height of Montaigne's popularity, it is unlikely that Descartes's approach would have found a responsive audience. However, after decades of war and violence, people were ready to hear what Descartes had to say.

---

[12] It should be noted, however, that the causes of the Thirty Years' War were not as strictly "theological" as some accounts have suggested. See William T. Cavanaugh, "'A Fire Strong Enough to Consume the House': The Wars of Religion and the Rise of the State," *Modern Theology* 11/4 (October 1995): 397–420.

As Toulmin's analysis of Descartes's historical context makes clear, the power of Descartes's influence is not found within the structure of his argument alone. Rhetorical analysis discloses the inseparable interdependence of a particular speaker, message, audience and channel of communication as they are embedded in a given historical context. If a message — a theological tract, sermon, biblical text, or prayer — is taken out of the context in which it was embedded and placed in the mouth of a different speaker addressing a different audience in a new context, this constitutes the creation of an entirely new message. Rhetorical analysis brings this process into greater focus.

A rhetorical perspective leads us to look at developments in theological thought with a careful eye on the historical context and the influences that were of greatest relevance to each theologian. By considering the ever-present rhetorical dimension of theology, we can better understand why theologians embrace certain doctrines while rejecting others, and sometimes change their commitments at different points in their career. Rhetorical analysis also helps us understand more fully why theologians are influential in certain contexts within a given historical period and not in others. Analyzing the dynamic interplay of factors involved helps students to understand that theology itself is contingent knowledge and cannot be described accurately as an embodiment of certain truth. Our individual, subjective experience has everything to do with why we find ourselves persuaded by one theology and not another.

Practical Reasoning and Human Rationality

If we accept the claim that objective analysis untainted by human perspective is impossible, it then becomes important to look at our assumptions about the nature of human rationality. As Toulmin notes in his analysis of Descartes, to understand why Descartes was so influential, we need to understand the thought processes of those who found his argument persuasive. Why was it considered rational for philosophers to adopt Descartes's point of view and forsake the perspective of previous philosophers, such as Montaigne?

The nature of human rationality is a fertile topic among rhetoricians today, as it is among scholars in many disciplines. From the perspective of practical reasoning or informal logic, rationality is constituted by one's ability to appropriately engage in and respond to reasons given for supporting or rejecting claims. The rules for practical reasoning vary in different contexts. However, within a given field, one's rationality is defined in terms of one's ability to engage in argumentation following the rules of reasoning honored by those who have respect and influence within that field. Rhetorician Walter R. Fisher points out that, from this perspective, human rationality is defined in terms of one's ability to create, evaluate, and respond to arguments that "feature clear-cut inferential or implicative structures" appropriate to a particular field of discourse.[13] The field of discourse may be a particular academic discipline, a legal context, a political context, or the discourse of those vested with decision-making power in the governing body of a religious organization. This perspective on human rationality is embedded in what Fisher calls the rational-world paradigm, a paradigm that assumes human beings reach their conclusions as a result of engaging practical reasoning and informal logic.

Over time, each field of discourse develops both implicit and explicit understandings of the forms of discourse that "count" as rational argument. From within the rational-world paradigm, a person is considered rational to the degree that that person is able to engage in the forms of argument defined as appropriate for a given context. For example, in order for an article to be published in a particular academic journal, the author must write in a way that reflects the reasoning and forms of argument that editors of that journal recognize as legitimate.

Rules for appropriate ways to engage in scholarly work and scholarly discourse vary in different fields, and in the same field over a period of time. Nevertheless, there are always rules — explicit and implicit rules — that guide editors' evaluations of articles submitted for publication. Consequently, it is not uncommon for scholars who challenge established assumptions, theories, research methods, and/or modes of discourse to be considered "irrational." Labeling a perspective as "irrational" because it is not consistent with the reigning view keeps scholars from giving serious consideration to new ideas. Thus, it is not uncommon for scholars on the leading edge of change within a discipline to be misunderstood, ignored, or ridiculed. The history of science is replete with examples of scholars such as Einstein who were shunned by the scholarly community when they first made their ideas public. As voices with new accents seek to be heard in theological disciplines, they too face pressure to conform their voices to the

---

[13] Walter R. Fisher, *Human Communication as Narration: Toward a Philosophy of Reason, Value, and Action* (Columbia: University of South Carolina Press, 1987), 59.

established norms of those who currently control the admission gate for participation in a given scholarly domain.

Broadening the Construct of Human Rationality

Fisher argues that the labeling of perspectives different from our own as "irrational" emerges from the view of human rationality espoused by the rational-world paradigm, in which rationality is reflected in one's ability to use the appropriate forms of argument valued in a particular context. Fisher offers an alternative — the narrative paradigm — as a more adequate way of conceptualizing rationality and guiding the general study of human communication, including contexts within which the forms of logical argument emphasized by the rational-world paradigm are featured. The narrative paradigm does not deny the important features of practical reasoning identified within the rational-world paradigm. Instead, it places all practical reasoning within a broader conception of human rationality. This conception allows us to provide a more adequate answer to the question, "Why is a particular audience finding a particular message — whether it be a theological perspective, biblical interpretation, sermon, or call for engaging in justice work — so compelling?" As Toulmin illustrates so clearly with his analysis of Descartes's influence, the answer is not found in the inherent rationality of the argument. People were taking far more into account than the close reasoning of his argument when they responded to Descartes, whether they were conscious of doing so or not. A broader rationality was at work. Fisher is grappling with helping us understand the nature of that broader rationality.

Fisher conceives of human rationality in terms of the metaphor of narrative. From this perspective, rationality involves recounting and accounting for human choice and action. Working with the metaphor of narrative, Fisher argues that "regardless of the form they are given, 'recounting' and 'accounting for' constitute stories we tell ourselves and each other to establish a meaningful life-world."[14] To distinguish his perspective from the prevailing rational-world paradigm, Fisher identifies his perspective as the narrative paradigm.

To grasp Fisher's perspective, we need to step back from thinking of narrative only in terms of the *genre* of narrative. Fisher, of course, acknowledges the significance of the genre of narrative; however, the

---

[14] Fisher, *Human Communication as Narration*, 62.

narrative paradigm points to a deeper and more inclusive aspect of all human communication, one that applies to all genres — including carefully argued scholarly work.

Fisher infuses the narrative paradigm with the insights of the preeminent rhetorician of the twentieth century, Kenneth Burke. Burke created a radical shift in the discipline of rhetoric by offering a significantly expanded understanding of the rhetorical process. In contrast to definitions of rhetoric that focus on intentional efforts to persuade, Burke argued that we are engaged in subtle forms of persuasion intentionally and unintentionally whenever we engage in the use of verbal or nonverbal symbols. He claimed that rhetoric is rooted in a natural, wholly realistic function of language itself; rhetoric is "the use of language as a symbolic means of inducing cooperation in beings that by nature respond to symbols."[15]

Burke's writings are complex and extensive. It is far beyond the scope of this essay to highlight even a few of his many contributions to the discipline of rhetoric. One aspect of his thinking that is particularly critical for the purpose of this essay, however, is his claim that the essential dynamic in any communication that is persuasive is the process of *identification*: "we persuade others by speaking their language, identifying our ways with theirs."[16] For Burke, the critical feature of persuasion is not the efficacy of a particular appeal, or the soundness of an argument's logic, but rather this process of identification between an audience and a rhetor. Without some degree of identification, whether realistic or fanciful, a person will not be influenced by another's message, no matter how carefully crafted and logically argued it may be.

To think about the implications of this claim, consider the theological and theoretic perspectives you find most compelling. Who has been influential in shaping your thinking? With whom have you identified? Why? We may never have met authors who have greatly influenced our thinking. However, we can ask what it is about their writing that has

---

[15] Kenneth Burke, *A Rhetoric of Motives* (Berkeley: University of California Press, 1950), 43.

[16] David S. Cunningham, *Faithful Persuasion: In Aid of a Rhetoric of Christian Theology* (Notre Dame, Ind.: University of Notre Dame Press, 1991); cf. Burke, *A Rhetoric of Motives*, 55–59.

allowed us to identify with their perspective — or to reject it when our deepest identifications lead us to an alternative vision of reality that we find more compelling. Identification is itself a complex process. We may identify with others for a great number of reasons: age, educational background, socio-economic factors, ethnicity, gender, use of language, familiarity of illustrations, attitudes expressed toward something that is deeply important to us, nonverbal behaviors, manner of dress, and so forth. We identify with different people in different contexts for different reasons.

The process of identification does not necessarily happen at the level of conscious awareness. We find ourselves drawn to one group of strangers rather than another when we enter a room without really thinking about why. We read one editorial writer regularly and ignore the one in the next column. We skim one journal, read another cover to cover, and leave another unopened. Certain sessions attract us at a professional meeting while others leave us cold. If we pay attention to such responses in our own lives, we can begin to notice patterns that suggest the myriad ways in which we are being and have been influenced by people — living or dead, fictional or nonfictional — with whom we have identified in the past or identify with in the present. According to Burke, when influence occurs, rhetoric is at work — and some degree of identification is involved.

Fisher assumes the validity of Burke's understanding of identification. When we identify with another, even partially, it carries implications for who we understand ourselves to be. Throughout our lives, our self-identity, the self-reflexive understanding we have of ourselves in terms of our autobiography, is continually reinforced or modified by the people with whom we identify.

From Burke's perspective (and the perspective of the narrative paradigm), the philosophical roots of rhetoric are ultimately ontological — not merely epistemological. Rhetoric includes our verbal and nonverbal, intentional and unintentional communication with others. It therefore not only contributes to what we know; at a more fundamental level, it actually *constructs* social reality, including our perception of ourselves. Our self-identity is constructed from our interaction with others. Human beings naturally respond to symbols; healthy babies engage in rhetorical processes from the first days of life — beginning, of course, with nonverbal symbols. The specific ways in which we use and respond to symbols, and the meaning and significance that we attribute to them, are, of course, socially constructed. But as human beings we respond to symbols without being taught the importance of doing so. The symbols to which we are exposed, and the interpretations that we come to adopt through processes of identification, create the world as we know it.

Fisher builds on this ontological grounding of rhetoric to expand the concept of human rationality. For Fisher, rationality is not limited to one's ability to understand and utilize the precise argumentative forms favored by a particular discourse. Rather, human rationality is reflected in our response to whether or not the "story" we are hearing "hangs together" and "rings true" in light of other understandings of reality we believe to be true.

Because of the potential confusion in terminology, it is important to repeat that the "story" that may not hang together or ring true need not be articulated in a form that falls within the genre of narrative. The *Book of Order* of the Presbyterian Church is a formal document that articulates rules to guide Presbyterians at all levels of church polity. When amendments to the *Book of Order* — such as those regarding acceptable sexual conduct of church leaders — are proposed, they are brought to the General Assembly for consideration. They may then be studied by local congregations and presbyteries. Whether or not a person finds proposed changes acceptable will depend on the "stories" one tells — about the nature of Christian faith and life, the role of the Bible, the nature of biblical interpretation, the nature of human sexuality, and so forth. People will offer carefully reasoned arguments for each aspect identified; however, the arguments in and of themselves will not determine whether or not people support a given amendment. Failure to explore the deeper issues influencing our responses to alternative perspectives limits our self-understanding of complex dynamics that have a great impact on the church and on local communities of faith.[17]

Similarly, when Presbyterians listen to candidates for moderator of the General Assembly of the Presbyterian Church (U.S.A.), they will hear each candidate offer a perspective, a "story," explaining the current state of the church, the proper role of the church, and the perspectives the candidate would encourage if elected. Presbyterians, regardless of their degree of formal education or experience with their denomination's polity and theology, will have an awareness of whether or not the "story" the candidate presents has narrative coherence. Does it "hang together"?

---

[17]See the case study, concerning exactly such an argument, that opens Wes Avram's essay in chapter 6 of this volume.

Secondly, those who hear and talk with the candidate will test whether what the candidate says has narrative fidelity. Does the candidate's story "ring true"? Does it make sense in light of other "stories" the person believes to be true as a result of years of being part of a local congregation? Who is telling the "Presbyterian story" in a way that resonates with who we understand ourselves to be as Presbyterians — and as Christians?

The point Fisher emphasizes is that without any formal education, people habitually respond to the presence or absence of narrative coherence and narrative fidelity of perspectives that are offered for their adherence. The claim is not that a person's response is necessarily correct. Rather the claim is that the response is *rational*. People have "good reasons" for responding the way they do. The informal logic of "good reasons" emphasized within the narrative paradigm recognizes that people have a concept of the "good" that guides their response to the stories that are offered for their adherence. We may disagree with another's sense of what the "good" is. However, if we recognize that people respond as they do for "good reasons," we are more likely to continue in conversation with them in an effort to understand those reasons and the stories in which they are embedded rather than just dismissing them as irrational.

Rhetoric, Rationality, and Theological Education

What difference might this concept of human rationality make if we were to consciously adopt it within theological education and within the church? From the perspective of this broadened understanding of rationality, people who are not persuaded by a particular candidate for moderator, a pastor, theologian, religious educator, or biblical scholar, would not be dismissed as irrational because they do not utilize the specific forms of argument that experts in a particular field employ. One of the effects of conceptualizing rationality in the terms offered by the narrative paradigm is that it gives more respect to the wisdom of laypeople, and legitimizes their participation in discourse that has generally been limited to those granted the status of experts.

This view of human rationality has important implications for local congregations. It pushes us to reflect, for example, on how we engage lay persons with different educational backgrounds. The wisdom of lay persons will not necessarily be offered by those who are best educated. Often congregational members with less formal education possess a wisdom that no number of degrees could provide. Unless we intentionally create safe, respectful environments for people of all educational levels to share in Christian education, church discussions, and church governance, we will be unlikely to benefit from the wisdom of those who feel hesitant to speak in the presence of those who have more formal education. If we are not intentional in creating inclusive processes, the church will simply reflect the hierarchy of status and authority that functions in the social reality of the surrounding culture.

Realities of Communication in Communities of Faith

Our concept of human rationality influences the ways we communicate with people of different backgrounds in the church. The verbal, nonverbal, intentional, and unintentional ways we communicate with one another in formal and informal settings constitute the social reality of each local congregation. If people in local congregations want to construct and sustain a social reality that is not merely a reflection of the social reality within the larger culture, they must be cognizant of the ways in which people communicate with one another in all the formal and informal interactions that take place among members of the community of faith.[18] These communication events — taken as an organic whole — constitute the social reality of a community of faith. As Jürgen Moltmann points out,

> the church of Christ must present itself as a 'derestricted area' amid the restrictions imposed by society. Schleiermacher meant by this a fellowship without an ulterior purpose; modern writers mean communication without repression. A 'liberated zone' of this kind in society would certainly fulfil that unfulfilled promise of the French revolution — 'fraternity.' The problem is that this 'fraternity' cannot exist without 'liberty' and 'equality.' *The idea becomes illusory when it overlooks these presuppositions for unrestricted communication, or simply assumes that they exist.*[19]

---

[18] I discuss examples of gender differences in communication and implications for communities of faith in Janet L. Weathers, "Gender and Small Group Communication in the Church," Jane Dempsey Douglass and James F. Kay, eds. *Women, Gender and Christian Community* (Louisville: Westminster John Knox, 1997), 117–28.

[19] Jürgen Moltmann, *The Church in the Power of the Spirit: A Contribution to Messianic Ecclesiology*, trans. Margaret Kohl (New York: Harper and Row, 1977; reprint, Fortress Press, 1993), 107 (emphasis added).

In my view, Habermas's theory of communication (to which Moltmann refers in this quotation) does not offer the most adequate insights into the processes of interpersonal communication. However, I believe that Moltmann is right in arguing that, in order to be the church of Christ, the church must constantly seek to be a "liberated zone" within which relationships embody liberty and equality. I also concur with Moltmann's claim that such relationships will not be possible if we overlook the specific nature of the day-to-day communication that is presupposed or simply assume that the communication that exists enhances liberty and equality among all members of the congregation.

Liberty and equality do not exist in the lived reality of vast numbers of people in the United States today, despite our national commitment to these values. Unless the church engages in the demanding work of creating and continuously supporting practices that engage the wisdom and contributions of all members — regardless of education, age, class, gender, race, ethnicity, disabilities or other variables that we use to create unrighteous divisions in the church — we will construct a social reality that simply reflects the social reality of the culture in which the church is embedded. The culture in which a community of faith exists will always be a major influence on any church community. We would be unwise to think we could avoid it. If we recognize the influences of culture, however, and intentionally choose practices and ways of communicating that reflect the values of the gospel rather than the culture, it is possible to create forms of community that stand in marked contrast to what is found in other institutions.

One of the contributions the discipline of rhetoric can make to our understanding of church practices concerns the construction of formal and informal hierarchies within the church. For several decades, feminists, black theologians, and liberation theologians have challenged the ways in which the hierarchies of society are replicated within many religious denominations, with preference and status given to males of western European ancestry.

Although the call to eliminate hierarchies is not uncommon, a rhetorical analysis suggests that it is not possible to eliminate hierarchies entirely. In a group of people of any size, some people will have more influence in relationship to certain issues and actions than others. The persons who have the most influence may vary easily and frequently. In other words, flexible hierarchies may emerge in different situations without becoming rigid and self-replicating. At any given point in time, on a given issue, however, there are going to be some "storytellers" who are more influential than others. From this perspective, an analysis of the flow of communication within a particular group will reveal ways in which perhaps quite subtle influence patterns function to establish a hierarchy among participants. In some groups the patterns of influence are quite obvious. For example, some persons are allowed to establish and change the topic of conversation, speak for longer periods of time, speak without interruption, receive respectful attention when they are participating, occupy more space, and influence the way a group decides to think about an issue. In any group, a careful analysis of the verbal and nonverbal communication of each group member relative to the other group members over a given period of time will suggest what may be either a temporary or fairly permanent hierarchy of status and influence. Burke believes that hierarchies are always present. He emphasizes, however, that acknowledgment that hierarchies always exist in no way justifies the existence of any particular hierarchy.

When we work to change an unjust hierarchy, we need to be aware that we will replace it with some other hierarchy. Eliminating an unjust way of structuring relationships does not lead automatically to liberty and equality. If we recognize the subtle ways in which hierarchies are created in social reality, even when they are not formally codified, we will be more likely to maintain vigilance in nurturing the quality of relationships within the church that we believe reflect God's will for the church. Local congregations, like all organizations and communities, are dynamic institutions that can change radically in a short period of time. A vibrant, faith-filled community may be demoralized and lethargic a few months from now. A dying congregation may be revived and begin to engage in dynamic ministry. As individuals within the community change, as people leave and new people join the group, the social reality must continuously be reconstituted to embody the values and commitments the congregation affirms. This dynamic process comes into focus when we engage the insights of rhetoric and communication theory.

People who are in positions of power and authority within any institution have the opportunity to empower others. Leaders with a captivating vision of a dynamic community of faith or a vibrant, educational institution can empower others to take the risks and make the effort required to embody such visions. When leaders have a narrow, ideological vision for the church or an educational institution, they are more likely to create a culture in which loyalty to the dominant ideology prevails and creative risk-taking efforts on behalf of a more dynamic vision are stifled. From a rhetorical perspective these different leaders are responding to very different "stories" of what the church, Jesus Christ, and theological education are all about.

If we follow Fisher's proposal for conceptualizing human rationality in terms of all people's ability to respond to the narrative coherence and narrative fidelity of "stories" they are offered for their adherence, we will be more likely to pursue and value the wisdom of people whose ways of thinking and communicating do not conform to the rules of the dominant discourse. The history of Christian religion in the United States provides good reasons for adopting Fisher's conceptualization of human rationality.

The Paradigm Exemplified: Challenging the Narrative Coherence of Slavery

The underlying narrativity of experience — as well as the intuitive human response in terms of narrative coherence and narrative fidelity — are illustrated by the responses of slaves in the United States to the gospel. Many uneducated slaves in the South accepted Christianity and responded with a deep faith that inspired courageous action. Albert J. Raboteau offers historical examples of slaves who began to understand the "story" of their relationship to their owners in a significantly different way as a result of their self-identification as Christians. In one example, Raboteau points out that

> when the master's will conflicted with God's, slaves faced a choice which was simultaneously an opportunity to assert their own free will and to act virtuously, even heroically, in the context of Christianity, in which disobedience to white authority, no matter the consequence, could seem morally imperative. . . . Beatings did not stop slaves from praying, and those prayers were symbols of resistance, symbols whose power was not underestimated by planters.[20]

Prayer was a particularly effective symbol of resistance, Raboteau points out, because both the slave and the slave owner believed in its power.

---

[20] Albert J. Raboteau, *Slave Religion* (Oxford: Oxford University Press, 1978), 307.

Slaves were also emboldened by the frequent experience of owners calling slaves to their bedside when they were dying. One slave, John Brown, wrote, "It is a common belief amongst us that all the masters die in an awful fright, for it is usual for the slaves to be called up on such occasions to say they forgive them for what they have done. So we come to think their minds must be dreadfully uneasy about holding slaves."[21] Raboteau points out that these experiences, and their Christian faith, not only gave slaves belief in "their moral superiority to whites but also a serious measure of psychological and emotional control over them."[22]

Raboteau's illustrations reflect ways in which uneducated slaves responded to the lack of narrative coherence in the story of Christianity and the stories of the world presented to them by white owners and pastors. "As early as 1774, American slaves were declaring publicly and politically that they thought Christianity and slavery were incompatible."[23]

Within the rational-world paradigm, experts are privileged as the ones who are able to make and evaluate rational arguments. From such a perspective, some white pastors asserted their superior ability to understand the Bible and sought to legitimize slavery and quiet any rebelliousness by pointing to the passages in the Pauline literature that admonish slaves to remain in slavery and conduct themselves as good slaves (Ephesians 6:5–9, for example). Within the rational-world paradigm, the challenge brought by slaves could be dismissed as uneducated and irrational because they had not been allowed to learn the forms of argument favored by those in power.

If one considers human rationality from within the narrative paradigm, however, the playing field is leveled. Many slaves knew intuitively there was something fundamentally incoherent in the story whites told to assert the compatibility of Christianity and slavery. The story didn't "hang together." Slave owners' death-bed efforts to extract forgiveness from their slaves were part of the story of reality that provided "good reasons" for the slaves' perspective. By approaching Raboteau's data using the expanded

---

[21] John Brown, *Slave Life in Georgia*, ed. L. A. Chamernvzow (London: 1855), 203–204. Quoted in Raboteau, *Slave Religion*, 292.

[22] Raboteau, *Slave Religion*, 293.

[23] Raboteau, *Slave Religion*, 290.

conceptualization of human rationality that Fisher proposes, we gain deeper insight into the rhetorical dynamics present in this part of Christian history.

Of course, not all slaves responded the same way. In fact, Raboteau points out that the same slave did not necessarily respond the same way at different points in his or her life. Raboteau argues that the relationship between Christianity and slavery is complex. He rejects as overly simplistic, however, the "story" of Christianity and slavery that points only to ways in which Christianity contributed to an other-worldly spirituality that supported slavery.

The story Raboteau tells in his analysis of slave religion resonates with the stories of uneducated lay persons in South America who began to challenge the relationship between the church and the governing powers that oppress the poor. Peruvian theologian Gustavo Gutiérrez' presentation of liberation theology was initially rejected by the Vatican.[24] However, Gutiérrez explains that when priests were told to stop preaching liberation theology, they had to explain to Rome that they could not stop liberation theology because it was coming from the people themselves and their "uneducated" insights into the good news of liberation found in the gospel. Eventually, Rome not only relented; the pope began to incorporate the perspective of liberation theology into his proclamation of God's "option for the poor." As Gutiérrez points out, the reason Rome could not stop the message of liberation theology was because the people were basing their demands on their reading of the Bible.[25]

Implications for Theological Education

Engaging the insights of twentieth-century rhetoricians and communication theorists leads to important questions we need to ask about every aspect of church practice and theological education that involves human communication. If we follow Burke's perspective that whenever meaning is generated, there is rhetoric, then we must conclude that there is a rhetorical dimension to every oral or written communication event. This

---

[24] Gustavo Gutiérrez, *A Theology of Liberation* (1971; reprint Maryknoll, N.Y.: Orbis, 1990).

[25] Gustavo Gutiérrez, Public lecture at Princeton Theological Seminary, Princeton, New Jersey, spring 1996.

claim does not imply that a rhetorical analysis exhausts what there is to be said about a given communication event such as worship, a session meeting, prayer group, student forum, formal lecture class, or small group discussion. Nevertheless, those who seek to understand such events will overlook critical dynamics if the rhetorical dimension is not explored. If we apply this perspective, along with Fisher's notion of the narrative paradigm, we will notice more details of the formal communication events that occur in the church, such as preaching, worship, and education. We need to look carefully at the intentional and unintentional, verbal and nonverbal aspects of these events. Many elements influence the process of identification, some of which we may not consider unless we are intentionally focusing on all the complexity of a particular communication event. The totality of communication will lead participants to perceive an overall "story" that may or may not coincide with the "story" the church or seminary wants to share.

When we communicate with one another to discern the better way, we seek to induce cooperation from others in several ways simultaneously. In beginning the dialogue, we invite others to participate. They could do otherwise. In choosing certain forms of communication and avoiding others, we influence the ongoing engagement of others in the process. Our choice to use language all will understand is part of the rhetorical process of seeking to induce others to communicate with us. If we choose to use language that others will not be able to understand, or that we know will offend them, that choice may influence others to drop out of the conversation or demand a change of communicative form.

Other people are influenced by the verbal and nonverbal forms through which we communicate, and by the substance of what we say (elements that in the final analysis cannot be separated). Consequently, rhetorical structures are in operation whenever influence is present — as it always is when two or more people communicate with one another. From this perspective, those who disparage the use of rhetoric and deny its legitimacy are engaged in the use of rhetoric themselves. We do not have the option of avoiding the process, if we are in the presence of others. Failure to recognize the presence of rhetoric does not constitute its absence. It only means that those denying the presence of rhetoric have forfeited some degree of self awareness in recognizing the nature and function of their own communicative behavior.

In order to understand responses to communication events in any institution, including the church and the seminary, we must recognize that all communication events — whether preaching, committee meetings, classes, Bible studies, prayer groups, or potluck dinners — occur within a dynamic environment. The environment consists of the fluid, and only partially controllable, flow of manifold, polysemous communication events that occur within the organic life of any institution. The boundary between one event and another is porous. Angry words shouted at a committee meeting will influence how people hear one another during a Bible study. What happens between the pastor and a group of parishioners on Thursday will influence, in at least subtle ways, how they hear the sermon on Sunday.

Similarly, the boundary between communication events within an institution and communication events in the wider social and cultural milieu, is also porous. Despite calls for Christians to join together in communities that challenge destructive cultural norms and influences, there is no way for us to insulate ourselves completely from the culture that has played a defining role in constructing our sense of self and our sense of reality. That cultural history, for better or worse, goes into the autobiographies in terms of which we understand ourselves. We will make changes in our self-reflexive autobiographies over time. We may have experiences and insights that even transform them radically. Although the formative influences of the past may be reinterpreted in significant ways, they can never be eliminated. The communication environment inevitably seeps into the communication events within the church; it influences what people know about, what they believe to be true, and how people respond to the narrative coherence and the narrative fidelity of the intentional messages that are communicated in worship and in educational contexts.

Within the seminary, these "communication events" include the textbooks that are chosen, and the ways in which these books are written; the ways in which faculty, students, and administrators communicate with one another in formal and informal contexts; and the ways in which people seek to adjudicate among diverse theological perspectives. The full range of communication events that occur in the life of a seminary community *necessarily* brings us into the realm of rhetoric. If we do not recognize the rhetorical dimension of our endeavor, we will fail to understand why we find some theological understandings compelling and reject others. We will fail to understand why some schools nurture healthy, dynamic relationships among students and faculty of diverse backgrounds and others deepen painful divisions.

A more adequate and holistic understanding of the rhetorical processes that constitute the life of the local congregation, as well as the seminary, will not solve the serious problems we face. Nevertheless, such an analysis will assist us in understanding more fully the realities that contribute to many of our problems. Such analysis will also help us become more aware of the ways in which the communication events that constitute the social reality of the church and its educational institutions serve or undermine the mission we seek to fulfill in our commitment to God.

Chapter 3

Rhetoric, Postmodernism, and Theological Education: What Has Vincennes to Do With Athens *or* Jerusalem?

A. K. M. Adam

In 1979, a relatively obscure French philosopher from the University of Paris VIII (Vincennes) published the results of a study of higher education, commissioned by the Conseil des Universités of the province of Quebec. Shortly thereafter, readers who would never crack the spine of *The Libidinal Economy* found themselves speaking confidently and expansively about Jean-François Lyotard's *The Postmodern Condition: A Report on Knowledge*.[1] Many of these savants seem to have appropriated little more from this work than a proclivity to define "postmodernity" as an "incredulity toward metanarratives." Such sloganeering shows little understanding of Lyotard's broader argument, and ignores the context in which he invokes that phrase.[2]

---

[1] *The Libidinal Economy*, trans. Iain Hamilton Grant (Bloomington, Ind.: Indiana University Press, 1993; originally published 1974); *The Postmodern Condition*, trans. Geoff Bennington and Brian Massumi (Minneapolis: Univ. of Minnesota Press, 1984).

[2] This famous phrase appears not in main text of the "report on knowledge" itself, but in the three-page introduction; Lyotard says, "simplifying to the extreme, I define *postmodern* as incredulity toward metanarratives" (xxiv). Both the immediate context ("simplifying *to the extreme*") and Lyotard's subsequent exposition of the postmodern condition (not to mention Lyotard's various other works) articulate a more nuanced presentation of postmodernity than many of

In any case, Lyotard's report became the touchstone in a discussion of what constitutes postmodernity, whether we inhabit a postmodern era, and similar questions.

But why should readers interested in the confluence of theology, Scripture, rhetoric, and theological education care about "the postmodern condition"? Although I expect that theologically-interested parties should have no particular stake in "postmodernism" *per se*, we should pay attention to postmodern interrogations of modern culture on numerous grounds. One very significant reason: Rather than simply thinking along *with* our culture — accepting without question that *its* assumptions and priorities should be *our* assumptions and priorities — we may examine those assumptions and priorities to see whether we ought thoughtfully and deliberately to promulgate them as Church leaders and educators. If we choose not to examine our assumptions, we will be promulgating them nonetheless — but we will be promulgating them heedlessly and uncritically, ignoring the biblical admonition to "test every spirit." On the other hand, we may opt to examine the characteristic underpinnings of our culture, to learn as much as we can about them, and then to decide whether these are sound assumptions on which we can contentedly rely, or whether some other assumptions are more fit for disciples of Jesus and teachers of the Gospel. Postmodernism shares with the rhetorical tradition an unwillingness to allow the shape and structure of the theological project to be determined exclusively by the assumptions of modern culture.

Lyotard's Critique of Modernity

Jean-François Lyotard's work represents a provocative contribution to a broad and deep argument about modern and postmodern cultural assumptions, and theologically-interested parties have ample reason to

---

Lyotard's ebullient supporters and facile detractors suppose — though he does frequently cite the decline (or demise) of belief in grand narratives of emancipation as symptomatic of postmodernity. For a richer account of Lyotard on postmodernity, cf. *The Postmodern Explained*, (Minneapolis: University of Minnesota Press, 1992), and a variety of articles on specifically postmodern concerns (and many other works pertinent to the topic), some of which have been collected into *Toward the Postmodern*, ed. Robert Harvey and Mark S. Roberts (Atlantic Highlands, N.J.: Humanities Press, 1993), and "A Svelte Appendix to the Postmodern Question," in *Political Writings*, trans. Bill Readings and Kevin Paul Geiman (Minneapolis: University of Minnesota Press), 25–29.

probe the relation of theological discourses and ecclesial practices to the cultures they inhabit. *The Postmodern Condition* teaches the useful lesson that modernity is no longer the only game in town; one can think differently from modernity without foregoing critical intellectual responsibility. Since one of the cultural assumptions most characteristic of modernity is its dismissive attitude toward theological premises,[3] theologians should have a strong motivation to investigate alternatives to modern assumptions. And this motivation will be doubly present for scholars and leaders who are seeking alternative models for reshaping not only their own particular disciplines, but the entire shape and structure of theological education.

Lyotard observes that once upon a time, "knowledge" came from authorities whose status depended on their *identity* as narrators (which might involve their location in the social structure, the awareness of the narrators from whom they learned, and their *ēthos* or character); he calls this "narrative knowledge," though one could reasonably argue that this category covers too many different modes of knowledge.[4] Here the transition from French to English curtails the breadth of Lyotard's thesis; Lyotard subtitled his book *Rapport sur le Savoir*, which was rendered *A Report on Knowledge* for the English edition. As Lyotard points out in the text of the book, however, *savoir* comprises not only the academic information that the English "knowledge" connotes, but also *savoir-faire, savoir-vivre, savoir-dire, savoir-écouter*: know-how, street smarts, and so on.[5] In this context, *savoir* might better be translated with the gerund "knowing": "A Report on Knowing."

Modernity favors a different sort of knowledge, which Lyotard characterizes as "scientific knowledge." The legitimacy of scientific knowledge depends on impersonal, technical criteria: whether it is produced and confirmed by accredited experts, subject to testing and falsification, productive of further research possibilities and of commercial

---

[3] As John Milbank observes in "Problematizing the secular — the post-postmodern agenda," in *Shadows of Spirit*, ed. Philippa Berry and Andrew Wernick (London: Routledge, 1992), 30.

[4] *The Postmodern Condition*, 18–23. Jeffrey Stout has given a rich account of authority in antemodern conditions in *The Flight From Authority* (Notre Dame: University of Notre Dame Press, 1981).

[5] *The Postmodern Condition*, 18.

benefits. Modern scientific discourse follows a strict order based on *denotation* — on data, number, and equations — rather than artfully crafted prose, speculation, ornamentation, or prescription.[6] A scientist's sphere of authority is, in theory, the domain of experimental data and empirical regularities; the character of the scientist makes no difference to the legitimacy of the scientist's conclusions, nor does the prose with which she specifies her claims, nor the practical consequences of her scientific claim. Further, modern discourses occlude other, non-scientific modes of knowledge. Lyotard points out that "the scientist questions the validity of narrative statements and concludes that they are never subject to argumentation or proof. He classifies them as belonging to a different mentality: savage, primitive, underdeveloped, backward, alienated, composed of opinions, customs, authority, prejudice, ignorance, ideology. Narratives are fables, myths, legends, fit only for women and children."[7]

Other kinds of knowing perdure nonetheless. Indeed, they *must* continue, since (in an ironic reversal) scientific knowledge depends on narrative legitimation to sustain its position as the uniquely authoritative discourse of truth.[8] Scientists invest considerable rhetorical energy in associating their work with humanity's progress from the gloom of ignorance to the bright light of ever-increasing knowledge in order to sustain science's prestige over against the recurrent threat that the defenders of science perceive in parascientific discourses (UFOlogy, astrology, alternative medicines, past-life regression, and so on). Adherents to modern ways of knowing hold that science provides a paradigmatic example of the appropriate, even *necessary* approaches for all other fields, disciplines, and areas of study to follow.

---

[6] *The Postmodern Condition*, 18–37.

[7] *The Postmodern Condition*, 27. One might correlate the pair of scientific knowledge and narrative knowledge with other epistelogical pairs such as the distinction between *technē* and *epistēmē*, or between *sapientia* and *scientia*, but such an endeavor would bear fruit only were one to pay painstaking attention to the differences among the discourses that frame these pairs.

[8] *The Postmodern Condition*, 27. "A crude proof of this: what do scientists do when they appear on television or are interviewed in the newspapers after making a "discovery"? They recount an epic of knowledge that is in fact wholly unepic. They play by the rules of the narrative game" (27–28).

The very notion that there are such things as "fields" where we study discrete entities called "theology," "biblical studies," and so on, bears on our work in countless ways. Not least of the ramifications of this compartmentalization is the enigma of how to connect theology to biblical studies appropriately — but we could multiply the examples indefinitely. The impetus to parse various topics into their own tightly-bounded specialized domains can seem inevitable and obvious. The divisions that vex us are not immutable facts of nature, however; to take but one apposite instance, the separation of dogmatic theology from biblical interpretation is a relatively recent development (Thomas Aquinas, after all, held a chair in *Sacra Pagina* at the University of Paris). The notion that the various areas of theological study should be separated from one another develops from the specifically modern notion that different sorts of inquiry diverge in such fundamental ways that they each possess a distinct logic, a distinct subject matter, and should be studied in distinction one from the other.[9] This premise generates a panoply of irksome conflicts between the departments in theological education, and debilitates students' capacity to see the ways that the topics of their curriculum always entail considerations pertinent to all the theological departments.

The modern divisions of academic labor derive much of their power over our imaginations from two features of the scholarly world: the expectation that anyone authorized to contribute to theological discourse be credentialed as an expert, and the expectation that these theological experts be productive. The criterion of expertise reinforces disciplinary isolation by requiring would-be scholars to specialize on ever-finer topics. And since it may be easier to generate new knowledge by looking at a smaller topic than by trying to bring new insight to a larger, more familiar topic, the criterion of productivity further underwrites the segregation of scholarly effort. These imperatives to seek expertise and productivity correlate to a modern sensibility that restricts "knowledge" to the province of experts who alone are qualified to authenticate or reject truth-claims. Then, modern experts are expected to demonstrate their expertise by

---

[9] The recent works of Hans Frei and David Kelsey illuminate this tendency in theological education: Frei, *Types of Christian Theology*, ed. William C. Placher and George Hunsinger (New Haven: Yale University Press, 1992); Kelsey, *Between Athens and Berlin* (Grand Rapids, Mich.: Wm. B. Eerdmans, 1993) and *To Understand God Truly* (Louisville, Ky.: Westminster/John Knox Press, 1992).

producing manifest results of one sort or another (whether these be publications, media appearances, patents, or discoveries).

Yet we would do well to ask the question (unthinkable for moderns), "Does theological discourse truly benefit from these proliferating bits of knowledge?" Is "productivity" in itself a desirable criterion for theologians? If we adhere without wavering to an ideal of productivity, we may risk running afoul of theological admonitions against pride and excess. At least some traditions of ethical reasoning would counsel that an unbridled appetite for publication signals a disordered set of priorities.

We might likewise "call the question," theologically, against the ideology of expertise. If, on modern terms, only experts provide legitimate guidance for understanding a subject area, then modern readers ought presumably to disregard the interpretive authority of *un*credentialed theologians such as Francis of Assisi or Sojourner Truth, or even of credentialed theologians who speak on matters outside their area of specialization. Ludicrous as such a prospect appears, modern premises incline forcefully against non-specialist knowing. For instance, histories of biblical interpretation typically condescend to (if they do not outright sneer at) ancient and medieval interpreters who produced readings of the Bible that do not measure up to what modern scholars have ascertained by "scientific" investigation. That very modern impulse, however, runs against a Christian tradition (and a rhetorical tradition) that has long held that one can appreciate both "knowledge" and "wisdom." Compare Francis's understanding of the Sermon on the Mount to that which Hans Dieter Betz articulates in his 700-page *Hermeneia* commentary[10]: to which representation of the sermon would we direct the Church for guidance in following Jesus?

We may demur from some of the specific features of modern knowledge that Lyotard proposes, but the general characteristics in his description correspond closely to features that the discourses of academic theology have adopted. The professional journals and research publications in theology and biblical studies tend to fit the pattern of "scientific knowledge" that Lyotard sets out. Colloquial usage ascribes to "science" the responsibility for determining actual conditions and facts. As Stanley Fish observes, "In our culture science is usually thought to have the job of

---

[10] Hans Dieter Betz, *The Sermon on the Mount*, ed. Adela Yarbro Collins, Hermeneia Series (Minneapolis: Fortress Press, 1995). The commentary (which covers both Matthew's Sermon on the Mount and Luke's Sermon on the Plain) actually comprises 692 numbered pages and 38 pages of front matter.

describing reality as it really is; but its possession of that franchise, which it wrested away from religion, is a historical achievement not a natural right."[11] Thus the humanities disciplines, often including theological studies, rush to append the modifier "scientific" to their reflections in order to highlight the modernity and authenticity of their conclusions. The (hard) sciences, by contrast, have shown little interest in adding to *their* cultural capital by appending the modifier "literary" or "historical" or "theological" to their names. (We see no sign, for instance, that biologists and zoologists are eager to reclaim the description "natural history" for their studies.) Modern, scientific knowledge rules the discursive roost.

Such a state of affairs generates serious problems for theological reflection. If the premises of science be established as criteria of knowledge and reality, claims about the existence of God (much less, God's triune nature) will attain at best a derivative authority: "It's not inconsistent with what we otherwise know about the world." This reverses the order of authority that the Christian tradition has characteristically ascribed to the stories it tells; Scripture, creeds and confessions have served as the fundamental definitions of what the Church knows, with other discourses elaborating things known on ecclesiastical authority. The Church has an admittedly poor track record in discerning how best to handle such matters as the Galileo affair or paleontological research; nonetheless, theologians need not conclude that they must submit their essays to departments of biology, chemistry, and physics for approval.

This is because, if Lyotard's analysis is right, scientists do not hold the copyright to knowledge. If we once allow that science provides only one of a variety of interwoven, *interdependent* discourses about knowledge, the imperative to measure all kinds of knowing by the canon of scientific legitimacy simply falls away. Other varieties of knowing, with different grounds for legitimation, provide a more congenial medium for cultivating theological wisdom. Indeed, theology, with its peculiar relation to revealed knowledge, to an immeasurable subject, to tradition and faith and hope, would appear to provide a cardinal example of a sort of knowing that

---

[11] Stanley Fish, *Professional Correctness* (Cambridge: Harvard University Press, 1995), 72. The fact that it occurred to Fish to describe science's predecessor as "religion" rather than "theology" or "the Church" suggests one element of his *own* professional location.

doesn't fit well under scientific rubrics.[12] Where scientific knowing thrives with empirical observations and quantifiable regularities, wisdom in the theological sense comes less from data and laws than from prayer, meditation, and attention to the very particularities that impede modern efficiency. Since theologians seem to speak a different language from scholars of religious studies, scholars of religion have translated theological claims into more familiar discourses such as structural functionalism in sociology, which can examine theological claims in terms of what effects they seem to have on human behavior. Still, Christians have typically thought hardest and struggled most about claims concerning such topics as the relations among the persons of the Holy Trinity, the relation of divinity to humanity in Jesus, the claim that Jesus was Christ and Lord. Such claims are remote from the sorts of questions science can address without changing the subject to fit a more scientific mode. To the extent that one addresses such questions to scientific investigators, one can expect only to learn the material causes and conditions that might give rise to convictions about theological topics; the topics themselves are opaque to scientific examination. Indeed, John Milbank has advanced a persuasive case for the thesis that various so-called "human sciences" — sociology, economics, political science — are themselves denatured theologies. That is, the social sciences try to give an account for human behavior in ways that depend on theological insights, but they replace God's providential agency with an "invisible hand" or "social pressures" or "market forces" or some other secular surrogate. Then, when the social sciences have extirpated the visible signs of their debt to theology, they return to demand that theologians submit *their* discourses to examination at the bar of social theory for scientific legitimation.[13] Modern theologians have fretted about the extent to which their teachings conflict with, or fit into, popularly-accepted scientific knowledge, but they might better concentrate on the extent to

---

[12] The academic religious-studies mainstream is undergoing a series of convulsive self-examinations as some scholars strive to become more truly scientific; thus where once one found the National Association of Biblical Instructors, one now finds the American Academy of Religion, which itself is insufficiently scientific for the North American Association for the Study of Religion, according to polemics documented in popular publications such as *Lingua Franca* and *The Atlantic Monthly*.

[13] *Theology and Social Theory* (Oxford: Blackwell, 1990).

which their theological tenets explain social phenomena to Christian observers more satisfactorily than do secular social studies.

Inasmuch as modern culture favors efficiency, productivity, and impersonal scientific knowledge, modern systems tend to treat people as instantiations of a Universal Subject, a human entity whose characteristics are intrinsic to "humanity" and whose deviations from the general features of humanity merit consideration mainly as impediments to the smooth functioning of state and commercial apparatuses. Modern ethical reasoning speaks *"human* rights" as its native language, asserting the fundamental interchangeability of any human person — though these are usually defined in markedly particular terms (citizens of the United States have "free speech" as a human right, but not adequate health care, whereas citizens of China have "adequate health care" as a human right, but not free speech).

The Universal Subject presents a myriad of subtle problems for theology. To the extent that such a hypothetical person is universal, of course, he[14] is no one in particular — but the God of Christian theology knows everyone *particularly,* so that to the extent that theologians permit a modern insistence on universality to dominate their doctrines, they collaborate with the modern proclivity toward homogenization (with its concomitant risk of assuming that all people should be *like us,* without interrogating "our" prerogative to determine the norm of human existence).

The modern subject situates itself at the peculiar intersection of its proper transtemporal identity (so that modern humanists can claim continuity with a "common humanity" discerned in Sophocles and St. Paul as well as Jefferson and Hammarskjold) and of the claim that modernity looks backward at its past across a vast abyss of time. Modernity treats the chronological gap as an ontological given; sometimes, by virtue of our humanity, we can clamber across for a moment's appreciation of ancient

---

[14] Although gender ought not make a difference in modern circumstances, the Universal Subject has typically taken an identity defined in androcentric terms; it has only recently figured out that women can be part of the modern project, too. From the beginning it was not so; the U. S. Constitution decreed that "all men are created equal," and France promulgated the Declaration of the Rights of Man. Feminist scholarship has shown over and over that this is not simply accidental, that the Universal Subject is, if not always male, at least always dressed in a man's suit. Here Luce Irigaray's *Speculum of the Other Woman,* trans. Gillian C. Gill (Ithaca N.Y.: Cornell University Press), remains the canonical analysis of cultural "hom(m)osexuality," or "monosexuality" (as she says in her later works).

insight, but under most circumstances the past is too far from modern experience to be seen without the aid of experts. One of modernity's defining moments took the form of a rebellion against the authority that antemodern culture ascribed to antiquity; in the *Querelle des Anciens et des Modernes* (in France) and the Battle of the Books (in Britain), adolescent modernity shook off the myth of classical superiority and set itself on a pedestal of its own construction. Modernity had not only *surpassed* its ancient forebears, but left them behind on the far side of a chronological rupture.

Such a gap is not simply *there,* of course (where would it be?); it is constructed by modernity's self-fashioned isolation from its precedents. While the modern world differs from ancient societies in certain respects — only a fool would dispute that — the gap is not temporal but cultural. One can readily find at this moment cultural spheres that are profoundly foreign to modern Euro-American ways, and some which are relatively close to the social world of antiquity. By the same token, certain dimensions of first-century lifestyles are not radically dissimilar from contemporary currents in New York or Paris, while other aspects of ancient culture are utterly alien. Where gaps impede our understanding of antiquity, time is only one of numerous possible obstacles to sympathy and apprehension.

Since the birth-struggles of modernity became firmly associated with its self-assertion over against ancient authority, time has also played an especially prominent role in the modern world-view. Time is the medium in which modern figures perform their hallmark gesture: that of surpassing what has gone before. Thus under modern conditions, one will tend to ascribe authority not just to contemporary sources but only the very most up-to-date sources. (Of course, this generates the modern paradox, wherein that which is truly modern is always already on the verge of becoming *passé,* and in order for a modern work to endure, it must be *ahead* of its time.) Modernity decrees anachronism a high crime, and banishes that which is out-of-date to the refuse-bins at the side of time's superhighway.[15] Whereas Jesus' adversaries in the Gospel of John always ask "Where is he from?" modern investigators ask "When was it published?"

---

[15] Indeed, "anachronism" now functions almost automatically as a term of abuse as much as the designation of a specific transgression. When you and I both propose rival "relevant" interpretations of a given passage, *yours* will be anachronistic, whereas *mine* will appropriately draw on an existing similarity between the ancient context and our contemporary setting.

In sum, the modern age has built its criteria for legitimacy into a self-portrait: modern scholars paint themselves as the jet-fueled protagonists of culture's drama who race ever forward, glancing behind only to see how far they have come. They never rest content with what others have discovered, but always break new ground. Unsentimental and skeptical, they resolutely search after facts, debunking one after another mythical narrative (except that on which their identities depend). Their private life is no business of ours; they are productive and efficient, unembarrassed by distinguishing particularities. They are *modern*, and if they harbor any theological inclinations, their creed keeps well within the bounds established by Newtonian physics, Darwinian biology, Freudian psychology, and functionalist sociology. These Universal Subjects of modern culture hold an ambivalent relation to faith in Christ; if they concede the idea cogency at all, they subscribe only to a fully demythologized (read: *re*mythologized) religion within the limits of reason alone, distancing themselves from Organized Religion.[16]

This composite sketch of modernity vividly highlights certain features and soft-pedals others. No one, of course, embodies all of the features described herein, nor does anyone embody all to an equal degree; yet the face of twentieth-century theological and biblical scholarship remains strikingly modern. The resemblance is especially arresting once one remembers that modernity harbors an ineradicable, *essential* resistance to any theology that presumes to say how matters stand, and why they stand as they do, in a divergent (narrative) mode of knowing. As Alasdair MacIntyre acutely remarked, in response to modernity "theists are offering atheists less and less in which to disbelieve."[17] Theologians are left with the choice of handing over the riches of their spiritual inheritance to the arbiters of modern knowledge or finding an alternative to modern criteria for legitimacy.

Theology Without Modernity

Granted all these considerations, readers who are interested in the convergence of biblical interpretation, theology, rhetoric, and pedagogy

---

[16] It should be noted that most *post*modern scholars likewise distance themselves from Organized Religion; such may be a sign that modern and postmodern are not so very different, or perhaps as a sign of the residual modernism that inhabits the scholars in question.

[17] Alasdair MacIntyre, in MacIntyre and Paul Ricoeur, *The Religious Significance of Atheism* (New York: Columbia University Press, 1969), 24.

have ample reason to step off the superhighway of modernity. Since "postmodern" instruction in Scripture and theology will not be just one thing — a new, improved *method* or a different canon of texts — scholars who adapt their approaches to avoid the limitations they discern in modernity will respond to the postmodern difference *differently*. Prominent opportunities for such theologians, biblical scholars, rhetoricians, and other interested parties include the possibility of pursuing biblical and theological studies as rhetorical (rather than scientific) practices, of a richer continuity of instruction in Bible and theology, of attention to instruction as a mode of the production and reproduction of theological knowing, and of critical attention to rhetoric, Bible, theology, pedagogy, as parts of daily life.

In all these areas one might construct "restorationist" antemodern (and *anti*-modern) models of Bible, theology, rhetoric, and pedagogy. Indeed, modern scholars are likely to regard *any* deviation from their institutional conventions as reversion to an allegedly pre-critical sensibility (I myself once read a paper situating the path of literary critical New Testament studies in a context framed with thematic reference to Paul de Man and Fredric Jameson — but was scolded for my "nostalgia" in subsequent panel discussion, on the ground that I had invoked the category of "allegory" in a discussion of biblical interpretation). Such a reflexive critique overlooks two points: first, that dissent from modern presuppositions does not imply placid submission to premodern principles, and second, that the critique itself tends to derive its cogency from specifically modern assumptions, so that the modern scholar accuses postmodern readers of a methodological failing — for not being modern. But that, after all, is the point of *distancing* oneself from conventional methods; the condemnation merely highlights the postmodern difference in attitude by emphasizing the modern interpreter's narrow, self-confirming criteria and the postmodern interpreter's deliberate deviation from modernity.[18]

---

[18] It is unlikely that most biblical scholars will be able to diverge much more than "deviating" from a modernity that has shaped not only the academy, but many culturally-prominent currents of everyday life. Few scholars are so loosely-rooted in modernity that they can, by force of theoretical will, separate themselves radically from modern culture. Readers who want to resist modern assumptions will usually be obliged not to banish modernity (which would result in the installation of a new, improved cultural formation — a frustratingly *modern* gesture), but to warp modern practices, to twist their interpretations, to propose varying *versions* (di-versions, re-versions, maybe even per-versions) of their modern interpretive tasks.

The preceding paragraphs noted various ways that modern assumptions had shaped the discourses of biblical and theological instruction. If, for instance, the borders that separate the lines of inquiry that belong to the four classical divisions of seminary instruction (biblical, historical, dogmatic, and practical theologies) were relaxed — if border crossings were less vigilantly policed — then there would be no less reason to write about the pastoral importance of dogmatic theology than about the extent of Sabellianism in the third-century church.[19] Such interdisciplinary ventures would appear less a *tour de force,* more a plausible outgrowth of an interest in Christian identity, vocation, and nurture. Biblical scholars would not assume that scientific critical research offers the *only* valid avenue for interpreting Scripture, such that credentialed biblical experts speak the last word on particular passages; instead, they would recognize that they stand to learn from the insights of their forebears in any century.

Moreover, although modern biblical and theological studies restrict their engagement with rhetoric to tightly delimited bounds, an approach that readily crosses these boundaries can identify "rhetoric" not exclusively as a feature of the texts being studied — "Paul's rhetoric" or "Nazianzen as rhetor" — but as a fundamental aspect of *knowing*. Thus Paul's rhetoric does indeed reward careful study, but our own study of Paul is every bit as much a rhetorical enterprise as Paul's letters themselves are. Critics who attend to the rhetorical dimensions of knowing will be less inclined to focus only on the criteria indigenous to what Lyotard identified as modern scientific knowledge, and more inclined to account for such elements of knowing as the purpose to which the knowledge would be put, as the character of the interpreter and readers, as the way that the study is pursued and represented, and as the effects that the study engenders. All of these elements are constituents of Lyotard's "narrative knowledge";[20]

---

[19] One oddity about the reception of Ellen Charry's *By the Renewing of Your Minds: The Pastoral Function of Christian Doctrine* (New York: Oxford University Press, 1997) is that this venture in church history, dogmatics, and pastoral theology should attract notice *simply for having been attempted* — when her thesis would suggest that these interests (which present academic practices make disparate) have, under other conditions, been profoundly integrated.

[20] *The Postmodern Condition*, 19–27, *passim*. Readers should also be aware that Lyotard has a significant interest in rhetoric, though I do not highlight those texts here — particularly in the ways that rhetoric counterbalances and complicates

these criteria are foreign, however, to the modern, scientific mode of legitimation.

In the remainder of this chapter, I want to provide one example of the possibilities that postmodern thinking offers us for the process of re-visioning theological education. I focus my attention on the specific area which has been known as "biblical theology,"[21] a no-one's-land between the disciplinary domains of dogmatic theology, biblical studies, historical theology, and church history.[22] Whereas the modern pursuit of "biblical theology" has labored to produce a discourse that employs the criteria of biblical criticism (conceived as scientific knowledge), a postmodern

dominant groups' capacity to dictate the terms for legitimate discourse. The touchstone essay for this interest is "Sur La Force des Faibles," originally published in *L'Arc* 64 (1976): 4–12, with various English translations: trans. A. K. M. Adam and David S. Cunningham, *Critical Theology* 1 (Epiphany 1989): 23–33; trans. Fred J. Evans in *Toward the Postmodern*, 62–72; a somewhat different text was translated by Roger McKeon in *Semiotexte* 3 (1978): 204–14. Lyotard alludes to this *topos* at various other points, including "Retortion in Theopolitics," in *Toward the Postmodern*, 120.

[21] Stephen Fowl proposes that the goals that have hitherto been sought under the heading of "biblical theology" be framed as "the theological interpretation of Scripture." This would have the advantage of evading the persistent (modern) argument over the *nature* of biblical theology, and of disabusing interpreters of the illusion that "biblical theology" is a *thing* that subsists apart from interpreters' efforts to articulate it. "Introduction," *Engaging Scripture* (London: Blackwell, 1998), 1–31.

[22] Theologians have already begun to explore the consequences of a rhetorical approach to theological knowing; cf. David S. Cunningham, *Faithful Persuasion: In Aid of a Rhetoric of Christian Theology* (Notre Dame, Ind.: University of Notre Dame Press, 1991) and *These Three are One: The Practice of Trinitarian Theology* (Oxford: Blackwell, 1998); Serene Jones, *Calvin and the Rhetoric of Piety* (Louisville, Ky.: Westminster John Knox Press, 1995); Don H. Compier, *What Is Rhetorical Theology? Textual Practice and Public Discourse* (Harrisburg, PA: Trinity Press International, 1999); and Stephen Webb, *Re-Figuring Theology: The Rhetoric of Karl Barth* (Albany, N.Y.: State University of New York Press, 1991). Biblical scholarship has made less headway to envisioning itself as a rhetorical practice, but Fowl's *Engaging Scripture* stakes out some of the possibilities. See also David S. Cunningham, "Rhetoric," in A. K. M. Adam, ed., *A Handbook of Postmodern Biblical Interpretation* (St. Louis: Chalice Press, 2000), 220–26.

approach to biblical theology permits other constellations of criteria.[23] It helps to illumine the role of the Bible in theological education for a postmodern, post-Christian era.

Biblical Theology:
Teaching the Bible under Postmodern Conditions

Biblical theology has often devoted vast intellectual energies to methodological questions, occasionally to the utter exclusion of any "theology" (biblical or otherwise). This comes as no surprise to postmodern critics of biblical scholarship, since scientific knowledge requires that the end of inquiry be internal to the investigative process: "The conditions of truth, in other words, the rules of the game of science, are immanent in that game, they can only be established within the bonds of a debate that is already scientific in nature."[24] The problem of method haunts biblical theology with especial poignancy. "Scientific" study of the Bible is thought to permit no discussion of God or God's purposes, no arguments for or against various church structures, no assessments of how people who take the Bible as Scripture ought to live out their lives; consequently, such matters are deferred as strictly irrelevant to the technical study of the Bible. The strain of connecting such an ascetically non-theological regime of knowledge to the constructive enterprise of framing claims about God, God's purposes, ecclesiology, and Christian ethics has constituted a grievous burden to biblical theologians. This burden is needless, however; interpreters who accept postmodern criticisms of modern accounts of "knowing" may demur from the widely-perceived obligation to propound only such interpretations of biblical texts as would pass muster for an issue of the *Journal of Biblical Literature*. The perceived *necessity* of a scientific foundation derives from specifically modern concerns. In response to modern demands for a legitimating method, a theologically-interested reader of Scripture may cite Camus's aphorism, "Quand on n'a pas de caractère, il faut bien se donner une méthode" ["If you lack

---

[23] In these paragraphs, I draw on arguments I make at greater length in *Making Sense of New Testament Theology* (Macon, Ga.: Mercer University Press, 1995).

[24] Lyotard, *The Postmodern Condition*, 29.

character, you'd better offer a method"].[25] The legitimacy of a theological interpretation derives not primarily from the method by which it was produced (as under modern conditions), but on its situation: its relation to the interpreter, the readers, the location from which it was produced, the ends for which it was produced, and the effects that it has (or may plausibly be anticipated to have). Thus, in the first instance, a biblical theology built with postmodern premises may relax its methodological obsession in favor of attending to the specific circumstances pertinent to the interpretation. Where modern biblical theologians worry that apart from scientific interpretive warrants there may be no valid criteria at all, postmodern interpreters face the challenge of a superabundance of criteria by which their endeavors might legitimately be assessed.

A second difference from modern biblical theologies arises when interpreters deliberately commit anachronism in order to make their case more persuasive on grounds other than those allowed by modernity. Anachronism can take at least three directions: anachronism in the rendering the purpose of the biblical texts, anachronism in interpreting the purport of the biblical texts, and anachronism in interpretive method. The first of these meets with little or no resistance among modern interpreters, perhaps because certain aspects of the historical interests with which many modern interpreters probe the Bible are themselves anachronistic.

The second of these, however, engenders fierce opposition. Since biblical interpreters so often struggle against anachronism when they aim at *historical* claims, they may fall into the habit of regarding anachronism as a flaw *tout court*. While historically-sensitive readers may find anachronism distasteful, however, it does not constitute a sin against the Holy Spirit such that no forgiveness may be extended to the transgressor. Anachronism serves rhetorical functions that are not intrinsically illegitimate, but — as is usually the case with rhetorical figures — depend for their legitimacy on broader considerations. If a biblical theologian reckons that the problems concomitant with a deliberately anachronistic approach — say, to investigating the possibilities of trinitarian theology in the book of Isaiah — are outweighed by the potential fecundity of such study, then anachronism itself is not the issue. The scholar's judgment (that such anachronistic exploration is warranted) is open to question: "Is it really that important to 'find' trinitarian theology in Isaiah?" The scholar's interpretation itself may

---

[25] Cited in Jeffrey Stout, "A Lexicon of Postmodern Philosophy," *Religious Studies Review* 13 (1987): 20.

be questioned ("That's not trinitarian!"), or the interests served by producing such a reading; but each of these criticisms is logically independent of the legitimacy of an anachronizing approach.

The third mode of anachronism evokes the most outright hostility among modern scholars. Few interpretive devices provoke such furious (and misplaced) outrage as allegorical interpretation, which modern critics have vehemently marked as an approach whose time has long since passed.[26] "By means of allegory," so the historicists say, "one can force a text to mean anything one wants" — a claim as hermeneutically confused as it is empirically implausible. Still, scholars protest that allegorical interpretation equals interpretive nihilism, which mocks reason and makes of Scripture a wax nose "and wrest[s] it this way and that way."[27] A wax nose, however, is still recognizable as a nose (rather than a football or a laptop computer), and there are limits on how far "this way and that way" one can wrest it without it losing the qualities that define it as a wax nose. Be it admitted: there is no Rule of Wax Rhinosity, which would determine

---

[26] My defense of allegorical modes of interpretation does not entail an utter rejection of the benefits that historical sensitivity has brought. On the contrary, I would argue that an acute engagement with the historical setting of biblical texts stands to enrich figurative interpretations, and *vice versa*. Historical study of the Bible has alerted readers in the late twentieth- and early twenty-first centuries that former depictions of Judaism were liable perniciously to distort the faith that Jesus held; Christian theological interpretations that attend to a (historically) sounder interpretation of Judaism will themselves be the stronger for their efforts.

The problem of allegory in contemporary biblical interpretation has drawn renewed attention of late; see especially Graham Ward, "Allegoria: Reading as a Spiritual Exercise," *Modern Theology* 15 (1999): 271-95; Mark Brett, "The Political Ethics of Postmodern Allegory," in *The Bible in Human Society: Essays in Honour of John Rogerson*, ed. M. Daniel Carroll R., David J. A. Clines, and Philip R. Davies (JSOT Supplement Series, 200; Sheffield: Sheffield Academic Press, 1995), 67-86; Stephen Fowl, *Engaging Scripture* (Oxford: Blackwell, 1998); and Frances Young, "Allegory and the Ethics of Reading," in Francis Watson, ed., *The Open Text* (London: SCM Press, 1993), 103-20.

[27] William Tyndale, quoted by H. C. Porter in "The Nose of Wax: Scripture and the Spirit from Erasmus to Milton," *Transactions of the Royal Historical Society* 14 (1964), 155. Porter notes that the "wax nose" *topos* seems to have originated with medieval expositor Alain of Lille, appearing also in Johann Geiler von Kasierberg in the fifteenth century.

scientifically when the waxen item makes the transition from "nose" to "misshapen lump"; nonetheless, one can't flatten the wax altogether and still claim it as a wax nose, and (to return to the topic) an allegorical interpreter can't wrest the Scriptures too far this way and that way before her work is no longer an allegorical interpretation.[28]

Modern biblical scholarship scarcely ever misses a chance to attack allegorical interpretations. William Irwin, to take but one instance, used his SBL Presidential Address in 1958 to denounce the "old errors we had supposed long-since deep buried,"[29] and to assert, "That [typology] is wrong in genesis and being there can be not the least doubt."[30] The vehemence of such assaults might lead one to conclude that a popular tsunami of allegorical interpretations was threatening the well-being of truly scientific criticism. This sinister tidal wave has yet to materialize. Irwin may have been right to worry, but perhaps there is more at stake than

---

[28] Karlfried Froelich has given a thorough account of the extent to which the practice of allegorical interpretation was rule-governed in his 1997 Warfield Lectures, of which the first, "'Aminadab's Chariot': The Predicament of Biblical Interpretation," has been published in *The Princeton Seminary Bulletin* 18 (1997), 262–78. Now, too, Henri de Lubac's *Medieval Exegesis* is appearing in English translation (Grand Rapids, Mich.: Wm. B. Eerdmans): vol. 1, trans. Mark Sebanc, 1998; vol. 2, trans. E. M. MacIerowski, 2000.

[29] "A Still Small Voice . . . Said, What Are You Doing Here?" *Journal of Biblical Literature* 78 (1959): 5. He did concede that the hermeneutic he decries is not merely a resuscitation of the discredited methods of the first century, or "crass medievalism."

[30] Ibid. One might object that Irwin here denounces *typology*, not *allegorical interpretation*. The difference between typology and allegory is subtle, and the extent of the difference is disputed; at the very least, however, one must allow that a sizable constituency of biblical critics have allowed typology as a risky but permissible sort of theological interpretation. G. W. H. Lampe — whose essay on "Reasonableness of Typological Exegesis" helped rehabilitate that mode (and evidently irritated Irwin) — commended typology in contrast to allegory; he finds allegory to be fanciful, "sheer rubbish," "tak[ing] no account of history"; "no allegorist can claim to be interpreting Scripture or to be a Biblical theologian" (!). See G. W. H. Lampe and K. J. Woollcombe, *Essays on Typology* (London: SCM Press, 1957), 31–33. If Irwin mistrusted the more innocuous typological approach, how much more abominable must allegory itself have seemed?

only disinterested concern to protect biblical criticism from interpretive nihilism.

For example, biblical scholars face an unusually fierce degree of contention from uncredentialed interpreters; since one does not need advanced academic training to become an allegorical interpreter, modern academic interpreters can uphold strict loyalty to scientific methods as one way of insulating themselves from their amateur rivals. Critics who demean allegorical criticism also distance themselves from cultural formations that do not spurn allegory — that is, most cultures other than modern Euro-America. Moreover, the various interpretive maneuvers that collectively constitute the repertoire known as "historical criticism" — the stock-in-trade of modern biblical criticism — are themselves thoroughly allegorical in form. Where frankly allegorical interpreters read their texts as correlative to doctrines and prescriptions, historical interpreters read the same texts as correlative to historical events and agents.[31] In both approaches, we construe a less-well-known text by mapping it to a corresponding better-known field of reference. The formal congruence of scientific biblical criticism and its anachronistic allegorical Other requires modern critics to differentiate their interpretive methods all the more vigorously from non-modern alternatives.[32]

I have indulged this lengthy digression on allegorical interpretation for several reasons. First, allegorical interpretation represents a familiar model for theological interpretation of Scripture. Revisiting allegory would not require expositors to start from scratch in their interpretive practice, but would offer a field within which to cultivate a theologically-trained imagination. Contemporary biblical scholarship scrupulously suppresses the exercise of imagination in order to avoid the "wax nose" of allegoresis,

---

[31] A. K. M. Adam, "The Future of Our Allusions," *SBL 1992 Seminar Papers*, Eugene H. Lovering, ed. (Atlanta: Scholars Press, 1992) 9–11, and Gerald Bruns, "On the Weakness of Language in the Human Sciences," in *The Rhetoric of the Human Sciences*, ed. John S. Nelson, Allan Megill, and Donald N. McCloskey (Madison: University of Wisconsin Press, 1987), 239–62.

[32] A practice of deliberate anachronism differs from carelessness in historical reasoning; the two are logically and practically separate from one another, and modern scholars would be hard-pressed to demonstrate that one leads to the other. For the record, I do not propose that historical scholars stop taking pains to avoid anachronism in their historical-critical reasoning.

the folly of supposing that we can enter into the consciousness of biblical characters to ascertain their feelings and motivations, the wish-fulfilling theological interpretations that stretch historical possibility in hope of bolstering the factuality of biblical stories. Even scientific reasoning requires a dose of imagination, however — and historiography requires more than a smidgen of imaginative writing. History-writing is a kind of poiēsis that always obliges authors to propose a persuasive plot for the main characters to enact, and requires both author and reader to exercise their imaginations to make connections among events, characters, and the probabilities of (historical) experience. Where biblical scholars aspire to abstemious restrictions on the role of imagination in their treatment of characters and theology, they often permit their imaginations to run wild in proliferating sources, laws of transmission, and conjectured editorial motives. A scholar who proudly repudiates any belief in the unseen God may passionately defend the intellectual *necessity* of believing in Q; postmodern critics may, however, doubt that Q is more pertinent to understanding the Beatitudes than is Aquinas. Biblical theology stands in desperate need of the disciplined exercise of faithfully-formed imagination, and the practice of allegorical interpretation provides one means to nurture this capacity.

Second, allegoresis makes no appeals to modernity's scientific modes of legitimation, but it legitimates its transmission in ways that better fit Lyotard's sketch of *narrative* knowledge. Perhaps allegorical knowing demonstrates its non-scientific character clearly in that its goal is not simply *better* allegorical interpretation, but always a more profound understanding of God and God's ways with us. Whereas modern knowledge ought to be *dis*interested, free from the impurities that extrinsic entanglements might insinuate into the process, the theological knowledge that allegoresis cultivates is *always* particular and interested. Allegorical explication includes among its elements the tropological and anagogical interpretations, each of which attends to ethical dimensions of hermeneutical practice. Tropology identifies ethical correlates to its biblical passages, and anagogy describes the fruit of faithful discipleship (or departure there from); each of these derives legitimation in part from the extent to which the interpreters authenticate their interpretation by the ways they live, and each provides counsel and guidance for believers who seek more fully to embody the faith they confess with their lips. Tropology and anagogy, along with the allegorical mode (as technically defined, the "doctrinal" dimension of the interpretive *quadriga*) draw further confirmation from their relation to the rule of the Church's faith. The contrast with modern biblical scholarship at this point could not be sharper, since the latter takes pride in its *freedom* from the constraints of theological (and ethical) accountability. Some proponents of interpretive heteronomy have gone so far as to suggest that any biblical interpretation that tends to confirm what the Churches believe is, by that circumstance, subject to suspicion until it is demonstrated beyond the shadow of a doubt.[33] Practitioners of allegorical interpretation, however, can aim frankly to support and strengthen the church's faith without a hermeneutical bad conscience; enriching and upholding theological claims is one of allegorical interpretation's principal purposes.

Finally, I invoke allegory because the same academic traditions that passed along this mode of theological exegesis simultaneously preserved the rhetorical tradition.[34] Indeed, the two topics were integrated in preaching manuals from Augustine's *De Doctrina Christiana* through Bede to Aquinas and the other Dominican teachers — and though one can never step into the same academic river twice, the antemodern confluence of rhetoric, Scripture, theology, and teaching in the medieval manuals provides a reference point from which postmodern pursuers of a like configuration of these discourses might orient themselves. Perhaps the medieval vision of an interpretive practice comprising diligent interpretive research, theological accountability, articulate instruction, and a faithful way of life provides a more sensible model for persuasive theological

---

[33] Even Leander Keck — an ardently committed defender of church and faith — argued (in a review article of Alan Richardson's *Introduction to the Theology of the New Testament*) that any portrait of the New Testament must "disturb comforting convictions" and "is itself suspect until it legitimates itself." Thus, he assigns to biblical theology the role of *disrupting* traditions. See "Problems of New Testament Theology," *Novum Testamentum* 7 (1964/65): 220.

[34] This point is no surprise to scholars working in the fields of Augustinian studies and of the history of exegesis; cf., for example, Robert W. Bernard, "The Rhetoric of God in the Figurative Exegesis of Augustine," in *Biblical Hermeneutics in Historical Perspective*, ed. Mark S. Burrows and Paul Rorem (Grand Rapids, Mich.: Wm. B. Eerdmans, 1991), 88–99; Joseph Anthony Mazzo, "St. Augustine's Rhetoric of Silence," *Journal of the History of Ideas* 23 (1962): 175–96; Michael J. Scanlon, O.S.A., "Augustine and Theology as Rhetoric," *Augustinian Studies* 25 (1994): 37–50. The coinherence of rhetoric, biblical interpretation, dogmatic theology, ethics, and practical theology remains concealed, however, from those who regard disciplinary boundaries as obvious, inescapable, and necessary.

interpretation of Scripture than any modern conglomeration of methods and facts, no matter how ornate its scientific theological veneer.

All of this suggests that a postmodern critique of the modern condition is much broader and more significant a phenomenon than many commentators have heretofore admitted. Moreover, this critique has implications for theology and for the future of theological education that we are only just now beginning to grasp. As I have attempted to suggest in this chapter, the philosophy of Jean-François Lyotard signifies in one part the lessons of this critique. In yet another part, however, Lyotard provides a passage to lessons from an earlier moment in the history of the University of Paris, a moment at which Aquinas expounded Scripture without differentiating his dogmatic, exegetical, practical, or historical observations. Under this earlier sign, we may remember a different wisdom from that which modernity has taught us; under the more recent sign, we can take the critical acuity that modern science has refined, and put it to work on behalf of the wisdom from above.

PART TWO

THE TASKS OF THEOLOGICAL EDUCATION

Chapter 4

Theology as Communication: Revelation, Faith, and the Church as Ongoing Dialogues

Bradford E. Hinze

The most basic theological reason rhetoric merits attention in Christian theology is that dialogue and communication constitute the very identity and practice of Christianity. This dialogue and communication is the kind of living discourse between persons, human and divine, that changes and nourishes the hearts, minds, and lives of individuals, and establishes and transforms entire communities and cultures. Exploring the dialogical and communicative character of revelation, faith, and the church enables us to appreciate the theological significance of rhetoric in Christianity.

There is more to be gained here than securing a theological rationale and perspective for the study and use of rhetoric in Christian life. The rediscovery of rhetoric in our day offers the prospect of deepening and enriching our understanding of God's revelation and the response of faith in the church. Indeed, it could be said that there is a grace in this opportune rediscovery of rhetoric. It is a grace that surely could be trivialized, spoiled, and abused by human sinful and finite purposes, especially in our own unstable age. But, it is a grace nonetheless, and the theological task is to be receptive and responsive to this grace by exploring the rightful and illuminating place of rhetoric at the very center of Christianity.

Revelation, faith, and the church are commonly understood in terms of the self-communication of God: in the cosmic theater of God's communicative action, women and men are invited into a dialogical encounter and saving communion with the divine persons of the Trinity and with a community of human persons. This communicative process is the crux of conversion, worship, and service to others. It is a fellowship that involves a dynamic exchange of listening and speaking, receiving and responding. In this fellowship, the human powers of reason and freedom, the imagination and the affections are touched by a divine power as they strive for and culminate in judgments, decisions, and actions that shape the lives of individuals and communities.

In short, dialogue is the medium of salvation and sanctification. Through communication people are freed and forgiven, redeemed and reconciled, restored and reoriented. Through communication people love and engage in works of love, and believers are drawn into the very life of friendship with God and into a community of friends. Through God's self-communication and the dialogical communion it generates, people are offered a glimpse, however cloaked in mystery and darkness, of the identity and purpose of God — and a sense of their own individual and collective identity and mission.

Christian experience is shaped by communication wherein messages are conveyed and received. *Communication* can refer to formal and structured modes of discourse in public settings — religious, educational, political, legal, and economic — where knowledge is transferred, and judgments and decisions made, where people through conversation strive to "reach an understanding" and sometimes even consensus.[1] In Christianity, these modes of "communicative action" are important for the transmission of beliefs and practices. But just as important in Christianity are those unstructured and informal modes of communication, where the reciprocal dynamic of dialogical relationships is pursued without agendas, objectives, and syllabi, and where the movement of dialogue is generated by the sharing of life, convictions, desires, concerns, hopes, dreams, and suffering. These formal and informal modes of communication are not

---

[1] See the influential work of Jürgen Habermas, *Theory of Communicative Action*, 2 vols., trans. Thomas McCarthy (Boston: MIT Press, 1985, 1987), and the theological appropriation of his work by Edmund Arens, *Christopraxis* (Minneapolis: Fortress, 1995).

simply things Christians do; they indicate who Christians are. In other words, Christians understand themselves in terms of dialogical relationships, based on the reciprocal dynamic of conversation.[2]

This being so, Christianity requires a dialogical, that is, a social and interpersonal ontology of personhood — one which describes the ways that processes of individuation and identity-formation, vocation and mission come to existence through bonds of intimacy and mutuality. Such bonds are experienced in community and in friendship where, through face-to-face relationships, knowledge, freedom, and love are intertwined. Accordingly, Christians can never ultimately be satisfied with a view of personal identity as static, assuming some essentialist, substantialist notion of the self; nor can they rest content with a sense of the self as entirely elusive, in a constant state of flux, fragmented, even composed of multiple selves. Instead, they are involved in a lifelong process of personal individuation, identity-formation, and integration through dialogue. Dialogical relationship is the defining characteristic of the Christian understanding of God and the human person, and this conviction cuts across every category in Christianity. The study of rhetoric serves to clarify the communicative and

---

[2] The significance of dialogue (conversation) and dialogical relationships have been emphasized by a wide range of twentieth century philosophers. Earlier in the century dialogue was stressed by Jewish and Christian personalist thinkers associated with the work of Martin Buber, Franz Rosenzweig, and Gabriel Marcel. Hans Urs von Balthasar accentuates this tradition in *Theo-Drama: Theological Dramatic Theory*, vol. 1, trans. Graham Harrison (San Francisco: Ignatius Press, 1988), 34–37, 626–648. So, too, Hans-Georg Gadamer has concentrated on dialogue, giving special attention to the Platonic dialogues and the work of R. G. Collingwood. Gadamer's contribution has been central for David Tracy in *The Analogical Imagination* (New York: Crossroad, 1981), and in *Plurality and Ambiguity* (Chicago: University of Chicago Press, 1987). While affirming the contributions of these two trajectories, I wish to give special attention to the importance of real difference and the diversity of voices in the dialogical situation as both an ethical and religious provocation in the various moments of communication: in rhetorical invention, in literary or oral works themselves, and in the history of receptions. Here the contributions of Emmanuel Lévinas, Mikhail Bakhtin, and Hans Robert Jauss move us beyond the earlier two understandings of dialogue. This broader vision of dialogue must be complemented by the insights born of ecumenical and interreligious dialogues.

dialogical character of Christianity, which has its most basic rationale in the nature of divine and human reality.

Exploring the dialogical and communicative nature of revelation, faith, and the church provides the simplest and most profound explanation for why rhetoric is so important for theology. Moreover, attention to matters rhetorical provides new intelligibility and new ways of being responsive to the work of the trinitarian God in the ongoing dialogue of Christianity. This chapter will examine the rhetorical character of revelation, faith, and church, especially in view of the threefold Aristotelian rhetorical topics of *logos, ēthos,* and *pathos*. It seeks not only to highlight some of the insights gained, but also to contribute to a cumulative case for the indispensability of rhetoric in theology.

The Rhetoric of Revelation

Divine revelation can be studied in terms of rhetoric for many reasons, but the most important theological justification for such an investigation is that Christians understand God and human beings in terms of communication and a dialogical ontology.[3] Christians profess that God is striving to communicate everywhere. God is the Original Rhetor, who seeks to convey God's identity and purpose and, by so doing, promotes dialogical communion. To this end, Christians believe there are countless manifestations and proclamations of God in the created cosmos and in

---

[3] Over thirty-five years ago, Ray L. Hart commended a rhetorical approach to revelation in *Unfinished Man and the Imagination: Toward an Ontology and a Rhetoric of Revelation* (New York: Herder and Herder, 1968). For him, that meant revelation is rhetorical because it is an event of language that provides the imaginative bridge, more by metaphors and symbols than narratives and arguments, between the ontic and ontological, the extensive and intensive dimensions of the human person. He presented revelation as the aesthetic vehicle for the eschatological journey of unfinished human beings that moves forward by way of thought and action. His position is advanced in the thick idiom of the Continental philosophical tradition — indebted especially to Edmund Husserl, Maurice Merleau-Ponty, and Martin Heidegger, but also to Hans-Georg Gadamer and Paul Ricoeur. Very little is explicitly said about rhetoric, and he does not address the specific treatments of rhetoric by Heidegger and Gadamer in the works he consults. Much has been done on the philosophical front since the publication of this work. See, as one example among many, Walter Jost and Michael J. Hyde, eds., *Rhetoric and Hermeneutics in Our Time: A Reader* (New Haven, Conn. and London: Yale University Press, 1997).

human history. Christians have been especially alert to God's self-communication in the history of Israel, in the history of Jesus of Nazareth, and in the pouring out of the Spirit upon Jesus' companions and upon the Church throughout the ages. At the same time, God's presence and agency in nature and in alien neighbors has also been acknowledged. Biblical and ecclesial traditions attest to these manifestations and proclamations and they serve to transmit basic beliefs and practices that are derived from them. In fact, the mediation of revelation in Christian tradition, both biblical and post-biblical, is by its nature a rhetorical process of communication. The very constitution of tradition is a rhetorical process. Biblical and ecclesial traditions have not only been generated by rhetorical acts, they have also been handed on to new generations, applied, explicated, expanded, and revised by such acts. The living discourse of the Christian tradition is rhetorical, and it cannot be otherwise.

At the core of these traditions is an invitation into a personal encounter with the triune God of Christian faith in everyday life. In the recollection of these traditions of beliefs and practices, the encounter, communication, dialogue with God is initiated anew and maintained in face-to-face meetings and in communal gatherings. Christians universally agree on *prima scriptura* — that biblical traditions provide privileged access to this process of communication at work. By means of the scriptures being read, prayed, dramatized, and ritualized, the dialogue of revelation, faith, and the church continues.

The communication of God's identity and God's saving purposes occurs in myriad ways through the human testimony of biblical witnesses. How these witnesses effectively convey a divine speaker and actor — through human speakers, writers, and editors too numerous to imagine — has been a source of much consternation, debate, and reflection over the last two centuries. The claim that God speaks in the scriptures is no longer typically identified with a theory of verbal inspiration which posits that God speaks directly in words and sentences to scribes. But that the scriptures attest to God's communication in the cosmos and in human history continues to be affirmed and cherished by Christians as a central conviction of their faith. And Christians remain convinced that the scriptures should be venerated as the word of God because they are an effective medium of God's self-communication. The living voice of God is heard regularly by ears of faith, read with eyes of faith, and received with hearts of faith when these biblical words are spoken and read. That genuine communication is mediated by sacred texts does not discount the fact that there are countless stumbling blocks, fragments, and even texts of terror in the scriptures that impede or distort conversation, and that in fact are unworthy of God and dangerous for the human community. Likewise, many believers who wrestle with the authority of selected biblical texts also insist upon the reliability of doctrinal and propositional truth-claims about God's identity and saving plan, conveyed in the scriptures and derivatively formulated and transmitted in church teachings. Study of the rhetorical character of revelation provides the means to respect the communication process involved in the divine economy that is mediated through these biblical traditions — and that continues on in the living tradition of faith — without denying its richness, complexity, and dangers.

The dialogue presented in the scriptures is not one in which God's declarative sentences are completed by the obedience of faith — in which God speaks and the reader agrees. Rather, the scriptures convey *various* messages about the identity and purpose of God, as they have been learned in communities and communicated by various speakers using a multitude of rhetorical devices. Moreover, the scriptures transmit a great diversity of responses of hearers and audiences: shock, disappointment, confusion, attraction, resistance, indifference, conversion, transformation, worship, service, love. Speakers, messages, and audiences are intertwined in the revelatory witnesses of the scriptures, which thereby exhibit their dialogical character. The dialogical process attested to in the scriptures does not end with the event of listening to or reading the scriptures. Rather, it continues in the living discourse of the church in various forms of proclamation: in preaching, catechesis, worship, and in the formation of official teachings — all of which communicate the doctrinal heritage of revelation. Attention to rhetorical matters helps us to reverence the details of these messages and responses and of the communal experiences they represent.

The role of rhetoric in biblical and ecclesial traditions has been in evidence since earliest Christianity, but has not always been appreciated. Since the 1970s, thanks to the work of many scholars of the Bible and early Christianity, a deeper appreciation of the use of rhetoric in the genesis, transmission, and ongoing development of the proclamation of the living gospel and of the doctrinal heritage has been gained. Recent studies have confirmed that a comprehensive understanding of revelation transmitted through biblical and post-biblical traditions is best acquired by attending to the various rhetorical components that comprise this communicative process.⁴ One can develop a greater understanding of the rhetoric of revelation by examining the three classic foci of rhetoric: *logos, pathos*, and *ēthos*.

First, discovering the rhetoric of revelation entails ascertaining the *logos* of tradition. In biblical exegesis this means attending to how figures of speech, narratives, and examples are configured in the development of persuasive arguments in these traditions. Moreover, one is required to identify the genre selections that are governed by the diverse needs of a given rhetorical situation: eliciting praise or blame of individuals or groups (epideictic), supporting basic community convictions and commitments, or bringing about a judgment on a contentious matter (forensic), or fostering deliberation about matters that merit communal decisions and actions (deliberative). These rhetorical considerations affected the development of teachings and arguments by Jesus, Paul, the gospel writers, and the many other texts that constitute the Hebrew and Christian Scriptures. The study of the rhetoric of revelation ought not to be reduced to one more exegetical technique helpful for determining literary form and genre. Rather such information would be best put in the service of illuminating the larger communicative process of revelation.

Being alert to rhetorical considerations in New Testament traditions cultivates a dialogical imagination by enabling one to enter into the multiple layers of dialogue at work in revelatory traditions: the face-to-face dialogue between actors in narrative texts, the dialogue between texts, readers, and communities of readers, and an ingredient in all of these, the dialogue between the Triune God and human persons.⁵ Let us consider some of these layers of dialogue briefly.

---

⁴Many of these works are cited throughout the present volume; I will not repeat them here. Reviews of the literature include Don H. Compier, *What Is Rhetorical Theology? Textual Practice and Public Discourse* (Harrisburg, PA: Trinity Press International, 1999), chapter 1; Bradford E. Hinze, "Reclaiming Rhetoric in the Christian Tradition," *Theological Studies* 57/3 (September 1996): 481-499.

⁵ As previously indicated, the approach to dialogue being espoused here draws on the history of recent reflection on dialogue in philosophy and theology; while we rely on the treatment of dialogue by an earlier generation of scholars, notably Martin Buber and Hans-Georg Gadamer, we also seek to incorporate the insights and impulses of a plurality of voices, the contestation of positions in the dialogical process, and the ethical dimensions of dialogue of the divine and the human in the of the work of Mikhail Bakhtin, Emmanuel Levinas, and Hans Robert Jauss.

On one level there can be gained a new recognition of the rhetorical power of Jesus' own teachings. His use of simple tropes and stories invite his audience to consider the power of God's reign and the impact it can have on one's life, like the seed received in rich soil that produces much fruit. His tropes and stories can amuse and disturb, challenging audiences' expectations about how God works: God's reign is like a banquet where the elite turn down the invitation and the unwanted are welcomed; when God reigns, the last are first, the poor are blessed, the people who work an hour are paid a full day's wage, and the despised outsiders are the good neighbors. Jesus is a rhetorically effective speaker: his discourse wins him close friends and followers, but also leads to conflicts and animosity.

At another level, through the gospel stories, we enter into dialogical episodes aimed to persuade us that the destructive, demonic powers of sin, anxiety, disease, derangement, social convention, economic hardship, and death itself, will not be victorious. The power of God's reign will triumph in the end: learn from sparrows, lilies, and little children; learn from Jesus who reaches out in compassion to those who are overcome by powers that threaten and stifle life. But in a special way, learn from Jesus how he faces his own death in the way of the cross: in generosity, in trust, in anguish, and in darkness. Once we have been touched and transformed by these dialogical encounters, then, and only then, will we be ready to absorb the full reality of the resurrection of Jesus — when the final enemy is defeated, and the rhetorical argument of Jesus' teachings and way of life is vindicated.

We are led by the very genres of the gospels to other levels of dialogical rhetorical insight. Certainly these genres lead the hearer or readers to praise (encomium, panegyric) the main character: indeed, to praise and reverence the work of God in Jesus. But these gospel genres — and here Mark's gospel offers an eloquent example — also invite the followers of Jesus to emulate the way of the Lord. They foster deliberation about what it means to be a follower of Jesus where his way presents a communal way, where standing firm and resistance can lead to martyrdom on the way to victory.

The rhetoric of revelation inevitably invites and leads receptive readers and hearers — through the gospels, the Pauline corpus, and the rest of the New Testament chorus — into the trinitarian dialogue that informs the identity and mission of God and the people of God. Jesus' dialogical encounter with the God he called Abba and with the Spirit that anoints with power are necessary to comprehend the identity and mission of Jesus. Here is the lure of God for humans to enter into a trinitarian friendship. The dialogical character of revelation is trinitarian at its core, and demands a trinitarian hermeneutic.

Awareness of these and other rhetorical concerns guided early Christian leaders in their preaching, worship, letter writing, biblical commentaries, and in their heated debates over doctrinal matters. When leaders disagreed about the identity of Jesus and the Spirit in relation to God the Father and Creator, or the need for God's grace for salvation, rhetorical arguments were the medium. These disputes resulted in the convocation of bishops charged to reach official judgments and led to finely crafted public teachings. These judgments were, in turn, rendered as propositional truth-claims — generated out of the scriptural witnesses, and presented in simple declarative form in official church teachings about the identity and purposes of God, about the nature of the human person and the hope of salvation. These official judgments and propositional claims constitute not the *end* of the conversation, not the *cessation* of the rhetorical process, but rather the beginning of a new phase in the living dialogue of a revelatory tradition. Symbols and conciliar statements, with their logical clarity and simplicity, are not the product of grammarians and logicians working in seclusion; rather, such prose is the result of rhetorical dialogue in a living community of faith about the very content of Christian faith and practice. In this process, leaders work together to fashion sentences that can meet the challenge of the day and that withstand the test of time. The study of the rhetorical character of official church teachings thus enables readers to hold together in a dynamic relationship the abiding power of a community's charter language and the social and historical process of reception, reinterpretation, and revision of this heritage.

The study of rhetoric came into currency in Hellenistic Judaism with rabbinic methods of interpretation of the scriptures, which were utilized in nascent Christianity in the genesis of its biblical traditions and the transmission and development of its ecclesial traditions. Rhetoric thus left its mark on the faith's formative traditions.[6] The contemporary rediscovery of rhetoric affords the opportunity not merely to reclaim rhetoric in the genesis of these traditions, but to utilize this information to recognize and

---

[6]David Daube, "Rabbinic Methods of Interpretation and Hellenistic Rhetoric," *Hebrew Union College Annual*, 22 (1949): 239–63; idem., "Alexandrian Methods of Interpretation and the Rabbis," *Festschrift Hans Lewald* (Basel: Verlag Helbing & Lichtenhahn, 1953), 27–43.

cherish the plurivocity of revelatory traditions as a living dialogue — spanning past and present, and reaching out into the future. The choice is not between propositional literalism and demythologizing; instead, we are invited to reverence the particulars of the living discourse of revelation by attending to the details of a rhetorical dialogue that is already underway.

Ethos refers to the construction and authenticity of the moral character or persona of a speaker or writer making a given rhetorical argument. The quality of the character making the argument lends credence or reliability to the argument being advanced: character generates authority. Whether it is Jesus in the gospel narratives, Paul in the letter to the Galatians, Athanasius against the Arian sympathizer, or Maximus the Confessor in his debate with the proponents of a monophysite Christology, in each case the quality of the character bears upon the quality of the argument. The same is true for every preacher, catechist, teacher — indeed, for every Christian who gives witness to Jesus Christ in the power of the Spirit: bearers of revelatory tradition must be people of character who teach with their lives as much as with their words. Orthopraxis is as important as orthodoxy. The character of individual Christians and church communities that bear this tradition are no doubt sinful and their vision finite; but since these individuals and communities are formed by God's grace, they are enabled to speak with authority (though always under divine judgment).

Rhetoric, finally, teaches speakers and writers to respect the *pathos* of the listening and reading audience. At issue is not simply how to reach an audience, but how to respect the authority of the audience. So, on the one hand, the rhetorical interest in pathos assumes a holistic anthropology that entails a respect for intellectual judgment and free decision, but that also does not undermine the important apprehension of the good, the true, and the beautiful through the affections and the imagination. On the other hand, respect for the passions of the audience entails honoring the common sense and collective memory of the audience, which reflects the repository of cultural wisdom. A local audience or community may be misguided at times, but their common sense and memory can never be dismissed when crafting arguments. The metaphors, stories, and examples of the heart are cherished resources that must be utilized in the service of the truth and the community. Rhetoric teaches speakers and writers that the listening or reading audience is always to be considered — for it is their reception, their reactions, their responses in affect, judgment, and decision, that complete the rhetorical process. The reception of the word of God — in human judgments, decisions, and actions — is, simultaneously, the work of the Holy Spirit.

In sum, the sense of the community is important not only in the formation or development of doctrine, but also in the reception of this doctrine. Lacking the living bond with the community, doctrine can become disconnected from the prophetic charism that is given to the entire community mediating the Christian tradition. Acknowledging the *pathos* of the community in communication requires honoring the authority of the audience in the formation of a communion of persons in the ways of orthodoxy, orthopraxis, and liturgy.

By attending to the rhetoric of revelation — to its *logos, ēthos,* and *pathos* — we gain access into the communicative process that constitutes the very nature of tradition, biblical and post-biblical. However, we are not simply identifying three discrete objects in a synchronic snapshot; nor are we trying to focus only on the author's intention, the text's literary structure, or the reader's or audience's response as isolated and privileged aims and norms, as some biblical scholars have advocated.[7] Rather, here we are offered the prospect for resolving the modern fragmentation of biblical and doctrinal hermeneutics into author-centered, text-centered, and reader-centered approaches: by concentrating on the rhetorical character of revelation, the entire diachronic process of living communal discourse comes to light.[8] The creative and critical work of writers and speakers is high

---

[7] See the critique of this approach offered by A. K. M. Adam in chapter three of the present volume; see also David S. Cunningham, "Rhetoric," in A. K. M. Adam, ed., *A Handbook of Postmodern Biblical Interpretation* (St. Louis: Chalice Press, 2000), 220–26.

[8] Over the past two hundred years there have emerged three basic approaches to biblical and ecclesial traditions: (1) author-centered, (2) text-centered, and (3) reader-centered. Many debates in biblical studies are between proponents of different approaches to interpretation, who emphasize one part on this complex reality of author(s), texts, and readers, often in isolation from other parts. But it is significant that representatives of each of these approaches have been taking an interest in the rhetorical composition of biblical texts. The debates among these various approaches are unavoidable, but perhaps they can become more focused and productive by concentrating on how the rhetorical character of Scripture unites authors, texts, and audiences in a dynamic and ongoing communal and historical relationship. Each part has its place in the traditioning process: author, text, and

lighted: the formation (invention) of persuasive public discourse addressed to communities in a given situation, as well as the communal reception of this speech, which is a process that recurs in variation through the ongoing transmission, reconfiguration, and reception of these revelatory traditions.

Thus, a rhetorical approach to tradition highlights the work of memory and creative imagination in addressing diverse social and cultural situations, and thereby provides an invaluable resource for the work of inculturation and contextual theologies.[9] And accordingly, the pedagogical plan of God through the global dialogue of Christianity amidst diverse religions and cultures, the so-called education of the human race, takes on new dimensions of meaning. A rhetorical approach to revelatory traditions fosters a deeper appreciation of and participation in a dialogical process.

The Rhetorical Character of Faith

Christian faith provides the means by which, through communication, persons become one with the Triune God (a communion of persons), and with the community of faith (which is called to be a communion of persons). The invitation into dialogical communion with God and others, through faith, is made possible because of the gracious offer of God and the communication of the living community of faith. Here, the living divine

---

audience; and no one approach controls the meaning of the biblical tradition. Concentrating on the rhetorical process at work in the genesis and reception of these biblical traditions facilitates a broader understanding of how communities and their public discourse interact in the genesis, transmission, and ongoing development of these traditions. See Hinze, "Reclaiming Rhetoric"; see also Stephen E. Fowl, *Engaging Scripture: A Model for Theological Interpretation*, Challenges in Contemporary Theology (Oxford: Blackwell Publishers, 1998), especially chapter 2, "Stories of Interpretation."

[9] Such a rhetorical understanding of revelation and the ongoing dialogue of Christianity would complement the work of Robert Schreiter, *Constructing Local Theologies* (Markyknoll, N.Y.: Orbis, 1985) and Stephen B. Bevans, *Models of Contextual Theology* (Maryknoll, N.Y.: Orbis, 1992). For an excellent case study, see Richard Clutterbuck, "Contextuality and Catholicity: Toward a Theology of Mediated Otherness," in David S. Cunningham, Ralph Del Colle, and Lucas Lamadrid, eds., *Ecumenical Theology in Worship, Doctrine, and Life: Essays Presented to Geoffrey Wainwright on His Sixtieth Birthday* (Oxford and New York: Oxford University Press, 1999), 136–47.

speaker is attested by the proclamation, worship, and action of the church. Faith is a dialogical process, wherein one's deepest identity and destiny is received and born in relationships with God and others. Faith engages the whole person and demands the response of the whole person.

The dialogical character of faith means that its classic articulations exhibit deep affinities with the nature of rhetoric. In fact, as with revelation, the very nature of faith can be illuminated in terms of the three-part division of rhetoric into *ēthos*, *logos*, and *pathos*. *Ethos*: Divine and human authorities elicit trust in order to evoke a firm assent to the truth and a conversion to a committed pursuit of the good. *Logos*: The movement to judgment and decision, to affirmation and commitment, is based on credible (but not irrefutable) forms of proof. *Pathos*: The affirmation of deep truths and the loving embrace of genuine goods by individuals and communities is also a response of human loves, affections, and moods under the influence of the divine power. This serves as the basis of any consensus and collective witness, and an impetus to individual and communal acts of love and of works for justice.

As is the case with revelatory traditions, classical rhetoric strongly influenced the earliest formulations of the nature of faith, which have echoed down through history. By gaining a fuller appreciation of the rhetorical character of faith, we can comprehend anew various aspects of the phenomenon of faith: the motivations for belief, the role of reason, freedom, and love in the act of belief. We can also better understand the role of the community in believing, as well as how acts of love, service, and work for social transformation are related to believing. All of these are aspects of the process of Christian conversion, which results from the free reception of the divine gift of faith and creates a new person and a new community.

The affinity between faith and rhetoric is evident in the New Testament. From the writings of Paul, to the gospel narratives, and on to Hebrews and James, the dynamic of faith is described in terms of trust, openness, and listening to divine and human speakers who address listeners and audiences with passions of longing and fear. It is described as an assent to a proclamation offered and an active reception that transforms the self and the community. These basic components of the New Testament understanding of faith correspond to basic features of the rhetorical process.[10]

---

[10] For further developments of this theme, see the essays by A. K. M. Adam and James Boyce in the present volume, chapters 3 and 9 respectively.

Indeed, the Greek understanding of rhetoric, as James Kinneavy has effectively shown, stands at the origins of the Christian understanding of faith in the New Testament. In Greek rhetoric, the word often translated as faith, *pistis*, is understood as a *product* — "a mental conviction of some certainty, freely chosen" — but also as a *process*, by which various kinds of appeal are made: ethical, emotional, logical, and extrinsic arguments. The Christian understanding of *pistis* combines these two: "a mental conviction of some certainty, freely chosen, incorporating trust, assent, knowledge."[11] Kinneavy goes on to examine New Testament texts in terms of *ēthos*, *pathos*, and *logos*. The good character, will, and sense of the speaker (God, Jesus, Paul, and the Evangelists) is one form of appeal (*ēthos*). The emotions of the listener and audience (*pathos*) are appealed to in terms of the hopes and fears, promises and threats that are associated with miracles and signs promised, with eternal life, and with justification. The subject matter of the proclamation is presented by examples, as in the case of parables; by enthymemes (partial logical argument), which Kinneavy identifies with miracles or signs reported; and topics, such as midrashic explanations (*logos*).[12]

It is significant that the theologians who have offered the most penetrating analysis of faith were those who exhibited great awareness of classical rhetoric: consider, for example, Clement of Alexandria, Gregory of Nazianzus, and Augustine.[13] Each understood that faith is a communicative relationship that entails trusting in a person of character, that faith is not a

---

[11] James L. Kinneavy, *Greek Rhetorical Origins of Christian Faith: An Inquiry* (New York/Oxford: Oxford University Press, 1987), 24. One may have reservations about Kinneavy's use of the classic Reformation understanding of faith as *fiducia, assensus,* and *notitia* as the template for analyzing New Testament views of faith, or about his interpretations of specific New Testament passages; nevertheless, his basic contentions about the role of rhetoric in the New Testament and his analysis of the New Testament texts in terms of *logos, ēthos, and pathos* seem warranted.

[12] Kinneavy, *Greek Rhetorical Origins*, 46, 49, 52, 107. He includes a treatment of extrinsic appeals, which in Greek rhetoric would be identified as torture, oaths, laws, contracts, witnesses, and which he compares to grace, father, spirit, and devil.

[13] On the rhetorical significance of the Fathers generally, and of Gregory of Nazianzus in particular, see the essay by Frederick W. Norris, chapter 10 of the present volume.

matter of strict logical demonstration, but of signs, of the testimony of others, of stories, and examples, and that what is to be believed is surely a matter of knowing, of firm assent, and judgment, but that it is likewise a matter of loving, of the affections, of commitment, and actions. It should not be surprising, then, that some of the most treasured statements about faith by these theologians reflect insights born of rhetorical thought. Since faith offers firm knowledge without necessary proofs of reason, Clement drew reassurance from the Septuagint version of Isaiah 7:9: "If you do not believe, you shall not understand"; Augustine offered his gloss on this passage: "we believe in order to understand."[14] Likewise, Gregory of Nazianzus points out the frailty of reason and the limitations of dialectic and philosophy, and, by attesting to the folly of the Cross and the wisdom bequeathed by the Spirit, affirms that "faith is what gives fullness to our reasoning."[15] Logical proof, irrefutable claims, and indubitable foundations are not the pathway of faith. Rather faith rests on trust and a way of knowing and acting that learns from a dialogue that takes place within the imagination and that moves reason, human freedom, and the affections in acts of faith and faith-inspired acts of love and work for justice.

The rhetorical character of faith both underlies and further promotes the perennial attempt to offer a full accounting of the dynamic interplay between knowledge, freedom, and the affections in the act of faith. Faith is a grace and a work of the Spirit that ultimately requires nothing less than a holistic anthropology. Attending to the intellectual, volitional, or affective components in isolation will not suffice. The history of theology offers a variety of attempts to describe the larger vision of faith. So Augustine says that "believing is to think with assent" in order to indicate that understanding and freedom cooperate in faith, that faith grasps and transforms the entire person by encountering the true and the good. Of course, the good is defined as that which we long to know and to love —

---

[14] See the historical analysis of the classic statements by Clement of Alexandria in *Stromata*, Book II, which offers the first sustained treatment of faith, Gregory of Nazianzus, and Augustine, by Avery Dulles in *The Assurance of Things Hoped For: A Theology of Christian Faith* (New York: Oxford University Press, 1994).

[15] Gregory of Nazianzen, *Faith Gives Fullness to Reasoning: The Five Theological Orations of Gregory of Nazianzen*, trans., ed., and commentary by Frederick W. Norris (Leiden: Brill, 1991), 29.21 (p. 269); see also 28.28. For further development of this theme, see Norris's essay in the present volume (chapter 10).

and indeed, to know *so as* to love, to love in knowing. Thomas Aquinas is remembered for emphasizing the role of the intellect in the act of faith, but he affirms no less the importance of trusting the divine speaker and being moved to love the divine good.[16] Martin Luther and John Calvin are esteemed for stressing the importance of trusting (*fiducia*) God as speaker and as giver of life and salvation, but this trust was not at the expense of the importance of knowledge (*notitia*) and free assent (*assensus*); and in fact these three components of faith were reciprocally related, and as such would result in "works of love." In the twentieth century, Karl Barth (invoking this same Reformation heritage), as well as Roman Catholic theologians (combining the Augustinian and Thomistic heritage), have striven to affirm the equal priority and dynamic reciprocity among knowledge, freedom, and love in the gift and act of faith.[17]

The basic point should be clear: theologians may emphasize particular aspects of the act of faith without necessarily denying its other dimensions. What does a self-consciously rhetorical analysis of the act of faith add? It serves a hermeneutic and phenomenology of faith that denies none of the

---

[16]When we think of the achievement of Thomas Aquinas, it is Aristotelian logic and physics, not rhetoric, which predominates. But if we analyze closely his treatise on the nature of faith in the *Summa Theologiae*, II-II, qq. 1–16, which self-consciously builds on the legacy of Augustine, we can glean affinities between his view of faith and the classical understanding of rhetoric. He affirms the persuasive and trustworthy character of God under the form of truth and as the revealer of the good. The material object of faith commands the attention of the entire person; it is affirmed in understanding, but also moved by the will. There are outward inducements to faith, miracles and human persuasion, but these are not sufficient, for there is need for the movement of God in the depths of the human person for faith (II-II.6.1; II-II.2.9 ad 3). Even though Aquinas's analysis may be logic-driven and focused on intricate causal analysis, the rhetorical character of faith and its holistic anthropology still shine through.

[17] Karl Barth utilized a dialogical approach to faith by describing it in terms of obedience — listening and receiving the word of the divine speaker — resulting in recognition, acknowledgment, and confession. *Church Dogmatics*, trans. G. W. Bromiley, (Edinburgh: T & T Clark, [1936–1960] 1975–1977), vol. I/1:227–47; vol. IV/1:608–42, 740–79. See also the contributions of Pierre Rousselot, *The Eyes of Faith* (New York: Fordham University Press, 1999) and Maurice Blondel, "Qu'est-ce que la foi?" (1906); partial translation in *Communio* 14 (1987):162–192. Rousselot and Blondel influenced the work of Karl Rahner and Hans Urs von Balthasar.

important facets of the act of faith: reasonableness, judgment, assent, the apprehension of value, and the attraction of the good. Moreover, it seeks to integrate these various components within a self-consciously dialogical and communicative view of God, the human person, and society.

Knowledge of rhetoric fosters new appreciation, not only of the act of faith, but also of the relationship between the objective nature or object of faith and the subjective act of faith — a topic which has long preoccupied theologians. This issue is broached by Augustine in his classic distinctions among *credere Deo, credere Deum,* and *credere in Deum*: believing God, believing about God, believing for the sake of God.[18] Thomas Aquinas also devoted considerable attention to distinguishing the object of faith and the act of faith. The classic distinction of *fides quae creditur,* the faith that is believed, and *fides qua creditur,* the faith that believes,[19] can easily be likened to James Kinneavy's rhetorical distinction of *pistis* as product and process. The former indicates the content of belief, while the latter the personal act of faith; the former is the objective character of faith, and the latter its subjective character. These two dimensions of faith are indispensable. By highlighting the rhetorical character of faith we are able to appreciate the fact that "the faith that believes" is based on trust, credibility, and conviction; yet it is neither indubitable, nor merely rationally verifiable. And, faith, like all rhetorically-based judgments and decisions, cannot be judged primarily on the basis of either the character of the speaker, the affections of the audience, or even a very strong rhetorical argument; instead, these judgments and decisions must ultimately be evaluated according to the faith which is believed, the objective content of faith, as well as by the actions which faith yields. Just as the use of rhetoric must be judged according to its service of particular beliefs and practices, so too the use of rhetoric to clarify the nature of faith must be judged by its coherence with the Christian view of God, the human person, and the world — the

---

[18] See the useful commentary on this distinction in Nicholas Lash, *Believing Three Ways In One God: A Reading of the Apostles' Creed* (Notre Dame, Ind.: University of Notre Dame Press, 1992), 19–22. For *credere in Deum,* Lash suggests the following rendering: "God is the object of our faith as heart's desire, as goal toward which all our life and thought is set" (p. 20).

[19] This distinction originates with Augustine and is echoed by Anselm, Peter Lombard, and Johann Gerhard. Karl Barth discusses the sources of this distinction in *Church Dogmatics* I/1, p. 236.

common but continually contested topics that define the identity of Christianity.

We have acknowledged the Christian conviction that faith yields a way of perceiving the world both for individuals and for a community of faith. This "sixth sense" provided by faith deserves a comment. The "sense of the faith" (*sensus fidei*) is a term used to describe the perceptive mode of apprehension that is attained by the human person through the divine gift of faith; "the sense of the faithful" (*sensus fidelium*) refers to the faith perception of the community of believers; and the "consensus of the faithful" (*consensus fidelium*) is the emerging oneness of mind and heart of believers in faith, proleptically present and yet only eschatologically realized.[20] These terms identify dimensions of faith that are consistent with and illuminated by the rhetorical interest in the *pathos* of the audience. By monitoring its audience(s), rhetoric affirms the significance of communal affections, memory, and imagination — not only in the creative formation of an argument, but in its communal reception as well. The theological interest in *sensus fidelium* has a counterpart in the rhetorical tradition's interest in "*sensus communis,*" which privileges a certain trust in the basic perceptions of the community (even though this confidence can sometimes be legitimately challenged).[21] The theological reason why *sensus fidelium* is more than *sensus communis* is based on the conviction that through the reception of the gift of the Spirit, which is ritualized in baptism, all Christians participate in the prophetic office of Christ. As such (and drawing on Calvin's formulation, which harkens back to early theological traditions), "the inner testimony of the Spirit" is in evidence in the active process of the reception of the gospel in faith. The sense of the faithful is thus a crucial ingredient in the ongoing dialogue of revelatory traditions through proclamation and witness, and through ongoing doctrinal dialogue. The sense of the faithful is, consequently, a theological source that warrants "consulting the faithful in matters of doctrine" (John Henry

---

[20] Following Daniel J. Finucane, *Sensus Fidelium: The Use of a Concept in the Post-Vatican II Era* (San Francisco/London: International Scholars Publications, 1996).

[21] Hans-Georg Gadamer commenting on Vico's understanding of the term "the sensus communis is the sense of what is right and of the common good that is to be found in all men; moreover, it is a sense that is acquired through living in the community and is determined by its structures and aims," *Truth and Method*, 19–30, here 22.

Newman) and fostering the reception of doctrine in the traditioning process.

Paul insisted that justification is by faith and not by works of the law, but he also acknowledged that this faith is manifest in works of love and in care for the poor. The letter of James sought to redress a misunderstanding of the Pauline legacy and insisted that faith without works of love is dead. Since the time of Pelagianism, theologians have sought to emphasize the gratuity of God's grace and faith: these gifts of God are not merited in any way. But it has likewise been acknowledged that faith is an act of freedom that is related to works of love and the promotion of justice. Faith is motivated by trust and governed by orthodoxy, but it is also judged by the practice of faith in actions of service, the promotion of justice, and love. The various aspects of character-building — not just isolated acts, but patterns of behavior, both of the individual and the community — are basic ingredients highlighted by a rhetorical approach to faith.

Rhetoric is at the origins of the Christian understanding of faith, but it also accompanies a person's lifelong journey of faith into deeper dialogical relationships with the Triune God and the human community in worship, in witness, in service, and in works of love. Christian faith initiates persons into, and sustains persons within, a dialogical communion of persons.

The Church as a Dialogical and a Trinitarian Communion

Finally, the importance of rhetoric in the daily life of the church gives sufficient reason for studying rhetoric in theology; but, beyond this, attention to matters rhetorical fosters a deeper understanding of the nature and mission of the church. The ongoing dialogue of revelation and faith takes place *in* the church. The Christian church is formed by the communicative acts of the proclamation of the gospel and the dramatic celebration of the sacraments of baptism and eucharist. The dynamism of dialogue informs every aspect of the church's life in its internal and external relations. The evangelical mission of preaching, catechesis, and all forms of witnessing, teaching, and learning depend upon rhetorical acts that create and shape individual Christians and the Christian community in every generation. Likewise, the social mission of the church relies on the rhetorical cogency of the church's witness and praxis in simple acts of loving service of those in need, in standing against injustice, and in working for social transformation in the public realm.

The church itself, and the use of rhetoric in the church, must be judged according to a divine measure. The Christian doctrine of God — both the personal identities (and missions) in the Trinity and the dialogical communion of divine persons — inspires and should ultimately determine the nature and mission of the church as a communion of divine and human persons.[22] Christians are called to share in the divine nature (2 Peter 1:4), and summoned to communicate persuasively the identity and mission of the trinitarian God by sharing in bonds of love and power that abide in the relations of the Father, Son, and Spirit (John 14:9–26; 15::8–17; 16:4–15). Consequently, the rhetoric of the church must be thought through precisely in terms of dialogical and trinitarian communion. Over the past twenty years, Catholic, Orthodox, and Protestant churches have come to realize this challenge and have espoused such a communion ecclesiology.[23] As a result, the nature and mission of the church is being articulated in terms of the communicative nature and mission of the triune God as a communion of persons. This "trialogue" among Father, Son, and Spirit, which constitutes the divine identity, provides the pattern of living communion. In this pattern, identity and mission flow from reciprocal relationships of gift-giver, gift, and reception of gift; speaker, message, listener; lover, beloved, and love.[24] The rhetoric of the church builds on this basic Christian

---

[22] See my essay, "Releasing the Power of the Spirit in a Trinitarian Ecclesiology," in *Advents of the Spirit: An Introduction to the Current Study of Pneumatology*, ed. Bradford E. Hinze and D. Lyle Dabney (Milwaukee, WI: Marquette University Press, 2001). See also the essay by David S. Cunningham, chapter 11 of the present volume.

[23] *On the Way to Fuller Koinonia*, Official Report of the Fifth World Conference on Faith and Order, Santiago de Compostela 1993 (Geneva: World Council of Churches, 1994); *Deepening Communion: International Ecumenical Documents with Roman Catholic Participation*, ed. William G. Rusch and Jeffrey Gros (Washington, D.C.: U.S. Catholic Conference, 1998); *Communio–Ideal oder Zerrbild von Kommunikation?* ed. Bernd Jochen Hilberath, Questiones Disputatae (Freiburg: Herder, 1999).

[24] The church has often and rightly been understood in terms of the identity and the mission of Jesus, the incarnate Son of God, both in terms of sacramental practices and leadership paradigms, with the church as a whole understood as the embodiment of Christ on earth. As the divine and human are distinct yet united in Jesus Christ, so too in the body of Christ. Equally important is the role of the Holy

affirmation of the church as a dialogical communion modeled on the *imago trinitatis*.

We can appreciate more deeply this dialogical communion by considering the nature of friendship. This affinity would not have been lost on some of the most important contributors to the study of rhetoric, such as Aristotle, Cicero, and Augustine, who also championed the significance of friendship in the moral and spiritual formation of individuals and communities. The dynamics of friendship provide a time-honored way of conceiving the Christian's relationship with God and others. Friendships are formed by dialogue; and, in their fullest form, these relationships cultivate a person's and a community's identity and mission. Likewise, through the living discourse of the church, people are invited into a friendship with God and to form a community of friends. This point is well illustrated by the stories of Jesus "befriending" various needy people and witnessing to this friendship by eating and drinking with them. Jesus' amicability is surely a personal trait, but it is also a social practice. As he forms communities of friends, Jesus encourages his companions to do the same.

Is there any real connection between rhetoric and friendship, or is it simply a coincidence that Aristotle, Cicero, and Augustine treated both topics well? Let us consider this possibility: rhetoric in its most noble uses not only serves the ends of pleasure and usefulness, but affirms the basic tenets of friendship between good people. Rhetorical relationships in their highest forms, like genuine friendships, foster communication based on mutual respect for the many dimensions of the human person (reason, freedom, imagination, affections). Moreover, the genuine bonds forged by common judgments, decisions, commitments, and loves, are based on a reverence for what is shared, while also respecting and even cherishing the

---

Spirit in the process of conversion, sanctification, ministry, and mission, wherein divine and human freedom act together. At times, christologically justified offices and pneumatically gifted individuals have been thought to be in tension; the rhetorical authority of office is set over against the rhetorical authority of charism. By focusing on both the Son and the Spirit, however, we gain an understanding of trinitarian *relations* — of the interpersonal character of identity formation and mission in the divine reality — that further clarifies the communicative character of the church in terms of mutuality and equality. For one view of some issues in trinitarian ecclesiology, see Miroslav Volf, *After Our Likeness: The Church as the Image of the Trinity* (Grand Rapids: William B. Eerdmans, 1998).

distinctive traits and contributions of each individual. For Aristotle and Cicero, both the highest forms of rhetoric and friendship are basic ingredients necessary for human happiness and a moral life.[25] And Augustine perceived the religious character of friendship: the Holy Spirit is described as the bond of friendship which unites the Father and the Son in the trinitarian relations, and who in turn draws Christians into the life of union with the Triune God.[26]

We now have a framework for conceiving the *logos* of the church, the *ēthos* of the church, and the *pathos* of the church. The *logos* of the church is based on the common belief in and love of the Triune God, the source and norm of its identity as a dialogical communion of persons, oriented toward a life of friendship and social practices aiming at individuation and communion. This characterizes the church's mandate of *apostolicity*.

The *ēthos* of the Christian church refers to the community's character and its call to *holiness*. Through individual and collective judgments, decisions, and actions, the community of believers witnesses to the truth of the gospel and thereby builds up the church as the body of Christ and the temple of the Spirit, as they also stand up in the public arena against injustice, resisting destructive powers, and promoting social transformation for the common good of God's creation.

The *pathos* of the church is the source of its *unity* and its *catholicity*. The church strives for dialogical communion by being open to the deep passions and convictions of Christian believers, perhaps especially those who may have been marginalized in the past; it is likewise challenged to broaden its receptivity and responsiveness to those beyond its current borders, including those in other communities of faith. The church fosters bonds of unity by promoting genuine dialogue among its members — even as it engages in intercultural, ecumenical, and interreligious dialogue as a means to continue to grow into its full identity as the people of God.

---

[25] Aristotle, *Nicomachean Ethics* (Indianapolis: Bobbs-Merrill, 1962), books 8–9. Cicero, *Laelius, On Friendship; The Dream of Scipio*, trans. and ed. J. G. F. Powell (England: Aris & Phillips, 1990).

[26] See Marie Aquinas McNamara, *Friendship in Saint Augustine* (Fribourg: University Press, 1958); John F. Monagle, "Friendship in St. Augustine's Biography: Classical Notions of Friendship," *Augustinian Studies* 2 (1971): 81–92..

Theology as Communicative Practice

Human beings are called from all eternity into dialogical communion, and so to individuate and collaborate in order to celebrate the greater glory of God. But the path of effective communication is too often obstructed; we experience frequently the failure of dialogue; rhetoric can be used for short-sighted and evil purposes.[27] Meetings of minds and hearts too frequently do not take place. Sometimes, all that is communicated are misunderstanding, anger, and hatred. Common loves and goals cannot be identified. Respect for differences is not conceded. It is true that sometimes the causes of dialogue's demise are benign. The contingencies of life and human finitude bring us up short. Distractions intervene. But there are also more pernicious reasons why dialogue fails and rhetoric destroys: times when the powers of selfishness, group interest, and bias are decisive, situations where pain and sorrow are left unaddressed and unresolved. Too many lives have been scarred, ruined, and even destroyed by the failure of dialogue and the rancor of rhetoric. Rhetoric in and of itself offers no remedy for humans harmed by a narrow human vision and a corrupt heart, as Paul and Augustine attest.[28] But in these cases dialogue or communication or rhetoric are not the cause of the problem; rather,

---

[27] Jean-François Lyotard has set his own rhetoric of "agonistics" as a defense of the *differend* and *dissensus* over against the "partisans of dialogue" and consensus in *The Differend: Phrases in Dispute* trans. George Van Den Abbeele (Minneapolis: University of Minnesota Press, 1988), 26. To transpose Lyotard's concern into a Jewish or Christian idiom, one must always make room for lamentation and prophetic critique. However, this legitimate concern need not undermine the quest for genuine dialogical communion that honors difference and individuation. For more detailed analysis of Lyotard's significance for the project of rhetoric and theological education, see the essays by A. K. M. Adam and Don H. Compier in this volume (chapters 3 and 7, respectively).

[28] Paul and Augustine admit that rhetoric can serve any message and therefore in and of itself rhetoric cannot save, but by their example they also teach that Christian rhetoric can assist and must be judged by the gospel of Jesus Christ crucified and risen — and by the dialogical God Christians profess: see 1 Corinthians 1:10–2:16; Augustine, *Confessions*, trans. Henry Chadwick (Oxford: Oxford University Press, 1991), Book 8.5; pp. 136–37; and Augustine, *De Doctrina Christiana*, ed. and trans. R. P. H. Green (Oxford: Clarendon Press, 1995), Book 4 *passim*, and particularly 4.4, pp. 197–99.

dialogue and the means of communication in the service of the gospel have not been allowed to work, or have not yet completed their task. The hard truth is that we stand under the judgment of a dialogical God, intent on communion. The rhetoric of revelation, faith, and the church will be judged by the Original Rhetor — not only for style but for substance, not only for character but for effect.

Chapter 5

Theology as Confession: Redeeming a Theological Trope for Pedagogy

Stephen H. Webb

The claims that teaching is an act of confession, and that students should be expected to confess their own personal positions in the classroom, have been in circulation for some time. Feminist scholars, for example, have drawn attention to pedagogical strategies that personalize the classroom. Nonetheless, those who teach religion and theology are often suspicious, not only of the practice of confessing in the classroom, but also of using confessional language to describe the art of pedagogy. Confessionalism has a specific history in Christianity; to some ears, it smacks of sectarianism, fanaticism, and subjectivism. Indeed, why is a good Disciples of Christ theologian (if I may be permitted to get "confessional" myself for a moment) talking about the value of confession, when we Disciples believe in "no creed but Christ"?[1] Surely *confession* is a term too overtly theological to name what goes on in the classroom. Or is it?

Confessionalists are often stereotyped as those who do not want to articulate a public theology and join in with mainstream opinions and conversations. They are thought stubbornly to pit "Christ against culture,"

---

[1] Although, as James Duke points out, to say that there is no creed but Christ is not the same thing as saying that there is no creed. See his "The Question of Confession Among Disciples," *Impact* (1990): 16–28.

as those categories are set up in H. Richard Niebuhr's typology. But is this the full story? Confessional theology is arguably the opposite of foundational theology (which accepts only those religious beliefs that can meet specific rational criteria). But just as not all foundationalism is logical positivism, not all confessionalism is fideism. To advocate confession is not to advocate an obscurantist rejection of all standards of rationality.

Confessionalism is not just an attempt to inoculate religion against the virus of secularity. If confessional approaches to theology make doctrines and beliefs incorrigible — that is, not subject to revision or reformulation — then confessionalism has no place in the academic classroom. I will argue, however, that confessional theology creates an open, not a closed, circle of theological reflection. By trying to bring all events into an interpretive framework that is grounded in a personal response to divine revelation, confessionalism will engage a wide range of alternative paradigms as it sharpens and expands its own criteria of how to appropriate new knowledge in order to deepen religious commitment.[2]

To the extent that confessional modes of pedagogy fail in the classroom, this is largely due to secular, rather than theological, versions of confessionalism. Taking a personal approach to religion by saying "that is just my opinion" can be a way of ending rather than beginning fruitful conversations. A theologically-informed confessional pedagogy, by contrast, will reconnect confession to the questions of responsibility (ethics) and truth (the reality of God). Theology thus can contribute a critique of current trends in pedagogy by presenting a fuller portrait of theological confession.

Tracing the Meaning(s) of Confession

In theological circles, the language of *confession* is frequently used in two very different contexts: the confession of sins and the confession of faith. The two are interrelated. Christians typically confess their personal sins in private, with a priest or directly to God; and they typically confess their faith in public, with others, in the church. But can a Christian can be involved in either of these practices without also being involved in the other? In Augustine's *Confessions*, for example, confessing one's story is equated with confessing faith in God; to know oneself is to know God. Every confession, even the most personal examination of one's private

---

[2] See Martin L. Cook, *The Open Circle: Confessional Method in Theology* (Minneapolis: Fortress Press, 1991).

faults and vices, entails a drive to know God, who is the author and guide of all life. By examining the conflicting desires that drive us, we demonstrate our longing for wholeness and healing. Self-interrogation enables a purging that makes possible a purity of the heart.

This double structure of confessional acts is broken apart in modern culture. We are no longer confident that the self is encompassed by a true end that transcends our conflicting desires, nor even that there is a true self amidst all of those desires. Perhaps that is why we endlessly talk about ourselves, in the hope that we will stumble upon who we really are. Today, ironically, the *public* confession of faith has been *privatized*, while the (normally private) confession of sin has been increasingly *publicized*. Indeed, we live in a hyper-confessional culture, in which many people seem to want to divulge their private lives, but nobody has anything really interesting to say. A public expression of faith can lower one's social status, but talking about one's flawed past can do just the opposite. Especially for the economically disadvantaged, confession is a way of saying "Here I am! Notice me, please!" For those with nothing left to lose, confession can be an empowering way of drawing attention and reclaiming some sort of dignity. Consequently, confessions are more likely to be about negotiating power than expressing the truth.

In this cultural form, however, the confession is not exactly a confession of sin; more typically, one confesses having been *sinned against*. People are anxious to divulge their most personal stories, because the language of victimization is so easily used to justify any deed. Nobody takes responsibility for sin, because somebody else is always to blame. People are so confident that they can find somebody to blame that they agree to "tell it all" on television talks shows. Indeed, the very act of confessing on television seems somehow to have an absolving effect. Jerry Springer, for example, ends each of his shows with a moral minute that is apparently meant to justify the carnival atmosphere that he hypes. He trades on the peculiar phenomenon that people are willing to admit to anything in order to get on television. "True confessions" are among the most basic building blocks of the entertainment industry.

Given this cultural climate, any classroom attitude suggesting that "anything goes" — any effort to encourage students to bring forth their personal opinions without subjecting them to critical examination — can be as much a form of disrespect as can a strategy of disallowing personal opinions altogether. Is the move toward personal confessions in the classroom merely a way of duplicating and reinforcing questionable societal trends? It may be true that many of us first learned to teach by watching Phil Donahue and later imitating his ability to be so concerned with the opinions of his audience; but do we want our classrooms to sound like a television talkshow? Our postmodern rejection of metanarratives and universal truths leaves us with the pedagogical criteria of trying to please the student — who is treated, in the absence of other ideologies, like a consumer driven by capitalist expectations. Under this logic, the content of a course does not matter, as long as the student's voice is heard and affirmed. In many cases, pedagogy has become little more than the pleasure of prompting, hearing, and making confessions. The classroom is the confessional, and every confession is "true."

Some conservative reactions to these pedagogical trends tend to lament the loss of hierarchical authority, to emphasize the need for personal responsibility, to proclaim the deleterious consequences of abandoning an account of truth as objective, and to grieve over the decline of modesty and reticence (both inside and outside the classroom). I do not necessarily share all of these concerns, but I am sympathetic to the student who resists the more overtly performance-oriented aspects of a form of teaching based primarily on student confessions. The secularization of confession results in an experiential expressivism (to use George Lindbeck's loaded phrase), privileging the subject as the beginning and end of all truth claims.[3] Given the widespread skepticism about every external constraint and demand on personal experience, the classroom becomes the place where confession is deritualized and normalized. It contains little more than a trace of the Christian emphasis on the personal responsibility of every person for self-examination and a public commitment of faith.

The Christian trope of confession, then, cannot be applied to the classroom without nuance, because it is an activity that has been appropriated and distorted by secular culture. Confession needs to be redeemed — that is, returned to its theological roots — before it can be used as an essential element in religious pedagogy. Is there a theological notion of confession that can save us from a culture that just loves to talk about itself, even when there is so little to talk about?

---

[3] George Lindbeck, *The Nature of Doctrine: Religion and Theology in a Postliberal Age* (Philadelphia: Westminster Press, 1984).

The Theological Roots of Confession

The view that Christian confessional practices stand at the source of modern views of selfhood has been emphasized above all by Michel Foucault. He focuses on sexuality, but his real interest is in the ways in which we learn to construct ourselves through divulging something interior and secretive. Christianity gave Western culture the idea of confession as a form of private piety that is virtually synonymous with self-examination. For Foucault, however, confession is not the expression of some prior state of being. Instead, it is a way of constructing who we are — indeed, of constructing new ways of being altogether. Confession is about the *invention* of the self, not deliberation over what the self should do or a disclosure of what the self believes. The confessional resembles, but eventually replaces, the judicial inquest as the model for getting at the truth. For truth, confession teaches us, lies in the stories we tell about ourselves. (Confession thus bears interesting parallels to the rhetorical process of *inventio*.)

To demonstrate the pivotal role of confession in the West, Foucault himself tells a story about its rise as a ritual and its proliferation as a way of life. One of the seven sacraments of the Catholic church, confession is recognized as a channel of grace. Through confession, the church asks every believer to, in Foucault's words, "transform your desire, your every desire, into discourse."[4] The Christian tradition has long practiced the communal confession of general sin during worship as a sign of spiritual need and transformation, but the church also recognized the need for a particularized account of sin that would lead to concrete signs of God's forgiveness.[5] During the early period of the church, penance was a public ritual of ecclesiastical reconciliation reserved for those Christians who had lapsed from the faith or who had committed grave sins. Introduced from Ireland and influenced by the custom of monks serving as spiritual directors, private confessions were institutionalized in the Roman Catholic Church during the Middle Ages. After the Fourth Lateran Council (1215) required

---

[4] Michel Foucault, *The History of Sexuality, Vol. 1: An Introduction*, trans. Robert Hurley (NY: Vintage Books, 1980), 21.

[5] For a thorough overview of this history of this sacrament, see Joseph Martos, *Doors to the Sacred: A Historical Introduction to Sacraments in the Catholic Church* (Liguori, Mo.: Triumph Books, 1991), ch. 9.

a yearly confession from all Christians who committed serious sins, confession became the primary means for enforcing social morality.[6] The legal rhetoric of penance — absolution as a judicial act and penance as a means of making satisfaction for sin — was strengthened in the Catholic Reformation by the Council of Trent (1551).

Protestants were suspicious of the power of confessors, with the priest functioning as an *alter Christus*, exercising the authority to judge and forgive. At their best, confessors are educators, teaching people how to reform their lives. The confessor serves to remind us that mercy does not come without justice. From the Protestant perspective, however, the penitential system smacked of blackmail and calculative exchange, which could only be rooted out by interiorizing the act of repentance. Nonetheless, Protestantism did not do away with confession itself. Indeed, by "liberating" confession from the penitential structure, Protestantism arguably made confession more ubiquitous. At its most daring, the idea of the priesthood of all believers transforms confession into something we share with each other (James 5:16), without the mediation of an authority figure who imposes upon us a specific remedy for our sin.

The Protestant reformers tried to retain the essence of confession without the support of church structures or of divine law, but the result was that the actual practice of confession soon fell into disuse. Confession continued in the Catholic church; but in the twentieth century, many Catholics found the legalistic framework of confession unhelpful in a time of great moral complexity and confusion, so that this ritual was administered only infrequently.

Secular Distortions of Confession

If the Christian churches no longer provide a framework for confession, secular culture has filled the vacuum with a vengeance. Shorn of its ritualized forms, confession has multiplied and spread to the point where it is hard to find cultural forms that are not confessional. In fact, Foucault argues that Western culture is characterized by an insatiable need for confession that has outstripped its religious context:

---

[6]Foucault exaggerates the importance of the Lateran Council of 1215 for the codification of penance and confession. See Pierre J. Payer, "Foucault on Penance and the Shaping of Sexuality," *Studies in Religion* 14 (1985): 313–20.

> The confession has spread its effects far and wide. It plays a part in justice, medicine, education, family relationships, and love relations, in the most ordinary affairs of everyday life, and in the most solemn rites; one confesses one's crimes, one's sins, one's thoughts and desires, one's illnesses and troubles; one goes about telling, with the greatest precision, whatever is most difficult to tell.[7]

Confession becomes a trope for truth — indeed, a trope for human nature itself. "Western man has become a confessing animal."[8] We determine who we are by deciding what we need to reveal about ourselves. Scrupulosity becomes a virtue. Confession is naturalized, so that we no longer see the obligation to confess as a power that is imposed upon us.

The diffusion of confession, Foucault argues, begins the Western world's slide into subjectivity. Selfhood comes to be seen as an internal world that requires articulation, rather than a public world of relationships that are formed through initiation and imitation. Foucault contrasts the confession of sexuality as it develops in the West with the *ars erotica* tradition more prevalent in the East, in which truth "is drawn from pleasure itself, understood as a practice and accumulated as experience."[9] The *ars erotica* tradition also regulates sexuality, but it places sexuality in the context of a practice that requires expertise, and thus a community and a tradition. The master transmits an esoteric knowledge that both disciplines and heightens the disciple's practice of pleasure. The science of sexuality that results from confession, by contrast, makes sexuality an interior secret whose very avowal constitutes the self in its most private relationship with itself.

Contrary to Foucault, we could say that the traditions of confession and *ars erotica* have met and joined hands in our secular culture. Sex has become an object of scientific scrutiny that nevertheless still titillates the imagination, a topos that incites a discursive explosion. We love to hear serious discussions of sexuality, precisely because they draw from a personal world that is ordinarily hidden from view. Of course, secular discourses gradually have come to take the place of theology, so that the

---

[7]Foucault, *History of Sexuality*, I:59.

[8]Foucault, *History of Sexuality*, I:59.

[9]Foucault, *History of Sexuality*, I:57.

unity that self-scrutiny can lead to is posited by the ideologies of psychology and other social and political sciences. More recently still, people seem to have less and less hope for any unity or healing in the interrogation of the self; yet the fascination with confession continues unabated. We are transfixed by those who bare their souls only to show us that the modern soul is, at best, a fiction — a story without an ending. We are voyeurs of other people's confessions, an obligation to which we anxiously attend, even with the foreboding that we are running out of things to confess.

There has been a gradual realignment, then, from the connection of confession to a cosmology of order and purpose to a confessionalism that is purely and merely anthropocentric. Contrition was once an integral aspect of confession, but the deritualization of confession makes it more of an act of self-exaltation than repentance. Confession originally was a ritual in which the speaker and the object of the discourse coincide for the purposes of purification and, ultimately, salvation. In traditional Catholic teaching, confession is connected to penance, so that words were intimately related to deeds (that is, one was held responsible for what one confessed to). To confess was not to negotiate a contentious narrative about who did what to whom; instead, confession was meant to put an end to such endlessly vindictive plays of power.

Today, the practice of confessing has become performance art, so that moral norms seem inappropriate and intrusive. Perhaps confession is inflated in our culture because there is no sense of what might constitute absolution. Without forgiveness, confessing becomes another form of rationalizing. We turn our failures into a coherent whole by dramatizing them through a plausible plot. We have aestheticized confession, so that watching a confession is like watching a play — though with rather less involvement than audiences normally bring to the theater. (Television remains a better analogy: it provides a safe distance, an on–off switch, and a good deal more melodrama.) Confessions are public, but only in the sense of blurring the boundary of what used to be private, making all of us into voyeurs. Confessions are not public in the sense of forming a community of those who seek the truth.

The strange and the bizarre have thus been normalized and even trivialized, so that the possibility of linking confession with penance has been almost totally erased from our culture. It becomes banal to confess something if everybody confesses everything. Confession is everywhere in our culture, but it follows a peculiarly scripted form, allowing people to delve into their own private lives with narcissistic abandon. (Notice how television viewers do not seem to mind that, evidently, many of Jerry Springer's shows follow a very precise script written by the producers, so that guests are encouraged to lie in the interest of dramatic effect.) Curiously, in an age that prizes individuality and confession as the means to therapeutic healing, everybody sounds alike — and nobody feels any better for it.[10]

A New Rhetoric of Confession

As theological educators who deal with some of the most significant aspects of our students' lives, we need to model in our classrooms a rhetoric of confession that can challenge and transform these longstanding and seemingly intractable social pathologies. The proper practice of confession in the classroom can go a long way toward restoring confession to its theological context.

Christian theologians need to recontextualize confession by reinstating its traditional boundaries. To confess is to believe, and it is also to open oneself to judgment. In a discussion of confession, Miroslav Volf emphasizes the connection of confession and commitment: "As a speech act, confession is essentially *commissive*; I commit myself to something by making this confession."[11] Broadly construed, confession can take nonverbal forms, as when a believer professes faith in Christ through works of righteousness. Conversely, as Volf points out, a false life can deny Christ as much or more than the confession of false doctrine. Confessions, then, do not simply unveil and illuminate the dark corridors of the inner life. Instead, a confession points to the future, by suggesting where the past has gone wrong and where one hopes to be.

The important biblical point about confession is that it is a public act, in that it always occurs *between persons*. Every confession is also at the same time an invitation — an interpersonal gesture of inclusion that is made

---

[10]For a sound defense of confession as therapy, see Sharon Hymer, "Therapeutic and Redemptive Aspects of Religious Confession," *Journal of Religion and Health* 34 (Spring 1995): 41–54.

[11]Miroslav Volf, *After Our Likeness, The Church as the Image of the Trinity* (Grand Rapids, Mich.: Wm. B. Eerdmans, 1998), 149.

possible by, and reinforces, a sense of community. Because of this social dimension, the confession of faith is often done according to established formulae. However, Volf insists that "every genuinely Christian speech act is, at least formally and implicitly, an act of confession."[12] The confession of faith is what Christians do; indeed, it is what the church *is*, in the sense that one person confessing the faith leads to another and finally constitutes the church. Volf emphasizes the importance of confession in order to defend a Free Church ecclesiology — a contestable argument that is beyond the scope of this essay. For my purposes, it is interesting to ask to what extent confession can constitute the classroom, and to make that inquiry by reflecting on the fundamental role of confession in the life of the church.

The practice of confession should link notions of human flourishing with the recognition that freedom can be found only in community. To confess oneself is to acknowledge that one is accountable to others. Nevertheless, confession by itself is not a magical way of creating community. Confession must be grounded in a community, reflecting its sense of moral consensus and ultimate truth, if it is not to lead to moral subjectivism. When practices of confession become thoughtless and routine, they can reinforce the sense that confession is about the self in its autonomy and isolation. The penitent looks inward rather than outward for the truth.

Confronting the relative absence of vital communities today, Foucault wants to turn back to a pre-Christian era when notions of subjectivity were so radically different. Foucault would replace confession with the arts of imitation and initiation — what he calls "technologies of the self" — relying on the pleasures of the body to guide human conduct. There is no deep self, Foucault and many other postmodernists insist; indeed, the notion of a deep self is a Christian invention, a result of the practice of confession. Instead, there are only bodies in motion and various ways of regulating, managing, and enhancing our embodied pursuits. For Foucault, the self is opaque until it invents itself.

This pagan restoration, with its antinomian ethos, is not open to the Christian theologian. Persons have infinite value and thus infinite depth because God is both creator and redeemer. It is true that, too often, Christian theology has spoken in almost gnostic terms about the human soul within and a ghostly afterlife. Theology too frequently has treated the human soul as an abstract entity that is essentially unrelated to anything but

---

[12]Volf, *After Our Likeness*, 150.

Theology as Confession ✜ 119

God. Nevertheless, the incarnation and the resurrection both affirm the utter materialism of the human body, and prophetic images of a new world acknowledge human dependence on nature as a whole. The practice of confession should lead us to a greater sensitivity to the various relationships that sustain human life. Confessionalism does not need to be attached to an ideology of subjectivity, especially if it is reconceived in terms of its original theological roots.

So how do we deal with personal confessions in a classroom where religion is being taught? This is one of those questions that raises a host of pressing pedagogical issues. Confessions, after all, are particular, so they raise the question of how we move from the personal to the public, and how we rationally scrutinize the personal without discouraging confessions altogether. Confessions need some type of policing, which can make everybody nervous. How do we decide what is and what is not appropriate in our classrooms? Moreover, all classes take place in a larger context — in an academic institution with its own mission and priorities; in such a context, no confession can be neutral or void of consequences. Every confession is also a statement about what should be or should not be said in the institution as a whole. We need to admit the existence of a "politics" of confession: who has the privilege of making confessions? What kinds of things are confessable?

These questions get at the heart of what theological education is all about. Consequently, the stakes are high; this in turn leads to a good deal of distrust about the role of personal confessions in the theological education classroom. Because the term *confession* is both pedagogical and theological, discussing it reveals one's interconnected passions about both teaching and theology. But some of the conversation about the term banks very heavily on the assumptions of modernity — as the following example makes clear.

Marginalizing Confession

In his book *Casuistry and Modern Ethics*, Richard B. Miller attempts to create a space for the doing of theology within a secular religious studies environment. Drawing on Wittgenstein and Geertz, he argues that religious studies has no essence, and therefore it cannot be kept pure from scholarly discourses that might "pollute" it. Miller takes a poetic or inductive approach to scholarship, and thus he wants to celebrate the many different discourses that constitute religious studies. The only criteria for what should count as legitimate in the study of religion concerns the skills that are being developed and practiced. Nevertheless, he is interested in establishing some boundaries for the study of religion. He appropriates some terminology from Stephen Toulmin to suggest that religious studies is not a "compact" discipline, capable of being judged at every stage by established canons and procedures; it is, rather, a "diffuse" discipline, which can conform loosely to the rigid requirements of scientific progress.

Nevertheless, even a diffuse discipline needs to be able to distinguish proper from inappropriate questions, issues, and methodologies, in order to make its researches productive. Thus, for all his poetic pluralism, Miller insists that one of the duties and obligations of the religion teacher is disciplining the study of religion by establishing its boundaries. The price of admitting theology into religious studies is that some form of theology has to be excluded. Miller accepts that every theological school is, to some extent, apologetical; but what he does not accept is confessional theology.

> Confessional theology is creedal, seeking to articulate the meaning and implications of an ostensive religion's beliefs. Typically, confessional theologians care little about whether they make sense to a wider public. But apologetical discourse is different: It attempts to defend religion according to wider canons of experience and rationality. . . . Insofar as confessionalists seek only to develop their truth claims from within the practices and beliefs of a particular religion, religionists have it right: Confessionalists seem to disavow canons of inquiry that might be shared by the nonbeliever, and so develop claims that are wholly 'from the inside.'[13]

Miller thus equates confessionalism with relativism, even though those on his list of confessional theologians — George Lindbeck, John Howard Yoder, William Placher, and John Milbank — would hardly accept that label.

Although he begins with a trenchant critique of essentialism, Miller ends up policing the field of religion, in order to keep it free of confessionalism. Rather than making an argument against confessionalism, he begs the question by assuming that confessionalists reject the mode of public inquiry so essential to academic discourse. Ironically, many of the

---

[13] Richard B. Miller, *Casuistry and Modern Ethics* (Chicago: University of Chicago Press, 1996), 208–209.

theologians he criticizes are writers who make use of his own authorities, such as Wittgenstein and Geertz. Nonetheless, Miller does not argue with confessionalists about what constitutes public inquiry and rational debate. Indeed, he tends to equate theological confessionalism with the narcissistic chatter that so often passes for confession in our secular culture. The confessionalists he identifies make strong arguments about the role of religion in society and the ways in which religion can best be understood, but these arguments go unanalyzed in Miller's sweeping dismissal.

In a footnote, he does make the condescending concession that confessionalists can be tolerated to some extent, which "parallels tolerating the intolerant in liberal political philosophy" (p. 288). But he also can sound the following warning: "Theologians who prefer a Religious Studies department to a seminary, divinity school, or theology department as a more desirable location for carrying out research and teaching elect that option at some risk" (p. 217). The risk is, evidently, that they might someday be told that they really do not belong. Miller says all this while admitting that very little theology done in the academy is intended for a parochial audience. Religious studies, in other words, has already succeeded in keeping itself pure by forcing theology into a rationalistic mode.

Reconstituting Confession

The problem with Miller's argument is that he essentializes confessionalism in order to avoid essentializing religious studies. That is, he treats confessionalism as a certain kind of thing with a very circumscribed agenda and set of presuppositions. I would suggest that it is questionable to think about confessionalism as a separate theological school, rather than as an inherent element within every faith — especially a faith like Christianity, which is so dependent upon trustworthy testimonies and witnesses. Even when confessionalism is thought of as a specific school of theology, its arguments must be taken as plausible and worthy of a critical response. A confessionalist like Stanley Hauerwas tries to base ethics upon a recovery of narrative and community, but others have come to a kind of confessionalism in theology from a feminist perspective, or even a postmodern critique of objectivity.

Confessionalists make strongly public arguments about the limitations to certain kinds of rational discourse and scientific approaches to religion. They might argue, for example, that religious discourse is best understood by the practitioners of that discourse, an argument not dissimilar to some things women say about women's studies or blacks say about black studies. Confessionalism also validates and defends the personal experience of the scholarly investigator, so that we are all confessionalists in the sense of admitting and clarifying the intersection of autobiography and research. After all, if the Heisenberg uncertainty principle teaches us that when we do physics, the position of the investigator determines how we isolate and measure an atom, how can we suppose that the subjectivity of the researcher of religion will be any less important?

Confessionalism is a tendency that runs throughout the academy, not just across the religions. Confessionalists are those who draw certain inferences from the confessional nature of all knowledge. They make the argument (publicly and rigorously) that there are no universal audiences or neutral observers, so that who one writes for, and what one believes, shapes what one has to say. To that extent, I would say that confessionalism is a dimension within *all* theology, but that it is frequently downplayed or minimized by some theological schools for epistemological reasons that are now largely unwarranted. In the postmodern academy, confessionalism in theology should become more accepted and popular just as it has become more standard in almost all other humanistic disciplines.[14]

Indeed, the field of ethics can be conceived as a way of teaching religion in the academy without being confessional. Most programs in ethics are still rooted in Christianity (courses in cross-cultural ethics are rare), but the fact that ethical issues are being examined, rather than doctrinal issues, gives these courses a veneer of objectivity and universality. Even though courses in ethics use Christian theologians, ethicists can always insist that the are using theology in the background while foregrounding the search for a reasonable and thus widely shared position on topics of universal concern. When Miller, for example, talks about the ways in which Augustine's *Confessions* can be taught in religious studies programs, he talks about Augustine's parallels with Freud, his role in intellectual history, and his

---

[14]Why confessionalism in theology should be singled out by Miller as a type of theology, an essence, that could pollute religious studies and therefore represents a danger to civil discourse is a mystery to me. Perhaps it has to do with Miller's own ultra-liberal Roman Catholicism, which attempts to follow St. Thomas Aquinas in illuminating the universal aspects of the human condition — without, however, accepting any role for special revelation or divine law.

hermeneutics of the self. What he does not mention is the question of God — which is, of course, the question that Augustine most relentlessly pursues.

Stanley Hauerwas has noted how biomedical ethics has given theology new life in the academy. Life and death issues naturally raise religious concerns and invite theological speculations. Hauerwas is skeptical, however, about ethical models that emphasize abstract principles. What if ethics is tied to what one believes? And what if one's beliefs are tied to a particular community and its tradition? And what if the ethicist took as her task the formation of ethical belief and conduct in her students? If so, then one would end up with a very different-looking course in ethics. Too often, these issues are avoided — especially in religious studies contexts, but also in seminaries, where theological questions ought to be at the forefront.

Unfortunately, the field of ethics is one of the last strongholds of liberal Protestantism in the academy (including the seminary). Ethics attempts to attend to theological influences, but also to speak to a wider audience on the basis of the broadest principles and premises. Maybe some day we will all be forced to admit that we speak out of particular situations and from personal commitments, which is what feminists have been arguing all along. Ethicists, after all, work out of particular traditions and raise questions of ultimacy and meaning that transcend the canons of materialism, naturalism, and secularism.

Confession in the Classroom

The theological dimension of confession cannot be directly translated into the classroom experience, because the classroom is not the church. The goal of teaching is to create a body of *knowers*, not only a body of believers. Yet at the same time, the lines between these two goals are not distinct; at the very least, "knowing" means knowing what you believe. It is appropriate, I think, not only to integrate personal confession into the classroom through the use of journals and story-telling, but also to make confession a more explicit aspect of theological education. Our students should be encouraged not just to tell their personal stories to each other, but also to *hold each other accountable* to the class and to its texts. In other words, students (and teachers) should be encouraged to think about the ways in which personal confessions are rooted in tradition and shaped by communities, so that they are no longer "private," but are part of the community's self-understanding.

Indeed, confessions are pedagogically useful precisely because the performative acts of students can never escape the actual history of religious beliefs and practices. Every confession is as much about the critical questions of religion as it is about the penitent's personal history. Especially in a course on theology, students could first read, discuss, and compare samples of ecclesial confessions, and could then talk about the role of confession in our culture. Next, they could try to write a confessional statement for the entire class, as a group project. Wouldn't that be an impossible task? How could all of the students ever agree on everything? What issues would be raised?

Of course, the classroom is not the church, so the confession would not be written in the context of an entire ecclesial community and tradition; but that would be the point that needs to be made. Confessions can only be made from a specific context; and to have students struggle with the act of public confession, and the extent to which they can agree about what is ultimate, would be a good way of teaching them what a confession is (and what it is not). The traditional task of a confession of faith is to publicize the personal in a communal context. To what extent that is still possible today in an academic setting would be a worthwhile task for any theology class.

Toward an Anti-Individualistic Confessionalism

Søren Kierkegaard represents for many people the zenith of nineteenth century subjectivism. The trends that Foucault outlines above come to culmination in his work. He defines the truth as subjective. He would agree with Nietzsche's own confession about the autobiographical nature of all thought: "It has gradually become clear to me what every great philosophy has hitherto been: a confession on the part of its author."[15] Indeed, even Kierkegaard's most theological works can be read as commentary on and distortions of his own autobiography, especially his broken engagement with Regina.

Nevertheless, Kierkegaard did not have a romantic notion of individuality. As David Wisdo points out, he rejected recollection as a romantic mode of self-understanding. Memory is not the sufficient stuff of selfhood. The person who artfully tries to craft episodic moments that transcend time, although seeking to ensure the consistency of the self,

---

[15]Friedrich Nietzsche, *Beyond Good and Evil*, trans. R. J. Hollingdale (NY: Penguin Books, 1990), 37.

actually risks losing the self's identity altogether. Such aesthetic moments do not carry temporal weight, so the self becomes disconnected from the very activities that tie us to the world and each other. Kierkegaard's entire critique of the aesthetic realm, then, is a rejection of inwardness as a criterion of authenticity. As Wisdo makes clear, for Kierkegaard, subjectivity is only possible if self-understanding is possible, and that is only possible for the self that stands before God. To confess before God is not to tell God something, because God is omniscient. Instead, it is to acknowledge that God already knows us, a knowledge that enables us to know ourselves. As Kierkegaard writes,

> To come to oneself is self-knowledge, *and before God*. For if self-knowledge does not lead to knowing oneself before God, then indeed there is something in what the merely human view says, that it leads to a certain emptiness which produces dizziness. Only by being before God can a man entirely come to himself in the transparency of sobriety.[16]

To confess, then, is to repent by acknowledging God's knowledge of us. God has chosen us; we do not choose ourselves. Kierkegaard's existentialism thus ends up with a traditional theological argument about the prevenience of grace.

Kierkegaard does not commit the error of exalting the self in its own subjectivity. The truth does not come from within. It comes from our transparency to the divine that is outside us. This is made clear in the *Philosophical Fragments*, that great book about teaching. Kierkegaard criticizes the Socratic theory of learning, which assumes that the student already knows the truth and the teacher is there merely to coax it from her. In Christian pedagogy, Kierkegaard reminds us, the learner is in untruth, and the truth is external to the personal. The truth, indeed, is disruptive and transformative, rather than appealing and confirming. Christian teachers, then, need to remember that we cannot give the students what they ultimately need. There has to be another other present when we listen to and share with our students their most significant responses to religion. For true confession to take place, it cannot simply be reduced to an act of mutual sharing, no matter how positively that act is portrayed. Confession creates authentic selfhood when it is done with others and before God.

---

[16]Quoted in David Wisdo, "Kierkegaard on Confession and Understanding a Life," *Journal of Religious Studies* 17 (1991): 92.

Otherwise, we are left with a postmodern fiction that begins anywhere and leads nowhere.

The most significant tasks for the Christian teacher, then, are to make room in the classroom for God, to remind students that God is more than just an object of discussion, and to prepare students to think about themselves in terms of their relationship to their creator and sustainer. We need to be ready to ask our students: What understanding of God does that opinion or argument entail? How would you make that point in an ecclesial community? Would you say that differently if you were putting it in the form of a prayer? And we can be ready to ask ourselves: toward what ends are we teaching? To whom are we ultimately speaking, when we walk into a classroom with the privilege of reflecting on matters of belief? The most important challenge for Christian pedagogy is to place our classroom confessions in a context that attends to God as our ultimate audience. Our failure to take up that challenge — indeed, the inevitable failure of every classroom, no matter how pious, to be pleasing to God — is where our personal confessions, as teachers, need to begin.

Chapter 6

Theology as Discernment:
Truth, Power, and Authority in Rhetorical Theology

Wes Avram

> God can no longer be arrived at by dialectics, by the 'discipline of truth.' . . . Hence the relationship of God to the world becomes, after Christianity, a rhetorical one.
>
> — John Milbank[1]

I am Presbyterian. Like most Presbyterian pastors, I was obliged to attend regional meetings of clergy and selected lay elders, first in 1997 and then again in 1998, to debate and vote on proposed changes in denominational wording regarding ordination. These proposals were prompted by concerns over what some believed to be laxity, and what others believed to be restrictiveness, regarding the sexual practices of candidates. My presbytery voted in the national minority each year. There was, nevertheless, controversy enough to prompt heated emotion and lively argument. The same large sanctuary was chosen each year to accommodate the larger-than-usual crowds. The sanctuary also had the odd advantage of two center isles. This allowed microphones separated from each other, with

---

[1] *Theology and Social Theory: Beyond Secular Reason* (Oxford: Blackwell, 1990), 429–30; cited in David Toole, *Waiting for Godot in Sarajevo: Theological Reflections on Nihilism, Tragedy, and Apocalypse* (Boulder: Westview Press, 1998), 60.

those "for" and "against" lining up in separate aisles. Persons adamantly opposed to each other could wait to speak without having to exchange breath.

Our debate was organized by rules that were pre-approved by committee and mailed to voters. Debate was restricted to the wording being voted on at the time, and would be limited to about an hour. Individual debaters would be invited to speak *for* or *against*, and only for a few minutes. Appeals would alternate between opposing microphones. Attached to the rules, mailed out in advance, were flysheets with titles like "Guidelines for discussion during times of conflict" or "When Presbyterians disagree."

I should note that I believe that most of the speeches were offered in good faith and with deep passion. I should also note that I did not speak, opting instead to participate as an observer. Among my observations: First, there was no microphone in the *middle*. Perhaps this was because our stated task was to come to a *yea* or *nay* on constitutional revisions, but the absence of an authorized center position remained instructive. Second, probably two-thirds of the speakers had to be warned when their time was up, and a handful elected to ignore requests from the moderator that they finish. My third observation is more anecdotal, and therefore interpretive: *every speaker but one* spoke either in agreement or defense of an already presented position, and spoke with the obvious intent of persuading the crowd to that position.

The one speech that stood out for me did take a position, but in a qualitatively different way than any of the others. No transcript of the remarks remains, so I paraphrase the brief speech from memory, with permission:

> I rise to speak against this proposal, not because I relish my opposition, but because I feel I must speak from my conscience — however well- or ill-informed my conscience may be at this point in my ministry. For so many reasons I wish I were comfortable seeing things differently, but from all that I have seen and heard, and from all that I have studied, and from all I know now of the Bible, I believe [the speaker described his position, then paused for a second or two].... But I may be wrong. I pray that if I am wrong I will come to know this and have the courage to change my mind.
>
> I invite you to join me, but not first in my vote. I invite you first to join me in the openness to the Holy Spirit I hope to keep, and also in mutual accountability. And I ask you to vote your conscience, and walk in the way

your own reading of scripture suggests. And I ask you to pray for the church. Thank you.[2]

It is easy to read this speech as confirming of whatever position a reader might bring to such a matter. But I've chosen to avoid identifying the position of the speaker because I believe this speaker was doing something different than simply making a case or proving a point — though he *was* engaged in the activity of persuasion. I believe he was speaking theologically in response to a rhetorical crisis (or rhetorically in response to a theological crisis), and that the contours of his speaking carried a *rhetorical and theological* significance different again from the other "passions seeking words" during those afternoons. That difference informs this essay.

The speaker and I are alumni of the same Presbyterian seminary, as were several other participants — including one of the architects of the rules that guided the afternoon debate. However well or poorly, the rhetorical choices made that afternoon — even my silence — were at least to some degree affected by the academic and pastoral training we received. But the connections between training and action are not always obvious. I do not recall any syllabus, sermon, lecture, or structured conversation during my studies with the theme of developing rhetorical sensibility *as such*. And I believe the words we speak, and the rhetorical decisions we make in shaping those words, are filled by something far more complex than the simple application of scholarly insights to verbal practice. I believe they are both more and less inventive than that, and that they are dependent on rhetorical *knack* in a way that is, at once, as ordinary as the day-to-day intrigues of communication and as mysterious as the Spirit who, according to the Church, fills bread and wine at each eucharistic feast. We have much to learn about the interlocking fates of rhetoric and theology — not least from the fact that the rhetorical dynamic in my speaker's remarks that I find noteworthy was, in my hearing, quite exceptional among statements made those afternoons.

---

[2]The speaker has authorized this paraphrase. He has also agreed with my request that the speech be included anonymously, so as to focus reflection on the rhetorical content of the text rather than prompt investigation into the position of its author on the topic. Whether my reconstruction is perfectly accurate historically is less important than what I believe to be its rhetorical accuracy to substance, sense, and significance.

I have presented the foregoing scene as an icon through which the urgency and curiosity of the relationship between the rhetoric and theology might be espied. I write both as a seminary professor and as a rhetorically-trained pastor. From this vantage point, I see a gap between how theological education has been organized and the contingencies most pastors must face day to day. I have a hunch that a strong and open-ended appropriation of a rhetorical-theological method might help us map the terrain of that gap. While no syllabus will be able to achieve training in rhetorical skill, we may yet be well served by more carefully considering how such skill affects, and is affected by, theological education.

I proceed in three steps. I start academically, discussing the *rapprochement* between rhetoric and theology and arguing for its significance. The next three sections — the core of my discussion — examine three themes for a constructive approach to rhetorical theology: truth, power, and authority. I argue for *the precedence of testimony* in matters of truth, for *a praxis of discernment over technique* in matters of power, and for an *ethics of decentered authorship* in matters of authority. Along the way I respond to criticisms of rhetorical theory as relativistic, subjectivistic, and manipulative. In a final section I return to the question of theological education, examining how it might begin to respond. The rhetor at my Presbytery debate remains in my mind throughout, even when not cited.

Theology's Rhetorical Turn

"My own belief," wrote David Tracy in 1994, "is that across the Christian theological spectrum there is occurring an event of major import: the attempt to free Christian theology from the now smothering embrace of modernity."[3] This event has been welcomed by some as a chance to displace the modern privileging of theory over practice.[4] Modern divisions between

---

[3]"Theology and the Many Faces of Postmodernity," *Theology Today*, 51/4 (April, 1994): 110. See also David Tracy, *Plurality and Ambiguity: Hermeneutics, Religion, Hope* (San Francisco: Harper & Row, 1987).

[4]"Philosophy is charged with the task of providing the root principles of all human knowledge, encompassing the realm of material nature and the region of the human mind. Descartes's arboreal metaphor of metaphysical roots became quickly aligned with an architectural metaphor of foundations (already in his own thought), further congealing the telos of philosophy as the discovery of ultimate and

theology and rhetoric are among the boundaries that are displaced or blurred in the process, producing a turn among certain theologians away from philosophical methods and toward rhetorical ones. "All forms of rhetoric agree that action of some kind is implied in communication," writes William Beardslee, "and those who are interested in theology will rejoice that we are moving toward an emphasis on thinking as a form of action or on the action that is intended as a result of thinking."[5]

From the theological side, rhetorical theology may include a simple interdisciplinary interest among theologians in themes or methods drawn from the rhetorical tradition.[6] From the side of rhetoric, however, the very

---

unimpeachable first principles. Within such a scheme of things, the subordination of the special disciplines in the arts and the sciences to philosophy is unavoidable, as they remain beholden to the foundational accomplishments of philosophical reason." Calvin Schrag,"Rhetoric Resituated at the End of Philosophy." *Quarterly Journal of Speech*, 71 (1985): 164–74; here, 165. See also Emmanuel Levinas, "God and Philosophy," in *Collected Philosophical Papers*, trans. Alphonso Lingis (Dordrecht: Martinus Nijhoff, 1987): "The philosophical discourse of the West claims the amplitude of an all-encompassing structure or of an ultimate comprehension. It compels every other discourse to justify itself before philosophy. Rational theology accepts this vassalage. If, for the benefit of religion, it reserves a domain from the authority of philosophy, one will know that this domain will have been recognized to be philosophically unverifiable" (153).

[5] "Theology and Rhetoric in the University," in David Ray Griffin and Joseph C. Hough, Jr., eds., *Theology and the University: Essays in Honor of John B. Cobb, Jr.* (Albany, N.Y.: State University of New York Press, 1991), 187. John Henry Newman argued in this direction in *An Essay in Aid of a Grammar of Assent* (London, 1870), but the point remained underexplored until recently. See David S. Cunningham's treatment of Newman in the first chapter of *Faithful Persuasion: In Aid of a Rhetoric of Christian Theology* (Notre Dame: University of Notre Dame Press, 1991), as well as Walter Jost, *Rhetorical Thought in John Henry Newman* (Columbia, S.C.: University of South Carolina Press, 1989) and Wayne Booth, "Rhetoric and Religion: Are They Essentially Wedded?" in Werner G. Jeanrond and Jennifer L. Rike, eds., *Radical Pluralism and Truth: David Tracy and the Hermeneutics of Religion* (New York: Crossroad Press, 1991), 62–80.

[6] See, for example, Stephen Webb, *Refiguring Theology: The Rhetoric of Karl Barth* (Albany, N.Y.: State University of New York Press, 1991); Serene Jones, *Calvin and the Rhetoric of Piety* (Louisville: Westminster/John Knox Press, 1995).

identities of disciplines being turned toward each other may be altered by the turning. As Michael Leff puts it, rhetoric can emerge as "the very medium in which social knowledge is generated."[7] This approach suggests a *praxis-oriented* approach to thinking — theological thinking included.

This praxis-oriented approach sees in discourse a particular sort of *dynamis* (potency, inspiration), and *technē* (skill, rule, technique), both flowing into an ongoing activity of discernment and practice (a *praxis*). Here all knowledge is taken to be formed *in the midst*. It is a creature of deficiency, contingency, and potential wonder; it is derived from a rhetorical engagement within concrete situations. Here, truth is not simply derived and then applied; it "arrives," it comes closer. In the theological realm, this can be described as a recovery of pre-modern forms of ortho*praxis* as an inherent dynamic within any ortho*doxy*.[8] Taken broadly, therefore, rhetorical theology can be defined as the discovery, performance, and interpretation of persuasive practice *in*, *for*, and *as* religious discourse.

One might call this praxial approach *theo-homilia*. The neologism comes from the Greek *theo* (of God), *homos* (the common discourse of the crowd), and *homologia* (an event of agreement or understanding indistinguishable from the process of its achievement). The rhetorical aspect of theo-homilia is not simply a set of aesthetic norms or instrumental techniques of application and embellishment — examples, metaphors and other tropes, or argumentative topics provided to truths it does not itself participate in discovering. Instead, this strong approach binds rhetoric and theology into an integrated activity in which the possibility of religious truth becomes a wager laid on a certain *way* or *manner* of social engagement. I take this wager to offer the deepest promise of rhetorical theology; it is the wager that my Presbytery speaker was making good on, at least in that moment.

A warrant for this strong approach to rhetorical theology might be found in the fact that, in the midst of whatever transition we making from modernity into postmodernity, theology is finding itself in an extraordinary flux of contingency and "dis-ease." This gives rise to what Hans

---

[7] "Cicero's 'Pro Murena' and the Strong Case for Rhetoric," *Rhetoric & Public Affairs*, 1 (1998): 63.

[8] Mary Carruthers borrows the term from Paul Gehl in her book *The Craft of Thought: Meditation, Rhetoric, and the Making of Images, 400–1200* (Cambridge: Cambridge University Press, 1998), 1.

Blumenberg calls the *prerequisites* of the rhetorical situation: "lacking definitive evidence and being compelled to act."[9] In such a situation, events like Presbytery meetings present a true burden to theological imagination. In them, we discover a chronic and perhaps unresolvable crisis in our discourse, and a pervasive sense of insufficiency.

One can discern rhetorical proofs for this situation according to the classic Aristotelian means of persuasion: *ēthos*, *logos*, and *pathos*. An emphasis on *ēthos* (authority, character, or agency) sees the crisis of theology as a crisis of rhetorical *credibility* in postmodern culture.[10] Theological argument lacks both evangelical persuasiveness and power to shape agreement because the voice of theology has lost the confidence of its audience. This crisis prompts discourse that is predominantly critical, political, or argumentative.

An emphasis on theological *logos* (meaning, substance, or logic) highlights the problem of theological *formulation*.[11] In this view, theological language requires continual reinterpretation in a context of conflicting worldviews and pluralistic communicative norms, and such reinterpretation requires vigilant attention to non-instrumentalist views of form and argument. This prompts rhetorical theologies that are

---

[9] "An Anthropological Approach to the Contemporary Significance of Rhetoric," trans. Robert M. Wallace, in Kenneth Baynes, et al., eds., *After Philosophy: End or Transformation* (Cambridge: MIT Press, 1987), 441.

[10] See Rowan Williams, "Postmodern Theology and the Judgment of the World," in Frederic B. Burnham, ed., *Postmodern Theology: Christian Faith in a Pluralist World* (San Francisco: Harper and Row, 1989), 92–112; Elisabeth Shüssler-Fiorenza, "The Ethics of Interpretation: De-Centering Biblical Scholarship," *Journal of Biblical Literature* 107 (1988): 13–14; and Cunningham, *Faithful Persuasion*. I would also argue that certain narrative theologians, Stanley Hauerwas the most prominent, have followed this direction by arguing for the significance of ecclesiology in Christian ethics as a way of restoring the credibility (*ēthos*) of the theological "audience."

[11] Prominent examples of this view would include David Tracy and David Klemm. For Tracy, see *Plurality and Ambiguity*; also *The Analogical Imagination: Christian Theology and the Culture of Pluralism* (New York: Crossroad Press, 1981). For Klemm, see "Toward a Rhetoric of Postmodern Theology: Through Barth and Heidegger," *JAAR* 55 (1987): 443–69; "Ricoeur, Theology and the Rhetoric of Overturning," *Literature and Theology* 3 (1989): 267–84.

predominantly hermeneutical, revisionist, and rooted in the metaphor of theology as an ongoing conversation with adaptable norms.

A third emphasis within rhetorical theology moves through a kind of indirection less apparent in the first two means of persuasion. In this third case, postmodern culture is taken to be less as a challenge to theology than theology's liberation, freeing a theological *pathos* (emotional or intuitive identification) that has been suppressed within modern attempts to distinguish clearly between comprehension and affect.[12] Here, the theological crisis is taken to be no crisis at all, but the very *essence* of positive theology. But to normalize a crisis necessarily *redefines* it: in what sense can we recognize a crisis, if "crisis" is characteristic of the age? This redefinition prompts rhetorical theologies that are predominantly aesthetic, paralogical (dependent on meanings that cannot be held by grammatical forms), and in certain ways deconstructive. Paralogical theology is marked by rhetorical effect before it is expressed within theological claims.

While a rhetorical theology will include all three approaches in some measure, holding the three means of persuasion in mind does allow for determining relative differences. It may also prove useful for a discussion of theological education. Truths inculcated and skills nurtured in theological education will shape a complex network of appeals, based on *ēthos*, *logos*, and *pathos*. And if we are fortunate, that complex network may begin to make some sense of how we talk together.

I now want to explore three themes that this rapprochement between theology and rhetoric now makes available. Principal among them is the place of *testimony* in a theo-homiletic meditation on the nature of theological truth. Alongside this is an interpretation of rhetorical theological power as a faculty of ethical *discernment* rather than as technical mastery of effect-producing argument. A third theme views theological authority as a form of *rhetorical positioning* — *vis-à-vis* the otherness of God.

---

[12]Examples here include Thomas Altizer and Mark C. Taylor. For Altizer, see *Genesis and Apocalypse: A Theological Voyage Toward Authentic Christianity* (Louisville, Ky.: Westminster/John Knox Press, 1990); "Total Abyss and Theological Rebirth: The Crisis of University Theology," in Griffin and Hough, eds., *Theology and the University*, 169–84. For Taylor, see *Erring: A Postmodern A/theology* (Chicago: University of Chicago Press, 1984), and *Alterity* (Chicago: University of Chicago Press, 1987).

Truth as Testimony

For readers schooled in a view of rhetoric as the study of persuasive form, with any form of closure suspended for the sake of "mere" effect, an invocation of *truth* may prove to be a stumbling block. Truth is often seen as the coherent description of reality by which contingent claims may be judged. Such a description would appear incompatible with rhetoric's concentration on influence, form, and undecidability. Must a thoroughgoing rhetorical theology render futile our striving for truth, abandoning theology to the abyss of relativism that is so often feared to be the underside of our postmodern situation? Shouldn't theology, of all disciplines, be preserving the dream of comprehensive knowledge and universally available reason, however fragile our hold on that reason might be?

Addressing Relativism

Any response to this concern should begin with a frank acknowledgment. Rhetorical practice certainly can imply a certain kind of relativism, but it is a relativism that is necessary to truth. There is no way of formulating theological claims, modern or otherwise, that doesn't risk this in some way or another; indeed, this is the danger of *any* use of language, whether plain or adorned. Rhetorical theology assumes that theological knowledge, and the truth is bears, is always *discursively* contextualized; but this does not cede truth's ground to relativism. Instead, this strong approach sees rhetorical theology as a thinking of God that is set *toward* truth, participates *in* truth, and simultaneously accommodates both provisional *and* absolute affirmations. But such accommodation is always *positioned*, arising *in the midst* of rhetorical engagement, and always spoken by real persons.

Here, the notion of *testimony* may prove useful; for one way in which both the absolute and personal character of truth might be rhetorically preserved is by lodging truth claims in the rhetoric of affirmation rather than argument. Rhetorical truth, *qua* theological truth, may take the form of truth *affirmed*. Rhetorical theology sets such absolute affirmation in the position of personal affirmation — in speech that is intoned by a person speaking, or a community living, or a tradition resonating. It is thus ethically charged and formative of those who bear it.

As such, the decorous form for theological affirmation may be *testimony* first, before advocacy. It resides in the courtroom of public judgment, neither as a lawyer (defending or accusing), nor as a judge sitting as a neutral, universal authority. It is, rather, in the position of a *witness*: it points, suggests, implies, gives account, answers, and remains responsible to context-specific norms. Yet while so responsible, it is also free to challenge the rule of the court when it is hampered from giving account to what it has seen or heard. But it often holds back some knowledge, for the sake of the court, and remains reticent to make claims it cannot support when questioned again. This not to lie, but to respect proceedings. The character of the speaker, witnessing rather defending, is always to some degree implicated in the testimony that speaker offers — even as the testimony does not originate in the initiative of the witness, but comes in the form of answering in *another's* trial.

Such witness is, finally, nonpresumptuous. It defers assessment and final verdict for another audience (another *jury*). So positioned, however, it has no less confidence in that to which it gives witness. Here rhetoric becomes, itself, the very practice in which knowledge of truth, and thus also knowledge of God, becomes possible. As such, the truth of God becomes a rhetorical, rather than logical, possibility — *rendered* before *proved*.[13]

Paul Ricoeur's treatment is instructive here. "The term *testimony*," he writes, "should be applied to words, works, actions, and to lives which attest to an intention, an inspiration, an idea at the heart of experience and history which nonetheless transcend experience and history." He goes on to suggest that the "philosophical problem of testimony is the problem of the testimony of the absolute or, better, of absolute testimony of the absolute. The question is only proper if the absolute makes sense for

---

[13]Note Franz Rosenzweig in "The New Thinking" (1923), in Alan Udoff and Barbara E. Galli, ed. and trans., *Franz Rosenzweig's 'The New Thinking'* (Syracuse, N.Y.: Syracuse University Press, 1999), 98: "God and the world and man. This And was the *alpha* [*das Erste*] of experience; this is must also return to the *omega* [*in Letzten*] of the truth. Still in the truth itself, in the final truth, which can be only one, there must be an And; this truth, different [*anders*] from the truth of the philosophers, which is permitted to know only itself, must be truth for someone. Should it be then, nevertheless, the only truth, it can be truth only for the One. And thereby it becomes necessary that our truth is manifold and that 'the' truth changes into our truth. Truth in this way ceases to be what 'is' true, and becomes that which, as true — wants to be verified [*bewahrt*]."

consciousness."[14] A rhetorical theology presumes this to be the case; and it acknowledges a "rhetorical problem" alongside the "philosophical" one, which is the question of how absolute affirmation is textured within ordinary discourse, rooted as ordinary discourse is in situations where communicators "lacking sufficient evidence" are nevertheless "compelled to act."

Much contemporary literature on testimony would suggest that the testifying moment is one in which a speaker uses a telling narrative of personal experience as a form of proof. Testimony is thus reduced to the telling of personal stories to correct hazards of supposed objectivity. The centrality of this kind of testimony in Post-Holocaust literature is a good example. This view of testimony tends to leave intact a view of truth as that which corresponds to the verifiably real, with testimony becoming a peculiarly privileged proof of what is "real" to a postmodern imagination.

While the theo-homiletic privileging of testimony that I am advocating does include a significant moment of subjectivity, it seeks to expand and reshape a definition of testimony along the lines suggested by Ricoeur. I am attempting to suggest that theo-homiletic truth is not the kind of truth *proven* by testimony. It is the kind of truth that *is* testimony, in the broader sense of that word: a texturing of absolute affirmation within ordinary discourse, shedding itself before rhetorical structures (over which it holds no authority), and submitting itself to criteria and cross-examination without fear. It is the "I believe" implied in any ontological "it is" statement. And it necessarily requires disciplines of subjective formation by which the "I" can become *worthy* of making testimony and prepared to do so as free as possible of both error and violence. Again, it may include using personal stories as telling examples or commanding expressive or experiential tropes, but the use of such stories or tropes is not what defines it as testimony. Ricoeur again:

> Testimony as story is thus found in an intermediary position between a statement made by a person and a belief assumed by another on the faith of the testimony of the first.
>
> It is not only from one meaning to another — from seeing to understanding — that the event is conveyed by testimony; testimony is at

---

[14]"The Hermeneutics of Testimony," in his *Essays on Biblical Interpretation*, ed. with an Introduction by Lewis S. Mudge (Philadelphia: Fortress, 1980): 119, 120.

the service of judgment. . . . The eyewitness character of testimony, therefore, never suffices to constitute its meaning as testimony.[15]

One might "tell one's story" and yet betray theo-homiletic testimony by using the telling to manipulate others and inhibit response (shutting down conversation through inappropriate appeals to empathy, for example, or hiding contestable claims within an indirect appeal to a listener's desire to remain in relationship). To the contrary, one might make an argument in what seems purely rational form, apparently absent any use of narrative or appeal to experience, and yet do this in a way that still exhibits the theo-homiletic character of testimony. It is a matter of rhetorical positioning, of *ēthos* within the *logos* of argument and moving within the *pathos* of humility and wonder. It operates before a dimension of transcendence in history and interpretation that cannot be encapsulated in logical description. Again, Ricoeur is instructive.

> Absolute testimony, on the contrary, in concrete singularity gives a caution to the truth without which its authority remains in suspense. Testimony, each time singular, confers the sanction of reality on ideas, ideals, and modes of being that the symbol depicts and discovers for us only as our most personal possibilities.[16]

I believe the statement made at that Presbytery meeting exhibits the characteristics of theo-homiletic testimony — at least in broad outline. Yet I haven't suggested where in the statement one might find such traces of testimony. Is it in the telling of the speaker's story ("From all I have seen and heard")? Is it in his providing certain limitations of scope ("not because I relish my opposition")? Is it because he intimates his own relationship to his words ("I wish I were comfortable seeing things differently . . . But I might be wrong")? Is it in the rhetorical presentation of congruence between struggle and appeal, ostensibly binding conviction to accountability ("I invite you to join me, but not first in my vote")? Or is it in a dynamic of delivery available only to a reader's imagination — in tone of voice, movement of body, pauses and emphases? If I am at all correct about this little speech, its status as theo-homiletic testimony surely lies in

---

[15]Ricoeur, "The Hermeneutics of Testimony," 123, 124.

[16]Ricoeur, "The Hermeneutics of Testimony," 122.

all these aspects — and maybe more. For there is a texture of self-reflexivity in this statement that works paralogically, rendering the ethical significance of the argument greater than the position it advocates. There is a hermeneutic congruence with a certain *sense* of God's claim on the speech, and it is to that *sense* of God's claim that the speaker gives witness. Therein lies its theo-homiletic surplus.

Addressing subjectivism

If accusations of relativism in a rhetorical definition of theological truth are countered through a robust view of testimony, do we not risk losing a sense of the *objective* in theological discourse? Again, one must at first cede the claim. Rhetorical theology, like any rhetoric, is suspicious of truth that limits itself within a naïve correspondence between objects and meanings, or truth and method. Quite the contrary, of course. Yet such chastening need not be extended to the point of an equally naive constructionism in which all exteriority collapses into a matrix of preferences.

This qualification is particularly urgent for rhetorical theology. For when explored theologically, rhetoric may be the very key to open the house of language, pointing us to meanings that cannot be encapsulated in a theme. Emmanuel Levinas writes that

> It is possible to show that meaning *qua* knowing has its motivation in a meaning that at the start is not a knowing at all.... This then suggests the idea of a dia-chrony of truth in which the said has to be unsaid, and the unsaid unsaid in its turn.[17]

Rhetorical theology may allow for a sense of the objective in the midst of rhetorical contingency by sensing a theological significance in certain forms of ineffability. Rhetorical theology will treat rhetorical struggles with "speaking the unspeakable" as signals of something other than conceptual failure or technical lack. Alongside an affirmation of the insufficiencies of human discourse, a theo-homiletic approach to rhetoric will also affirm a certain *super*sufficiency. Language, in the context of its use, does more than what the rules of discourse would help it to do — even as it does less. This is a transcendence signified in the very possibility, or trace, of a pure surplus of meaning (or non-meaning) weaving through discourse.

---

[17] Levinas, "God and Philosophy," 158, n. 4.

This surplus may catch a speaker up short at the very moment she is searching for words. It may signify a paralogical "Glory to God!" when the breach of distorted meanings is mended for a moment, or a "My Lord!" when, in the midst of desperate appeals, we somehow hear ourselves called by name (as did Mary in the garden with the Risen One). Or it may come as an expectant silence, in which sorrow turns to a peace the origin of which one cannot know. There is a wager in rhetorical theology — noted at the beginning of this essay — that this excess resides *within* our lack. And this wager is doubled by a hope that this superlative object is, itself, pregnant with words we do not yet know. It overflows from the insufficiency of theology into the supersufficiency of prayer and liturgy.

This rhetorical excess is *pathos*-oriented to the extent that it vigilantly comes alongside, opens up, and redirects ethical and the logical discourse. This rhetorical excess is *ēthos*-oriented to the extent that it positions persons as responsive, responsible, and so *voiced* even in their own brokenness — not because of something relative to our experience but out of our responsiveness to the sheer and potentially divine possibility that runs *through* our experiences. And this dynamic is *logos*-oriented to the extent that tropes, figures, and topics of speech interpret it — not by limiting it within ontological understanding, but by preserving its difference (its holiness?) *within* understanding. This is the otherwise-than-comprehensible within the comprehensible (which is not the same as the incomprehensible). This outsidedness may also be the space of revelation. For Christian thinkers, Christology itself may require just such a conception of truth.

Theo-homiletic testimony opens up to this dimension as if revealing a loophole in persuasive argument. That loophole opens to the truth that testimony bears but cannot contain. To say that theo-homiletic truth is testimony, therefore, is not to say that Divine Truth is reduced to personal description, but to say that there is a dimension of truth that human discourse can only bear in the *form* of courtroom-like witnessing. The loophole at the center of theo-homiletic testimony preserves the freedom of the Holy Spirit to act, just as it preserves listeners' freedom to respond.

Power as Discernment

There is yet another objection to be overcome before imagining a robust rhetorical theological education, and this is also related to the mistaken notion that rhetoric is unable to address questions of truth. This is the concern that the *ēthos* of rhetoric (both as a practice and as a theory) is inevitably one of manipulation and abuse of power — of "making the worst case most pleasing," according to the critique of Plato's *Gorgias*. Of course, rhetoric can become a tool of domination; but the fact that such abuses are *possible* is not reason enough to negate rhetoric's methodological usefulness for theology. After all, dialectical, propositional, liberation, and other theological methods are also implicated in regimes of power and dominance — despite their differing intent.

Even as rhetoric can give way to violence and separation, it can also give way to agreement; as such, it is a praxis of peace as much as it is a tool of domination. In fact, while it may be used as one among many tools of dominance, it may be, at the same time, the most definitive praxis of peace. For rhetoric holds within itself norms of decorum and judgment that not only encourage, but in certain ways require, the nonviolent resolution of conflicting claims. It hinges peace on the preservation of the other's freedom to be freely persuaded, rather than coerced; and so also requires safety for those who cannot freely choose. Violence or coercion, therefore, may be considered anti-rhetorical — even if rhetorical tools are often recruited to their ends.[18]

The defining presence of an *audience* in rhetorical discourse, for example, can be analogized into an acknowledgment of the rhythms of questioning and answering, apprehending and erring, claiming and resisting — all of which help to constitute a sociality that refuses violence. Because rhetorical invention is always concerned with these rhythms, it can bring the potential for violence remarkably close to the generative potential for reconciliation. Rhetoric, at its fullest, is a faculty for discerning these differences — even when the differences are subtle.

This view of rhetoric — as a faculty of discernment in the work of nonviolent persuasion — contrasts with later notions of rhetoric as fixed rules of tropes in composition, or as a limited set of repeatable topics in argument. But I take it to be consistent with Aristotle's view.[19] Seen as a faculty of discernment, rhetoric moves within vernacular practices with a

---

[18]See David S. Cunningham, "Theology as Rhetoric," *Theological Studies* 52/3 (September 1991): 407–30; here, 421–22.

[19]See Thomas Farrell, *Norms of Rhetorical Culture* (New Haven, Conn.: Yale University Press, 1993).

more adaptive sensibility than what might be allowed by more technical approaches.

My discussion of testimony offers a clue again, as it seems that *praxis*-oriented norms in rhetorical theology are norms of *responsiveness*, opening loopholes in the midst of argument, rather than techniques for shaping ideology through effective appeal. Theo-homiletically significant testimony may require a rhetorical norm of self-application, by which a claim invites the same forms of judgment upon itself that it makes on other claims, and invites such judgment as a warrant for the very argument it makes. Because I witness to grace as a surplus to meaning, I acknowledge the insufficiencies of my own meanings, even as I testify to the One who is source of the very grace graciously received. I can only seek to offer such testimony *graciously* — however imperfectly I do so. I accept judgment upon that basis, and let such judgment enhance, or even participate in, the very witness I seek to make. Testimony is thus judged by its *ēthos*. Christian theologies of redemption — struggling as they do to preserve, interpret, and give form to the relationship of violence and infinite possibility in the biblical story — may require just such a communicative practice.

Authority as Rhetorical Positioning

I return again to the courtroom, this time as a way of describing theo-homiletic authority. Locating theo-homiletic truth on the witness stand necessarily shifts the locus of authority in theological affirmations. By saying this, I am not simply reiterating the helpful and now familiar arguments against privileges of gender, class, ecclesiastical status, or schooling in doing theology — as important as those arguments are. There is no doubt that many factors both effect and affect rhetorical ethos. But as present as these factors are, they may cut in several directions simultaneously; and they are not always as easy to describe as some theories would claim. I want to bracket them here to look at a rhetorical dynamic that may cut across them, though it is never unaffected by them.

Within this use of the courtroom metaphor, one surely needs to pay attention not only to the witness, but to other characters as well. There is a dimension of truth-telling that is the unique charge of the one accused. Indeed, sometimes the one giving testimony is also the one accused. There is also a truth uniquely charged to the judge whose responsibility is preserving the forum in which judgment might be rendered truthfully. And one might note that when the forum is challenged, the judge herself might become the one accused — or, in reference to her own credibility or interpretation of the law, she might herself be put in the position of the one giving testimony. A similar complexity would hold for a prosecuting advocate and, in its own way, for the one judging (a jury or a substitute for a jury). Yet while a theo-homiletically responsive speaker may provisionally move her rhetorical positioning among judge, advocate, defendant, jury, prosecutor, or even alleged victim, she will only do so at the service of her position as *witness*. She must eventually shed any other authority she may momentarily take on. Control over the cases being made, over the structure and preservation of the forum, and even over the ability of charging, pleading, or judging is finally shifted back to others. The authority of theo-homilia, as such, is the authority of *response*. And this is a peculiar authority indeed.

This odd authority is, first, an *obligation*. Save for rare circumstances, one is under some degree of compulsion to respond. At the outset, the questions come *to* the witness — well before a witness might ever be free to offer questions in return. One has little freedom to orchestrate the forum of discourse, even as one has an obligation to affect it. Freedom to refuse self-incrimination may serve as one check on all of this: a witness may use silence to give testimony to broken rhetoric, double-bound language, or unjust confusion of witness and defense. It is one way, albeit an imperfect one, for a witness to name a potential injustice against testimony itself. Aside from that, however, the witness has rather circumspect rhetorical license, even while maintaining significant rhetorical potency. She may make proximate decisions in response to a line of questioning, but she has little *strategic* freedom. Even when a witness believes he is being used for purposes at odds with just judgment, he remains under obligation to respond. This obligation remains, even when the witness is relatively unaware of what judgment is open to question or how a line of argument is unfolding.

Second, the authority to respond is dependent upon a sense of an "I" that can make a bold claim to knowledge while still shedding power over both how that knowledge will be received and how it will, finally, be assessed. The "I" of the witness is unlike any other "I" spoken. Consider the move in the Robert Bolt's *A Man for All Seasons*, in which, in the wake of Henry VIII's separation from Rome, Thomas More bases his defense of Catholic authority on a rhetorical move. When challenged by his friend the Duke of Norfolk over his assertion of Apostolic Succession, Bolt's More makes an ontological claim that is immediately repositioned as testimony through two intonations of the same phrase. The difference is instructive for the kind of "I" that is germane to theo-homilia. When Norfolk retorts that Thomas is resting his view on merely a theory, More replies: "Why, it's a theory, yes; you can't see it; can't touch it; it's a theory. But what matters is not whether it's true or not but that I believe it to be true, or rather, not that I *believe* it, but that *I* believe it."[20]

The rhetorical distance between More and his interlocutor widens as he lodges his assertion in a *responsive* subjectivity. He does so by backing away from an ontological instinct to wedge his relationship with his friend, as well as his claim on his friend's own loyalty, solely on the basis of the verity of his belief. By positioning himself in relation to his actions in a way that implicates only himself, without implying privileged access to a universal logic, he frees an *other* to remain in responsive relationship (even in disagreement). And he does so without sacrificing his own freedom to make a strong claim — perhaps even stronger than the one that rested solely on the object of his belief. This is rhetorical distance, requiring a context of interlocution and testifying proclamation. It is a "here I stand," lodged within the widening intrigues of conviction. Such a responsive subjectivity is not passive, however; for in order to avoid rhetorical violence, it requires a listening sensibility rooted in the discipline of self-application. My "I" must be open to other "I"s, and thus as open to being persuaded by just arguments as it is passionate about claiming its own right to argue.

The irony here is that to a common hearing, the second "I" — what I am calling the "I" of responsive subjectivity — speaks conviction in a way that may sound stronger and more arresting, even while being the most freeing of the other. Once again, I hinge this observation on its status as testimony. On the witness stand, one may be able to claim reason and make the strongest of assertions without doing violence — both because one eschews control over the one to whom one is speaking, and because one has made a prior pubic declaration of one's intention to avoid lying. But it should be noted again that what one eschews is *control* — not responsibility, obligation, or relation.

Finally, the authority to respond is oriented toward the past before it is about either the present or future. The witness surely changes the present

---

[20]Robert Bolt, *A Man for All Seasons: A Play in Two Acts* (New York: Random House, 1962), 91.

by her testimony, just as she shapes the future by affecting judgment. But this is the result of another's assessment of what she tells about the past. She speaks of what she believes, sees, experiences, knows, reasons, presumes about what precedes her — and even then, only about what her own powers of perception give her ability to remember or intuit.[21]

In sum, the authority of testimony is the authority of *authoring* rather than of *controlling*. It is a response to questions that one may not have formed, and to results over which one may not have much input. We shed our selves before those to whom we bear witness, retaining a sense of obligation to our interlocutors without presuming either agreement or empathy. And we have the potential, or potency, to change it all — even as we refuse, or are refused, power. It may, therefore, be incumbent upon the church to work toward creating rhetorical cultures of care in receiving and evaluating such testimony — both out of respect for the authority of other "I"s, and out of evangelical concern to prepare space for the peculiar authoring called Christian proclamation. We not only proclaim; we work to nurture a culture in which our witnessing proclamation can be received without violence, fear, or, when possible, misunderstanding.

Rhetorical Theological Education

What difference does any of this make for theological education? In order to imagine an answer to this question, I want to ask how the communal activity of theological education can remain textured by a Spirit-filled kind of *gasping* while maintaining a rigor-filled *grasping* for comprehension and deliberative judgment. This is to ask how the systolic rigor of teaching and learning can be held fast to the diastolic beat of ineffable faith, without collapsing one into the other. For me, this suggests a handful of small disciplines within the broader structure of theological education. Broader possibilities might present themselves as these smaller practices begin to affect our work.

---

[21]The category of "expert witness," whose testimony is to his or her opinion regarding something at stake in a trial may be an exception to my claim that witnesses normally testify about the past. Granted that problem, I am not trying to do comprehensive forensic rhetorical theory. I am following Ricoeur in using the courtroom as a collection of metaphors for a theological purpose. What one might do theologically with the practice of "expert testimony" will be left to the reader.

Consider first the *ēthos* of rhetorical theological education. It is revealed in the forms of attention given to both implied and inferred relationships among speakers and hearers in every word spoken or action taken — including tradition and novelty, culture and critique, teaching and learning, conviction and uncertainty, knowledge and praise. This may begin by acknowledging complexity. In writing this I am remembering Simone Weil's description of intellectual reductionism in "The Power of Words."

> In every sphere, we seem to have lost the very elements of intelligence: the ideas of limit, measure, degree, proportion, relation, comparison, contingency, interdependence, interrelation of means and ends. . . . Our lives are lived, in actual fact, among changing, varying realities, subject to the casual play of external necessities, and modifying themselves according to specific conditions within specific limits; and yet we act and strive and sacrifice ourselves and others by reference to fixed and isolated abstractions which cannot possibly be related either to one another or to any concrete facts. In this so-called age of technicians, the only battles we know how to fight are battles against windmills.[22]

Though the "myths and monsters" of contemporary theology may be different than the political ones Weil saw in the 1930s, with terms like "the Christian Right," or "Liberalism," or "patriarchy," or "justice," or "Biblical," or even "theology" itself being among our God- or Devil-terms, our flirtation with abstractions incongruous with lived experience may yet be similar to what she saw. Do we not tend to rush too quickly to a kind of essentialism in our theological debates, by which we fill our various God- and Devil-terms with whatever implied content might short circuit arguments from measure or conditions? And if so, what comes of the ethos of our discourse but a battle of rectitudes? The call to discursive nonviolence, which I want to emphasize, would raise the question again of how disciplines of qualification and interpersonal respect might shape the ethos of judgment in theological education.

I imagine communities of discourse in which relations among truth, power, and authority are established neither by suppressing nor by naïvely privileging undecidability. As I have argued here, one approach to this may involve cultivating the language of testimony. For theological discourse

---

[22]"The Power of Words," in Sian Miles, ed., *Simone Weil: An Anthology* (New York: Weidenfeild and Nicolson, 1986), 222, 223.

may tend to trust ontological language too much, in which the theological voice rushes too quickly to describe reality *as such*. Every "it is" statement necessarily carries with it a set of far more contingent beliefs than what a speaker's description of reality would imply. Cultivating such communities may require finding new ways of authorizing and welcoming statements that invoke Thomas More's distinction: "I *believe* . . . no, *I* believe." Possible truth meets possible truth in the metaphorical courtroom of witnesses, speaking and listening with varying levels of rhetorical skill. This ethos will be marked by a common fear of either mandated relativism or indecorous abstraction. It will also fear distortions of empathy, forced civility, presumptuous generalizations, and other kinds of rhetorical violence.

Such theological education may be characterized by a kind of two-tracked discourse. Persons engaged in it may simultaneously talk of God and talk of *how* they are talking of God. Always doubling back, we will trust that as the space between theological object and theological subject is opened the truth of the object will manifest itself — revealed, concealed, and then appropriated in both individual and communal judgment. Such work is textured by regular pauses for revisiting both *form* in the use of tropes and figures and *premise* in our choice of topics.

I imagine regular co-curricular opportunities to reflect on the educational process. These would constitute such pauses on a sort of macro level, when all members of a theological conversation stop to interpret the very activity in which they are engaged. We may come to recognize such pauses to be more than merely meta-reflections; we may come to embrace them as both an essential component of theological education itself, and a necessary gesture in the interpretation of radical otherness that *is* theology. They may become a form of educational *testifying*, shedding naïve confidence in the educational process for a moment when those engaged in it might reaffirm that their work is *derived* — bound to time, limited in space, and ever humbled by ineffability. It is a way of remembering our rhetorical situation.

Self-reflection of this kind requires enormous discipline. It also requires a common spirit that will remain open to shifting patterns of authority in truth-telling. It will also be skilled in receiving theo-homiletic testimony without collapsing into inappropriate loss of privacy in the telling of secrets, or loss of judgment through endless processing of contradictory convictions, or loss of generative silences through coerced interaction.

Perhaps such *praxis* is best held liturgically — in the rhythm of learning, worship, and contemplation that *is* the seminary. Here the theory upon which the curriculum is built is humbled, in the best sense of humbling, before that which might render the work both faithful and useful: the work of prayer, both public and private, that keeps teaching from falling into gossip;[23] the work of worship, that binds inquiry to tradition and personalities to communion; the work of gathering, to both welcome and send, feast in celebration and fast in loss, to remember our need for God, both to calm down and to open up. The end of *liberation* is a proliferation of worship and the passing of peace. The end of *formulation* is confession of faith in gratitude for words uninvented. The end of *identification* is recognition of the grace that winds its way through the obvious, holding both the *logos* and the *ēthos* of theological education fast to the anachronistic *givens* that gives them rise: tradition, scripture, faithfulness of the church past, hope for the church future, power within the church present, and God's passion for the world.

This may mean deferring the distinction between theological reflection and the practice of ministry upon which much of modern theological education has been built. By that, I do not mean collapsing one end into the other, which is usually taken to mean trying to get more "practical." Quite the contrary, in fact. I mean to ask that we cultivate the habit of refusing to make the distinction at all because of its way of reinforcing anti-rhetorical presuppositions.[24]

I believe that in whatever academic discipline or liturgical practice it is cultivated, rhetorical theological education involves the development of a faculty of discernment — responsive to the infinite possibility of God in Christ, in service to the community of discourse called the church, for the sake of the world.

---

[23]I am grateful to Philip Turner for the insight that "theologizing without prayer" may be the equivalent of gossip.

[24]See Richard R. Osmer's essay on "practical theology," chapter 8 of the present volume. Franz Rosenzweig's 1919 call for a non-Idealistic, "new" way of thinking, called both "speech-thinking" and "radical empiricism" also comes close to what I am trying to describe here. In addition to "The New Thinking," see *The Star of Redemption*, trans. William W. Hallo (Notre Dame, Ind.: University of Notre Dame Press, 1985). On theme, also consider what Mikhail Bakhtin described as dialogized authorship. See his *The Dialogic Imagination: Four Essays*, ed. Michael Holquist, trans. Caryl Emerson and Michael Holquist (Austin: University of Texas Press, 1981).

Chapter 7

Theology as Testimony: Rhetoric, Public Theology, and Education for Ministry

Don H. Compier

Half a century ago theologian Reinhold Niebuhr appeared on the cover of *Time* magazine, hailed as a leading intellectual of the Cold War.[1] In the same era his one-time colleague Paul Tillich appealed to a generation of academicians of various disciplines, who felt that his reinterpretation of Christian symbols allowed them to embrace the faith without loss of intellectual integrity.[2] In different ways, then, two prominent theologians were very public figures.

It is somewhat difficult to imagine the recurrence of this scenario today; we witness a growing public marginalization of the theological disciplines. If representatives of the popular media take any cognizance of religious thought, they generally feature spokespersons from the extremes of the spectrum: either the "Religious Right" (Gary Brauer, Jerry Fallwell, Pat Robertson) or radical revisionists (John Shelby Spong, Matthew Fox, Robert

---

[1]*Time*, March 8, 1948. For more details, see Richard Fox, *Reinhold Niebuhr: A Biography* (San Francisco: Harper and Row, 1985), 233.

[2]At a symposium at the Graduate Theological Union a few years ago I enjoyed a conversation with the psychologist Rollo May, in which he described what Tillich's thought had meant to him and his contemporaries.

Funk). Only rarely will a talk show invite a professor from a "mainline" seminary.[3] Even when religious academicians and groups address public issues, their message often falls on deaf ears. In 1994, for instance, several theologians, as well as practically every denomination and ecumenical organization in California, went on record in opposition to Proposition 187, a ballot initiative depriving "illegal aliens" of schooling, health care, and all other public services. Yet poll data indicates that the measure received support from a large majority of the state's Protestant voters, as well as almost half of California's Catholic electorate.[4] Such experiences suggest that the standard secularization thesis will not suffice as an account for theology's loss of public influence. On the one hand, even those who identify themselves as Christians apparently don't pay much attention to the public pronouncements of their academic and ecclesial leaders. And on the other hand, some studies suggest that U.S. citizens do not object on principle to the church's involvement in political debates, and some lament that religious institutions miss opportunities to exercise civic leadership.[5]

---

[3] And even then usually due to other factors. For instance, Philip Wogaman of Wesley Seminary frequently appeared, but he was President Clinton's minister. Recent figures on church membership and attendance make one wonder how long we can continue to call the traditional Protestant denominations the "mainline." Pentecostals, fundamentalists, and various non-denominational "super churches" have a better numerical claim. The decline in membership of the former "mainline" no doubt contributes to the increasing marginality of the intellectuals who represent those traditions. For helpful assessment of the causes and consequences of theology's loss of public influence, see Van A. Harvey, "On the Intellectual Marginality of American Theology," in Michael J. Lacey, ed., *Religion and Twentieth-Century American Intellectual Life* (New York: Cambridge University Press, 1989), 172–92; and Owen C. Thomas, "Parish Ministry: A Theologian's Perspective," *Sewanee Theological Review* 40 (1997): 444–56.

[4] "Immigration Debate Divides Christians," *Christianity Today*, February 6, 1995, 42–43. 69% of Protestants and 49% of Roman Catholics voted in favor of Proposition 187. One example of theological reflection on the issue is Alex García-Rivera's "Jesus, Mary and Joseph Were Illegal Immigrants," *U.S. Catholic*, April 1995, 32–34.

[5] Gustav Niebuhr, "Public Supports Political Voice for Churches," *Religious Studies News* 11 (September 1996), 1, 3, 11. Cf. Elizabeth Lynn and Barbara G. Wheeler, *Missing Connections: Public Perceptions of Theological Education and Religious Leadership*, Auburn Studies, No. 6 (September 1999).

Obviously the matter requires further analysis. Little wonder, then, that a considerable body of recent literature addresses the question of "public theology." The debate is far from settled: not everyone agrees that practitioners of systematic reflection on Christian doctrine should worry about its public reception, and the motives of those arguing for the recovery of "publicness" (D. Tracy) do not always coincide. Some seek greater respectability for theology within the universities; others hope that as public intellectuals, theologians will address broader cultural concerns or participate in debates about public policy.

This essay seeks to make a small contribution to this growing sub-field of theological discourse. My perspective differs from that of other proponents of public theology in several ways. First, though they are usually persons with profound commitments to the Christian faith, many of the leading thinkers in this field work in university settings. At the time of writing this chapter, I was employed by a free-standing denominational seminary in an ecumenical consortium. I am certainly not uninterested in debates with colleagues from other academic disciplines; my involvement in the education of doctoral students requires regular engagement in interdisciplinary conversations. However, most of my hours each working day are devoted to the formation and training of seminarians. In this essay, then, I explore what kind of public theology should be pursued within theological education. How does our intellectual labor in this mode support the mission of the churches that we serve? And in particular, how will our pedagogical practice be shaped by a commitment to public witness?

Second, in the context of this volume, I wish to demonstrate the relevance and utility of classical rhetoric in the articulation of public theologies. While leading contributors to this debate (notably David Tracy) are familiar with the oratorical tradition, I contend that this emerging field has yet to make full use of all that rhetoric can offer. In fact, I would go so far as to say that unless publicly-minded theologians pay more attention to the persuasive arts, it is very unlikely that we will succeed in escaping from our intellectual ghetto.

Critics may argue that I take the necessity of public practices of theology far too much for granted. I concede that the enterprise of public theology requires more intellectual justification and defense than I can offer in this short space. Briefly put, I contend that theology must become public for no other reason than to act on behalf of the world that God loves. David Carroll implicitly challenges Christian theologians when he asks: "What are the responsibilities of thought in relation to politics in general, and more specifically in relation to injustice, especially of the most extreme, unthinkable kind?"[6] The classical rhetorical tradition is certainly familiar with the temptation to enjoy the luxury of quiet retreat in the search for truth. Fighting this tendency in himself, Cicero insisted that "it is the part of the wise to concern themselves with public affairs," in spite of the uncertainty and rancor of such an undertaking.[7]

Cicero's claim has relevance for us today. In a time characterized, for instance, by growing evidence of a global environmental crisis, a theology influenced by both Biblical themes and the spirit of classical rhetoric would effectively seek to join the fray in defense of life. While in this process Christian orators will certainly have much to say to the academy and to church, in such theological praxis "public" will refer to political engagement in the broadest classical sense of the term.

Whether or not my readers accept these claims, I hope that, for now, it will suffice to make two points. First, several Christian traditions have long assumed that the church should have a voice in debates about the common good.[8] In support of these churches to which we are accountable, then, theological educators should find ways to assist denominations, judicatories, and local congregations to bear a more effective public witness. Second, this volume as a whole makes a case for a rhetorical approach to theology and to theological education. I simply wish to underscore a point

---

[6]"Foreword: The Memory of Devastation and the Responsibilities of Thought: 'And let's not talk about that,'" in Jean-François Lyotard, *Heidegger and the Jews*, trans. Andreas Michel and Mark Roberts (Minneapolis: University of Minnesota Press, 1990), xvii.

[7]*De Oratore*, in *Cicero on Oratory and Orators*, ed. J. S. Watson (Carbondale and Edwardsville: Southern Illinois University Press, 1970).

[8]This is certainly true of the Anglican Communion, which I serve. The Church of England (as well as its successor bodies in many colonial situations) was, after all, at one time the state church. In the twentieth century Desmond Tutu has been a leading example of Anglican political witness. Those interested in public theology should also consider the life and work of Archbishop William Temple (d. 1944). See F.A. Iremonger, *William Temple, Archbishop of Canterbury: His Life and Letters* (New York: Oxford University Press, 1948); and Temple's *Christianity and Social Order* (New York: Penguin Books, 1942).

already made previously:[9] the rhetorical tradition is public in its very essence. This civic spirit was underscored in the work of Cicero and other Roman orators, but it was already evident in the earliest Greek rhetors and in Aristotle's influential synthesis of the persuasive arts. Scholars and educators who adopt a rhetorical model of authorship and pedagogy, then, cannot refuse to engage in speaking and writing which transcends the bounds of academic discourse. The adoption of rhetorical methodology entails a public practice of the theological disciplines. In what follows I offer one vision of what a rhetorical conception of the task of public theology might look like.

Some Guiding Principles: Decorum and Deliberation

As other chapters of this book point out, the oratorical traditions offer a great many resources that can be put to a variety of uses in theological praxis. Here, I want to highlight the importance of that cardinal rhetorical value which Cicero called decorum. This principle of adaptation or accommodation demands careful attention to the specific character of particular speakers and audiences. If we take this rhetorical notion seriously, we will understand the impossibility of developing hard and fast rules applicable to any and all situations. Theological education, then, does not consist of a transmission process by which students are crammed full of facts, schemas, methods, and ethical and doctrinal rules, which they are expected to memorize and repeat on tests. To be sure, we should offer information and encourage research that can help ministers to understand themselves and those whom they seek to address. Given the enormous variety of contexts in an ever more complex and pluralistic world, however, our goal should be to produce theological *artists*, skilled in a diverse repertory of specific performances of communication. Our seminaries and our books can contribute to a process of formation by which persons (including teachers!) acquire not only knowledge but wisdom. We often speak about vocational discernment; attention to the critical role of decorum will lead to the realization that ministry is a constant spiritual process of discerning what is appropriate (both godly and effective) in multiple, ever-shifting contexts and occasions.

---

[9] See the discussion, particularly of Roman rhetoric, in chapter 1 of the present volume.

In envisioning public theology as a series of pedagogical and compositional activities, then, we realize that the "publicness" of our discourse cannot be established once and for all. Its practitioners must time and again exercise influence in the polis through specific persuasive performances. Their success depends upon their ability to have a clear sense of the audience being addressed, and of their own persuasive resources. We envision who the listeners will be; we determine (as well as we can) their character, inclinations, and tastes; and we discern how the received traditions can address the concerns of this audience. The skilled orator will discover, construct, organize, and refine arguments tailored to this concrete group on this unique occasion.

Careful attention to the principle of decorum will alter assumptions often held by systematic theologians. For example, we are inclined to believe that we address a universal audience. David Tracy, a leading proponent of public theology, insists that "a public discourse discloses meanings and truths which in principle can transform all human beings."[10] From the perspective of classical rhetorical theory, however, it is unclear how any individual speaker could address an audience comprised of every other human being. How could the orator possibly accommodate all the divergent interests and passions in a single rhetorical performance, or even a series of them?[11]

---

[10] *The Analogical Imagination: Christian Theology and the Culture of Pluralism* (New York: Crossroad, 1981).

[11] It is true that Ch. Perelman and L. Olbrechts-Tyteca discuss the universal audience. But they refer to "unanimity imagined by the speaker" corresponding to a claim that (s)he considers a matter of "objective fact" or a "true and even necessary assertion." In other words, they are speaking of an argumentative strategy, not a rhetorical situation in which the orator seeks to address all other human beings. They also note that "the universal consensus invoked is often merely the unwarranted generalization of an individual intuition." When others refuse to be persuaded, the universal audience can quickly become an "elite audience" of those with sufficient mental endowments to perceive the "obvious" truth. *The New Rhetoric: A Treatise on Argumentation*, trans. John Wilkinson and Purcell Weaver (Notre Dame, Ind.: University of Notre Dame Press, 1969), 31–33. See the discussion of the universal audience in David S. Cunningham, *Faithful Persuasion: In Aid of a Rhetoric of Christian Theology* (Notre Dame, Ind.: University of Notre Dame Press, 1991), 60–64 and 68–75, with attendant bibliography.

Moreover, our modern hermeneutic of suspicion, so ably discussed by Tracy himself, inclines many persons to skepticism in the face of claims to universal discourse. And as literary critic Charles Altieri points out,

> Ciceronian rhetoricians must begin with a recognition that claims about tradition are aspects of the *topoi* they manipulate in order to develop the kinds of consensus that serve their interests or projects. The more general the argument about tradition, the more likely it is to be in the service of some particular program. It is prudent, therefore, to distrust all general claims about tradition.[12]

Altieri contends that rhetoric and theology are incompatible, for the former "has to face the fact that the author is interested and partial (even if seeking consensus).... Understanding involves how we stage utterances within a theater composed of human wills vacillating between cooperation and conflict." The latter, on the other hand, "produces its absolute object because of the unreasonably ideal and abstract demands it makes on our concepts of understanding."[13] In other words, both rhetoric and theology are pursuits driven by specific human interests, but the former admits this fact up front, while the latter — at least during the modern era — has often sought to hide it. Altieri follows Kenneth Burke in suspecting that the generality of theological formulations functions as a rhetoric of legitimation, so that arguments couched in the broadest terms are still persuasive strategies pursuing specific ends.[14] On the other hand, a number of recent theologies — notably postmodern proposals and the various discourses of liberation — do admit their interested and situated character. A rhetorical approach to public theology, respectful of the principle of decorum, will support this trend.

My attempts to be attentive to contemporary audiences suggest that in one respect the classical rhetorical traditions may not serve us well. The

---

[12] Charles Altieri, "Toward a Hermeneutics Responsive to Rhetorical Theory," in Walter Jost and Michael Hyde, eds., *Rhetoric and Hermeneutics in Our Time: A Reader* (New Haven, Conn.: Yale University Press, 1997), 96.

[13] Altieri, "Toward a Hermeneutics," 96.

[14] See Burke's *The Rhetoric of Religion: Studies in Logology* (Berkeley: University of California Press, 1970).

Roman orators, who so decisively shaped legal practice in the West, demonstrated a marked preference for the judicial genre. As a result Western rhetoric tends to display a strongly combative, agonistic tenor.[15] One can certainly think of contemporary situations in which this fighting spirit represents an appropriate stance. And as my lawyer friends insist, their training does incline them to appreciate the argumentative merits of opposing viewpoints. Nevertheless, judicial rhetoric always involves contests — demanding that one position be deemed right and other perspectives wrong — and results in winners and losers. Its practice polarizes and divides persons from one another. In today's highly pluralistic social context, in which those acting for the good of the polis must forge coalitions and alliances, I believe that the recovery of rhetoric as a mode of public theological discourse cannot proceed primarily along judicial lines. Epideictic, the rhetoric of praise and blame, will not suffice either. Though its entertainment value sets a light tone, and may encourage an aesthetic appreciation, encomium and diatribe still tend to establish oppositions and contrasts unfavorable to many human actors.

Instead, we must pay increased attention to the most underdeveloped genre in ancient rhetorical texts, namely deliberative rhetoric.[16] This was the form operative in the legislative assemblies, appropriate when actors with different interests had to forge majorities in favor of specific policy initiatives. Since such bodies only rarely had much power in the ancient world, we can understand why this mode of oratory received so little attention. Today, however, we cannot excuse such neglect. One only has to watch any of a number of popular shows featuring political pundits, or spend a few minutes tuned to C-Span, to become painfully aware of our society's lack of skill in deliberative discourse.[17] Perhaps one of the greatest services theology in our context could provide would be to offer

---

[15]Kenneth Burke, *A Rhetoric of Motives* (Berkeley: University of California Press, 1969), 52.

[16]In his sweeping history of ancient rhetoric George Kennedy has material for only a few pages on this topic: *The Art of Persuasion in Greece* (Princeton, N.J.: Princeton University Press, 1963), 203–206; and *The Art of Rhetoric in the Roman World* (Princeton, N.J.: Princeton University Press, 1972), 18–21.

[17]Cf. Deborah Tannen, *The Argument Culture: Moving from Debate to Dialogue* (New York: Random House, 1998).

encouragement and concrete models as our society struggles to reestablish the possibility of civil discourse which can respect difference while finding avenues of cooperation and common endeavor.

I am convinced that an increased emphasis on deliberation offers distinct advantages in our current highly pluralistic cultural situation. Other proponents of public theology have certainly attempted to face our social reality without flinching. David Tracy, for instance, demonstrates much interest in fostering a more deliberative culture; he champions the model of conversation as a way of understanding human inquiry. He examines an extraordinarily broad range of texts and cultural phenomena. Interlocutors of the most diverse viewpoints are invariably treated with respect. Tracy's students report that in seminars and other pedagogical interactions he consistently fosters a genuine collaborative spirit.[18] The irenic tone of his work is refreshing.

Yet Tracy repeatedly expresses his belief that public conversations can only occur when a broad degree of consensus already exists among participants. Partners in dialogue must hold a "shared concept of reason."[19] Much of Tracy's *The Analogical Imagination* revolves around the concept of "the classic," those texts all members of a society should consider authoritative and of lasting value. These are the works that continually disclose truth to any and all engaged readers. And when he turns to our specific cultural situation in North America, Tracy claims that all who would participate in public discourse in this context inevitably pay homage to "two classical traditions": the legacy of the American Enlightenment, or Jeffersonian democracy, and the religious heritage of "the Puritan covenantal tradition."[20] In summary, it seems that, for Tracy, consensus is

---

[18] I am grateful to my own mentor Rebecca Chopp for stories about Tracy, and for continuing the warm collegial approach he represents.

[19] "Theology, Critical Social Theory, and the Public Realm," in Don S. Browning and Francis Schüssler Fiorenza, eds., *Habermas, Modernity, and Public Theology* (New York: Crossroad, 1992), 19.

[20] "Afterword: Theology, Public Discourse, and the American Tradition," in Lacey, ed., *Religion and Twentieth-Century American Intellectual Life,* 201–202.

the indispensable ground or starting point that alone enables dialogue in our pluralistic society. In its absence, no public discourse can emerge.[21]

If one accepts these premises, public theology today would appear to be a nearly impossible task. For Tracy himself has written extensively about the breakdown of a unified view of human reasoning. He is fully aware of the postmodern challenge, with its insistence on incommensurable language games and irreducible "differends" (J-F. Lyotard[22]). The debate about "the Western canon" is raging throughout the academic world.[23] I perceive no consensus about what works should be included, or even about whether an authoritative list should exist at all. And we now live in a society containing many non-Western and non-Christian persons. I am extremely dubious about the prospects of the Jeffersonian and Puritan traditions as a common social glue in this new century.

Since no agreement exists at present on a number of key foundational issues, Tracy's assumptions lead to the conclusion that diverse interlocutors have little to talk about. In this schema it appears that the public theologian's only recourse would be to insist on a prerequisite — namely, that all who wish to enter the conversation must first accept a particular mode of rationality, a prescribed canon, and the authority of Jeffersonian and Puritan cultural traditions. This is precisely the type of discursive move contested by postmodern theorists. Jean-François Lyotard, for instance,

---

[21]Other proponents of public theology share similar biases. William Dean calls for the construction of a new "myth of America" which can offer all residents a sense of common purpose grounded in "a more viable spiritual culture" (note the singular); *The Religious Critic in American Culture* (Albany, N.Y.: State University of New York Press, 1994), 180. And Ronald F. Thiemann expresses his confidence in the unifying values of "liberal democracy" and speaks of how churches can inculcate values which pursue a society expressive of the "American dream;" *Constructing a Public Theology: The Church in a Pluralistic Culture* (Louisville, Ky.: Westminster/John Knox Press, 1991), 24, 43.

[22]See the detailed analysis of the significance of Lyotard's work for a rhetorical approach to theological education in the essay by A. K. M. Adam, chapter 3 of the present volume.

[23]To obtain some sense of this battle's ferocity, consult Harold Bloom's *The Western Canon: The Books and Schools of the Ages* (New York: Harcourt and Brace, 1994).

consistently denounced the tendency to impose a premature consensus, thereby silencing the expression of unique individual voices.[24] While his thought underwent a series of significant modifications, his determination to establish justice by preserving genuine difference never wavered.

I am convinced that in his later work Lyotard was at pains to demonstrate that he did not wish to shut down conversation between heterogeneous interlocutors altogether, as some claim.[25] I suggest, rather, that his project shared affinities with the genre of deliberative rhetoric. Simply put, in such discourses consensus is the *telos* sought by our conversation, but we cannot and should not assume that it exists already at the beginning as ground. For that presupposition will in the long run impede the possibility of genuine cooperation by failing to acknowledge and respect the uniqueness and alterity of each dialogue partner. If we enter discussions assuming that others think like we do, we invariably distort their positions and imply that their own self-understandings are, in certain respects, in error. I would suggest, then, that the task of public discourse involves finding ways to *construct* genuine consensus. The first persuasive strategy must be to refuse to impose or assume agreement where none exists.[26] "Dissensus," then, is no disaster, but the challenge and opportunity grasped by the deliberative enterprise.

But couldn't one argue that my proposal reflects a certain naïveté? Doesn't recent epistemology, as well as theological reflection on revelation, demonstrate that people "can only understand what they, in some sense, already know"?[27] Given this fact, how can we avoid perceiving those who

---

[24]Perhaps most famously at the conclusion of *The Postmodern Condition: A Report on Knowledge*, trans. Geoff Bennington and Brian Massumi (Minneapolis: University of Minnesota Press, 1984), 65–67.

[25]I recommend the helpful overview of the evolution of Lyotard's thought by Stuart Dalton, "Lyotard's Peregrination: Three (And-a-Half) Responses to the Call of Justice," *Philosophy Today* 38 (Fall 1994): 227–42.

[26]In the previously cited passage from *The Postmodern Condition*, Lyotard also insisted on the local and provisional character of consensus. It should not be imposed on those who were not a party to the agreement.

[27]Steven Mailloux, "Articulation and Understanding: The Pragmatic Intimacy Between Rhetoric and Hermeneutics," in Jost and Hyde, eds., *Rhetoric and*

are different according to our own image? As anthropological analysis of the virtually universal phenomenon of ethnocentrism would suggest, we cannot avoid this obstacle entirely, at least not at the outset. Yet in the process of genuine dialogical encounter, spaces for the reception of otherness can open up. Steven Mailloux suggests that

> Boundaries are crossed in interpretation when one culture becomes the conversational topic or interpretive object of another; boundaries are maintained as the interpretive act in its rhetorical exchanges figures and persuades within the context of the interpreting culture; and boundaries are moved as interpretation changes the shape — trivially or dramatically — of the culture in which the interpretation is produced and received. To understand an act within a foreign culture, the differences must be found in the margins of our own...as the marginal comes into focus or even moves toward the center, the boundaries of our horizons can shift and even be expanded by the other within. Another way of putting this: as we interact with other communities, traditions, cultures, we can reweave our webs of belief to take account of the other...A rhetorical hermeneutics claims that this cultural context cannot be completely transcended but it can be slowly and significantly changed.[28]

A deliberative approach of this type offers little in the way of final answers or even a clearly marked path to pursue. It sounds very much like "muddling through"! And yet this realistic approach does sketch a way of achieving consensus while continuing to recognize necessary boundaries between different traditions and worldviews. I am suggesting that we take Tracy's preferred metaphor of conversation with radical seriousness to include open-ended discussions about the rules of engagement. We should also follow Kenneth Burke in envisioning a constantly shifting set of interlocutors and subjects — in short, an absolute absence of finality.[29] If

---

Hermeneutics in Our Time, 382.

[28]Mailloux, "Articulation and Understanding," 389.

[29]A famous passage about the "unending conversation" may be found in Burke's *The Philosophy of Literary Form: Studies in Symbolic Action*, 3rd ed. (Berkeley: University of California Press, 1973), 110–11. For a specifically theological application, see David S. Cunningham, *These Three Are One: The Practice of Trinitarian Theology* (Oxford: Basil Blackwell, 1998), 336–38.

meetings of very diverse minds are to occur in our society, we cannot control the flow of dialogue by recourse to canonical mechanisms — the rules cannot be set in advance! Tracy himself sometimes uses similar language to describe the nature of conversation.[30] I am simply arguing for a more radically consistent commitment to the principles of deliberation.

How might these general principles of decorum and deliberation affect the actual practice of public theology in seminary settings? In the concluding section of this chapter, I would like to provide a rough sketch of a theology and pedagogy informed by rhetorical principles and precedents.

A Vision for the Public Practice of Rhetorical Theology and Pedagogy

In the seminary setting, the "theological mode of production" involves two primary interrelated activities: writing and teaching. In sketching my concrete proposal for a public rhetorical practice, I will address each dimension in turn. Clearly this separation, perhaps necessary for expository purposes, is somewhat artificial. For isn't authorship the extension of teaching to an audience beyond the classroom? Don't research and writing affect our teaching and offer an instructive model for our students?

Writing

In light of the general principles developed above, a public theology will inevitably find articulation via discrete utterances marked by partisanship, particularity, and occasionalism.[31] I contend that no theologian either can or should hold her- or himself responsible for making claims rationally defensible according to some imagined standard of "universal reason." I have noted the impossibility of such labor from the rhetorical perspective. More importantly, I believe that the record of biblical revelation points in a different direction. There we encounter "the scandal of particularity," in that God singles out an initially rather marginal group, the

---

[30]As in *Plurality and Ambiguity: Hermeneutics, Religion, Hope* (San Francisco: Harper and Row, 1987), 18 and 20.

[31]H.R. McAdoo speaks of the "occasional nature" of the tradition of Anglican divinity in which I stand. *The Structure of Caroline Moral Theology* (London: Longmans, Green, 1949), 8.

people of Israel. Furthermore, according to the Christian faith, God's supreme revelation takes place in a specific human individual at a particular historical juncture and in a concrete culture. The contextual character of Christian theology is a response to the way God makes the divine self known in human history.[32]

By embracing particularity and historical concreteness, Christian theology does not necessarily give up on the idea of universality. Israel did become a light and a blessing to all nations, and God's revelation in Jesus of Nazareth has transformed people in many times and places. As Justo González notes, a corresponding theology pursues "a very different sort of universality that is achieved, paradoxically enough, by being very concrete."[33] If we respond faithfully and skillfully to the unique demands of contemporary situations, the results of our labors may become candidates for classical status. No one can know in advance, however, and we must be motivated by the needs of creation, not by a wish to make declarations valid always and everywhere.[34]

I would contend that most, if not all, of the works we actually revere as Christian classics emerged from engagement in very specific historical debates. Irenaeus attempts to reestablish order in the badly divided church of Gaul. Augustine's *City of God* defends Christianity from charges that its practitioners were guilty of the recent fall of Rome. Calvin's *Institutes* seeks to clear French Protestants of the slanderous accusations which led to fierce persecution.[35] Schleiermacher promotes the place of theology in the culture and university curriculum of post-Enlightenment Germany. Barth responds to the collapse of modern German culture and the rise of Nazism. All these contributions and many more become part of the great stream of tradition,

---

[32]For a thorough defense of such claims, see Douglas John Hall, *Thinking the Faith: Theology in a North American Context* (Minneapolis: Fortress Press, 1989).

[33]*Mañana: Christian Theology from a Hispanic Perspective* (Nashville: Abingdon Press, 1990), 52.

[34]Cf. Thiemann's reflections in the chapter entitled "I Have Heard the Cries of My People: Discerning the Call of God in the Cries of God's People," *Constructing Public Theology*, 96–111.

[35]A point I argue at considerable length in *John Calvin's Rhetorical Doctrine of Sin* (New York: Edwin Mellen Press, 2001).

but the latter is best understood as what Robert J. Schreiter has called a "series of local theologies."³⁶

Rhetorical theologians, then, simply cannot know in advance which audience(s) they must address. As Luther might say, we will have to pray for the discernment to detect that particular place where the battle rages. Theological production will have to occur on the fly, often in great haste. We must try to know and respond to our audiences as effectively as possible, but we cannot avoid considerable guesswork and arguments with uncomfortably ragged edges. Theologians such as Barth have often acknowledged the provisional nature of their work, but a rhetorical conception of method will increase the draft quality of all theological writing.

Publishers probably won't be pleased with such developments, and neither will tenure committees who look for traditional modes of "productivity." The primary vehicles for the expression of rhetorical public theology will only infrequently be books; instead, it will tend to appear in newsletters, websites, and other more ephemeral media. Such a development would not necessarily sound the death knell of the lengthy systematic tome. However, the purpose of this traditional genre would undergo modification. Returning to one classical model, these texts could serve as storehouses of theological commonplaces, offering a compendium of distinctively Christian arguments applicable in a variety of concrete circumstances.³⁷

Nor does a rhetorical public theology have the luxury of ignoring critical theoretical debates. Cicero engaged in considerable philosophical inquiry, for he recognized that the varying pursuits of wisdom offered rhetorically useful ways of analyzing human predicaments in depth.³⁸ As I have already insisted, theologians should devote considerable time and effort to reflection on the nature of deliberation. Though I have offered some critique of their work, theologians such as Tracy are on the right track

---

³⁶*Constructing Local Theologies* (Maryknoll, NY: Orbis Books, 1985), especially 93–94.

³⁷Philip Melanchthon's *Loci Communes Theologici* is a prominent example of such a collection. See Wilhelm Pauck, ed., *Melanchthon and Bucer*, Library of Christian Classics (Philadelphia: Westminster Press, 1969), 3–152.

³⁸Hall also calls for renewed attention to philosophy. *Thinking the Faith*, 315.

when they ponder the nature of public Christian witness in an increasingly pluralistic culture. Theologians traditionally insist on a balance between identity and relevance, or what Hall refers to as the tasks of profession and confession.[39] While maintaining the distinctive core of Christian proclamation, for the common good we must find reasons and ways to respectfully cooperate with persons who do not share our convictions or moral vision.

Today's public theologians must find ways to maintain theoretical sophistication while regaining a capacity to find a broad readership. Here the specific techniques and strategies taught by rhetoricians can perform a tremendous service to our discipline. All too often, today's theological tomes contain very dense and difficult prose, with multiple allusions to complex scholarly debates, constant use of specialized technical terms, and copious footnotes. Our books and essays place strenuous demands even on highly educated readers. No wonder we bore people — even those who possess much initial curiosity about theological subjects. Our writing style unnecessarily eludes the comprehension of many persons in the pews and in the streets. Our theology will only become truly public when, under the tutelage of the ancient art of persuasion, we are willing to relearn the craft of writing.[40]

Teaching

One can scarcely overestimate the importance of pedagogy in the implementation of the vision that I am presenting. A rhetorical conception of public theology requires that we reform the practice of theological education in North America. First, while declining enrollments understandably make seminary personnel nervous about demanding prerequisites, we

---

[39]In the last two volumes of *Christian Theology in a North American Context*, entitled *Professing the Faith* and *Confessing the Faith* (Minneapolis: Fortress Press, 1993 and 1996).

[40]The recent research of theologian William C. Placher should provide useful material for this task. See his preliminary reports, "Taking Risks to Reach a Popular Audience," *Religious Studies News* (November 1998), 20, and "Helping Theology Matter: A Challenge for the Mainline," *The Christian Century* 115, no. 29 (28 October 1998): 994–98.

should find ways to encourage the old ideal of a thorough liberal-arts education as an indispensable precondition for theological study. At a time when rhetoric experiences a revival in many university disciplines, we should expect our entering students to acquire familiarity with the traditions of classical and humanist pedagogy. For a time, at least, we will probably have to supplement their undergraduate education by introducing seminarians to classical rhetoric — and not only in homiletics!

Second, we must break with the expectation that ministry should primarily or even exclusively attend to the private needs of individuals. We must develop and encourage theologies that stress the church's public responsibilities in the life of the world. Undoubtedly this attitudinal sea-change will only occur if theological education actively involves the laity as well as present and prospective clergy.[41] It will need to operate across the theological subdisciplines, receiving attention from biblical studies, history, theology, ethics, and practical theology.

Third, I contend that we should move rhetorical hermeneutics to the center of our pedagogical practice. The history of rhetoric included as part of chapter 1 of this volume demonstrated that hermeneutics played a particularly key role in the education of orators: by determining how previous authors addressed their audiences, one learned by example. Much of classroom time, then, was occupied by what we would call case studies. Through much practice a student might acquire a well developed sense of decorum and have the judgment to successfully perform in ever new situations.[42] At my former seminary, for instance, my colleague Rebecca Lyman and I redesigned our history and theology curriculum to show students how Christian thought emerges in and responds to the requirements of specific historical moments. Rather than stressing the supposed universal and transhistorical nature of encounters with the revelatory power of the classics, we hope that our students will perceive how authors from the past practiced decorum, adapting their composition

---

[41]Owen C. Thomas offers helpful insights on this point in "Parish Ministry."

[42]Victoria Kahn, "Humanism and the Resistance to Theory," in Jost and Hyde, eds., *Rhetoric and Hermeneutics in Our Time*, 149–70; and Kathy Eden, *Hermeneutics and the Rhetorical Tradition: Chapters in the Ancient Legacy and its Humanist Reception* (New Haven, Conn.: Yale University Press, 1997).

to the needs of particular audiences.⁴³ As seminarians acquire practice in tracing "contextualizations" from patristic to modern times, we find that they are more prepared to make their own constructive moves in accordance with current demands. Case studies of various types can be utilized in all areas of instruction. The art of decorum requires continual practice and reinforcement.

Fourth, a rhetorical approach can counter the frequently heard complaint about the impracticality of theological education. Following the precedent of classical oratory, we would be less interested in meaning for its own sake (probably a very modern concern!) and more concerned about fostering persuasive action. Like Augustine, we would then teach our students to interpret symbols, the Christian scriptures, and classical texts precisely so that they may employ this knowledge to preach the powerful Gospel, which moves hearers to conversion.⁴⁴ Through explicit attention to decorum, we will foster our students' capacity to develop the practical judgment needed to adapt to ever varying audiences. By showing seminarians how previous orators crafted their arguments to suit concrete historical situations, rhetorical theological education develops the very practical faculty of discernment, preparing theologians for active engagement in the affairs of the world that God loves.

Fifth, we can indeed do more to familiarize students with contemporary cultural and political debates. I endorse Ronald F. Thiemann's suggestion about the integration of public policy analysis in theological education, but we should not neglect other ways of encouraging greater understanding of potential audiences beyond the confines of our churches. For instance, the arts (literature, drama, popular music, etc.) can tell us a great deal about the spiritual state of many contemporary persons. Van Harvey has made the interesting suggestion that we should ponder what Reinhold Niebuhr knew, and then determine how we could help our students to acquire his familiarity with the American context.

---

[43]On this point, see the essay by Bradford E. Hinze, chapter 4 of the present volume — particularly its conclusion.

[44]See the comments on allegorical interpretation by A. K. M. Adam in chapter 3 of the present volume.

We will no doubt hear the complaint often voiced about rhetorical education, namely that we are simply demanding too much.[45] If public rhetorical theology is seen as the work of individuals, that charge would possess considerable merit. But I envision a team approach which enlists the various strengths and gifts of diverse members of the body in a common effort. Not incidentally, this approach requires and fosters a deliberative approach. If the church can learn to embrace difference and yet retain a sense of communal purpose, perhaps it can indeed become a model and instrument for the recovery of a truly civil culture. At the very least, pedagogy appropriate to a rhetorical public theology might help return the theological task to the all the baptized members of Christ's body. And that would be no mean achievement.

---

[45]Kahn (in "Humanism and the Resistance to Theory") argues that the decline of rhetorical pedagogy in the seventeenth century was in large part due to the arguments of new educators who insisted that the high requirements of humanism constituted a kind of elitism that deprived most people of a readily accessible training. We hear similar complaints about theological education today.

PART THREE

RE-VISIONING THE THEOLOGICAL ENCYCLOPEDIA

Chapter 8

Rhetoric and Practical Theology: Toward a New Theological Paradigm

Richard R. Osmer

> How, then, does Protestantism raise the question of God and how does it seek and find its answers to its problems? How does the problem of God present itself to us who work in this living tradition? It comes to us as an eminently *practical* problem, a problem of human existence and destiny, of the meaning of human life in general and of the life of self and its community in particular.
>
> — H. Richard Niebuhr[1]

Niebuhr echoes here an affirmation central to Protestant Christianity from the beginning: it declares that the purpose of theology is practical. It raises the question of God as a practical problem, one of human existence and meaning. Throughout the modern period, however, it has been far easier to make this claim than to honor it in practice. As modern science gradually became the standard for rational inquiry in the university, theology was faced with a difficult question: How could it justify its place in the university as a scientific enterprise, on the one hand, and maintain its practical orientation, on the other? It responded in terms of the encyclopedic paradigm of theology, a pattern in which the scientific and practical tasks of theology were pursued through a division of labor. Three

---

[1]H. Richard Niebuhr, *Radical Monotheism and Western Culture* (New York: Harper & Row, 1943), 115–16.

of the branches of theology — biblical studies, church history, and dogmatic/systematic theology — were charged with the scientific work of theology.[2] A relatively new branch of theology called practical theology was given the task of integrating and applying the research of the other theological disciplines to congregational life.

The recent rhetorical turn — the focus of the present volume — throws new light on this way of holding together the scientific and practical tasks of theology. At the heart of this turn is a broadened understanding of rhetoric as a comprehensive theory of persuasive discourse, giving rise to a new model of rationality. This essay will explore the possibilities this model holds for a new, post-encyclopedic approach to theology, giving special attention to the role of practical theology in a paradigm that no longer confines concern for practice to a single field of theology. It will proceed in three steps, examining: (1) the emergence of practical theology as a discipline, with special emphasis on Schleiermacher's description of this field in his theological encyclopedia; (2) the contribution of the rhetorical turn to new models of theological rationality, including a brief exploration of its implications for theological education; and (3) the implications of a rhetorical model of theological rationality for practical theology.

Practical Theology in the Theological Encyclopedia

The term "practical theology" first appeared in the writings of Gisbert Voetius in his *Selectae Disputationes Theologicae*, published in five volumes between 1648 and 1669.[3] Use of this term remained relatively rare, however, until the latter part of the eighteenth century, when it became a standard

---

[2]Throughout this essay, I will use the term "scientific" to refer to the scholarly research of academic theology, keeping the reader mindful of the paradigmatic status of science in the university across the modern period. For an extended discussion of the emergence of specialized research programs in academic theology during this period, see Edward Farley, *Theologia: The Fragmentation and Unity of Theological Education* (Philadelphia: Fortress Press, 1983).

[3]Voetius' *Selectae Disputationes Theologicae* is translated in part in *Reformed Dogmatics: Seventeenth Century Reformed Theology through the Writings of Wollebius, Voetius, and Turretin*, ed. and trans. John Beardslee (Grand Rapids, Mich.: Baker Book House, 1965), 265–334. For a discussion of the early history of practical theology, see my *A Teachable Spirit: Recovering the Teaching Office in the Church* (Westminster/John Knox, 1990), ch. 8.

part of the encyclopedic paradigm of theology emerging in the context of the modern research university. Its widespread use in this historical and institutional context was no accident. Broadly speaking, the modern research university was the product of two social trends: institutional differentiation and the rise of scientific culture. The university, like many other institutional contexts, was emerging as a relatively autonomous sphere of life with its own norms and practices independent of the church. These were deeply influenced by the rise of scientific culture, which, increasingly, was granted authoritative status across all modern societies by virtue of the impact of scientific breakthroughs in medicine, farming, industry, and other areas of life.

Theology suddenly found itself in the position of having to defend both its place in the university and the role of religion in a rapidly secularizing world. It mounted its defense by adopting the increasingly important genre of *encyclopedia* to describe its work. The history and transformation of this genre in the modern university have been extensively described by others, and there is no need to trace this story in detail here.[4] Suffice it to say that adoption of this genre allowed various theologians to forge a rhetoric in which the scholarship of theology could be defended as scientific, on the one hand, and as practical, on the other, as making an essential contribution to the positive functioning of religion in the newly emerging modern context. The scope and purpose of practical theology was given shape within the larger contours of this rhetoric.

The most brilliant expositor of theological encyclopedia in the early modern university was Friedrich Schleiermacher. As a professor and leading member of the faculties of Halle and Berlin, he knew well the challenges modernity posed to Christianity. In his *Brief Outline on the Study of Theology*, he drew on themes developed more extensively in other writings and lectures to describe both the scientific and practical orientation of theology

---

[4]Two of the most important accounts of the incorporation of the encyclopedia into theological studies are offered by Farley, *Theologia*, cited above, and Charles Wood, *Vision and Discernment* (Atlanta: Scholars Press, 1985). Discussion of the encyclopedic paradigm more broadly is found in Alasdair MacIntyre, *Three Rival Versions of Moral Enquiry: Encyclopaedia, Geneaology, and Tradition* (Notre Dame, Ind.: University of Notre Dame, 1990).

within the encyclopedic genre.⁵ This theme is taken up in the very first page of the *Brief Outline* in Schleiermacher's description of theology as a positive science. This is his way of locating theology amid the various forms of scientific inquiry found in the university. He describes a positive science as follows:

> Generally speaking a positive science is an assemblage of scientific elements which belong together not because they form a constituent part of the organization of the sciences, as though by some necessity arising out of the notion of science itself, but only insofar as they are requisite for carrying out a practical task.⁶

This linkage of the scientific and practical appears repeatedly throughout the *Introduction*.⁷ A positive science is an academic discipline that draws on the research of a number of fields to address the practical concerns of a profession important to society. Jurisprudence, medicine, and political science are positive sciences in this sense.⁸ By employing this line of argumentation, Schleiermacher accomplishes two things simultaneously.

First, he provides his most important justification for theology in the university on practical grounds. Theology is important because the education of church leadership is important to society. Schleiermacher's argument at this point is enthymematic. His unstated premise is the continuing importance of religion in modern societies. He argues explicitly for this premise elsewhere, criticizing the Enlightenment's reduction of religion to knowledge or ethics and describing it as something that is *sui*

---

⁵Friedrich Schleiermacher, *Brief Outline on the Study of Theology*, trans. Terrence Tice (Richmond, Va.: John Knox Press, 1966).

⁶Schleiermacher, *Brief Outline*, par. 1.

⁷See, for example, paragraphs 5 and 9.

⁸Schleiermacher describes each of these as positive sciences in his lectures on practical theology. See, Friedrich Schleiermacher, *Christian Caring: Selections from Practical Theology*, eds. J. Duke and H. Stone (Philadelphia: Fortress Press, 1988), 85–86.

generis in human life.⁹ An educated clergy is important, he argues, not merely for the well-being of the church, but for the well-being of society as a whole. No society, including those of the modern age, can thrive without religious institutions that cultivate the religious dimension of human life.

Second, this description of theology as a positive science allows Schleiermacher to describe, in general terms, the very complex relationship he posits between the various branches of theology and science proper. As the definition cited above makes clear, the relationship between various forms of theology and cognate forms of science is not straightforward. Each of the three branches of theology he describes stands in a somewhat different relationship to science proper.

It is worth pursuing this line of thinking a bit further, for it clarifies the unique position of practical theology within Schleiermacher's theological encyclopedia. Schleiermacher constructed his system of the sciences in his *Ethik* by identifying two major sciences, the sciences of nature and reason, and two modes of knowing, speculative and empirical.¹⁰ Speculative knowing focuses on knowledge of essence; empirical knowing focuses on knowledge of existence. The crossing of these two modes of knowing with the two major sciences results in a fourfold system that can be diagramed as follows:

	Speculative (knowledge of essence)	Empirical (knowledge of existence)
Nature	Physics	Natural Science
Reason	Ethics	Historical Science

---

⁹As early as his first major book, *On Religion: Speeches to Its Cultured Despisers*, Schleiermacher writes of religion: "Without being knowledge, it recognizes knowledge and science. In itself, it is an affection, a revelation of the Infinite in the finite, God being seen in it and it in God" (p. 36). In his masterwork, *On Christian Faith*, Schleiermacher would make this same point by describing the religious dimension of human existence as a "feeling of absolute dependence," a primordial awareness, embracing cognition and emotion, that life is a contingent gift.

¹⁰Friedrich Schleiermacher, *Schleiermachers Samtliche Werke*, Part III, Vol. 5: "Entwurf eines Systems der Sittenlehre," ed. Alexander Schwizer (Berlin: Raimer, 1835), pars. 55–60 and 108–109. See Walter Wyman's brief but extremely helpful discussion in *The Concept of Glaubenslehre: Ernst Troeltsch and the Theological Heritage of Schleiermacher* (Chico, Calif.: Scholars Press, 1983), 181–84.

It is Schleiermacher's discussion of the two sciences of reason (ethics and historical science) that are of interest to us, for it is here that he locates theology. He describes the relationship of ethics and the historical sciences through an analogy. History is the "picture book" of ethics, and ethics is the "rule book" of history. Using speculative reason, ethics deduces the stable forms of cultural and moral life representing the "rules" of history: the state, the family, religion, and so forth. These ideal constructs can be actualized in an infinite number of ways. The task of the historical sciences is to set forth the concrete manifestations of these forms as they have appeared empirically, that is, to serve as the "picture book" of history. Located between ethics and history are two disciplines which mediate speculative and empirical inquiry. The second half of the above diagram is therefore expanded to include these two additional features:

Speculative	Mediating Disciplines	Empirical
Ethics	critical disciplines; technical disciplines	Historical Science

The critical disciplines mediate this relationship speculatively, attempting to identify the essence of a historical movement or institution.[11] The technical disciplines mediate this relationship empirically, setting forth the practical conditions determining how a particular form of life is actualized historically.

Schleiermacher describes three branches of theology in the *Brief Outline* in terms of this system. Philosophical theology is a critical discipline, situated between a description of the essence of religion in ethics and an examination of the empirical manifestations of particular religions in the historical sciences.[12] As a branch of Christian theology, its task is to set forth the essence of Christianity as both a distinctive mode of faith and as a religious community.[13] Historical theology is a part of science proper,

---

[11]Quoted in Wyman, *Concept of Glaubenslehre*, 182.

[12]A particularly clear statement of philosophical theology which echoes the language of his system of the sciences described above is found in Schleiermacher, "Entwurf eines Systems," pars. 21 and 35.

[13]Schleiermacher, "Entwurf eines Systems," par. 24.

located squarely in the modern historical disciplines.[14] Here, Schleiermacher locates an array of theological subdisciplines, including biblical studies, church history, dogmatics, and church statistics (an early form of the sociology of religion). Each is to employ the scientific methods of historical research appropriate to its particular area of study.

Practical theology is a technical discipline, charged with formulating the *Technik* of the tasks of church leadership.[15] In his description of the kind of reflection appropriate to this branch of theology, Schleiermacher repeatedly uses the German term, *besomnene*, ("deliberative" in the English translation). This term was commonly used by German ethicists during this period to translate the classical Greek term *phronēsis* and the Latin *prudentia*, both of which designate the practical reasoning by which judgments are made in situations of practice — situations that do not lend themselves to the kinds of conclusions that can be drawn by science proper.[16] Closely related is his frequent use of the term "rules of art" to describe the *Technik* of practical theology, a term also appearing in classical literature to describe the guidelines developed for practical arts like ethics, politics, and rhetoric. Schleiermacher seems to be groping in his use of these terms for a way of describing the kind of reflection that is appropriate to practical theology as a technical discipline. It is not merely a mechanical applied theology, on the one hand, nor is it fully scientific, on the other. Rather, its core task is the formulation of rules of art that can guide the deliberation of clergy in their leadership of various facets of church life.

As Friedrich Schweitzer and others have noted, Schleiermacher's unpublished lectures go beyond his description of practical theology in the *Brief Outline*. In the lectures, he adds two further elements (1) the construction of a comprehensive theory of ecclesial practice within the context of modernity; and (2) the construction of an empirical/practical ecclesiology by which practical theology can assess and reconstruct the present practice of the church.[17] Here, Schleiermacher calls attention to the

---

[14]Schleiermacher, "Entwurf eines Systems," par. 69.

[15]Schleiermacher, "Entwurf eines Systems," pars. 257–76.

[16]See Tice's note to this effect on p. 91 of the *Brief Outline*.

[17]Schweitzer, personal correspondence and public lecture.

kind of *reflection on ends* that, also, was a part of practical philosophy in the classical period. Rhetoric, for example, as described by Cicero and Quintillian, did more than marshal practical precepts for persuasive speech. It also included reflection on the social and moral ends to which persuasion should be directed.[18] So too, Schleiermacher argues, practical theology as a technical discipline should formulate rules of art that are animated by a vision of what the community of faith both is empirically and might become ideally in its own time and place.

Schleiermacher's description of practical theology remains, I believe, the most promising approach yet formulated within the encyclopedic paradigm of theology. His sustained attention to this field in his writings and lectures almost single-handedly established its legitimacy within the modern European university, a legacy that has been maintained on the continent to the present day. The translation of the *Brief Outline* into English and the incorporation of its description of practical theology into the influential encyclopedias of Philip Schaff and Karl Hagenbach allowed this field to become a standard part of American theological education during the middle of the nineteenth century.[19] As brilliant and influential as Schleiermacher's description of practical theology proved to be, certain problems can be discerned from a perspective informed by the contemporary rhetorical turn. Our retrieval of certain aspects of his understanding of this field can only take place within the context of a quite different intellectual framework. The difficulties of his position are rooted

---

[18]For a brief discussion of the relationship between wisdom and eloquence in their theories, see George Kennedy, *Classical Rhetoric and Its Christian and Secular Tradition from Ancient to Modern Times* (Chapel, Hill, N.C.: University of North Carolina Press, 1980), 90–96, 100–102.

[19]Philip Schaff, *Theological Propaedeutic: A General Introduction to the Study of Theology — Exegetical, Historical, Systematic and Practical, Including Encyclopedia, Methodology, and Bibliography: A Manual for Students* (New York: Charles Scribner's Sons, 1893). Karl Hagenbach's encyclopedia came into English by way of George Crooks and John Hurst, *Theological Encyclopedia and Methodology on the Basis of Hagenbach* (New York: Phillips & Hunt, 1884). For an excellent overview of the introduction of the encyclopedic paradigm into American theological education, see Robert Lynn, "Notes toward a History: Theological Encyclopedia and the Evolution of Protestant Seminary Curriculum, 1808–1968," *Theological Education*, vol. 17, no. 2 (Spring 1981), 118–44.

in three basic assumptions of the rhetorical genre in which he worked: the encyclopedia.

First, Schleiermacher assumed that an integrated system of knowledge could be projected in which philosophy played a key, if not *the* grounding role. An image used commonly by the encyclopedic movement to describe the system of knowledge was that of a tree. Each field was viewed as organically related to every other field. Philosophy typically was portrayed as providing the roots (or foundations) of knowledge, setting forth the epistemological principles grounding and unifying science as a whole. Often, a descriptive hierarchy was used to order the various branches of knowledge. Specialized inquiries in particular fields were portrayed as twigs of a larger branch attached to the trunk of knowledge as a whole.

Schleiermacher used the image of the tree in the first (1811) edition of the *Brief Outline*, going so far as to describe practical theology as the "crown" of the tree.[20] He did not, however, place philosophy in a foundational role, placing the speculative and historical sciences in a mutually-influential, dialectical relationship. He does, however, graft theology onto his projected system of the sciences. Indeed, his encyclopedia can be seen as a kind of "encyclopedia within an encyclopedia." On the basis of his description of a fourfold system of science, with two mediating disciplines, he locates the rational operations of each of his three branches of theology. Throughout, his commitment is to defending the place of theology in the university by locating it in a comprehensive system of knowledge.

Second, Schleiermacher's encyclopedia is dominated by the rhetoric of science. Theology is portrayed as a positive science with no distinctive rational orientation of its own. It takes over the findings and methods of fields viewed as scientific in a fundamental sense (as in historical theology) and mediates the fundamental sciences along critical and technical lines to the specific interests of the Christian community (as in philosophical and

---

[20]Schleiermacher uses the image of the tree in the 1811 edition of the *Brief Outline*, but dropped it in his revised 1830 edition, fearing that readers would mistakenly view philosophical and historical theology as subordinated to practical theology. He continued in his lectures, however, to refer to the latter as the "crown of theology." For a discussion of Schleiermacher's use of this image, see Duke and Stone, *Christian Caring*, p. 22 and his continuing use of the crown metaphor, p. 99.

practical theology). The rhetoric of science displaces the rhetoric of theology.

Third, the paradigmatic status of scientific rationality in the encyclopedia, even when located in a broader framework, made it exceedingly difficult for Schleiermacher to give an adequate account of the practical grounds of theoretical research, on the one hand, and the theoretical tasks of the practical disciplines, on the other. Within his threefold description of theology, it is practical theology that stands in the closest relationship to ecclesial practice. It is the site of integration of the findings of the other theological disciplines and their mediation along the lines of a technical discipline to the contemporary life of the church. It alone develops rules of art guiding the deliberations of the reflective practitioner. As the "crown" of theology, practical theology is the discipline in which theological knowledge as a whole comes to fruition, enabling theology to make good on its commitment to practice as a positive science.

Beyond the Theological Encyclopedia

From the perspective of the contemporary postmodern intellectual scene, serious questions can be raised about each of these three assumptions. In this section, we will examine each in turn, pointing to both the critique posed by a rhetorical model of rationality and the alternatives it opens up. We will begin by focusing on the second — dominance of the rhetoric of science — for it is here that the impact of the rhetorical turn is most immediately evident.

Beyond the Hegemony of Science:
From Universal Rules to Situated Context

One of the most powerful critiques offered by the new rhetoric is its criticism of a rule model of rationality.[21] This model portrays reason as securing true knowledge by following a set of universal rules. In its classical, premodern form, these rules were conceptualized along the lines of formal logic. Throughout the modern period, the more comprehensive operations of empirical science have replaced formal logic. Stenmark aptly

[21]Harold Brown, *Rationality* (London: Routledge, 1988), ch. 1 and Mikael Stenmark, *Rationality in Science, Religion, and Everyday Life: A Critical Evaluation of Four Models of Rationality* (Notre Dame, Ind.: University of Notre Dame Press, 1995), chapter 3.

dubs the latter "formal evidentialism" and describes it as a two step process: (1) the gathering of empirical evidence and its articulation in the form of observation statements, and (2) the linking of this evidence to propositions and, subsequently, to theories on the basis of "appropriate" rules.[22] Across the modern period, there has been debate about how these rules are best conceptualized — as the following of inductive logic, probabilistic reasoning, or the logic of falsification.

At the heart of the rhetorical turn is a critique of the rule model of rationality in all its forms. Put simply, it rejects the notion that a set of universal rules, transportable from one context to another, actually informs the ways scientists and scholars in other fields carry out their work.[23] It "naturalizes" rationality, calling for the study of the ways scholars actually carry out inquiry.[24] More importantly, it reconceptualizes rationality as a special form of communicative action in which good reasons are formed on the basis of the rhetorical norms and epistemic values of different rational enterprises. There are three dimensions to this model.

First, rationality is conceptualized as a form of communicative action and as inherently social. Frequently, this communication is conceptualized along the lines of argumentation. It is portrayed as a dialogical exchange in

---

[22]Stenmark, *Rationality in Science, Religion, and Everyday Life*, ch. 3.

[23]Criticism of formal evidentialism has emerged from a number of sources. In the contemporary philosophy of science, Thomas Kuhn in *The Structure of Scientific Revolutions*, published in 1962 and now in its 3rd edition (Chicago: University of Chicago Press, 1996), was only the first of many who pointed out that idealized notions of scientific rationality are far removed from the way scientists actually work. He called for the "naturalization" of scientific reasoning: the study of the history and practice of the ways scientists actually form and regulate their beliefs and choose their theories. As Kuhn pointed out, theory-choice is not undertaken on the basis of well-established rules and the history of science reveals drastic changes in the rules governing criteria of explanation, testing, and inductive inference.

[24]For an extremely helpful discussion of the naturalization of rationality, see John S. Nelson, Allan Megill, and Donald N. McCloskey, eds., *The Rhetoric of the Human Sciences: Language and Argument in Scholarship and Public Affairs* (Madison, Wis.: University of Wisconsin Press, 1987) and Herbert W. Simons, ed., *The Rhetorical Turn: Invention and Persuasion in the Conduct of Inquiry* (Chicago: University of Chicago Press, 1990).

which claims are put forward, challenged, and defended.[25] Some scholars, rightly, have pointed out that an exclusive focus on argumentation and its conflict orientation is too limited.[26] Rather, rationality is best conceptualized on the model of an open conversation in which good reasons are formed through a process of mutual sharing and searching. Challenge and defense may play a role in such communication, but it is a limited one. More fundamental to the construction of good reasons are attitudes of mutual openness, truth-telling, and a willingness to revise one's position in light of new information and insights.

Second, this model broadens rationality to include the rhetorical norms in which rational communication takes place. Cunningham's discussion of Aristotle's model of rhetoric is helpful at this point, recasting its three means of persuasion.[27] Rational exchange involves not only *logos*, the explicit reasoning or argumentation proffered, but also, *pathos*, the way a particular audience is constructed and engaged, and *ēthos*, the interests and values by which a community evaluates and authorizes the position put forward. Toulmin makes a closely related point by drawing attention to the ways rational communication varies in different "argument fields."[28] One

---

[25]The Ur-sources of this discussion are Stephen Toulmin, *The Uses of Argument* (Cambridge: Cambridge University Press, 1958) and Ch. Perelman and L. Olbrechts-Tyteca, *The New Rhetoric: A Treatise on Argumentation* (Notre Dame: University of Notre Dame Press, 1969). Also important are the following: Stephen Toulmin, Richard Rieke, and Allan Janik, *An Introduction to Reasoning*, 2nd edition (New York: Macmillan Publishing, 1984); Jürgen Habermas, *The Theory of Communicative Action*, Vol. 1, *Reason and the Rationalization of Society* (Boston: Beacon Press, 1984), part I; James Freeman, *Dialectics and the Macrostructure of Arguments: A Theory of Argument Structure* (New York: Foris Publications, 1991); and Charles Willard, *A Theory of Argumentation* (Tuscaloosa, Ala.: University of Alabama Press, 1989).

[26]David Tracy, *Plurality and Ambiguity: Hermeneutics, Religion, Hope* (San Francisco: Harper & Row, 1987), ch. 2.; Iris Marion Young, "Communication and the Other: Beyond Deliberative Democracy," in *Democracy and Difference*, ed. Seyla Benhabib (Princeton: Princeton University Press, 1996), 12–135.

[27]David S. Cunningham, *Faithful Persuasion: In Aid of a Rhetoric of Christian Theology* (Notre Dame: University of Notre Dame Press, 1991); see also chapter 1 of the present volume.

[28]Toulmin, Rieke, and Janik, *Introduction to Reasoning*, ch. 25.

does not argue a legal case in court, for example, in the same way one writes up a scientific lab report for a journal or formulates a managerial policy for a business. Rational communication in each field is governed by the socially-established rhetorical norms of that field: the genres of writing and speaking, accepted patterns of reasoning and warranting, and shared standards of judgment.[29] Argument fields, moreover, typically have more than one forum: distinct settings in which different types of reasoning and argumentation take place.[30] In a rhetorical model of rationality, thus, the social conditions making rational communication persuasive in a given argument field and its various forums are explicitly included in the model. Rationality is not conceptualized as a set of universal rules transportable from context to context but as a field-dependent set of rhetorical norms in which specific methods and procedures (i.e. rules) have their place.

This opens out to a third dimension of this model: the epistemic values informing a particular argument field. Once more, Toulmin is helpful, pointing out that a society's most important argument fields are located within relatively stable social systems designed to meet particular human needs.[31] To use his terms, they are part of larger "rational enterprises" that pursue different social goals. The epistemic values of a given field are shaped by these goals. The value placed on prediction and control in scientific experimentation, for example, rests on the commitment of science to providing an accurate, comprehensive account of the workings of nature. The epistemic values of the legal system in a constitutional democracy are quite different, seeking ways of gathering and presenting evidence in various forums in order to ensure equal treatment before the law. The epistemic values of the production and appreciation of art are different still.

---

[29]Two particularly helpful studies of the role of genre in rational communication are Charles Bazerman, *Shaping Written Knowledge: The Genre and Activity of the Experimental Article in Science* (Madison, Wis.: University of Wisconsin Press, 1988) and Carol Berkenkotter and Thomas Huckin, *Genre Knowledge in Disciplinary Communication: Cognition/Culture/Power* (Hillsdale, N.J.: Lawrence Erlbaum Associates, 1995).

[30]Toulmin, Rieke, and Janik, *Introduction to Reasoning*, 15–17.

[31]Toulmin, Rieke, and Janik, *Introduction to Reasoning*, 271–75. Jürgen Habermas criticizes Toulmin for resting content with a purely historicist account of rational enterprises. See his *Theory of Communicative Action*, 24–42.

In each case, the larger purposes of the rational enterprise in which rational communication takes place shape the kind of knowledge constructed and the ways it is appraised.

As many have noted, the replacement of a rule model of rationality with one that is rhetorical represents a recovery of practical reason.[32] Indeed, it calls into question the longstanding distinction between theoretical and practical reason, which, in various forms, has characterized Western rationalism. Instead of conceptualizing theoretical or scientific reasoning as arriving at necessary conclusions on the basis of an agreed-upon set of rules, it recognizes that rationality inevitably involves a complex series of practical judgments about the sort of argumentation likely to be effective in a particular act of rational communication, the genres and other rhetorical norms by which it is typically conducted in a given forum and field, and the larger purposes of the social system in which it takes place. In short, the rule-governed rationality of modern science is replaced by the practical reasoning of situated rhetoric. Three important implications for a post-encyclopedic approach to theology can be noted.

First, it will no longer do to conceptualize some branches of theology as scientific (or scholarly or theoretical) and others as practical. In a fundamental sense, all theology is practical, involving the practical judgments inherent to forging a rhetoric appropriate to a particular time, setting, and audience. A second, closely related implication is recognition that theology is socially-situated. There is no single, timeless form that theology must take. Even a cursory glance at the history of theology through a rhetorical lens reveals a wide range of genres and patterns of argumentation appropriate to different social locations. The *Summa* of the Middle Ages, for example, forged a rhetoric responsive to the rediscovery of Aristotle, the practice of disputation in the medieval universities, and patterns of divine descent/ascent found in medieval spirituality.[33] The theological encyclopedia forged a very different rhetoric, responsive to a

---

[32] See, for example, Stephen Toulmin's "The Recovery of Practical Philosophy," *The American Scholar* 57/3 (Summer 1988): 337–52.

[33] An excellent discussion of this development in Thomas Aquinas is found in James Weisheipl, *Friar Thomas D'Aquino: His Life, Thought, and Works* (Washington, D.C.: Catholic University Press, 1974). See also, G. R. Evans, *Old Arts and New Theology: The Beginnings of Theology as an Academic Discipline* (Oxford: Clarendon Press, 1980).

very different set of circumstances. The challenge before theology today is the crafting of a new theological rhetoric appropriate to our postmodern and globalized context. This opens out to a third implication: the articulation of the epistemic values that guide theological rhetoric as a distinctive rational enterprise. What is the purpose of theology? What social goals guide the construction of its knowledge and its standards of judgment? What is the function of religion in general and the Christian community in particular within the emerging global community? Theology can no longer answer these questions in an encyclopedic fashion, relying on the rhetoric of science or cognate fields to determine its own rational orientation.

Beyond Foundationalism: Interdisciplinary and Global Perspectives

This brings us to the first assumption of the theological encyclopedia: the belief that theology could be located in a comprehensive, philosophically-grounded system of knowledge. It is precisely on this point that the postmodern trajectory of the rhetorical turn offers its most compelling insights.[34] It calls into question all grand systems and metanarratives that seek to comprehend human knowledge as a whole, elevating some fields or perspectives to positions of power and marginalizing others.[35] Knowledge, according to the advocates of this trajectory, is best seen as local and contextual.[36] The entire encyclopedic project of a philosophically-grounded system of knowledge must give way to a radical pluralism of perspectives that cannot be taken up into a unified, comprehending whole. Already, the contemporary theological scene is

---

[34]See, *inter alia*, Jean-François Lyotard, *The Postmodern Condition: A Report on Knowledge* (Minneapolis: University of Minnesota Press, 1984) and Michel Foucault, *Power/Knowledge: Selected Interviews & Other Writings: 1972–1977* (New York: Pantheon Books, 1980).

[35]See the development of this perspective in several of the essays of the present volume, particularly those by Janet L. Weathers (chapter 2), A. K. M. Adam (chapter 3), and Don H. Compier (chapter 7).

[36]An especially illuminating study of science from this perspective is Joseph Rouse, *Knowledge and Power: Toward a Political Philosophy of Science* (Ithaca, N.Y.: Cornell University Press, 1987).

characterized by a remarkable pluralism, leading us to speak of *theologies*: feminist, Barthian, process, or liberation (to name but a few). Each gives answer to the fundamental questions of theology noted above along somewhat different lines.

Some critics have expressed anxiety about any affirmation of this pluralism, assuming that it necessarily leads to insularity — that theology will become "merely" local and unable to speak outside its very narrow boundaries. However, two contemporary realities seem likely to prevent the contextual approach that I have described here from devolving into a strategy of insularity or withdrawal. The first is the growing importance of cross-disciplinary conversations: under such conditions, distinctive argument fields have no choice but to engage one another.[37] The second is the reality of globalization: the emergence of systems of transportation, communication, and economic exchange that are knitting the world into a single time and place.[38] These concerns pose important questions to a post-encyclopedic paradigm: Is it possible to project comprehensive ways of mapping the range of human knowledge without lapsing into a covert form of encyclopedic foundationalism? What is the best way of forming general yet non-universal theories to assist us in comprehending and guiding the emerging global whole? Two possibilities are particularly promising.

The first is the emergence of a relatively new literature on multidisciplinary thinking.[39] Here, methodological pluralism and inquiry are viewed as necessary to the comprehension of complex systems. As

---

[37] This issue is raised in a particularly helpful way by J. Wentzel Van Huyssteen in *Duet or Duel? Theology and Science in a Postmodern World* (London: SCM Press, 1998), ch. 1. See also Richard Osmer, "A New Clue for Religious Education? Cross-disciplinary Thinking in the Quest for Integrity and Intelligibility," in *Toward a New Religious Education in the Next Millennium*, ed. James Michael Lee (Birmingham, Ala.: Religious Education Press, 2000).

[38] The literature is enormous. Two helpful introductions: Peter Beyer, *Religion and Globalization* and Roland Robertson, *Globalization: Social Theory and Global Culture* (Thousand Oaks, Calif.: Sage Publications, 1994 and 1992, respectively).

[39] Stephen Jay Kline, *Conceptual Foundations for Multidisciplinary Thinking* (Stanford: Stanford University Press, 1995); Nancey Murphy and George Ellis, *On the Moral Nature of the Universe: Theology, Cosmology, and Ethics* (Minneapolis: Fortress Press, 1996).

Stephen Kline points out, in the face of extremely complex systems, especially open systems with emergent properties, no single theory or field can comprehend the whole and its various parts.[40] The data and perspectives of many fields are needed. Multidisciplinary thinking attempts to map the relationship and unique contribution of different fields both to one another and human knowledge as a whole. It does so without recourse to a unifying philosophical system, however, relying on historicist accounts of the present state of human knowledge and the *ad hoc* contribution of different fields to different problems.

Equally promising is recent work in evolutionary epistemology.[41] Here, the relatively late emergence of human life on earth is located in an unfolding, evolutionary process that comprehends the universe as a whole. Human rationality is placed within the broader framework of biological evolution and portrayed as dependent on the development of cognitive mechanisms that allow humans to cope with their world intelligibly.[42] These biologically-based mechanisms are species-wide; in a very real sense, they undergird the diversity of ways humans attempt to understand and cope with their world. Without eliminating cultural and field diversity, this perspective invites us to discern the resources of rationality that are shared across the human community.[43] Rational communication within and between fields and cultures is viewed as part of the unfolding conversation of humankind in its quest for intelligibility.

The brevity of this chapter makes it impossible to pursue either of these lines of thinking further. Suffice it to say they point to ways theology might conceptualize its rational communication as participating in a wide array of interdisciplinary and multidisciplinary conversations extending far beyond the Christian community. A rhetorical model of theological rationality developed along these lines has the potential of moving beyond

---

[40]Kline, *Conceptual Foundations*, 62.

[41]The best introduction to this literature is Franz Wuketits, *Evolutionary Epistemology and its Implications for Humankind* (Albany, N.Y.: State University Press of New York, 1990).

[42]Van Huyssteen, *Duet or Duel?*, 139.

[43]Ibid, 148–49. See also, Calvin Schrag, *The Resources of Rationality: A Response to the Postmodern Challenge* (Bloomington, Ind.: Indiana University Press, 1992).

the foundationalism of the older encyclopedic paradigm while continuing to engage the full range of human knowledge and culture.

Beyond Application: Rethinking "the Practical" in Theology

This accent on conversation that stretches beyond tight disciplinary boundaries is equally important in thinking our way beyond the third assumption of the encyclopedic paradigm: the division of labor between the so-called scientific branches of theology, engaged in scholarly research and theory-construction, and the practical fields, engaged in the application of their research to the life of the church. This pattern continues to exert enormous influence on contemporary theology as practiced in academic institutions. Rhetorically, it can be described in terms of the primary audiences of different fields. Scholars in biblical studies, church history, and dogmatic theology continue to address the specialist audiences of the guild; scholars in practical theology, those providing leadership for congregations.

The overall effect of this pattern on theology has not been entirely positive, leaving much academic theology cut off from the church and other communities of practice important to the healthy functioning of civil society. Moreover, it often distances theology from the innovative force of new social movements. The flow of communication is conceptualized as moving in one direction: from the academy to the church, or from the academy to society. It fosters the idea that theology is the province of academic specialists alone. Moving beyond this highly institutionalized pattern will be not be easy. A rhetorical model of theological rationality, however, points in several promising directions.

Perhaps most importantly, it breaks up the division of labor between scientific/academic and practical fields by locating the specialist scholars of all theological fields in a series of rational conversations stretching beyond the academy. Already, some trajectories of contemporary theology have moved in this direction and do not follow the institutional pattern described above. Liberation and feminist theologians have long called attention to the importance of engaging base communities and other social movements beyond the academy. Theologians and ethicists attempting to recover the public face of theology, likewise, have begun to address medical, scientific, corporate, and other communities beyond the church.[44]

---

[44]For a good analysis of the promises and limits of this process, see the essay by Don H. Compier, chapter 7 of the present volume.

Liturgical scholars have entered into dialogue with worship innovations in widely diverse congregations — from the new baptismal liturgies of feminist communities to the seeker services of evangelicals. In each case, the audience is not merely specialist scholars of the same field. Nor is the flow of communication in one direction. Scholars learn from these conversations as well as contribute to them. They address matters of practice, as well as theory. How are we to conceptualize these developments? As aberrations from the "real" tasks of theological scholarship?

A rhetorical model views these developments positively. It accounts for them theoretically by broadening our understanding of theological rationality —where it occurs and what it looks like. One of the most important gains of the new rhetoric, especially as developed in contemporary argument theory, is the broadening of our understanding of rationality to include activities taking place in everyday life.[45] Quite frequently in the course of everyday interaction, individuals are challenged to explain and defend the claims they have put forward or to engage in rational conversation. I tell my daughter that the movie *Life is Beautiful* is clearly the best of the year. After seeing it with her boyfriend, she says: "Why did you think that movie was so great? Ted and I thought it inappropriately made light of the holocaust." Her challenge to my evaluation of the movie is an invitation to articulate the reasons I found it so powerful. If I listen to her very different evaluation, I may rethink my original position. She may alter her response to the movie in light of the reasons I offer.

This sort of rational communication takes place quite frequently in everyday life. For this reason, many contemporary argument theorists have expanded Toulmin's notion of an "argument field" to include sites that are not typically identified with rationality. What if we were to take this broadened understanding of rationality seriously? We would begin to notice that theological reflection takes place quite frequently in congregational settings — in preaching and teaching, in the various decision-making processes of church committees, and in conversations with persons considering church membership (to name but a few). We also would begin to notice that Christians quite frequently find themselves having to address issues of ethical import in a range of non-church settings:

---

[45]In addition to Stenmark and Willard, cited above, see also Frans van Eemersen, Rob Grootendorst, Sally Jackson, and Scott Jacobs, *Reconstructing Argumentative Discourse* (Tuscaloosa, Ala.: University of Alabama Press, 1993).

the decision to terminate life-support for a loved one in the hospital, the PTA's support for a new multicultural curriculum in the public schools, and a conversation with friends about the presidential impeachment hearings. Here, many Christians struggle to offer good reasons for their actions and decisions to non-Christians — reasons informed by their faith.

Clearly, practical theologians are not the only academic specialists who have something to contribute to and learn from this sort of rational exchange in everyday life. At the very least, a rhetorical model of theological rationality allows us to move beyond understandings of "the practical" in theology that confine it to a specific discipline concerned with application after the "real" work of theology has already taken place. Forging lines of rational exchange with various communities of practice ideally is distributed across all fields.

Indeed, a rhetorical model of theological rationality is more radical still. Theology is not concerned with "the practical" exclusively when it turns to communities of practice or attends to everyday life. It views every attempt to construct theological rhetoric that is persuasive to a particular audience in a particular forum as inherently practical, from the most technical dogmatic tomes to a lecture on medical ethics to a group of doctors. In seeking to persuade its audience, theological discourse invariably must concern itself with matters of practical import — making judgments about the sorts of reasons this particular audience will find compelling, the communicative genres in which they are best expressed, and the epistemic goals and values guiding rational communication in this concrete forum. All theology is practical, as H. Richard Niebuhr pointed out in the quotation with which we began — but for reasons he did not foresee.

Implications for Theological Education

The potential implications of a rhetorical model of rationality for theological education are many. Most importantly, it points to an understanding of Christian leadership that can serve as an integrative center of theological education without eliminating the pluralism characterizing the current theological scene. *It views the goal of theological education as the formation of Christian rhetors* — leaders with the rational and communicative competencies to articulate a persuasive understanding of the Christian faith across a number of different settings and to engage in meaningful rational exchange with persons and groups who are culturally, morally, and religiously different from themselves.

While the ideal of the Christian rhetor is not new, informing the educational ideals of Augustine and various Reformers like Sturm and Melanchthon in the sixteenth century, the sort of theological education being pointed to here transforms this educational tradition in certain ways. Especially in the Reformation Latin academies and universities, the rhetorical ideals of Renaissance humanism were very influential. Students were to learn both piety and eloquence through the imitation and practice of the "classical" models of the past, allowing them to internalize the socially-shared body of knowledge and precepts standing at the heart of the classical tradition. It is precisely the whole notion of a determinant cultural tradition with a fixed body of authoritative texts and practices that was called into question by modernity. It was replaced by the research orientation of the modern university in which the educational ideal was the ongoing production of new knowledge, typically modeled along the lines of scientific progress. It was this ideal that eventually gave rise to the specialization of the academic disciplines, including those standing at the heart of theological education.

Nevertheless, neither the contemporary collapse of modernist assumptions nor the vindication of the rhetorical tradition will provide comfort for those seeking some kind of reactionary return to the ideals of ancient educational paradigms.[46]

There are many reasons for this. To take but one, the intensification of pluralism in our postmodern intellectual scene renders the older humanism's commitment to a determinant cultural tradition, with fixed authorities and boundaries, deeply problematic. Today, we think of living traditions in more dynamic and open categories, as embodying ongoing arguments between a range of positions (MacIntyre), for example, or as the source of preunderstandings enabling new insights and interpretations in the present (Gadamer).[47] Rhetorical competence on the far side of these

---

[46]While the vindication of tradition takes place among a large number of contemporary authors, it is Jaroslav Pelikan who coined this term in his *The Vindication of Tradition* (New Haven, Conn: Yale University Press, 1984).

[47]Alasdair MacIntyre, *After Virtue: A Study in Moral Theory*, 2nd edition (Notre Dame, Ind.: University of Notre Dame Press, 1981); Hans-Georg Gadamer, *Truth and Method*, trans. Joel Weinsheimer and Donald G. Marshall (New York: Continuum, 1989).

more dynamic and flexible understandings of tradition depends less on the mastery of a determinant cultural inheritance than on three other factors: (1) the ability to articulate a position within a tradition critically, with an awareness of alternatives and the ability to provide good reasons for the stance one takes; (2) acquisition of core dispositions making possible rational conversation within and across traditions of a variety of communities — dispositions such as hospitality, mindfulness, mutuality, humility, and truthfulness;[48] and (3) a commitment to ideals of truth, goodness, or beauty that transcend their embodiment in any particular tradition at any given time, ideals that keep the rational conversation and argumentation of communities open to fresh forms and insights.

The formation of persons with these kinds of excellences opens out to many changes in theological education as it currently is practiced in North America. Three lines of change can be pointed to here to illustrate the more comprehensive transformation of theological education it potentially opens up. First, the cultivation of these kinds of rhetorical competencies provides an *integrative center* across all courses of the curriculum. Rather than viewing the defining center of departmental courses as an introduction to the specialized research languages and problems of different fields, the common goal would be the cultivation of the *resources of rhetorical rationality* that are shared by all departments and courses across the curriculum. Students would be taught to think rhetorically: to analyze the arguments of the books they read, to recognize their implied audience, and to assess the effectiveness of their appeal. Student writing and classroom discussion would be viewed as exercises in rational communication, in learning how articulate a position, to defend it when challenged, to listen mindfully to those whose perspectives are different, and to welcome these alternate perspectives with charity. Students would be encouraged to reflect on the ends (or epistemic values) informing the disciplined study of Scripture, church history, Christian doctrine, and contemporary Christian practice. What is the purpose of disciplined, rational communication in the Christian community and how it is related to that of other fields like science and moral philosophy? In these and other ways, the shared resources of rhetorical rationality across the curriculum would work together to form

---

[48]In the ancient rhetorical and ethical traditions, these dispositions were categorized under the heading of "the virtues": see Aristotle *Nic. Eth.* books 2–7; cf. Aristotle *Rh.* I.9–15.

Christian rhetors who can function competently in pluralistic congregations and communities and who have acquired the habit of rational persuasion in their leadership, rather than psychological coercion or conformity to social convention.

Closely related is a second line of change in the contemporary practice of theological education: the development of *rhetorical sensitivity*. This is an attempt to move beyond one of the most destructive aspects of the encyclopedic approach to theological education: the widely perceived gap between the academy and the church. Students in Master of Divinity degree programs experience this gap most directly. They have enormous difficulty relating what they have learned in theological education to the practice of ministry. A kind of "forgetting" takes place in their transition from the academy to the church. They stop reading serious academic books. They come to rely on managerial techniques learned in short-term continuing education offerings with little theological content.

Consequently, in addition to teaching students how to stake out a position and argue for it, theological education must also develop students' rhetorical sensitivity. This is the ability to make judgments about context and audience, particularly the kinds of persuasive strategies that are most effective in different situations. One of the real gains of the movement beyond the theological encyclopedia's limitation of "the practical" to the so-called "application disciplines" (i.e. practical theology) is a new openness to these kinds of concerns across the curriculum of theological education. Concern for audience is no longer the special province of preaching or Christian education.[49] It is not uncommon, for example, for professors of the Bible to invite students to consider the rhetorical impact of "texts of terror" on contemporary audiences, or for dogmatic theologians to explore the pastoral function of doctrine in the shaping of Christians' lives. Conceptualizing these sorts of concerns as the cultivation of rhetorical sensitivity allows professors to attend explicitly to the differences between a specialist audience and the many different audiences Christian leaders must address in their preaching, teaching, and involvement in civil society. It is not enough to initiate students into the discursive practices of the guild. The more important task is the formation of leaders who are adept in

---

[49]See especially the discussion by Donald Juel and Patrick Keifert concerning the audience-oriented focus of the curriculum at Luther Seminary (in the conclusion of the present volume).

moving back and forth between the conversation of scholars and those of church meetings and the school board.

A third implication for theological education follows closely. Taken seriously, the perspective we have been developing would alter the way the academy evaluates the members of all departments for tenure and promotion. Instead of consistently rewarding the academic specialist, it would also reward the rhetorically competent scholar: the person with the ability to participate in a range of in-depth conversations across fields and communities of practice. Cross-disciplinary facility, rather than hyper-specialization, would be the most sought-after scholarly trait. The ability to write and speak persuasively to a wide variety of communities—from congregations to the health-care professions—would be prized.[50] The ability to enter into sustained dialogue with new social movements would be viewed positively. Rhetorical competence of this sort is not a sign of academic weakness. On the contrary: if the Christian academic community is to play a role in shaping church and world in the highly pluralistic, complex social context of postmodernity, rhetorical proficiency is precisely what is needed most.

Practical Theology in the New Paradigm

What, then, are we to make of practical theology? Everything said to this point appears to make it superfluous in a post-encyclopedic approach to theology. In this final section, I will argue that this is not the case. Perhaps the best analogy for our thinking about practical theology should be taken from rhetoric itself. The rhetorical turn has broadened our understanding of rhetoric to include a comprehensive theory of persuasive discourse with implications for the rationality of all fields. This has not, however, eliminated the importance of rhetoric as a *specific* set of activities — that is, as a practical art concerned with the performance and analysis of speaking and writing in public forums, including the modern media. Analogously, the recovery of practical reason in all fields of theology on the basis of the rhetorical turn does not eliminate the distinctive focus of practical theology as an argument field. Rather, it points to its

---

[50]On this point, see the comments of Don H. Compier in chapter 7 of the present volume, and particularly his citation of the work of William C. Placher on this question.

transformation. Let us take Schleiermacher's very promising model of practical theology and reconstruct it in a post-encyclopedic paradigm.

What would it mean for practical theology to move beyond the rhetoric of science and forge a theological rationality appropriate to it as a distinctive argument field? Recall Schleiermacher's description of practical theology as a *technical* discipline, charged with formulating rules of art that can assist the deliberation of clergy in their leadership of the church. These guidelines were portrayed as descriptions of how to perform certain actions and practices in light of both the actual empirical condition of the church and a vision of what it might become in the emerging modern context. This description, I believe, captures well the heart of practical theology. Among the fields of theology, it focuses directly on *how to perform* certain actions and practices. Where Schleiermacher ran into difficulty was in conceptualizing how practical theology could maintain this performative orientation and still be scientific. How could it be both theoretical and practical?

As we have seen, a rhetorical model of theological rationality displaces science as the paradigm of rationality and examines the ways different argument fields actually carry out inquiry and argumentation. The question before practical theology in a post-encyclopedic mode, thus, is: How have practical theologians held together the performative orientation of their field — the construction of rules of art — and the theoretical and research components appropriate to academic argumentation? They have done so by constructing *theories of practice*. There is no question of having to choose between empirical research and theological/ethical reflection, on the one hand, and practical precepts, on the other. The explicit goal of theory-construction and research is the development of a *framework that guides and reconstructs specific fields of action*. The rhetoric of practical theology, as such, is explicitly performative. It is argumentation about how and why to perform certain actions and practices in some ways and not others.

As we have seen, a rhetorical model of rationality challenges practical theology to forge a rhetoric that is *theological* but does not close itself off from rational conversation with other fields. Especially with the emergence of the social sciences, practical theology carried out its work in the face of powerful theories that claimed the mantle of science. At times, it has capitulated in the face of these alternative perspectives, losing its explicitly theological focus in theories of religious education, pastoral psychotherapy, and sacred rhetoric. The challenge before it today is reclaiming its theological orientation in the context of cross-disciplinary conversation.

A concrete example of what this entails may be helpful. Contemporary theories of religious education almost invariably define the nature and purpose of this field in terms of philosophy and the social sciences. This general theory of education is, then, applied to different religious communities. In contrast, a rhetorically-informed practical theology would begin with a theologically-defined understanding of the nature and purpose of its field, focusing on concepts like the teaching ministry, the teaching office, or Christian education. Its theory of practice, as such, would take its bearings from the nature and purpose of the church located in the context of the missions of the Triune God. As a field of theology, it would join contemporary debate and discussion of the other theological fields over these kinds of issues. This would not prevent it, however, from engaging in a wide range of cross-disciplinary conversations.

In dialogue with contemporary theories of modernization and globalization, for example, it might develop a socio-historical understanding of the contemporary context in which the teaching ministry takes place. It might come to realize that across the modern period religion has been confined to the private sphere in the face of secularization and institutional differentiation, trends giving greater freedom to individuals in constructing their religious identities. In light of recent theories of globalization, it might also realize that this pattern is increasingly viewed as *Western* — and that, across the globe, Christianity and other religions are playing an important role in structuring sectors of life beyond the private sphere. Accordingly, it might project a contemporary theory of the teaching ministry that is not confined to congregations alone — addressing individuals, families, and institutions responsible for the education of the various publics of national and global communities.

In this hypothetical example, practical theology projects a theory of practice that is explicitly grounded in theological understandings of the ministry, church, and God, but it, also, engages as conversation partners various non-theological disciplines. It takes up the question of interdisciplinary and multidisciplinary thinking across argument fields, a question that different practical theologians will answer in quite different ways.[51] In so doing, it begins the process of locating its theory of practice

---

[51]Within contemporary practical theology, interdisciplinary conversation is conceptualized in a wide range of ways, including Hans Frei's *ad hoc* correlational method, Calvin Schrag's notion of transversal rationality, Paul Tillich's method of

within the broader conversation of humankind, describing the contribution of the Christian community to the human community's quest for intelligibility and understanding.

Informed by the rhetorical turn, practical theology, also, will carry out its constructive work in dialogue with concrete communities of practice — drawing on the insight that rational communication does not take place in the academy alone. While it is not the only branch of theology vitally engaged in this sort of conversation, it necessarily engages communities of practice for two reasons. First, the development of a theory of practice in practical theology is in the service of the construction of rules of art: open-ended guidelines designed to help individuals and communities perform activities and practices along certain lines. It is inconceivable that these could be developed without extensive engagement of the fields of practice toward which they are directed. To pick up the example offered above, development of rules of art for the teaching ministry of families in light of the globalization of the economy would involve actual work with families: listening to their hopes and fears, their time-constraints, and the specific challenges they face. In a very real sense, the validity of the guidelines offered would rest in part in their persuasive effect on real families. Similarly, it is would be misguided for practical theology to develop principles for assessment of the teaching of religion in public schools without first entering into conversation with teachers and curriculum writers involved in this forum.

Practical theology engages concrete communities of practice for a second reason: the importance of empirical research in its construction of theories of practice. Obviously, it can rely in part on the empirical research of the social sciences. As van der Ven, Heitink, and other Dutch practical theologians have made clear over the past two decades, however, this research frequently does not address issues of greatest importance to the church.[52] Moreover, when such research is available, it is rarely focused in

correlation, David Tracy's and Don Browning's revised correlational method, and Rebecca Chopp's and Matthew Lamb's revised praxis correlational method.

[52]See Johannes van der Ven's comprehensive treatment of this topic in *Practical Theology: An Empirical Approach* (Kampen: Kok Pharos Publishing House, 1993). For an example of the way van der Ven carries his empirical approach out in relation to ecclesiology, see his *Ecclesiology in Context* (Grand Rapids, Mich.: William B. Eerdmans, 1993).

a way that is sensitive to the religious self-understanding of its subjects, making its implications for contemporary religious practice unclear.

The Princeton Theological Seminary Institute for Youth Ministry, for example, has recently undertaken an extensive, cross-cultural literature review of the impact of globalization on the religious identity of adolescents. It has found virtually no significant research on this subject. As a result, it has begun to design its own large-scale investigation of this topic, drawing together practical theologians from around the world. Practical theology must carry out this kind of empirical work on an ongoing basis, framing its research in ways that have direct implications for the contemporary practice of the Christian community. Research focusing on faith development theory, congregational studies, a comparative analysis of theological education, and abuse in different religious communities also are examples of the kind of empirical work that practical theology has carried out in recent years.

In a post-encyclopedic paradigm, thus, practical theology will not be the only field of theology to take up matters of practice. As other fields address communities of practice within and beyond the church, they too will provide guidance for the Christian life. Practical theology, however, will do so explicitly as a research program, seeking to develop theories of practice and rules of art that are informed, not only by its engagement of particular communities of practice or specific clinical settings, but also, by sustained empirical investigation that cuts across a number of such settings. It is here that practical theology may make one of its most important and distinctive contributions to theological discourse as a whole. It will lift up trends, innovations, and questions emerging from the living text of the Christian life. These are matters of importance for other theological fields, affording a richer understanding of the various audiences they hope to address when venturing beyond the academic guild. Such research might even prompt new lines of thinking within the guild itself.

Prospect

In this chapter, we have traced the emergence of practical theology as an academic discipline in the context of the theological encyclopedia. We have pointed to the assumptions of the encyclopedic approach to theology and the ways these have been challenged by the rhetorical turn. At present, the encyclopedic pattern of theology remains firmly in place in most academic institutions of theological education. Even as theologians have begun to think their way beyond the encyclopedic approach to their fields, they teach and work within departmental patterns and academic standards that prevent actualization in practice of what they believe. But such persons can take heart from Thomas Kuhn's description of paradigm shifts in scientific communities.[53] Such innovations, he notes, often, begin on the margins of the community, and become compelling only when it is clear that the older patterns cannot respond adequately to the most pressing problems of the field. With every passing day, the decline of mainline Protestantism in the West and the emergence of new forms of global community make it increasingly apparent that the inherited ways of practicing theology no longer work. Can it be long before the new approaches pointed to in this book begin to take hold?

[53]Kuhn, *The Structure of Scientific Revolutions*.

Chapter 9

Rhetoric and the Word of God: Treasure in Earthen Vessels

James L. Boyce

> But we have this treasure in earthen vessels, to show that the transcendent power belongs to God and not to us.
> — 2 Corinthians 4:7

In these words of Paul, a crucial argument is being developed. At stake are Paul's ministry, the manner of his life, and the power of his preaching. At stake, too, are the nature of belief and the proper perception of the Word of God. For Paul, these issues are inseparable: Word of God and faith are intimately bound up with life experiences. Though the Gospel is veiled, and in spite of the embarrassment of Paul's sufferings, the eye of faith can see life at work in the very signs of death. Paul here testifies to the hidden marks of the God's eternal power — treasure hidden in earthen vessels — and so links his experience with that of the psalmist: "I believed, and so I spoke." Belief and speaking belong together.

Paul clearly equates his own speaking with the word of God; but the recognition and acceptance of this equation is not to be taken for granted.

> We refuse ... to tamper with God's word, but by the open statement of the truth we commend ourselves to every person's conscience.... Even if our gospel is veiled, it is veiled only to those who are perishing (2 Cor. 4:2f.).

As soon as this claim is made, Paul is compelled to marshall arguments in its support — using a variety of topics and techniques familiar to the student of rhetoric. For example, he assumes a metaphysical and hierarchical distinction between the seen and the unseen, relying on the traditional rhetorical *topos* of "more and less" and granting a greater degree of reality to the unseen than to the temporal and visible (4:17-18). He argues by analogy and by appeal to tradition when he characterizes his own experience and preaching as of the "same spirit of faith" as the psalmist (4:13). He appeals to his own authority and experience, employing the "ethical" appeal of classical rhetorical theory. He has renounced all methods that are underhanded, disgraceful, or cunning; he commends himself to the judgment of his hearers' conscience (4:2-3). His arguments play on the emotions of the audience, the appeal strengthened by references to his own perseverance in the face of adversity, comparing his bodily distress to the very sufferings of Jesus (4:8-10). Finally, the appeal is cemented in a denial of personal interest and the assertion of an overriding concern for those who are Paul's hearers: "we preach not ourselves, but . . . as your servants . . . it is all for your sake" (4:5,15). The whole is captured and summarized in the maxim-like statement which recalls the argument's beginning and serves as a pivotal hinge of transition and propulsion: "But we have this treasure in earthen vessels to show that the transcendent power belongs to God and not to us" (4:7).

This example helps us recognize the essentially *rhetorical* character of the New Testament witness. Its goals are *persuasion* and *adherence* — in response to a witness that is never self-evident, but is ambiguous and obstructed by competing claims. Paul's argumentation shows what observers of classical rhetoric know well: successful persuasion hardly ever relies on only one argument or one kind of argument. Audiences and speakers are complex entities, varying in mind, emotion, character, and experience; and their internal differences are matched by the complexities of language itself. Arguments must be personal and various, in order to address those complexities.

The foregoing example could be extended to the whole of the New Testament — and, for that matter, to the whole of Scripture. It thereby reminds us of the importance of rhetoric, and of its implications for understanding and proclaiming the biblical message.

Rhetoric and the New Testament

Although there has been a growth of interest in rhetorical criticism in biblical studies, this work still reflects a narrow understanding of rhetoric that restricts it primarily to matters of style and structure.[1] But as the opening three chapters of this volume make clear, rhetoric is not a monolith. We can, however, generalize about the benefit that rhetoric has to offer, and the desired effects pursued by those who have sought its aid: namely, its power to persuade an audience. Since persuasion makes sense only when there is a possibility of disagreement, the subject matter of rhetoric might described as *the probable*.

Most definitions of rhetoric, whether from classical or contemporary sources, reflect this view. As noted in Chapter 1, Aristotle defined rhetoric as the "faculty of discovering, in the particular case, the available means of persuasion."[2] In this definition, two features are worthy of note. First, rhetoric is not described as persuasion itself, but is rather a process of developing persuasive arguments. The task of discovery or discerning, called *inventio* in the later handbooks, encompasses fully two of the three books of Aristotle's *Rhetoric*; only in the relatively brief third book does he address matters of arrangement and style. This balance in Aristotle's theory is particularly significant, given that many modern approaches to "biblical interpretation through rhetorical criticism" have reversed that emphasis by identifying rhetorical criticism primarily with stylistic concerns.[3] Yet precisely in its consideration of matters of "invention" can rhetorical criticism most benefit the task of interpretation. Moreover, the linkage (in Aristotle's definition) of the task of "discovery" of arguments to "the particular case" reminds us of the importance of the rhetorical situation — and of the role of the audience in interpretive theories.[4]

The discussion of rhetoric throughout the present volume should at least establish a theoretical basis for its usefulness and appropriateness for

---

[1] This is especially true since the invitation of James Muilenberg; see his SBL Presidential Address, "Form Criticism and Beyond," *JBL* 88 (1969): 1–18.

[2] *Rh.* 1.2.1355b.

[3] As a case in point, see many of the essays in the volume edited by Jared J. Jackson and Martin Kessler, *Rhetorical Criticism: Essays in Honor of James Muilenberg* (Pittsburgh: Pickwick Press, 1974).

[4] See Lloyd F. Bitzer, "The Rhetorical Situation," *Philosophy and Rhetoric* 1 (1968): 1–14, and responses, some of which are noted in Alan Brinton, "Situation in the Theory of Rhetoric," *Philosophy and Rhetoric* 14 (1981): 234–48, with bibliography.

interpreting the New Testament as a literature of persuasion. That justification is further strengthened when supported by arguments which take note of (1) the overwhelming influence of rhetoric in education and culture in the historical environment of early Christianity; (2) the essentially oral character of the New Testament even in its written form; (3) the arena of New Testament argumentation as the realm of the probable; and (4) the nature and intent of the New Testament literature as a literature of persuasion.

Why have rhetorical approaches to the Bible become more popular of late? Among the factors that have stimulated this work, we might include: dissatisfaction with the fragmentation resulting from traditional methods of source-, form-, and redaction-critical studies; a growing influence in biblical studies of literary-critical approaches, with their rhetorical insights and their emphasis on the unity of literary composition; and the reappropriation of classical rhetorical theory by the proponents of "new rhetoric" such as Chaïm Perelman and Kenneth Burke.[5] A positive stimulus was certainly the creative treatment of the New Testament writings from a rhetorical perspective by Amos N. Wilder, who argued for the essential interrelationship of form and substance in the creative vitality and variety of the New Testament language.[6]

Examples of rhetorical treatments of the New Testament include the work of Wilhelm Wuellner and Hans Dieter Betz on the letters of Paul, and of Vernon K. Robbins and George A. Kennedy on the Gospels.[7] Wuellner

---

[5]See the discussions in chapter 2 above, with attendant bibliography.

[6]See his Haskell Lectures at the School of Theology at Oberlin College given in 1962, published as *The Language of the Gospel: Early Christian Rhetoric*. (New York: Harper & Row, 1964), reissued in 1971 as *Early Christian Rhetoric: The Language of the Gospel* (Cambridge: Harvard University Press).

[7]For Wuellner, see "Greek Rhetoric and Pauline Argumentation," in William R. Schoedel and Robert L. Wilken, eds., *Early Christian Literature and the Classical Intellectual Tradition* (Paris: Editions Beauchesne, 1979); "Paul's Rhetoric of Argumentation in Romans." *Catholic Biblical Quarterly* 38 (1976): 330–51; "Where is Rhetorical Criticism Taking Us?" *Catholic Biblical Quarterly* 49 (1987): 448–63; "Der Jakobusbrief im Licht der Rhetorik und Textpragmatik." *Linguistica Biblica* 43 (1978): 5–66. For Betz, see *Galatians: A Commentary on Paul's Letter to the Churches in Galatia*, Hermeneia Series (Philadelphia: Fortress Press, 1979). A preliminary introduction

argues that a rhetorical approach is a crucial key to the interrelation of form and content in Paul's letters, stemming from their argumentative intention to influence the audience's adherence to certain theses. Betz has sought to apply this approach to the whole Galatians letter. Unfortunately, his interpretation is spoiled by his negative and narrow view of the nature of classical rhetorical theory. This is mostly due to his reliance on the later stylized traditions and his failure to recognize the variety of options presented by classical theory. He mistakenly says, for example, that judicial speech theory limited persuasion only to rational argumentation, and further characterizes rhetoric as a kind of sneaky, underhanded tool which banks on hoodwinking an unsuspecting audience.[8]

to the approach later reflected in the commentary can be found in "The Literary Composition and Function of Paul's Letter to the Galatians," *New Testament Studies* 21 (1975): 353–79. See also "The Sermon on the Mount: Its Literary Genre and Function." *Journal of Religion* 59 (1979): 285–97 and "The Problem of Rhetoric and Theology According to the Apostle Paul," in A. Vanhoye, ed., *L'Apôtre Paul.*, BETL 73 (Leuven: Peteers/Leuven University, 1986). For Robbins, see *Jesus the Teacher: A Socio-Rhetorical Interpretation of Mark* (Philadelphia: Fortress Press, 1984), and his review article with John H. Patton, "Rhetoric and Biblical Criticism," *The Quarterly Journal of Speech* 66 (1980): 327–37. For Kennedy see his preliminary remarks in "An Introduction to the Rhetoric of the Gospels," *Rhetorica* 1/2 (1983): 17–31, which are incorporated into his fuller treatment in *New Testament Interpretation Through Rhetorical Criticism* (Chapel Hill: University of North Carolina Press, 1984).

[8]"Rhetoric, as antiquity understood it, has little in common with the truth, but it is the exercise of those skills which make people believe something to be true.... [It] is preoccupied with ... psychological exploration and exploitation of the audience, but it is not interested in establishing the truth itself. Consequently, people who are interested in the truth itself must be distrustful of the 'art of persuasion,' because they know of its capacity for intellectual manipulation, dishonesty, and cynicism. The effectiveness of rhetoric depends primarily upon the naïveté of the hearer, rather than upon the soundness of the case. Rhetoric only works only as long as one does not know *how* it works." Betz, *Galatians*, 24. Unfortunately, Betz's attitude toward rhetoric continues to prevail, as was evidenced in a recent seminar at a meeting of the Society of Biblical Literature. The conversation was guided by the interpretive assumption that wherever Paul is most rhetorical, there he is being deceitful and cannot be trusted to be expressing his true opinion. The rhetorical tradition, on the other hand, would suggest that where Paul is most rhetorical is precisely the place where the argument is most crucial.

A more positive approach has been argued by George Kennedy,[9] who proposed a method encompassing (1) determination of the rhetorical unit as it is focused by some integrity of action or argument; (2) definition of the rhetorical situation as that specific condition or complex of persons, events, objects and relations that call for some response; (3) identification of the arrangement or disposition of the various parts of the unit to fit with persuasive strategies to produce religious conviction with different varieties of audiences and situations; (4) identification of stylistic devices that support the argumentation; and (5) evaluation of the whole with a view to a sense of the meaning consistent with the persuasive content and situation.

The story of rhetoric's role in the study of the biblical text is clearly an uneven one. Nevertheless, the scholarly attention that rhetoric has received presents, at the very least, a *prima facie* case for its usefulness for teaching biblical studies in the seminary context. But there are other good reasons for biblical theology to take a rhetorical turn — a few of which will be explored in the remainder of this chapter.

The Language of Religion

Rhetorical criticism provides a valuable perspective for understanding how religious language functions. First, the meaning of a religious statement is seen primarily in the use that is made of it. The emphasis is not on some absolute standard as its basis, but on the function or purpose of the language, its objective and its relation to other systems of language that we use. Religious language assumes a family of systems of meaning, involving ethical claims, attitudes and their formation, and personal commitments — each with its own significance for the life of a believer.[10]

Religious language involves three further characteristics. Questions of truth or falsehood, while important, have a different basis than is true for other kinds of statements. Religious statements contain empirical assertions, but they generally refer to attitudes and personal characteristics, rather than to data as such. And religious statements commonly have a message to

---

[9]Kennedy, *New Testament Interpretation*, 33–38.

[10]James I. Campbell, *The Language of Religion* (New York: Bruce Publishing, 1971), 41. Cf. Ludwig Wittgenstein, *Culture and Value*, ed. G. H. von Wright and Heikki Nyman, trans. Peter Winch (Chicago: University of Chicago Press, 1980), 85.

convey.[11] Religious statements usually assume a personal commitment, and so are not assumed to be simply objective or neutral information.

Within these characteristics, religious statements can assume a wide variety. They can include statements which are historical, definitional, emotive, prescriptive, invocative, accusatory, recollective, persuasive, invitational, or descriptive. Although these different emphases may be noted, we might also say that, along with all language, religious language is typically intended to persuade; and in that sense it is rhetorical. Its rhetoric, similar to that described for Paul above, relies on authority (either the authority of the speaker or some past authority), and argues by analogy to the present situation. It further relies on the congruity of the argument with aspects of the experience of the hearer.[12]

Religious discourse thus recognizes the importance of the authority of the person speaking, or even of certain collections of texts — as well as the possibility of an almost intuitive response to the message. Often religious language contains absolute demands that seem to stand precisely in contrast to or demand rejection of the reason of the world. Paul says, "Has not God made foolish the wisdom of the world? ... Jews demand signs and Greeks seek wisdom, but we preach Christ crucified, a stumbling block to Jews and foolishness to Gentiles" (1 Cor. 1:20, 22–23).

On the other hand, both in the specificity of its texts and in the oral proclamation that underlies it, there is a tradition that assumes that it is precisely within time, within the context of human experience, that the particular religious language has meaning. Its pronouncements and its proclamation are not "timeless truths." Like Paul's letters or the Gospels, they are addressed to specific persons in real or concrete situations. Like rhetorical speech everywhere, they are a dialogue that breaks in with an urgency to the particular human situation of the "here and now" and seeks to form a new order of reality in a community of those human beings involved in that situation. They seek to create a new reality through the medium of persuasion.

Because it takes place within the specific context of human experience, religious language partakes of some of the same characteristics as does language in general. Robert Funk has described these as aspects of the

---

[11] Campbell, *Language of Religion*, 55.

[12] Campbell, *Language of Religion*, 90.

perception, the problem, and the promise of the functions of language.[13] Language imposes limitations of perception; it classifies and molds our environment. Once those perceptions are established and joined with particular formulations of language, they have a durability in tradition that often outlasts the original meaning in context. In a new context, the same words do not have or convey the same meaning. "Biblical literalists are those who insist on the original words but not necessarily the original meaning."[14] Like other language, religious language becomes a problem when fixed traditional perspectives exercise a tyranny over a new context, in which both language and perceiver have drifted to a new stance in relation to the object of memory or the meaning it sought to reflect. Abstractions become formulated in language that drifts free from its original context and can blind us to the particular and the new. Words and sentences do not always convey the same associations or meaning to a new generation that they conveyed to an earlier one. That is especially true for the interpreter who seeks to understand the literature of the New Testament, which not only bespeaks a different cultural perspective, but does so over a gap of almost two thousand years. But language also holds promise when it is reborn or reassembled around fresh contact and examination of experience in the real world — when language is allowed to shape and organize human experience, and to place it in new contexts of meaning.

All of these aspects of religious language highlight its rhetorical function.[15] Its traditional perceptions and its visions of new promise are anchored within language that is part of the common human experience. Its statements are made in such a way as to ground them as widely and deeply as possible. Its goal is to exhort and to persuade to a particular perspective, attitude, or action. At this point, religious language is not different from all language in its motivating force; whenever people use language, even in its most trivial instances, it is somehow acting as a goad to bring about some

---

[13]Robert W. Funk, *Parables and Presence: Forms of the New Testament Tradition* (Philadelphia: Fortress Press, 1982), 8–18.

[14]Funk, *Parables and Presence*, 13.

[15]"Religious tradition, then, consists of language which presides over perception which precipitates problems when habituated, and which, when renewed and fresh, may produce promise." Funk, *Parables and Presence*, 18.

motion within the act of communication.[16] The upshot is that one cannot escape the problem of religious language, either by denying its validity or by assigning to it a character that is completely distinct from other forms of human language, argument, and persuasion.

Rhetoric and the Language of the New Testament

Religious language in general, and the language of the New Testament in particular, is rhetorical: its goal is persuasion or adherence. It may therefore be useful to examine that language with attention to the three classical rhetorical notes of speaker (or writer), audience, and message (whether oral or written). These three aspects are united in one communicative event; this event has its roots in the original context of the speech or writing, but its argumentation and response is repeated and renewed in each new hearing. The particular character of the New Testament message is reflected in these three aspects of speaker, speech and audience.

Speaker

The speaker is most associated with argument by *ēthos*: ethical argument focuses on the person who seeks to persuade, and on how that person inspires the trust and confidence of the audience. In the language of the New Testament, it bears upon the complex matter of *authority*.

The New Testament writers certainly lay claim to authority; moreover, in the New Testament, as in all Scripture, ultimate authority resides in God. Throughout the biblical writings, God is ultimately the speaker — and in this sense, the ethical appeal is immediate and ultimate. Awareness of God's authorship is most evident in those passages where God speaks

---

[16]Kenneth Burke thus sees a close analogy between the rhetoric of religious language and the rhetoric of all language. The difference between them may only lie in what Burke calls the "thoroughness" of theological language; religious language thus has a claim to the ultimate nature of its language in a way that common human discourse does not. Otherwise, Burke would not seem to press the distinction of religious language so thoroughly. In fact his whole argument in *The Rhetoric of Religion: Studies in Logology* (Berkeley: University of California Press, 1970) proceeds from the premise that study of the nature of use of religious language provides insight into the nature of the way in which all language functions (pp. 2–3).

directly in the first person; it is also obvious when a prophet professes to speak directly for God. This awareness would also have been more obvious in Scripture's original oral context — and even when one hears the message at each new proclamation or reading.

Interestingly, however, instances in which God is represented as speaking directly are much rarer in the New Testament than in the Hebrew scriptures. Such representations as do occur are mostly connected to incidents in the life of Jesus (e.g., his baptism). Otherwise, the New Testament has already begun to transmit the words of God less directly: through the quotation of the prophets and the citation of the Scripture. These were traditions of transmission that were handed down within the community; already a part of the Hebrew Scripture, they are employed much more consistently in the New Testament.

When one listens to a contemporary sermon, one can sometimes be moved such that, with no great stretch of religious fervor, one might claim that God has spoken. At other times, no religious fervor or imagination — however great — can bring one to such a claim. Though some persons on occasion might declare that they have heard God speaking to them directly, we tend to regard such claims with suspicion.

A similar situation occurs when we regard the New Testament writings. There is a sense in which God is the ultimate speaker and authority. Yet from a rhetorical perspective, it may not be so easy to answer the questions, "Who is the speaker?" and "Upon what authority is the audience addressed?" Certainly one would describe Paul as a rhetor in his letters; and similarly for the authors of the Gospels and for certain characters who appear within the Gospels (and Acts). In fact, throughout the New Testament, the author or speaker plays the most significant role. The authority of God, which a hearer may attribute to the text, is actually dependent on an authority granted to the text's author — including judgments about that author that have been rendered by a particular religious community. Our granting of authority to Paul or to Matthew rests in the conviction that these writers offer a word from God; and that conviction rests in turn on the church's judgment, through its canon, that the words of Paul and Matthew are part of our authoritative literature.

These considerations affirm the critical role of the speaker in the persuasive moment of the New Testament. Ultimately, whether orally or in texts, Christians have no access to the words of God except through the words and minds of those who claim to speak in God's name and with

God's authority. We cannot penetrate to a meaning that is beyond theirs, as it is reflected in the particular argument of their message.[17] This means that authorial intent is not an irrelevant issue when it comes to our understanding of the New Testament witness. It is an integral part of the nature of these particular texts; and even though we may not be confident of that intent, it is certainly an appropriate part of the total understanding of the persuasive goal.

Speech or Text

It is clear that one cannot talk about word of God without talking also about those particular texts that claim to be Word of God in a special sense: the texts of the New Testament. These texts lay claim in a special way to being the Word of God for us today. That claim extends to those texts not only as they were originally spoken, but also to their nature in the Christian community as "sacred" texts that continue to claim a particular authority.

As noted in the previous section, their authority resides, in part, in the *ēthos* of the one who addresses the hearer in these texts — be that the ultimate address of God, or the address of the author and the Christian community who passed on and shaped the traditions. But the authority of the text also resides in the message itself — in the particular shape and content of its argumentation. Part of that shape is its essential unity within the canon. The canon assumes that there is a unity of intent, if not always of particular focus.

At the beginning of this chapter, I noted that Paul's argumentation in 2 Corinthians is complex and diverse. Paul is not unique in this respect; throughout the New Testament, arguments tend to mushroom into a variety of forms. Even when a particular occasion makes one form of argument dominant, multiple shapes are employed. The argumentation employs the common topics of persuasive argument as identified in classical rhetorical theory. It relies on the external evidence of testimony, often established in turn by ethical considerations of the authority of the speaker. Finally, it relies on the admissibility of the corroborative evidence of the experience of the hearers.

The significance of the text or argument itself is underscored by the very existence of the text of the New Testament, the process of its selection

---

[17]Compare G. B. Caird, *The Language and Imagery of the Bible* (Philadelphia: Westminster Press, 1980), 61.

as canon, and its history within the Christian community through the centuries. At times it has obscured the fact that the proclamation was originally oral, that these texts were originally meant to be heard, and that this process of hearing is extended even to the contemporary community in the context of public worship and proclamation. Consideration of the relative implications of the orality or the textuality of the New Testament may shape the way in which we hear the text; but it will not alter the fact that, on either count, the content of the discourse is argumentative and persuasive. The texts have a goal and a purpose; and they always assume an audience.

Audience

The Scriptures repeatedly speak of the *power* of God's word — which they describe as able, by its very nature, to accomplish that which it intends. That this intention is directed toward an audience is evident in the very description of God's activity as involving communication and language. Language is a particularly human activity, and to speak of God's word is to assert that God is about the matter of seeking the adherence of those who are addressed.

To focus on the audience is to raise the issue of faith. The audience is always present in the hearers, and especially in their actuality or potentiality as a believing community. This believing community — its disposition of faith, its common adherence to a perception of reality — ultimately accounts for the perception of the New Testament as the Word of God. Because particular hearers experience particular words as persuasive, the texts function as "sacred" literature. Indeed, in the experience of many who have been persuaded, this literature has been *effective*; it has accomplished that for which it was intended. The power to persuade is never absolute; it depends upon whether a given hearer or community can be drawn into a common bond of thought and action. "Do not be hearers only, but doers of the word" is the common exhortation — much as Augustine saw the active and persuasive intent of the rhetoric of the scriptures as that of awakening the active adherence of faith through instruction, pleasure, and encouragement to action.

The New Testament understanding of faith has been described as a complex interdependence of intellect, assent and commitment in attitude and action of the total person. Calling the audience to such faith is the focus of the persuasive intention of the scriptures. The scriptures always address an audience with an explicit or implied "in order that...": for example, the author of the Gospel of John writes, "These things are written in order that you may believe" (20:31). Paul's letters never simply add important information to the religious stockpile; he consistently integrates into his argumentation an exhortative "therefore" that assumes a change or new orientation. The narratives of Jesus' ministry and his preaching consistently call attention to the division of "those who hear" into two groups: those who accept his call, and those who reject it. In much the same way, Matthew's argumentative climax occurs in the parable of the sheep and the goats, with its explicit call to action — and in the Great Commission's "Go therefore and make disciples" (28:19). Such a posture towards an audience shows that, in some sense, the New Testament writings assume the possibility of judgment and decision. Argumentative discourse assumes the interplay of competing opinions and the possibility of free and open judgment. Although the New Testament may represent that adherence as a response to the power and grace of God, it is, nevertheless, also a response of the *hearers*, in faith.

Precisely here — in the ambiguity of opinion, in the interplay of doubt and faith, of grace and decision — the Christian experiences the complexity of the language event that is the New Testament. As much as we might sometimes wish it were so, religion and religious discourse does not rescue humans from existence in this world. Language does not simply declare objective truths, because part of being human and fallible is the inability ever to look at reality completely objectively. Language, and the reality it describes and shapes, is always true and meaningful within contexts — and in the midst of relationships.

The New Testament message refuses to rescue the hearer from that ambiguity. Life in the Kingdom is life in this world. We may see dimly, but still we see. The story of God's new creation ("genesis") in a Son is couched in the words of a "book" (Matthew 1:1,18). The culmination of the story is even in this world, as the "New Jerusalem" of the elder's vision comes down to this place.

It is *in this world* that the Christian life is created, takes shape, and is lived. Here, the word as word of God is understood and appropriated in the interplay of author, discourse and audience — of God, sacred text, and believer. The words that convey this word must be constantly reshaped into new and relevant meanings. Christian faith and existence is, at its heart, rhetorical: it demands faithful response and adherence to a word of God, mediated through specific arguments and stories, which call upon the hearer to respond in faith to the address of God's love and mercy.

Treasure: Transcendent Power in Earthen Vessels

Although rhetorical criticism might be described as essentially secular, its application to the New Testament literature is anything but neutral or objective. To seek to understand these documents fully is to be open to the particular perspective that shapes their argument from beginning to end. They are not neutral or objective; they not only seek adherence to a particular way of understanding, but promise that, in the hearing of the word, the hearer will be transformed.

Those who would preach or teach the message of these documents most ably will be convinced of the treasure that lies within them. The treasure that Paul describes is the presence, for the hearer of any age, of the transcendent power of the Word of God in all its deceptive weakness. All human language has power: power to describe and order reality; power to remember a reality now past; power to imagine new realities for the future. Yet, to hear and respond to the message of Scripture is to acknowledge its testimony to a word that is *beyond* human language, and yet finds expression *in* human language. The language of God is present in the powerful word of creation. "In the beginning was the Word" (John 1:1); God spoke and the world came into being. God's word goes forth and accomplishes that for which it is intended. For the New Testament, the ultimate mark of the power and effectiveness of that word is that "the Word became flesh and dwelt among us" (1:14). In Jesus, within the arena of human experience and language, the address of God has become tangible. Wherever that word is heard — wherever author, discourse, and audience are recreated and bound up together — that transcendent power is present. "Where two or three are gathered in my name, I am there among them" (Matt. 18:20).

Yet according to Paul, this treasure — this transcendent power that belongs to God — is "in earthen vessels." The word "in" should be construed both in the sense of "contained in" and in the sense of "composed of or consisting of." It is the "in" of Luther's "in, with and under," and is analogous to the understanding of the sacraments: transcendent power resides in and through earthly signs, and the two cannot be separated or distinguished. Without both, there is no sacrament.

In similar fashion, the New Testament message — in spite of the novelty of the events of faith that are described therein — is always bound up in language. The medium of revelation is the common language of human beings.[18] "Treasure in earthen vessels" implies that the revelation of God is enmeshed in the human experience of this world — words and all — with all its imperfections and ambiguities, with all its rhetorical perspectives, problems, and promises.

The consistent emphasis in the New Testament is on *testimony*. That testimony ultimately resides in the persuasive power of God; God is the ultimate authority. To this fact, Paul bears witness. Yet it is *Paul*, and his words, that bear witness to the Corinthians; it is the disciples and apostles, the letter-writers and story-tellers, who are called to bear witness "to Judea, to Samaria and to the uttermost parts of the world" (Acts 1:8). This witness is still couched in the persuasive rhetoric of human language, addressed to this audience of potential believers. Through the same human language, the call is extended to those who hear and read today, and are persuaded to respond to its call.

Paul's metaphor of the "earthen vessel" of language is a particularly apt one. As anyone who has spent some time on an archaeological dig in Palestine will readily recognize, the "earthen vessels" of which Paul is speaking are the common, everyday clay vessels that formed the common material of shipping and packing and household vessels for cooking, eating and storage. Clay containers were certainly as pervasive a phenomenon among Paul's contemporaries as was language. Although clay vessels could be formed and decorated in such a way that examples are still admired and treasured for their beauty, for the most part the earthen vessels were consistently utilitarian — as simple and unobtrusive as the clay of which they were made. They were suitable to the moment and to the need, made to be used, and frangible, just as readily discarded for a new replacement. Like language, these clay pots were not always perfect, even in their simplicity. They could be nonfunctional; they could have leaks or broken handles; they could be misshapen or misfired, aesthetically unpleasing, and misinterpreted or unappreciated by a new generation. Yet when one looks at ancient pottery one is amazed at the durability of the medium, and amazed also at the durability of a particular model, shape or form — so much so that new models consistently seek to follow the shape of their predecessors, even when original uses for the ware may long have passed

---

[18]Wilder, *Language of the Gospel*, 26.

away. So persistent are these types that archaeologists can use them to locate pottery geographically, and to date it.

So it is with the word of God that Paul describes as being "in earthen vessels." It is suitable first of all for the moment and the day; it partakes of all the idiosyncrasies and ambiguities of human speech, including its rhetorical power; new models and a new day will tend to replicate the old tradition, which will still be heard, but in some cases will no longer be useful in the same way, and will need to be discarded. Like new pots, the human language in which the word of God is couched will necessitate a new word for each day — but one which is shaped, guided, identified by a persistent schema. That schema is the one of which Paul speaks in Philippians: that Jesus "took the form" of humanity (2:7–8). That form gives shape to the language of the New Testament, in that the "word of God became flesh and dwelled among us" (John 1:14). As the greatest works of art are frequently those which are couched in the specifics of a particular situation, so the word of God is seen both in its greatness and in its simplicity — couched in the human language of everyday experience.[19]

Paul's "earthen vessel" — the common language of humanity — was and still is the medium of revelation. Jesus' speech identified with his followers and hearers. Its newness and power may have forced new images and metaphors on the current idiom, but it was still consistent with that idiom and rooted in the secular media of contemporary and ordinary speech. That revelation was consistently intended for persuasion; it was rhetorical. As it had called Moses and the prophets, so it addressed the disciples with a "follow me." It confronted Saul on the Damascus road, and summoned Peter to visit Cornelius. Human speech requires the persistence of the old conventions; but it also allows the freedom of the new to break in with dreams, thoughts, and actions never before imagined. Still, the historicity and the down-to-earth character of the common language — the "earthen vessels" through which that power is available — is a check against an intoxication of the spirit that would wish to abandon this world.[20] The history of faith and theology, the sojourn of the Christian church (in both its life and its scriptures), is bound up with the history and the fate of

---

[19] See the comments of Kenneth Burke, *Counter-Statement* (Berkeley: University of California Press, 1968), 84–85.

[20] Compare the comments of Wilder, *Language of the Gospel*, 62, 78.

language. Just as the word of God in promise is subject to evaluation in later fulfillment, so the word of God in purpose and meaning always assumes the judgment and the experience of human language. Revelation always remains in, and bound up with, that judgment and experience.

We have spoken here first of "transcendent power" and only then of "earthen vessels." In light of what we have said about human language as the medium of revelation, we might well have reversed the order. On the other hand, this order has been chosen to underscore the assertion that, finally, only here in human language is the Word of God met. Human language has the first and last word, insofar as human experience of the transcendent is concerned. But we first affirm our conviction of a transcendent power in these texts, because there are some who, however readily they might recognize the human character of their rhetoric, might not be so willing to assign them the transcendent power that their role as Christian scripture demands.

One might object that such a position removes the spontaneity and the power of God — that it precludes the reality of direct mediation of the Spirit or the experience of ecstasy, that it asserts ultimately a closed world not open to transcendent power. It is important to note, however, that we are not speaking of the origin of revelation, but about *how* that revelation can be known and experienced by human beings within this world. In that context, even the most ecstatic of religious experiences can only be comprehended and interpreted, even those who experiencing it, within the framework of human discourse and language. Human language provides the categories and images with which we understand. Without the appropriate language the experience remains unthinkable and ultimately unknowable by the individual or the community. It reveals nothing. Interestingly, even ecstatic utterance is spoken of as *glossalalia*: it is "another tongue" which bears witness in the experience that language is the framework of all religious experience. Without language there is no religion; without the persuasive power of language to call forth human commitment and response, there is for us no God. Radical as that may seem, it is simply to state from the other side the reality that is testified in the Christian confession that from creation to the consummation, human existence is bound up with the "word" and address of God. That Word becomes flesh for us in the particular human words that tell the story of the life, death, and resurrection of Jesus — and tell it as a story that is ultimately to, and about, *us*.

Can the revelation of God to us, and ultimately our own story, be so at risk, so bound up with the ambiguities and perversities of human language? Such a claim is unnerving to some, as was illustrated for me recently when I was reading a library copy of Amos Wilder's book, *The Language of the Gospel: Early Christian Rhetoric*. In a section in which Wilder is emphasizing how the narratives of the New Testament remind us that Christian existence is bound up with the historicity of particular language, with particular tellings of a story, he comments:

> Perhaps the special character of the stories of the New Testament lies in the fact that they are not told for themselves, that they are not told only about other people, but that they are always about us. They locate us in the very midst of the great story and plot of all time and space, and therefore relate us to the great dramatist and storyteller, God himself.[21]

Within the margin alongside this particular paragraph an earlier reader had written in quotes with a large exclamation mark, "Rot!" Perhaps the affront is that such transcendent power should be limited by such a fragile and unassuming "earthen vessel" that just as well might be relegated to the "rot" of a garbage heap as be the bearer of the refreshing water of life. As clear as the rhetorical character of the New Testament makes it that Christian existence and experience is always bound up with language and so with history, it remains so "irreligious" and unthinkable that students of the New Testament — and those who proclaim its message — must be reminded of it again and again.

Word of God and Human Words

Word of God in earthen vessels constantly calls attention to the rhetorical mode of Christian existence and faith. The Christian life always involves persuasive arguments that seek adherence and commitment in the face of choices that are ultimately matters of probability. Language is also part of that risk, that witness, and that life. God is ever new, and each day presents new possibilities for understanding what God is doing in this world. There is truth, yes; but it is not unambiguous. Truth, even the truth that we call revelation, is always truth for a particular historical context, for a particular people of God. It is constantly moving. Like the language that

---

[21]Wilder, *Language of the Gospel*, 65.

contains it, it needs to be hammered out in constant dialogue with the scriptures (the language of the tradition), and the world (the language of the present), in order that it may be constantly fresh with images for tomorrow. As in human life in general, seeking to understand what the word of God is for today is never the search for an absolute "truth" hidden for all eternity, but a search for clues to the transcendent power of God, which we are convinced is active in the reasonable, the probable, and the contingent of life in this world.[22]

A number of aspects of this rhetorical mode of Christian existence are important for the interpreter of the New Testament. The Christian existence that those texts describe is historical as well; the people who originally proclaimed those particular words (which, in their written form, we now call the Scriptures) were as bound up in history as are we. The words which the biblical writers spoke and wrote partake of that same character. Alongside the historicity of Christian experience stands the historicity of the scriptural texts.

This implies that life is a matter of probabilities, not certainties. It consistently involves choices and decisions; the relative value and persuasive appeal of each is presented and weighed by individuals with themselves or by groups within communities through the exercise of human words and language.

Human beings are not automatons; perhaps the best proof of that fact is the persuasive and argumentative character of language. We must make choices, and we offer arguments to support these choices; this implies that we have multiple options. Christian witnesses today need to recognize that the word of God, entrusted as it is to human words, is never self-evident or unambiguously verifiable. It takes its chances in the arena, along with all other competing claimants, in seeking to win allegiance and adherence.

This implies that Christian witness is never free of the complexities of rhetoric. In the original occasion of the scriptures, the intricate interdependence of speaker, audience, and discourse means that each interprets and shapes the other. Similarly, the present-day speaker (inter-

---

[22]Compare Perelman's comments on the impact of dialectic as a way of understanding the role of argument and rhetoric within the ambiguity of human life's constant choices and opinions. See William Kluback and Mortimer Becker, "The Significance of Chaïm Perelman's Philosophy of Rhetoric," *Revue Internationale de Philosophie* 33 (1979): 33–34.

preter) and audience will reshape and rethink that discourse, shaping each other in a new historical context and a new event of revelation. The linking of the two rhetorical events is never simply that of formal or logical demonstration. Neither revelation nor proclamation is ever merely the unpacking of the kernel of truth or the logic of the text and making them available. Rather, the treasure is always hidden within the unassuming common language of human speech or in the actions of human beings towards one another as interpreted within the framework of language. It involves a persuasive argument, an invitation to a point of view, an image of reality.

That point of view or image of reality is also rhetorical; it is an agreed-upon worldview or perspective within the context of other competing perspectives. It is a community of discourse to which we have been persuaded and to which we have given our commitment. We say we have been called into a community; our expressions of commitment or faith are a "speaking together," a "con-fession." Life in that community, with its own specialist language, is much like life in any other human society or political group. To use the New Testament term, it is life in the "Kingdom."

Lutheran theologians have traditionally resorted to talk of two kingdoms as a way of describing the character of that life. The "kingdom on the left" is the historicity of human life in this world; the "kingdom on the right" is that life, beyond death and sin, that belongs ultimately by God's grace to the final consummation. Word of God in human words, treasure in earthen vessels, is part of the kingdom on the left. It asserts that there in the midst of the ambiguity of human life is where life is now, where preaching and faith take place.

A rhetorical perspective is thus an anti-dogmatic interpretive principle that allows for the renewing power of life and spirit over the binding threats of the letter. The word of God in human language, just as in the human life of Jesus of Nazareth, comes as a radical adversary; it is a persuasive word of life, to which assent is never automatic. And what is spirit and life to us today can become "mere letter" tomorrow, when new events call for a new language and a new word. Rhetoric and language are always for a particular moment and a particular hearing; they call for a particular response.

That call for response, implicit in the New Testament literature, can be more clearly heard when the texts are examined from a rhetorical perspective. The New Testament, like all human language, is not individualistic; it is, however, intensely personal. Its indicative announcement and its imperative exhortation are couched in the dialogue of first and second person, in the dialogue of speaker and hearer. With that address comes a challenge. Here, rhetorical criticism can be helpfully distinguished from a literary-critical model. Appreciation of the "images," the "story," the "characters" and their interplay — the "art" of the text — may allow the story or the characters to "come alive" for the modern reader and may even call forth admiration or appreciation for the story or the characters. But it may also take place while still enabling a disregard for the call to adherence — the claims to obedience, identification, and transformation that faith in the text requires. "Something happens to us in listening. . . . We come to view and review our world as infinitely more open and unfinished than we first imagined because the world is an arena where God is busy making good on his promises."[23]

The argument for the helpful perspective of rhetorical criticism is a crucial one that strikes at the heart of the New Testament and its message. The nature of the Word of God, and the nature and destiny of human existence in this world, are at stake; a rhetorical perspective enables the interpreter and preacher to see and understand such matters.

A rhetorical vision for biblical interpretation offers an openness to the living and changing Word of God as it takes shape in human words appropriate for each new day. It develops from an understanding of human community within which the meaning and function of language takes place. Language exists and is meaningful only within the context of community; thus, the Word of God is persuasive and meaningful only within the particular experience and realm of discourse of a Christian community that supports its persuasive argument. A rhetorical perspective also recognizes the danger of human language that exists in its ambiguity. History has

---

[23]William H. Willimon, "'Eyewitnesses and Ministers of the Word': Preaching in Acts." *Interpretation* 42 (1988): 166. Willimon also notes how in reading the scriptures we are moved beyond the "what does it say," to the dynamic concern for what God is "using the Bible to do to us." See also the remarks of Krister Stendahl on the "normative expectation" of the scriptures that can too easily be overlooked by a literary-critical approach. Stendahl says that "The normative nature of the Bible requires . . . a serious attention to the original intentions of the texts," and that the more intensive the normative expectation, the more concern is needed for attention to "what it meant" as it is reflected in the intention of the authors. Krister Stendahl, "The Bible as a Classic and the Bible as Holy Scripture," *Journal of Biblical Literature* 103 (1984): 3–10.

shown that the persuasive power of human language can be the agent of tyranny and oppression; its function and its meaning depend on "how it is heard," which in turn is determined by the rhetorical interplay of speaker, hearer, and discourse.

A rhetorical perspective also recognizes the *promise* of language. Because it is not bound to the past, it calls for the birth of imagination, of a creative vision that allows the ability of human language to see beyond the limits of the past or the present, and so to have the eyes and ears of a heart that is open each day to the working of God in community and world.

And finally, a rhetorical perspective is a reminder that language is important. Word of God is first, last, and always about speaking and about texts. The particular texts of scripture, historically conditioned as they are, are the particular place where we hear that Word. They belong to a particular community of language of promise and persuasion; they are not externally validated in the way that a theater ticket or a birth certificate, a voter registration or an ordination paper may be validated. They are validated by the way in which their particular message of speaker, audience, and discourse combines in effective argumentation, enabling response and commitment in each new proclamation.

Chapter 10

Rhetoric and Historical Theology: Gregory the Theologian

Frederick W. Norris

Rhetoric lost.

My Microsoft Word spell check program does not know: Cicero, Demosthenes, Gorgias, Hermogenes, Isocrates, or Quintilian. Aristotle and Plato it knows, but not because someone insisted that they had significant things to say about rhetoric. Yet at the same time, *rhetoric* is receiving significant notice these days; for example, there are no compelling definitions of "postmodernism" that do not include some attention to rhetoric. Interest in the subject exploded late in the twentieth-century after it had been nearly obliterated. At the beginning of that century rhetoric was a solid component of education, whether it was pursued in Europe and North America or in China and India. The ability to write and speak well, to persuade audiences, had been included in the dominant conceptions of political and cultural life. Even within small, one-room schools in agricultural Indiana, my grandmother and great aunts taught rhetoric formed by Cicero and Aristotle.

The old, misunderstood Greek debate between philosophy and rhetoric — Plato against Gorgias — has been won, at one level, by philosophy. "Rhetoric" in common parlance is the camouflaging verbiage employed by politicians and used-car salesmen to trick their hearers. Outside the revival of different senses for the word in academia, that sense rules among the general North American public. In the seminary where I teach, wide-eyed students of quite diverse backgrounds and ages question initially any use of the term — whether in biblical studies, constructive theology or homiletics courses — because opening it up creates for them an unbearable stench.

In spite of all these obstacles, however, I want to suggest that the obliteration of foundations that has marked the emergence of postmodernism should recall us to a new appreciation of the ways in which rhetoric and theology belong together. Their interrelationship becomes most obvious in those cultural contexts in which no one is certain that Cartesian foundationalism is any answer at all. In the present chapter, I examine the confluences of rhetoric and theology through an exploration of the work of Gregory Nazianzen (c. 330–390). His example demonstrates that former giants, who have been considered not even bothersome pests in the twentieth century (Microsoft Word doesn't know him either), may again take their places in positions of honor.

At the Council of Chalcedon in 451, sixty-one years after his death, Gregory of Nazianzus was called "The Theologian." In Eastern Orthodoxy that is a title he shares only with the author of the Gospel of John — a title that has just a few variations in the entire history of Byzantine theology.[1] Indeed, Nazianzen's stamp on the nature of theology is consistent throughout Eastern Orthodox theology up through the contemporary period. John Meyendorff, in presenting a modern systematic treatment of Byzantine theology, conceded that Gregory Nazianzen's type of ordered presentation was seldom attempted within Orthodoxy.[2] Neither Gregory of Nyssa nor John of Damascus reached for the level that marked the great medieval work of Thomas Aquinas (who absorbed and recast Damascus), nor the multi-volumed presentations of Protestant Orthodoxy, nor the exemplars of twentieth-century theology (whether Orthodox, Catholic, Protestant, or Free Church).

Rather commonly, Greek Patristic and Byzantine theologians were uncertain that any philosophy was true and powerful enough to enclose

---

[1] *Acta Conciliorum Oecumenicorum* 2,1,3,114,14. Symeon "The New Theologian" also stands in that line.

[2] John Meyendorff, *Byzantine Theology: Historical Trends and Doctrinal Themes*, 2nd ed. (New York: Fordham University Press, 1987).

and reshape the Gospel. In that conviction they resemble Gregory the Theologian, who could eclectically employ all manner of insights from Hellenistic philosophy but always by critically appropriating its fragments. He found Plato not only fascinating, but also — on occasion — speaking truths about God; yet Nazianzen disliked his theory of ideas, his views on the re-embodiment and cycles of our souls, his theory of knowledge as recollection, and his stories of distasteful love-affairs between men and boys. The Theologian depended upon much of Aristotle's sense of rhetoric; but he attacked his conception of providence, his artificial and overly-technical logical system, his view of the soul's mortality, and his reductionistic humanism. Pythagorians, Epicureans, Stoics and Cynics also took their lumps from his hands, but in each case he also found something useful.[3]

The modern Western sense that one should first discover the most profound philosophical system of the day and then do theology from within it finds no support in Nazianzen's works. And in return, he has remained primarily on the periphery of Enlightenment-oriented theologies of quite varied types.

Within Eastern Orthodoxy, particularly in its Russian revivals early this century (like that of Georges Florovsky), Gregory was given a distinguished place.[4] Part of that influence grew out of a deep concern that the Orthodox heritage might be lost altogether if it were forced to find its primary arena in the West — away from fascist oppression, but suppressed nonetheless by Enlightenment foundationalism. The arena was to be formed by the Christian Tradition with its liturgy and confession, and with the truth and beauty of ritual, icons, and music. These revivals of Orthodoxy warned against succumbing to rigid logical constructions and to a theology that defined itself as truth stated in propositions, demonstrated in syllogisms,

---

[3] *Or.* 27.10, *Patralogia Graeca*, ed. J.P. Migne and his successors, Vol. 36 (Paris: Garnier Fratres, 1885), 24B–25A, *Grégoire de Nazianze, Discours 27–31 (Discours théologiques)*, ed. Paul Gallay, Sources chrétiennes 250 (Paris: Les Éditions du Cerf, 1978), 94–8.

[4] Georges Florovsky, *Collected Works of Georges Florovsky*, 14 vols., ed. Richard Haugh, particularly Vol. 7 *The Eastern Fathers of the Church*, Vol. 8, *The Byzantine Fathers of the Fifth Century*, and Vol. 9, *The Byzantine Fathers of the Sixth to the Eighth Centuries* (Vaduz: Büchervertriebsanstalt, 1987).

organized into systems. For Florovsky, the Christianization of Hellenism — rather than Harnack's account of the Hellenization of Christianity — was the key.[5]

Among the sources of that project, Nazianzen led the way — and was able to do so because, as I define him, he was a rhetorical theologian. His mastery of ancient philosophical and technical rhetoric was so complete that Byzantine Christian professors of rhetoric taught the subject by replacing examples of Demosthenes with ones from the Theologian. Students learned a Hellenistic rhetoric dominated by phrases from Gregory and thus had little difficulty in finding his theology in sync with their rhetorical educations. John of Sicily, one author of such a rhetorical handbook, says that, in terms of his command of rhetoric, Gregory "excelled Plato in the virtues of speech as much as in theology, and he made Demosthenes seem a mere child."[6] In a similar fashion, George Kennedy, a modern proponent of ancient rhetoric who is not partial to any particular school of theology, says that Nazianzen's speech on Basil is probably the greatest funeral oration since Demosthenes' death.[7]

The relationship of rhetoric and theology was viewed as an even deeper reality among some Byzantine theologians. For them the two were one; indeed, rhetoric itself was referred to as a "sacrament," a *musterion*.[8] Rhetoric, and not philosophy, was the handmaiden of theology.

In the short compass of this essay, I cannot attempt to set out what a "postmodern" theological education might look like — even in its rhetorical aspects. Other contributors to this volume take parts of that task in hand.

---

[5] Florovsky, "Christianity and Civilization," *St. Vladimir's Seminary Quarterly* 1 (1952), 13–20.

[6] In *Rhetores Graeci*, ed. by Christian Walz (rpr. Oznabrück: Zeller, 1968), Vol. VI, 99, trans. by George Kennedy, *A History of Rhetoric*, vol. 3, *Greek Rhetoric under Christian Emperors* (Princeton: Princeton University Press, 1983), 238.

[7] Kennedy, *Greek Rhetoric under Christian Emperors*, 237.

[8] Doxaprates, *Prol. Syll.* 80.12-6; John of Sicily, *Prol. Syll.* 394.12-4. For further secondary interpretation of this phenomenon, see George Kustas, *Studies in Byzantine Rhetoric*, Analecta Vlatadon, 17 (Thessaloniki: Patriarchikno Hidryma Paterikon Meleton, 1973), 117–26.

What I propose is to show how remarkably this ancient theologian fits our postmodern situation — precisely because he is a confessing Christian and a master rhetorician. He knows the power of rhetorical theology and embodies it in his practice. He has absorbed the philosophical rhetoric of Plato and Aristotle, neither of whom allowed the study of rhetoric to be confined to technical maneuvers.[9] Plato fiercely attacked Gorgias, but in his *Phaedrus* he indicated that the ways that positions were expressed had no small influence on whether or not an audience accepted them. As too many students of his philosophy forget to emphasize, he used dialogue form and rich depictions of conversations to make his points. Similarly, Aristotle designed his rhetoric, specifically the enthymeme, to deal with human questions that were not susceptible to formal syllogistic treatment.[10]

There is little doubt that Nazianzen was in extraordinary control of most all the techniques available to a rhetorician; yet he despised a narrow definition of rhetoric that limited it to techniques. Only hacks depended upon technical rhetoric alone. The compelling issue was how humans faced numerous questions that could not be worked out through a single logic with universally valid results. That was particularly true of the overwhelming queries of theology. For Gregory, rhetoric provided theology with an alternative epistemology.

---

[9] I have treated Gregory's acceptance of philosophical rhetoric in *Faith Gives Fullness to Reasoning: The Five Theological Orations of Gregory Nazianzen*, Supplements to Vigiliae Christianae 13 (Leiden: E.J. Brill, 1991), 17–39. The conception of "philosophical rhetoric" as opposed to "technical rhetoric" is best found in the description of Plato's work by George Kennedy, *A History of Rhetoric*, vol. 1, *The Art of Persuasion in Greece* (Princeton: Princeton University Press, 1963), 61–66, 74–79, 82–114. Also see William Grimaldi, "Studies in the Philosophy of Aristotle's Rhetoric," reprinted in *Landmark Essays on Aristotelian Rhetoric*, eds. Richard L. Enos and Lois P. Agnew (Mahwah, N.J.: Lawrence Erlbaum Associates, 1998), 15–159 and his *Aristotle, Rhetoric I: A Commentary* (New York: Fordham University Press, 1980).

[10] Aristotle well may have been at his best when he recognized that dialectic was a "greenhouse flower" while rhetoric was a "plant growing in the open air of the city and public places" (Jacques Brunschwig, "Aristotle's *Rhetoric* as a 'Counterpart' to Dialectic," *Essays on Aristotle's Rhetoric*, ed. Amélie Oksenberg Rorty [Berkeley: University of California Press, 1996], 51). Christian theology often made its appeals in cities.

In Gregory's view, a confessing Christian begins with a rather sophisticated sense that our knowledge of God is limited. We know what God lets us know, because our minds are far to small to encompass who God is. God's existence is clear enough, but exact, complete definitions of God are impossible.[11] The point is not that all theology must be entirely apophatic, always saying only what God is not. There are things about God that must be stated in kataphatic form; if you want to talk about two times five, it would be better to say "ten" on occasion rather than "not one," "not two," *ad infinitum*.[12] Therefore, confess that God is Father (but not male),[13] both Trinity and Unity.[14] Recognize that God is the great persuader who cajoles and woos in an attempt to convince creation to return to the ways instilled in it — and instilled particularly in the people God originally formed. God went through two covenants, slowly treating us as would a teacher or a doctor.[15]

God's nature is not revealed only in alpha-privative nouns: impassible, uncreated, unbegotten, and so on. From Nazianzen's perspective, one of the odd things about his opponents, the Neo-Arians, is that they apparently claim to know the nature of God so thoroughly that they understand it as well as God does. When reading the debate, one suspects that the charge may be false (or at least trumped up). Yet the Neo-Arians do insist that their knowledge of God's nature is encapsulated in the word "unbegotten" — that God is ultimately describable in a term that designates what God is not. When they speak positively, they assert that names designate essences (although sometimes names can be used in proper and improper senses). Gregory wonders how one determines such issues. How do I know that a "dog" is more "dog" than a "dogshark"? "Nothing attached to the names

---

[11]*Or.* 28.6, *PG* 36, 32C–33B, *SC* 250, 110–12.

[12]*Or.* 28.9, *PG* 36, 37B, *SC* 250, 118.

[13]*Or.* 31.7, *PG* 36, 140D, *SC* 250, 288.

[14]*Ors.* 28–31, *PG* 36, 25C–172A, *SC* 250, 100–342 contain a significant number of references to trinitarian subjects.

[15]*Or.* 31.25, *PG* 36, 160D–161B, *SC* 250, 322–24.

forces that conclusion.... No, things of the same and things of a different status can have the same name."¹⁶

For the Theologian, such strife over words is dangerous nonsense. The great mystery of our faith may be severely weakened by finicky professions that presume to offer complete accuracy and unshakable foundations. What he sees people facing in the fourth century has strong similarities to what we face in the twenty-first century. His Oration 28 has a rather simple outline, developed with delicate detail. It resonates with the book of Job. When well-educated theologians look at nature, they find a series of conundrums that are unsolvable. They do not know nature well enough to say that it is entirely knowable and under human control. At an even deeper level, human nature is quite illusive. As people look within themselves, they discover neither clearly defined nor unquestionable principles stating whence they came and whither they are going. If nature around them (and human nature within them) has so many mysterious features, how could anyone claim to have precise, complete, and incontestable knowledge of God?

Any theology that begins with the utterly inconceivable character of God's ultimate nature provides a rich context for contemporary postmodern discussions. Gregory has things to assert about God, including long discussions of titles for the Father, Son and Holy Spirit; but much of what Scripture and Tradition state remains in a confession of the mystery — the unfathomable essence of the divine. No discussions of God can begin on a foundation that all people will intuitively grasp and universally accept.

It also bothers him that his opponents train inexperienced young men in logic and foist them on the Church as theologians. None of them understand that

> discussion of theology is not for everyone.... Nor, I would add, is it for every occasion, or every audience; neither are all its aspects open to inquiry. It must be reserved for certain occasions, for certain audiences, and certain limits must be observed. It is not for all, but only for those who have been tested and have found a sound footing in study, and more importantly, have undergone, or at the very least are undergoing, purification of body and soul. For one who is not pure to lay hold of pure

---

¹⁶*Or.* 29.14, *PG* 36, 92B–C, *SC* 250, 204–206. The translation is by Lionel Wickham in Norris, *Faith Gives Fullness to Reasoning*, 253–54.

things is dangerous, just as it is for weak eyes to look at the sun's brightness.[17]

The three-point rule of speaker, audience, and topic — along with the frequently-added fourth point, occasion[18] — reflects part of Aristotle's *Rhetoric*; it reinforces Gregory's accusation that neither the Neo-Arian teachers nor their students have grasped even the most basic points of rhetoric. Furthermore, they do not understand that theology should be formed by those who have matured in both study and purification. Gregory's point is not that being mindful of God is an infrequent practice; indeed, it is more important than breathing. But while faith is universal, theology is not for everyone — nor for every time, every place, or every topic.[19]

> It is not the continual remembrance of God I seek to discourage but the continual discussion of theology. I am opposed neither to theology, as if it were a breach of piety, but only to its untimely practice; nor to instruction in it, except when it goes to excess.[20]

Pagans have enough sense not to divulge all their mysteries to an unprepared audience, and their mysteries are not so grand as ours.[21]

In terms of twenty-first century postmodern assumptions, Gregory knows in a particular way that the readers' responses, and the hearers' perceptions, are deeply important. Pagans do not understand the words that theologians use; instead, they think of (what seem to us to be) the oddest associations when they hear Christians arguing. Christian debate

---

[17] *Or.* 27.3, *PG* 36, 13C–16A, *SC* 250, 76. The translation is by Frederick Williams in Norris, *Faith Gives Fullness to Reasoning*, 218, very slightly altered.

[18] On this point see the essay by Janet Weathers, chapter 2 of this volume.

[19] Aristotle in his *Rhetoric* 1356A discusses three of the four. He does not seem to be interested in "occasion" as Gregory is.

[20] *Or.* 27.4, *PG* 36, 16C, *SC* 250, 80. The translation is by Frederick Williams in Norris, *Faith Gives Fullness to Reasoning*, 219, very slightly altered.

[21] *Or.* 27.5, *PG* 36, 17B–C, *SC* 250, 82.

about the begetting of the Son by the Father is heard in the context of Kronos, who begat his offspring from his thigh and then ate them when he saw them as a threat.[22] According to Gregory, it is better to serve such audiences in acts of loving kindness with arms outstretched and tongues silent, until they can be given some chance of understanding. Practice comes first.

Another fruitful insight that the Theologian gained from his rhetorical study was the importance of poetry. He wrote forty-four orations of beautiful structure and phrasing, most of them homilies prepared for worship settings within the context of understanding that made them come alive. But he also authored a number of epigrams and 17,000 verses of poetry, including a sensitive autobiography that surpasses Augustine's *Confessions* (not in content, but in form). Because theology is confessional and occasional, its best practitioners should provide, indeed create (*poieō*), images and words that evoke deeper reactions from their readers and hearers.

> Our noblest theologian is not one who has discovered the whole — our earthly shackles do not permit us the whole — but one whose mental image is by comparison fuller, who has gathered in his mind a richer picture, outline, or whatever we call it, of the truth.[23]

Again, this view connects with contemporary discussion of rhetoric within postmodernism by noting that no human being can encompass the entire subject of theology. It also insists that the better the mental image, the richer the picture, the fuller the theology. Gregory's own orations, and particularly his poetry, show how much he himself took this advice to heart.

To balance his view, however, we must see that Nazianzen was not only a wordsmith but also a "lifesmith." The Theologian criticizes all who are overly focused on theological debate: "Why do we keep our hands bound and our tongues armed?"[24] He and the other Cappadocians, particularly

---

[22]*Or.* 31.16, *PG* 36, 152A, *SC* 250, 306.

[23]*Or.* 30.17, *PG* 36, 125A, *SC* 250, 260. The translation is by Lionel Wickham in Norris, *Faith Gives Fullness to Reasoning*, 274.

[24]*Or.* 27.7, *PG* 36, 20B, *SC* 250, 86.

Gregory of Nyssa, Basil of Caesarea and their sister Macrina the Younger, were deeply concerned about Christian practice. The three men wrote sermons concerning the poor, primarily centered on a desperate famine that struck the region. Both on the basis of Christ, who gave his life, and on the basis of the Greco-Roman sensibility of a patron, they implore the rich to provide for the poor rather than make a financial profit from their hoarded grain. Macrina created a convent that cared for the needy.

Twenty-first century liberation theologies can find support in what the Cappadocians tried to accomplish through the persuasive power of orations concerning the poor, ones that have seldom been translated into English because Western church historians often have not found such themes interesting. According to the Cappadocians, however, a theologian who does not serve is not a theologian. Basil of Caesarea went so far as to build a new city centered on a church, a monastery, a bishop's palace, and a hostel for pilgrims. The hostel grew into a hospital particularly for lepers and then, during a severe famine, became a large refuge for the starving and homeless. The new city was so successful that old Roman Caesarea eventually was abandoned for Basil's new city.[25]

Gregory of Nazianzus is also concerned with theory as we usually think of it, but he tends to use the word *theōria* in at least two senses. It can be compared and contrasted with practice in terms we might employ. But it can also speak of intellectual apprehension and/or spiritual meditation. Occasionally the two are put together or viewed as a further unity of *theōria* and *praxis*.[26] At the same time Gregory knows that a theologian who does not create images and analogies — who does not ransack the culture's

---

[25]Nazianzen in *Or.* 43.35–36, *PG* 36, 500B–501B, *Discours 42–43*, ed. Jean Bernardi, *SC* 384 (1992) describes this venture. In *Eps.* 94, 150 and 17, *Saint Basil: The Letters*, trans. Roy Deferrari, Loeb Classical Library, vol. 2 (Cambridge: Harvard University Press, 1962), 148–52, 360–70 and 458–60, Basil gives his own account. The best description of this project is the 1998 North American Patristic Society Presidential Address by Brian E. Daley, "Building a New City: The Cappadocian Fathers and the Rhetoric of Philanthropy," *The Journal of Early Christian Studies* 7 (1999), 431–61.

[26]For the unity and diversity of theory and practice see Thomas Spidlik, "La *theoria* et la *praxis* chez Grégoire de Nazianze," *Studia Patristica* 14 (1976): 358–64.

literature, philosophy and science for the best possible pictures to make aspects of the great mystery intelligible — is less than the best theologian.

Theology cannot rely upon a universal logic, for there are multiple logics. Aristotle's insistence on a law of non-contradiction, his "excluded middle," is false. When faced with an opponent who insists that the truth must be either A or non-A, one or the other, the educated, experienced philosophical rhetorician — who has studied much logic — knows that there are other options. Both A and non-A could be false or both could be true. The form of such a distinction does not constitute a compelling argument that imprisons all interested parties within its apparent conclusions.

Thus when the Theologian confronted Neo-Arian opponents (who insisted that the Son must either exist or not exist when he was begotten), Gregory replied that he would not fall into the trap. Apparent contradictories like the liar's paradox ("I am now telling a lie"), or questions of whether or not we are present to ourselves, or whether time is or is not "in" time, demand the consideration of what the paired statements might mean — meanings that are much wider than his antagonists suggest. It is not the case that one is true and the other false. They could also be either both true or both false.[27]

The rejection of a universal logic to which all theology must submit looks very much like some postmodern appeals — whether they occur within a totally relativistic context, or within a missional approach of contextualization or inculturation. Humans do not all think alike even when they are thinking correctly. Nazianzen did not work with several languages and cultures; he was primarily a Hellenist. However, we do not know (at least, not so well as we would like to know) how much Iranian influences still had force within his native Cappadocian family; nor do we know how much he knew of the indigenous Cappadocian language. He thought that Latin was an impossible language in which to do theology because it lacked the sophistication of Greek[28] — not an insight that many would defend

---

[27]*Or.* 29.9, *PG* 36, 85A–B, *SC* 250, 194. See my *Faith Gives Fullness to Reasoning*, 141–42 and Lionel Wickham's translation, 250–51.

[28]*Or.* 21.35, *PG* 36, 1124C–1125A, *Discours 20–23*, ed. Justin Mossay, *SC* 270 (1980), 184–86.

now. In any case, reason for him came in different packages, not just in one universally described and accepted form.

Because of his nagging sense of relativity, he has unexpectedly open views on other religions — ones that have seldom been grasped. In secondary works, the Theologian is noted for his vitriolic attacks on the emperor Julian's attempts to revive Greco-Roman religion. He had felt the fear that Julian inspired in Christians; near the time of the emperor's death; he had savaged him in two orations.[29] Yet there are other places within Gregory's work where he points out the truths which can be found among other religions.[30] The most pointed example relates to his father, who grew up in a Hypsistarii family within a religion that had Iranian roots and had effectively Hellenized its rites in various areas of the Roman empire. In the funeral oration for his father, a form that invited him to talk about his subject's grand family and early virtues, Gregory said:

> Even before he was of our fold, he was ours. His character made him one of us. For, as many of our own are not with us, whose life alienates them from the common body, so, many of those outside are on our side, whose character anticipates their faith, and need the name for the work they do. My father was one of those, an alien shoot, but inclined by his life toward us.[31]

This is reminiscent of Karl Rahner's conception of anonymous Christians; but its power lies primarily in an insight that should be read not *only* in terms of Rahner's developed analysis. Gregory's view does sit in a twenty-first century context rather lightly, insisting that truths are there in persons and communities of other faiths — even though mission, and thus the "name," are still important. At the very least, Nazianzen must not always

---

[29] *Ors.* 4–5, *PG* 35, 532A–719A, *Discours 4–5, Contre Julian*, ed. Jean Bernardi, SC 309 (1983).

[30] See my "Gregory the Theologian and Other Religions," *The Greek Orthodox Theological Review* 39 (1994), 131–40.

[31] *Or.* 18.6, *PG* 35, 989C–993A. Translation adapted from Charles Browne and James Swallow, *A Select Library of Nicene and Post-Nicene Fathers of the Christian Church*, 2nd Series (reprint Grand Rapids: Wm. B. Eerdmans, 1954), Vol. 7, 256.

be put within the framework of the old saw that insists that early Christianity accepted the philosophical heritage of Hellenism but overwhelmingly denied its religions. Gregory was critical of his era's received philosophy and religion, but could find important insights in each. He did not think that anyone could command all the truth or provide all proper expressions of the truth.

He had the appropriate and limited relativism of a rhetorician who knew that there was no one argument for every speaker, occasion, audience or case. That kind of relativism, however, was modified by his rhetorical education. I have shown elsewhere that the larger structure of his argument in Oration 33 apparently depends upon Hermogenes' *stasis* theory, concerning how one would argue a case before a judge or a senate. In the first part of the speech he attacks his opponents as if he were a prosecutor; in the second part, he speaks on his own behalf as a defense attorney. As a prosecutor, he insists that the facts of the case are clear. His antagonists had attacked his congregation while it was assembled in worship, and had even killed some of its people. The charges against the adversaries are certain and complete; there is neither a legal nor a rational defense for such actions.

In the second part, he speaks in his own behalf as a defense attorney. Here, the charges against him are certain but incomplete. He did grow up in a small town. His appearance is disappointing and his speech rustic. But the definition of the charge may be reshaped. Many biblical heroes are not remembered for their good looks. Neither did they grow up in large cities and gain the sophistication engendered by life in a metropolis. The citizenship of Christians is in the new Jerusalem, not Constantinople.

The reader of this oration is forced to the conclusion that Gregory's technical prowess is remarkable. He leaves no doubt that he has a range of tools at his disposal through which he, like a good lawyer, could argue any side of a case to his and his clients' advantage.[32]

---

[32] See my "The Theologian and Technical Rhetoric: Gregory of Nazianzus and Hermogenes of Tarsus," *Nova & Vetera: Patristic Studies in Honor of Thomas Patrick Halton*, ed. John Petruccione (Washington, DC: The Catholic University of America, 1998), 84–95.

At times his powers of grammatical analysis remind one of the insightful (post?)modern linguistic analysis of Ludwig Wittgenstein.[33] Along side Nazianzen's sense of grammar is an understanding that often the Christian community must present the gospel through deeds. But when God's fullest nature is unknowable, when other religions contain some truth, when there is no obvious public square in which all final decisions will be made, it is precisely *images* that evoke strong reactions and produce the best theology. Liturgy does not merely stand in the background in such theology; it is intimately a part of theology, because theology is driven by images. Gregory shows himself to be a master at this level as well. He preaches within the liturgical year at the various festivals, and opens different ways into history and heaven.

> Again my Jesus, and again a mystery; neither deceitful nor disorderly, nor belonging to Greek error or drunkenness (thus I speak of their rites, and so I think will everyone of sound judgment); but a mystery lofty and divine, and allied to Glory above. For the Holy Day of the Lights, to which we have come, and which we are celebrating today, has its beginning in the baptism of my Christ. He is the true Light who enlightens everyone who comes into the world and purifies me and assists that light which we received at our beginning from him above, but we darkened and confused by sin.... At his birth we properly keep the festival, both I, the leader of the feast, and you and all those in and above the world. With the Star we ran and with the Magi we worshiped, and with the Shepherds we were illuminated, and with the angels we glorified him and with Simeon we took him up in our arms, and with Anna, the aged and chaste, we made our responsive confession. And thanks be to him who came down to his own in the guise of a stranger because he glorified the stranger. Now we come to another action of Christ, another mystery. I cannot restrain my pleasure; I am rapt in God.[34]

---

[33] See my "Theology as Grammar: Gregory Nazianzen and Ludwig Wittgenstein," *Arianism after Arius*, ed. by Michel Barnes and Daniel H. Williams (Edinburgh: T. & T. Clark, 1993), 237–49.

[34] *Or.* 39.1 & 14, *PG* 36, 336A & 349B–352B, ed. Claudio Moreschini and trans. Paul Gallay, *SC* 358 (1990) 150 and 178–82. The translation is adapted from Browne and Swallow, *NPNF*, Second Series, Vol. 7, 352 and 357.

And again:

> God is light: the highest, the unapproachable, the ineffable, that can neither be conceived in the mind nor uttered with the lips, that gives light to every reasoning creature. He is, in the world of thought, what the sun is in the world of sense; presenting himself to our minds in proportion as we are cleansed; and loved in proportion as he is presented to our mind; and again, conceived in proportion as we love him, contemplating and comprehending himself and pouring himself out upon what is external to him. That light, I mean, which is contemplated in the Father and the Son and the Holy Spirit, whose riches are their unity of nature and the leaping out of their brightness.[35]

The Theologian can also put his talent to work on singular words or phrases. He is the first to use *perichōrēsis*, "interpenetration," as a term for the unity of the two natures in the person of Christ.[36] Within trinitarian theology, an analogous conception continues to be employed today.[37] At the end of Oration 31 he looks at a series of images for the Trinity, discusses the strengths and weaknesses of each, then returns to a Biblical analogy.[38] In ways that are most suited to the style of his time, he stacks images on top of each other, with the plan that some of them will make his point. Selected phrases still have their merit.

> What is the right time [for theology]? Whenever we are free from the mire and noise without, and our commanding faculty is not confused by

---

[35] *Or.* 40.5, *PG* 36, 364B–C, *SC* 358, 204–206. The translation is adapted from Browne and Swallow, *NPNF*, Second Series, Vol. 7, 361.

[36] *Ep.* 101.31, *PG* 37, 101C, *Lettres théologiques*, ed. Paul Gallay, *SC* 208, 48.

[37] See, for example, Leonardo Boff, *Trinity and Society*, trans. Paul Burns (Tunbridge Wells: Burns and Oates; Maryknoll, N.Y.: Orbis Books, 1988), 5–7, 134–48; Catherine Mowry LaCugna, *God For Us: The Trinity and Christian Life* (San Francisco: Harper/Collins, 1991), 270–78; David S. Cunningham, *These Three Are One: The Practice of Trinitarian Theology*, Challenges in Contemporary Theology (Oxford and Cambridge: Basil Blackwell, 1998), 180–81.

[38] *Or.* 31.31–33, *PG* 36, 169A–172A, *SC* 250, 338–42.

illusory, wandering images, leading us, as it were, to mix fine script with ugly scrawling, or sweet-smelling scent with slime.[39]

There is a creative poet at work in his brilliant description of Christ, built on a mass of Biblical phrases, but balanced so that a full Christology of human and divine natures is played out in a growing crescendo. His opponents have argued that Christ is not of the same divine nature as the Father, discussions that he thinks have been improperly formed. But the power of the liturgy, the balance that he finds in a mass of Biblical texts, can rectify the problems:

> As man he was baptized, but he absolved sins as God; he needed no purifying rites Himself — his purpose was to hallow water. As man he was put to the test, but as God he came through victorious — yes, bids us be of good cheer, because he has conquered the world. He hungered — yet he fed thousands. He is indeed "living heavenly bread." He thirsted — yet he exclaimed: "Whosoever thirsts, let him come to me and drink." Indeed he promised that believers would become fountains. He was tired — yet he is the "rest" of the weary and the burdened. He was overcome by heavy sleep — yet he goes lightly over the sea, rebukes winds, and relieves the drowning Peter. He pays tax — yet he uses a fish to do it; indeed he is emperor over those who demand the tax. He is called a "Samaritan, demonically possessed" — but he rescues the man who came down from Jerusalem and fell among thieves. Yes, he is recognized by demons, drives out demons, drowns deep a legion of spirits and sees the prince of demons falling like lightning. He is stoned, yet not hit; he prays, yet he hears prayer. He weeps, yet he puts an end to weeping. He asks where Lazarus is — he was a man; yet he raises Lazarus — he was God. He is sold, and cheap was the price — thirty pieces of silver; yet he buys back the world at the mighty cost of his own blood. A sheep, he is led to the slaughter — yet he shepherds Israel and now the whole world as well. A lamb he is dumb — yet he is "word," proclaimed by "the voice of one crying in the wilderness." He is weakened, wounded — yet he cures every disease and every weakness. He is brought up to the tree and nailed to it — yet by the tree of life he restores us. Yes, he saves even a thief crucified with him; he wraps all the visible world in darkness. He is given vinegar to drink, gall to eat — and who is he? Why, one who turned water into

---

[39]*Or.* 27.3, *PG* 36, 16A, *SC* 250, 76. The translation is by Frederick Williams in Norris, *Faith Gives Fullness to Reasoning,* 218.

wine, who took away the taste of bitterness, who is all sweetness and desire. He surrenders his life, yet he has power to take it again. Yes, the veil is rent, for things of heaven are being revealed, rocks split, and dead men have an earlier awakening. He dies, but he vivifies and by death destroys death. He is buried, yet rises again. He goes down to Hades, yet he leads souls up, ascends to heaven, and will come to judge quick and dead, and to probe discussions like these. If the first set of expressions starts you going astray, the second set takes your error away.[40]

Gregory is also a good storyteller. For him, narrative has the place that it often does in ancient rhetoric, particularly in the shape of funeral orations. Within a series of speeches on his father, his brother, and his sister, as well as a group of saints, he tells the stories of the family tradition behind the person honored. Furthermore, he has the good sense to understand the narrative structure of the Gospel itself — even when it is expressed within the various liturgical festivals that provide the context for a number of his most moving orations. At the same time he does not seem to worry about whether or not the best story is the one closest to the "facts" even as he knows them. He massages here and there, and is sometimes just utterly wrong (perhaps not knowingly), as when he speaks of great Cyprian and conflates stories about Cyprian of Carthage with those about Cyprian of Antioch. Indeed when he writes a long funeral oration on his friend Basil of Caesarea, the text works with Basil's biography in terms of the expectations of a Hellenistic funeral oration. But underneath is a subtext that argues for his own reputation, after he had resigned from the bishopric of Constantinople and was still angry at those who forced that move.[41] He seldom writes any straightforward text that does not have various layers within it. The more one knows of rhetoric and the Hellenistic milieu of the

---

[40]*Or.* 29.20, *PG* 36, 100C–101C, *SC* 250, 222. The translation is by Lionel Wickham in Norris, *Faith Gives Fullness to Reasoning*, 258–60. The same kinds of parallels in a shorter passage appear in his *Poemata Arcana* 2, *PG* 37, 406A–407A and Claudio Moreschini and David Sykes, *St Gregory of Nazianzus: Poemata Arcana*, Oxford Theological Monographs (Oxford: Clarendon Press, 1997), 8–9.

[41]See my "Your Honor; My Reputation," *Greek Biography and Panegyrics in Late Antiquity*, eds. Tomas Hägg and Philip Rousseau (Berkeley, CA: University of California Press, 2000), 140–59.

fourth century, the more one knows liturgy and scripture, the more one learns from what Gregory says.

It is not difficult to see how the postmodern shift, with its acute interests in rhetoric, can find in the Theologian an ally in framing rhetorical theologies shaped by something like his philosophical rhetoric. God is never well enough known to be described in logical propositions, syllogistically argued and organized into a final system — even if that system is meant only for a particular age. Theology's roots should be closer to scripture and liturgy than any universal logic, not the least because the latter does not exist. If theology is confessional, it must be rhetorical: intimately related to its authors, occasions, audiences and topics. It is not formless, nor toothless; it is a much more sobering and sophisticated process than many have understood. The limited relativism of rhetoric suits theology's needs. There is a point to every oration, poem, and aphorism; but that point cannot be expressed in one single way. Indeed all our senses of knowledge and our logics are plural. In the end, only faith gives fullness to reasoning:

> When we abandon faith to take the power of reason as our shield, when we use philosophical inquiry to destroy the credibility of the Spirit, then reason gives way in the face of the vastness of the realities. Give way it must, set going, as it is, by the frail organ of human understanding. What happens then? The frailty of our reasoning looks like a frailty in our creed. Thus it is as Paul too judges, smartness of argument is revealed as nullifying the Cross. Faith, in fact, is what gives fullness to our reasoning.[42]

Human beings have no choice but to live inside a practicing community that speaks within its own confines of its own hallowed mysteries. This is not just the case for Christians, but for every human community. Such a community moves only with great care into a public square where it understands it must speak; it makes its case best when it does so with its hands untied and its tongues disarmed. It knows that its dearest images and words are often heard as nonsense: they may become reasons for ridicule or emerge as bases for the establishment of what it considers to be horrid conceptions. Gregory's theory and practice of rhetorical theology can help

---

[42] *Or.* 29.21, PG 36, 101D–104A, SC 250, 224. The translation is by Lionel Wickham in Norris, *Faith Gives Fullness to Reasoning*, 260.

us think through this process of moving from within the interpretive community to outside it.⁴³

The Theologian's faith is orthodox; he deepened the sense of the Holy Spirit as God. He has a gospel to preach. But he was a man of his times, and is not always a sufficient guide for contemporary problems. He cannot be appropriated romantically as the prime example of how premodernity anticipates all postmodern concerns. Personally, he was something of a whiner, proud and too often wounded (*ēthos*). Educationally he was so enmeshed in his Hellenistic culture that he cannot clearly provide many of the cross-cultural insights demanded by our recognized multi-cultural worlds (*pathos*). Hermeneutically, he sometimes employs texts in ways which moderns and postmoderns would find questionable (*logos*). Other points indicate that he plays with what some would identify as deadly modern concerns. Foucault would find his choice of ascetic discipline and well-defined propriety to be anything but postmodern.⁴⁴

Yet when he conceptualizes what God reveals and states it so that his audiences (originally hearers, and now, readers) join in the process of understanding, he overflows with insight. He finds being a theologian devilishly hard work, yet ultimately a gracious gift from the Spirit — best received in response to our pious life, "in but not of" the world. For Gregory, it also demands the deepest study of culture that anyone can imagine. How do people think? In what ways do they express themselves? He is certainly right on one important count: rhetorical theologies are the only games in town.

---

⁴³See Don Compier's essay on "Public Theology," chapter 7 of this volume.

⁴⁴In *Or.* 27.4–5, *PG* 36, 16B–17C, *SC* 250, 78–84, those concerns loom large for Gregory. Foucault, within many of his works, has found such things to be devastatingly misguided. In one of his rebukes of the propriety of Christian asceticism that appears in *Essential Works of Foucault 1954–1984*, Vol. 1, *Ethics: Subjectivity and* Truth, ed. Paul Rabinow, trans. Robert Hurley et al. (New York: New Press, 1997), 207–208, he scolds Athanasius, Evagrius and John Cassian. I listen to Foucault's critiques and at times find them persuasive, but here I read Gregory's concerns neither as narrow nor as misplaced.

Chapter 11

Rhetoric and Christian Doctrine: Trinity and Teaching

David S. Cunningham

The contributors to this volume are convinced that the faculty of *rhetoric* has something significant to offer to the task of theological education. In support of this claim, they offer a number of warrants — including, for example, explorations of the rhetorical features of the biblical texts, examples of classical theologies that have employed a rhetorical approach, and analyses of the *usefulness* of rhetoric for the tasks of theology (such as testimony, discernment, and communication). In this essay, I want to offer a different kind of warrant — a *doctrinal* warrant, in fact — for a rhetorical approach to theological education. I want to propose the (perhaps rather audacious) claim that Christian teachings about *the very nature of God* provide us with good reasons for looking to the rhetorical tradition to provide an integrated vision for theological education.

This chapter comprises four parts. The first part offers a thumbnail sketch of classical trinitarian doctrine, focusing on the language of *processions* and *relations* in God that developed as part of the medieval synthesis. In the second part, I describe the traditional theological process through which these trinitarian claims are understood as infusing Christian life and thought (and indeed, the entire created order): the tradition of identifying "triune marks" (or what Augustine called *vestigia trinitatis*). The third section constructs some parallels between classical trinitarian doctrine and the classical rhetorical tradition, suggesting that the latter can be understood as a triune mark. In the final section, I offer some concrete proposals as to how theological education, by becoming more "rhetorically" structured, might simultaneously become more "trinitarian" — and therefore more coherent with Christian claims about the nature of God. In this way, the theological work of "teaching" can come more into line with perhaps the most important "teaching" (*doctrina*) of the Christian faith.

Classical Trinitarian Doctrine

For a description of the *processions* and *relations* that have helped to form traditional trinitarian theology, I turn to the *Summa Theologiae* of St. Thomas Aquinas. Thomas is clearly drawing on the tradition he has inherited; many of his claims could be just as easily illustrated from the work of Sts. Gregory of Nazianzus or Augustine (though in those cases, certain details would vary). But Thomas has already put this account together for us in a rather tidy package, so we can make a start by listening to the story as he tells it. I will also offer a number of interpretive comments of my own.

Thomas begins by considering what we may know of God on the basis of what has been revealed to us. He answers that we may know that there are two processions in God: the procession of the Word, which he calls generation or begetting (*generatio*), and the procession of Love, which — because it is the procession of the Spirit — is called "spiration" (*spiratio*; Leonardo Boff translates, more helpfully, "breathing out"[1]). Despite the fact that Thomas employs abstract terms, the processions are fundamentally based on the biblical account of God's revelation through Christ and the Spirit. Indeed, Thomas's first argument (ST Ia.27.1) for the whole idea of "processions in God" is a quotation of John 8:42 — the words of Jesus, "I came forth from God."[2]

God, then, is an internally self-differentiated being. At first, this seems similar to the neo-Platonic descriptions of "emanations" that flow forth

---

[1] Leonardo Boff, *Trinity and Society*, trans. Paul Burns (Tunbridge Wells: Burns and Oates; Maryknoll, N.Y.: Orbis Books, 1988), 90–91.

[2] Quotations, cited by part, question, and article, are from the Blackfriars edition: St. Thomas Aquinas, *Summa Theologiae*, 60 vols. (New York: McGraw-Hill Book Company; London: Eyre and Spottiswoode, 1963–70).

from God, forming a great chain of being in which all beings participate to a greater or lesser degree (depending on their distance from God). But that picture is decisively altered in the Christian tradition, in that the divine emanations do not flow forth and animate the created order; rather, they are described as wholly *internal* to God.[3] Moreover, this is not merely an act of self-duplication on God's part; it is an act of self-abandonment, a giving up of oneself in order that there might be an Other to oneself.[4]

The idea of an "internally self-differentiated being" is a difficult one; in the created order, there are no perfect analogies to describe it. Yet because Thomas's discussion of this matter is highly technical, a concrete example will be needed, however imperfect it may be. The best example, in my view, is one that was not available to Thomas:[5] it is the example of pregnancy. The formation of the children in a woman's womb is a good example of "going forth from oneself," which is the notion behind the divine processions: the mother gives her own self to the "other" within her, becomes "other" to herself, yet does not thereby diminish herself. Again, the analogy is not perfect; she does not do this as a pure act of her own will, and the production of the "other" is not entirely internal, since it requires at least one sperm cell. Nevertheless, despite its imperfections, this analogy will help us think about the concept of internal, self-differentiating processions. We will return to it again as Thomas develops his argument.

The processions within God would seem to imply relations within God; and in question 28, Thomas examines the idea of "real relations" (*relationes reales*, ST Ia.28.1.). A "real" relation is not merely logical or external; it belongs to the very nature of an act (as in the relations of giving a gift and receiving it), and is not merely accidental (as in the relations among the books scattered across my desk). Real relations also arise when something has the same nature as that from which it comes; in that case, "both that which issues and that from which it issues belong to the same order; and so

---

[3]John Milbank, *Theology and Social Theory: Beyond Secular Reason*, Signposts in Theology (Oxford: Basil Blackwell, 1990), 428.

[4]See Hans Urs von Balthasar, *Theo-Drama: Theological Dramatic Theory*, vol. III, *Dramatis Personae: Persons in Christ* (San Francisco: Ignatius Press, 1993), 518, 526.

[5]Not available, because of the biology of his era, which claimed that the woman was a merely passive vessel in matters of reproduction, and therefore gave nothing of significance to the child.

must have real relationships with each other" (ST Ia.28.1). Since the divine processions are of the same nature as the source from which they come, they give rise to real relations in God.

Note that Thomas has not yet spoken of divine "persons"; indeed, in these questions he mentions the traditional terms *Pater, Filius,* and *Spiritus Sanctus* only rarely. The real relations described here are not relations *among* individuals; rather, they are deduced from the internal divine processions. If there are two processions, there must be four real relations; each procession implies two relations, signifying the two perspectives from which each procession can be viewed (for example, the bestowal of a gift can be characterized as a relation of giving or a relation of receiving). Thomas names these relations *paternitas, filiatio, spiratio, et processio* (ST Ia.28.4), which I translate: initiation, fruition, issuance, and emergence.[6]

I want to underscore the *active* way in which these relations are here described. This is not the static language of fixed and isolated entities; the processions and relations tend to imply one another, and thus to evoke movement and flux. These active forms are primary for Thomas, and are solidly in place when he turns to discuss substantive terms for God (ST Ia.29). He does so by examining the Latin word *persona* (which traditionally designated that of which there were three in God). He asks whether it signifies a relation; and is answer his that it does, and specifically, a *subsistent relation* (*significat relationem ut subsistentem,* ST Ia.29.4).

To "subsist" is to be self-grounded, to exist in and of oneself, and not to be dependent on some other thing. A "subsistent relation" is thus not an easy concept to grasp, since we are generally accustomed to thinking about individual entities who *have* relations, or who *enter into* relations, rather than about relations that just "are." Relations, to us, seem to be dependent upon the presupposed "beings" that are "in relation"; but this habit of thinking results from our increasing tendency to assume that nouns are the basic building blocks of language. We like nouns because they seem imply some degree of fixity and permanence in the midst of the swirling, chaotic

---

[6]An *apologia* for these idiosyncratic translations appears in David S. Cunningham, *These Three Are One: The Practice of Trinitarian Theology* (Oxford: Blackwell, 1998), 65–71, from which some of the reflections in this chapter are drawn.

realm of language. They have, in Catherine Pickstock's words, "a hardness as of cut stone."[7]

But our enthusiasm for the supposed permanence of substantives appears to be a relatively recent development.[8] Thomas still lived in the age of the triumph of the verb, an age in which active, "verbal" relations *precede* the substantive entities that are "in" relation. Likewise, Thomas emphasizes that the "threeness" of God is not an instance of three individual entities who enter into a relation. The divine "Three"[9] are a secondary and derivative concept; the divine processions are primary. The Three are not "individuals" who come into relation; they are not "endpoints," between and among which there are relations; they are, rather, "relations without remainder."[10]

As I noted above, Thomas is building on the insights of St. Augustine, the Cappadocians, and an entire tradition of trinitarian thought; his claims here are not particularly new.[11] But to modern readers, they are (as I have

---

[7]Catherine Pickstock, *After Writing: On the Liturgical Consummation of Philosophy*, Challenges in Contemporary Theology (Oxford and Cambridge: Basil Blackwell, 1997), 89–95.

[8]See the comments of Michel de Certeau concerning "the de-throning of the verb" in *The Mystic Fable*, vol. 1, *The Sixteenth and Seventeenth Centuries*, trans. Michael B. Smith (Chicago and London: University of Chicago Press, 1992), 125. My thanks to Nicholas Lash for pointing me toward this passage; note also Lash's own use of verbal forms throughout his book *Believing Three Ways In One God: A Reading of the Apostles' Creed* (Notre Dame, Ind.: University of Notre Dame Press, 1992).

[9]The use of the phrase "the Three" is my tentative solution to the vexed question of what substantive to use to describe that of which there are three in God. For a critique of the contemporary English alternatives, and a justification of this term as a substitute, see *These Three Are One*, 27–29.

[10]Nicholas Lash uses the phrase "relationship without remainder" to describe God in *Believing Three Ways in One God*, 32.

[11]Cf. Gregory of Nazianzus *Or.* 29.16; Augustine *de Trin.* 5–7; for a summary of Augustine's views, with bibliography, see J. N. D. Kelly, *Early Christian Doctrines*, 5th ed. (San Francisco: HarperSanFrancisco, 1978), 274–75; on its importance, see John Milbank, "Can a Gift Be Given? Prolegomena to a Future Trinitarian Metaphysic," *Modern Theology* 11/1 (January 1995): 119–161; here, 150–54.

just noted) somewhat counterintuitive. As Robert Jenson comments, "our inherited ways of thinking suppose that — obviously! — there must first be *things* that in the second place may be variously related. But there is nothing intrinsically obvious about it; in fact, by biblical insight it is the other way round."[12] In the biblical narratives (as in most narratives), individuals are not defined in the abstract and then shown to be related to one another; the character of persons becomes apparent only by means of their relatedness to others. This biblical insight was the starting-point for the systematic formulation developed over the centuries (which Thomas systematizes here).

I will not provide a detailed description of Thomas's extremely technical account of why, if there are *four* real relations in God, there are nevertheless only *three* subsistent relations. Suffice it to say that this difference is related to the Western insistence that the Spirit proceed from the Father *and the Son* (*filioque*), and that this theological presupposition necessarily leads to the numerical difference that he describes.[13] Of more interest to us here is the fact that Thomas does not use the same words to describe the subsistent relations as he used to describe their corresponding real relations. For the latter he used the more verbal and relational terms *paternitas, filiatio*, and *processio*; but for the former he uses the rather individualizing substantives *Pater, Filius*, and *Spiritus sanctus*. This move is understandable, because (1) Thomas wants to provide a mark of difference between the real relations and the subsistent ones; (2) he wants to provide a reminder that the subsistent relations are self-grounded, that they have at least a temporary stability, allowing us to refer to them as entities (which is easier to do with substantive names than with verbal, relational forms); and (3) he wants to describe them by using the names for the Three that are woven into the biblical narratives and that have therefore dominated the history of the tradition. Unfortunately, however, in the process, he dispenses with any need to continue to employ the strongly verbal (and thus, more active and relational) terms that he first used to describe them (I translated them *initiation, fruition*, and *emergence*). These verbal terms are

---

[12]Robert W. Jenson, *The Triune Identity: God According to the Gospel* (Philadelphia: Fortress Press, 1982), 123.

[13]Readers anxious to delve into the details may consult *These Three Are One*, 60–62.

replaced with relatively static substantives. These terms still imply relation at some level, but the hearers of these terms rarely bring those relational elements to mind.

Thus, when we hear the English words offered as ordinary translations of the Latin substantives — *Father, Son,* and *Holy Spirit* — we do not normally call to mind the real (and verbal and active) relations from which, as Thomas insists, these names are ultimately derived. Instead, we think of them as separate entities, as distinct centers of consciousness — in short, as isolated individuals. And as a result, one of the most important claims of trinitarian theology — that the divine Three are most fundamentally *relations* — is lost from our view.[14] (We could note a similar problem with the use of substantives to designate the relations in pregnancy: once we begin to speak of "mother" and "child," we tend to assume that they can be defined in isolation from one another — a tendency that is evident on all sides in the current politics of pregnancy.)

I do not mean to blame St. Thomas for our tendency to "miss" the notion of relationality with which he hoped to invest the words *Pater, Filius, et Spiritus Sanctus.* In his context, their relational qualities may have been clearer; and we may, by means of thoughtful translation, help to repristinate those qualities.[15] On the other hand, it may simply be the case that *any* naming of the divine persons by static substantives will make it difficult to remember that the Three are *relations*. As readers and listeners, when we hear three nouns, we think of three entities; any relations, we assume, would need to be *among* these entities. But when we hear three verbal forms, such as "initiation, fruition, and emergence" — we are probably less likely to think in terms of stasis and potential isolation, and more likely to think in terms of motion and relation.

We have now followed the rather arduous path that was trod by a great many trinitarian theologians through the early and medieval eras of Christian thought, as summarized by St. Thomas. We began with the biblical affirmations of processions in God; from them we derived the real

---

[14]Its significance is underscored by Robert Jenson, who describes it as "the main place at which the metaphysically revolutionary power of the gospel breaks out in Western theology" (*Triune Identity*, 123).

[15]See, for example, my use of the formula "Source, Wellspring, and Living Water" throughout *These Three Are One*.

relations; and we noted that three of these are subsistent relations. We concluded by noting that our substantive terms for the divine Three tend to obscure their active, relational nature.

Having traced this process, we are in a better position to find ways of resisting the tendency to think of the Three as isolated individuals who *have* relations, or who make a decision to *come into* relation. Instead, we can begin to understand the Three as "relations without remainder," constituted by the two processions that are internal to God. And having done so, we are better prepared to consider the implications of trinitarian doctrine for theological method in general and for the task of theological education in particular.

For if the doctrine of the Trinity is as central to the Christian faith as theologians have often declared it to be, it should impinge on every element of Christian life and thought. We should expect theological method, biblical interpretation, historical theology, preaching, and pastoral care to bear a "trinitarian" character. And this in turn would suggest that theological education must also bear this character — not only within each of its subdisciplines, but also with respect to its overall structure. But the claim that these theological tasks must be *trinitarian* will need to mean more than simply invoking the name of the Trinity when carrying them out. Rather, we should be considering how the trinitarian character of the Christian faith might come to permeate all that we do. Fortunately, one possible way of thinking about this question has already been provided for us.

Triune Marks[16]

In Book 13 of the *Confessions*, Augustine complains briefly about the endless debates and quarrels in which Christians seem to be engaged concerning their various speculations on the Trinity. He suggests an alternative:

> I wish that human disputants would reflect upon the triad within their own selves. These three aspects of the self are very different from the

---

[16]Much of this section appears in a slightly different form in David S. Cunningham, "Interpretation: Toward a Rehabilitation of the Vestigia Tradition," chap. 7 in *Knowing the Triune God: The Work of the Spirit in the Practices of the Church*, ed. James J. Buckley and David Yeago (Grand Rapids, Mich.: William B. Eerdmans, 2001), 177–200.

Trinity, but I may make the observation that on this triad they could well exercise their minds and examine the problem, thereby becoming aware how far distant they are from it.[17]

Here Augustine sounds a theme that he will take up again, in much greater detail, in *De Trinitate*. There, he draws on Romans 1:20 in particular as an invitation to offer a triadic reading of structures in the created order — but one that refers back, constantly, to the Triunity of God: "As we direct our gaze at the creator by understanding the things that are made, we should recognize the Trinity, whose mark appears in creation in a way that is fitting."[18]

The word that I have here translated as *mark* is the Latin *vestigium*, from which we also derive the English word *vestige*. In English, it has two standard definitions: (1) a visible sign of something that is no longer physically present, or (2) a very slight amount of one entity that is present in another. Unfortunately, neither of these definitions is wholly satisfactory as a rendering of Augustine's concept. The first one would depict a God who creates the world and then abandons it (leaving us the task of deciphering the divine fingerprints); the second one would suggest that God places little bits of divinity into the created order, vaguely reminiscent of some of the gnostic redeemer myths. Since neither of these clusters of meaning can adequately describe Augustine's project, I will not use the English word *vestige* to describe it. In fact, the two definitions contribute to a false dichotomy — suggesting that God must either be "in" creation in some sort of quasi-pantheistic sense, or else that God must be wholly absent from creation, like a divine watchmaker who now has better things to do. Neither story is the Christian story; we believe that the God who created the world (as something radically other-than-God) is the same God who became flesh in order to redeem the world, and who is poured out on all flesh in order to sanctify the world. God's full-scale engagement and

---

[17] Augustine, *Confessions* XIII.xi; trans. Henry Chadwick (Oxford: Oxford University Press, 1992), 279.

[18] Augustine *De trin.* VI.10(12). Translation (slightly altered) from *The Works of Saint Augustine: A Translation for the 21st Century*, vol. 5, *The Trinity*, ed. and trans. with an Introduction by Edmund Hill, O.P., (Brooklyn, N.Y.: New City Press, 1991), 213.

involvement cannot underwrite a sharp dichotomy of identity-or-absence. God is wholly other than the world, yet constantly involved with it.[19]

In an attempt to avoid the "presence-or-absence" dichotomy posed by the typical uses of the English word *vestige*, I have instead employed the word *mark*. Even though a person who "made a mark" or "left a mark" is no longer *physically* present, the very act of deliberately "leaving one's mark" can imply both an *interest* in the other (a mark can be left *for* someone) and a degree of *personal involvement*. These latter aspects of the word's usage suggest that the *source* of the mark can continue to have an influence — perhaps even a certain "presence" — in spite of certain signs of "absence." In employing the phrase "triune marks," I may not evoke all the resonances that Augustine hoped to call to his readers' minds by means of the phrase *vestigia trinitatis*; nevertheless, this translation seems an improvement over the current alternatives.

As is well known, Augustine goes on in the later books of *De Trinitate* to offer a large number of threefold *vestigia*: the lover, the beloved, and love; the mind, its knowledge, and its love; memory, understanding, and will; man, woman, and child; and many others (twenty different ones are listed in the index to a recent translation of *De Trinitate*[20]). Some of these Augustine mentions only briefly, then quickly discards; others he develops at great length. In every case, though, he eventually observes that the particular *vestigium* fails to mirror the Trinity perfectly, and that each one has specific inadequacies in addition to the more general point that no *vestigium* can provide a complete and unmistaken account of that which produced it. "There are not a number of such trinities, experience of some of which could enable us ... to believe that the divine Trinity is similar."[21]

---

[19] Here it may be useful to consider the traditional category of divine "missions" — the incarnation of the Word and the sending of the Spirit. The word *mission* itself tends to evoke *engagement* in spite of *otherness*; "going on a mission" requires us to care enough about a task to leave our comfortable surroundings and venture into foreign territory.

[20] Joseph Sprug, indexer, in Hill, ed., *The Trinity*, s.v. trinities, 469.

[21] Augustine *De Trin.* VIII.8, trans. from *Augustine: Later Works*, ed. John Burnaby, Library of Christian Classics, vol. 8 (Philadelphia: Westminster Press, 1955), 46.

Augustine picks up the same theme, in a more condensed form, in *The City of God*. Here, he suggests that the doctrine of creation itself grounds the expectation that *vestigia* will appear in creation.

> If the divine goodness is nothing other than the divine holiness, then certainly we are being reasonably diligent, and not excessively presumptuous, in inquiring whether, in the works of God, this same Trinity is not suggested to us (in an enigmatic form of speech, intended to catch our attention) whenever we ask of each creature: 'Who made it? And by what means? And why?'[22]

Augustine then discusses the role of the whole Trinity in creation, suggesting that the Three correspond, respectively, to the three questions that he raises at the end of this passage: they are maker, means, and purpose. Consequently, says Augustine, "the whole Trinity is revealed to us in its works."[23] He notes echoes of this revelation in the created order, and especially in humankind — created the image of God.

In encouraging us to "read the created order" with attention to its triune marks, Augustine is not suggesting that the creation will "lead us" to its Creator. Rather, he believes that, if we become *active interpreters* of the world around us, our knowledge of God will become sharper, more acute. When we inquire about the maker, the means, and the purpose of creation, the wholly other God is, in some sense, "made present" to us — albeit in veiled and cryptic ways. In the very process of our interpretive acts, God's triune character is enigmatically suggested to us. God is neither immanent in creation nor simply absent; rather, God is active in creation in ways that have certain effects, such that one might reasonably speculate on the relationship between the created effects and the One who produces them.

Augustine's description of the *vestigia* tradition can help us think about the implications of the Christian doctrine of God for a wide range of Christian practices. Unfortunately, however, in spite of the good use to which Augustine and many others have employed this tradition, it has been

---

[22] Augustine *De civ. Dei* XI.24; my translation.

[23] Augustine *De civ. Dei* XI.24. Translation, altered, from that of Marcus Dods in *The City of God* (New York: The Modern Library, 1950), 369.

the subject of significant critique.[24] Indeed, it is often dismissed as a relic of the theological past; Colin Gunton, for example, speaks of the "famous and futile quest for analogies of the Trinity in the created world." Their "weakness," he claims, "is their employment as attempts to illustrate the divine Trinity: the world is used to throw light on God, rather than the other way round."[25] The familiar dichotomy once again rears its head: the assumption seems to be that theological knowledge has its origins *either* in God alone, *or* in the world alone — and that the former is legitimate while the latter is illegitimate. This further implies that the practice of *interpreting the created order* cannot actually contribute to our knowledge of God; for this would be to usurp a task that is properly God's alone.

But if we recognize the falseness of this dichotomy, we can develop a coherent response to the critique of this tradition. I have elsewhere offered such a response at length;[26] I will not attempt to repeat that argument here, except to say that, once we have extricated ourselves from the false dilemma of God's "presence in or absence from" the world, Augustine's faith in the *vestigia* tradition seems clearer and more justified. Admittedly, the exploration of God's "triune marks" must be undertaken with caution; we must always reason *from* God *to* the created order (and not the other way around). But when we do so, we employ an important tool for understanding how the doctrine of the Trinity can infuse every aspect of Christian thought and practice.

Rhetorical Invention as a Triune Mark

In this section, I want to explore the possibility that the process of rhetorical invention might be considered a *vestigium trinitatis* or "triune mark." By "rhetorical invention," I mean that preparatory process, prior to

---

[24]The most influential of these critiques is probably that of Karl Barth, in *Church Dogmatics* (Edinburgh: T. & T. Clark, 1958–1969), volume I/1, section 8.2 ("The Root of the Doctrine of the Trinity").

[25]Colin Gunton, "Trinity, Ontology, and Anthropology: Towards a Renewal of the Doctrine of the *Imago Dei*," in *Persons, Divine and Human*, ed. Christoph Schwöbel and Colin Gunton (Edinburgh: T. & T. Clark, 1991), 55, n. 18; see also *The One, The Three and the Many* (Cambridge: Cambridge University Press, 1993), 144, n. 23.

[26]Particularly the essay "Interpretation," cited in note 16, above.

the presentation of a persuasive appeal, in which a person attempts to "discover" all the means of persuasion that might be available in a particular case.[27] In Roman rhetoric, this process was called *inventio* — the "invention" or "creation" of an argument (as opposed to the processes of memorization, delivery, and so on). One might think of an attorney planning a summarizing statement, or a politician getting ready to deliver a campaign speech, or a pastor preparing a sermon. (The argument applies to the process of writing as well, with certain necessary changes; but for clarity and simplicity, I will here focus on oral communication.[28]) My focus here is not on the "empirical" process of persuasion that takes place when someone stands(for example) at the bar in a courtroom, behind the podium at a political rally, or in the pulpit of a church. Rather, I want to attend to the activity of those who are *preparing* to persuade a particular audience to take a certain course of action. I want to suggest that the process of rhetorical invention can be understood in parallel to the description of the divine processions and relations.

The General Form of the Analogy

The process of rhetorical invention includes two activities in which such persons must "go forth from themselves" and become "other" to themselves. These two "processions" concern (1) the formulation of the words that will be written or spoken; and (2) the process of "stepping outside oneself" into the position of the audience, so that one can imagine how the language will be received. We can refer to these two processions as "the production of language" and "the construction of the audience."

Persuasion takes place through some form of communication. Its goal is to move the audience to take particular actions — such as returning a certain verdict, voting for a certain candidate, or living a certain kind of life. In these instances, at least, communication requires the use of language — though we would probably want to define language in the broadest possible way. It could be any system of symbols; a gesture, such as hand waved

---

[27]See the exposition of this concept and its importance in chapter 1 of the present volume.

[28] This is not to deny to extraordinary differences between writing and speech, explored at length in the work of Walter Ong, Jacques Derrida, Catherine Pickstock, and many others.

in the air, could be language in this respect. Often it is a combination of words and gestures; but the gestures are often meaningful only because of a certain form of words that has accompanied or preceded them. In any case, persuasion involves the production of language.

We can consider this production from two perspectives — depending on whether we are thinking about the process from the "inside looking out" or from the "outside looking in." This gives rise to two relations, which we could name as "speaking" and "being spoken." Note that these two relations are wholly dependent on each other; we can imagine an event of "speaking" only if something is "being spoken," and something is spoken only if someone speaks.

Of course, in our ordinary discussion of this activity — as I noted above with respect to trinitarian language — we tend to move immediately from these verbal, relational forms to specific names; thus, we usually describe the process of the production of persuasive language *not* as "two relations" of speaking and being spoken, but as something that requires a speaker and a speech. Notice, however, what happens as a result: we quickly forget that these two are dependent on one another. We assume that we can abstract the speech from its context — and then reprint it, circulate it, ask someone else to deliver it, and so on. And we assume that the speaker can walk away from this process, going on about her daily business — most of which has nothing to do with her relation to this particular speech. But this picture is faulty, because (as was more clear when we were using verbal terms), the speaker and the speech depend upon each other for their very definition. Once the speech is reprinted, circulated, and so on, it is no longer what it originally was — that is, a discourse of words spoken by *this* person in *this* particular context. And once the speech has ended, the speaker is no longer a speaker. She may continue to be many other things (a human being, a worker, a daughter, a mother), but she is no longer the "speaker" in terms of the relational language we are using here.

The production of language is a necessary condition for persuasion, but not a sufficient one. By itself, without an "other" to whom it is directed, this language cannot persuade (nor even communicate); the relations of "speaking" and "being spoken" remain enclosed within a solipsistic world in which no one is "moved" to a change of will (which is, after all, the goal that persuasion seeks). The speaker may be speaking, but this language need not be intended for anyone in particular. Perhaps the speaker speaks a language of his own invention — a language no one else understands (others might not even recognize it as language). What is lacking in this scenario is an *externality* or *difference* — indeed, a "second difference," to use John Milbank's apt phrase.[29] The situation requires something that can bring the production of language out of its self-contained world and allow it to encounter that which is truly *other* to itself. In order for persuasion to occur, there must be more than a begetting of words. This process of language-production must go beyond itself — must "process," to use the theological term — so that it can be received and witnessed.

This other "procession" in the process of rhetorical invention also requires a "going-forth-from-oneself" — an act of stepping outside oneself, postulating oneself as an other. In this case, one must step into the position of the audience who will hear the speech. This is always a somewhat speculative endeavor, since the audience can never be known perfectly — and especially not ahead of time, when the various means of persuasion are being developed and discovered. One must ask oneself a number of very important questions about how the audience will receive the speech. Will they understand the language I am using? Will they recognize my references to literature, to current events, to popular culture? Will they remain interested enough in my speech to listen to it until the end? Will they ultimately be persuaded? In some cases, answering these questions may be mere guesswork; but one's success in answering them depends also on the ability to move outside oneself, to become "other" to oneself, so that one hears the speech from the other's point of view, and not merely from one's own.

Of course, the audience being "constructed" here may bear very little resemblance to the empirical audience that actually hears the speech. That group may be very different than that which has been speculatively "constructed" ahead of time — which helps us to understand why some efforts at persuasion fail, even if the form of language that they use is well-reasoned and insightful. The construction of the audience is a procession *within* the process of rhetorical invention, in which a person "becomes" other to him- or herself, in order to "hear" the speech from the audience's perspective and make judgments about its persuasiveness. In this procession, we can again speak of two relations: constructing and being constructed. As was the case with the first pair of relations, the very

---

[29] See John Milbank, "The Second Difference: For a Trinitarianism Without Reserve," *Modern Theology* 2, no. 3 (April 1986): 213–34.

grammar of the words make them clearly dependent on one another (the same verb is used, in active and passive voices). They require each other, and cannot exist in isolation from one another.

Again, however, we need to observe what happens when we move from these verbal terms to substantives: we usually speak simply of "the speaker" and "the audience." As in the previous case, this obscures the close mutual relationship between the two; we tend to assume that they could exist in isolation from one another. In addition, in this second case, something even more troublesome occurs: we forget that the audience is, at least in the first instance, an imaginative construction of the speaker. We tend to jump ahead to the empirical entity that actually hears the speech — an entity that is wholly external to the process of rhetorical invention. This further exacerbates our tendency to think of these two entities as wholly separable, rather than the mutually dependent realities named by the relations of "constructing" and "being constructed."

Summarizing, then: in the process of persuasion there are two activities, the production of language and the construction of the audience. We can in turn think of these as four relations: speaking and being spoken, and constructing and being constructed. These relations differentiate the process of persuasion, such that we can understand certain activities as taking place within it, "internally" as it were. Our substantive terms for these relations — words such as *speaker*, *argument*, and *audience* — are less cumbersome, and are therefore useful (as we noted above, with reference to names for God). Such substantives provide some "temporarily stability" to discussions of a complex, differentiated, relational whole. But in doing so, they take on "a hardness as of cut stone." They are less clearly interdependent (implicated by and implicating one another) than are the verbal forms from which they are derived. These substantive terms tempt us to abstract speaker, speech, and audience from their context, treating each one as an isolated entity. This, however, is an artificial separation. All three are necessary; if one is missing, the entire process of persuasion vanishes.

The Analogy Exemplified: Trinitarian/Rhetorical Co-Equality

The analogy that I am developing here will, I think, become clearer through an illustration. I want to examine one parallel between trinitarian doctrine and rhetorical theory — a parallel that allows each enterprise to clarify certain aspects of the other.

One of the central claims of classical trinitarianism is that the Three are radically equal to one another; none is in a position of superiority over the others. In order to rule out Arianism and other forms of subordinationism, the Nicene Council rejected a whole variety of attempts to place the Three in an hierarchical order — logical, causal, temporal, or otherwise. The Council's clarity on this point is especially visible in the Nicene anathemas, which claim that there was no time when the Word "was not." And in order to make it clear that the "begetting of the Son" need not imply temporal order, the Creed states that this begetting takes place "eternally." Nor is there a *logical* hierarchy among the Three; they all imply one another and are dependent on one another, so that no one of them can be understood in a position of primacy over the others.

This is a difficult concept to grasp, not least because most things in our experience *can* be expressed in causal or temporal order. But the Three are not "entities" in the normal sense of our experience; they are *relations*. Relations are not independent entities that can be arranged in temporal or logical sequence; they implicate one another and are dependent upon one another. Two of the three relations are commonly given names that attempt to preserve this mutual dependence — the two that we usually translate "Father" and "Son." At first, we might assume that a father precedes his son, both logically and temporally; but this is an illusion. Certainly, the older man precedes the younger man; but the older man does not become a *father* until he has a *child*. Without a child, no parent — and without a parent, no child. "The advent of the child, in a sense 'gives birth' to the father."[30] This aspect of divine relationality was emphasized in later Greek trinitarian theology, where the parental-filial language was thought to provide an especially clear description of two entities whose very existences were wholly dependent upon one another.[31] Similarly with respect to causal sequence: while there is a certain sense in which a parent is a *cause* of a child, there is an equally valid sense in which the child is the cause of the

---

[30] Janet Martin Soskice, "Trinity and 'the Feminine Other,'" *New Blackfriars* 75, no. 878 (January 1994): 2–17, here, 11.

[31] "For the Cappadocians the idea of an original that only *is* through its imaged presentation is a necessary further spelling out of 'essential fatherhood'": John Milbank, "The Second Difference," 220.

parent — for unless there is a child, the parent is not a parent! Such other-constituting relations are "retroactively causative."[32]

Even in some of the most important trinitarian speculation of the early period of Christian history (for example, that of the Cappadocians), this radical equality was not always made completely clear. While emphasizing the lack of any temporal sequence in God, they still spoke of an "order" [*taxis*], and sometimes spoke of only one of the Three as the cause [*aitia*].[33] They are not always completely consistent in these matters; nevertheless, such language tends to diminish the full equality of the Three, so that (for example) in later Orthodox theology, one of the Three gets raised to the status of "the principle of unity" in God, or the ultimate ground and origin of the Godhead. This in turn has been taken over by a number of Western theologians; Walter Kasper, for example, goes out of his way to establish God as, fundamentally, a single transcendent person (the Father).[34] As John Milbank has noted, this tendency "obscures the really interesting and rigorous notion of an absolute origin that is 'always already' difference and succession."[35]

Finally, the radical co-equality of the Three has also been obscured by the common practice of describing them with ordinal numerals as the "first," "second," and "third" persons of the Trinity. As useful as this language may be, it very strongly suggests a logical or temporal sequence, and students of trinitarian doctrine can thus be forgiven for assuming that the "first person" is, in some way or another, "first."

The trinitarian notion of a radical, relational co-equality is also a feature of the process of persuasion. Here, we also speak of three: the rhetor, the argument, and the audience. Here too, there appears at first glance to be a temporal or logical sequence; we assume that the rhetor is "first," and that the argument comes later (and the audience later still). But if we concentrate

---

[32]Ibid., 219.

[33]See, e.g., the discussion in Frederick W. Norris, ed., *Faith Gives Fullness to Reasoning: The Five Theological Orations of Gregory Nazianzen*, trans. Lionel Wickham and Frederick Williams, Supplements to Vigiliae Christianae, vol. 13 (Leiden: E. J. Brill, 1991), 45–46.

[34]Kasper, *The God of Jesus Christ*, part 1, and especially section 1 of part 2.

[35]Milbank, "The Second Difference," 218.

on the process of rhetorical invention as described above, we may be able to recognize the fully relational, and thus the fully equal, nature of these three elements. The rhetor does not *become* rhetor except through the production of language and the construction of the audience. The audience is not a last-minute addition to the process, but must be constructed even as the argument is being developed. And the argument only exists in having been produced *by* someone and *for* someone.

Thus, the three are fully and mutually dependent on one another; all three must be present in order for any of them to be present. We can *imagine* them as isolated entities, but only by abstracting them from the very process from which their names are derived. A person can stand alone in a room and offer an impassioned plea for some cause or another, but if the words are not intended to be heard by anyone — if the speaker has not even imagined a possible audience — then "rhetorical invention" is not really taking place. There is no sense in which this person is a *rhetor*; there is no goal involving persuasion. Nor is the language employed in such a circumstance an "argument," except in some proleptic sense; it is not intended to move anyone to action.

Thus, the relationship among rhetor, audience, and argument mirrors that among the divine Three: the rhetor becomes a rhetor only when producing an argument for an audience; the argument becomes argument when so produced; the (constructed) audience becomes audience upon being postulated as the target of the argument by the rhetor. Certainly, the human being who is about to take on the role of rhetor pre-exists the rhetorical context; but that person cannot be named by a relational term such as *rhetor* until the other elements of the process of rhetorical invention are also in place. Only then do the relations of "speaking" and "constructing" play a role. Similarly, a group of people assembled in a room, waiting, is not yet an "audience" in any strong sense; and even when they do hear the argument, they are not its "original" audience, for an audience first had to be constructed in the mind of the rhetor in order for the argument to be formed. Each of the three is thus fully dependent upon the other two; none can be separated from the others and leave the process of rhetorical invention intact, even in the most elementary sense. Each causes the others and is simultaneously caused by the others; there are no logical, temporal, or causal hierarchies among the three. And just the same goes for the Trinity: the Three implicate one another, making one another what they are.

Trinity and Teaching: Implications for Theological Education

Where does this analogy between trinitarian doctrine and rhetorical theory leave us? For one thing, it helps to provide a *theological* warrant for the claim that has been made throughout this volume: namely, that rhetorical categories are altogether appropriate for the doing of Christian theology. Not only in this chapter, but throughout this book, contributors have cited a number of *theological* features of the rhetorical tradition; that tradition flows alongside, and often intermingles with, the stream of Christian theology. Rhetoric is thus not simply a "helpful" and "useful" way of approaching theological questions (though it is that, as well); it is a *theologically justified* methodological tool.

Elsewhere, I have explored some of these matters at greater length.[36] In the few pages that remain in the present chapter, I want to turn to the question of theological education, and in particular, to how we might rethink some of our *practices* in light of the rhetorical and trinitarian categories that I have delineated here. While I cannot describe these practices in much detail, I hope to offer enough ruminations that my readers can imagine some possible "next steps" in the ongoing reformation of theological education.

Pedagogical Implications

The relational nature of God argues for a relational approach to the study of God and to the things related to God. This suggests a theological rationale for moving away from a purely didactic process in which the instructor states "the truth" and the student's task is to "receive" the wisdom that is thereby transmitted. Such philosophies of education rely heavily on what is sometimes called a "sender-receiver" model of communication.[37] According to this model, the originator of a message places it into a hermetically sealed vehicle, which is then transported to the receiver — who removes the message intact. Even the various modes of

---

[36] At the general methodological level in *Faithful Persuasion: In Aid of a Rhetoric of Christian Theology* (Notre Dame, Ind.: University of Notre Dame Press, 1991); and with respect to the Christian doctrine of God in *These Three Are One*.

[37] Walter J. Ong, *Orality and Literacy: The Technologizing of the Word*, New Accents (London: Methuen, 1982), 176.

electronic communication (through which this analogy gains so much persuasive power) have an effect on the content of the messages they transmit; how much more is this the case for the networks of human relationships that are involved in so much of our processes of communication. Recognizing the inappropriateness of the "sender-receiver model" — as well as working to replace it with a more rhetorically-nuanced understanding of how communication works — must be among the first steps in rethinking our understanding of theological pedagogy.

Students need to learn to negotiate the relations among the theological "arguments" that they are being taught, as well as among the speaker-audience relationships within which these arguments will be explicated. As suggested in other essays in this volume, courses in biblical or historical studies need to be attentive to the rhetorical context in which arguments were originally developed. When students learn about a particular doctrinal controversy (say, Arianism), they should not be asked simply to memorize relevant biblical cruxes and the names and dates of authors who engineered the turning-points in the debate. Rather, they need to know why a particular argument was persuasive in a particular context — and to whom, and under what assumptions. Only such an approach to doctrinal controversy will adequately prepare students to reason theologically about "reappearances" of the same (or a closely-related) controversy in our own age.

Similarly, in courses on systematic theology, instructors need to inspire students to go well beyond the mere description of a particular doctrine. Relevant questions become: what will a particular teaching or interpretation "sound like" to an audience of catechized Christians? How will this differ from its impact on an audience of Gen X-ers who are cynical about the Church? How will a given audience "hear" a particular theological claim differently, if it is propounded by a doctor or a lawyer rather than by a pastor? These questions become more salient when we remember that the reality of theological claims, like the reality of God, is found also in the *relations*, and not just in the *essence*.

Rethinking the Subdisciplines

The Christian doctrine of the Trinity suggests that God is always about the business of "giving place" to what is Other within God, always allowing its multiplicity to coinhere or interpenetrate. A relational account of God tends to emphasize the degree to which the Three participate in one another, such that we can never speak of them in isolation from one another. This is sometimes referred to under the heading of *perichōrēsis* — the claim that the Three interpenetrate one another to such a degree that one can never separate them one from another.

This reality calls us to develop a similar approach to the theological subdisciplines. This question has already received some attention in the present volume. For example, in chapter eight, Richard Osmer suggests that we need to move beyond the theological encyclopedia that was constructed within the heart of modernity, and to re-vision the relationships among the subdisciplines for a postmodern, post-Christian world. He also demonstrated how the rhetorical tradition might point us in some useful directions for pursuing this goal.

Here, I want to suggest that the parallels between rhetorical theory and trinitarian doctrine provide us with further warrant for such a reconfiguration. What would it mean to imagine a "perichoretic" curriculum, in which scripture, ethics, history, and practice all included one another in intentional ways? We might think about some concrete ways of doing this. Perhaps each subdiscipline could include one text from another subdiscipline in its required reading, and/or include guest lectures from colleagues. Team-teaching is another alternative. But my point here is not so much to provide practical suggestions; that will need to be done in each particular educational setting, in ways that are appropriate for that setting. I simply want to observe that such alliances are warranted not just by pedagogical theory and the desire for collegiality, but by the doctrine of the Trinity, which insists on *perichōrēsis* as a fundamental feature of God.

"Academic" in What Way?

As has been observed frequently by the contributors to this volume, we have tended to think of theological education along the model of the modern academic institution (University of Berlin *et seq.*). This perspective suggests that our goal is to prepare individual scholars who are capable of working on their own, publishing their findings, and declaiming truth from a university lectern. But those who graduate from our seminaries are not, by and large, headed to academic posts; and in any case, we can legitimately ask whether the typical American academic post allows for the kind of individualistic assumptions about scholarship for which the early-modern German universities provided the model. And if this is true in the academic setting, it is doubly so for pastors — who are expected to work cooperatively, engage in conversations, and listen to the reactions of their audiences. All of this raises doubts about basing theological education on analytic modes of discourse, as if the first principles were self-evident and the process of deduction straightforward. Instead, we need to develop a rhetorical model of theological education, admitting the lack of agreement about the principles by which we operate, and recognizing that all new knowledge is generated through the complex interaction of speakers, audiences, and texts.

Perhaps one of the subliminal reasons that the University of Berlin tended to promote analytical models of knowledge was that Trinitarian theology was so marginalized at the time. Think of Schleiermacher's *The Christian Faith*: there, the Trinity only makes a brief appearance, as a sort of appendix.[38] In this sense, Schleiermacher reflects the spirit of the age, in which a monistic doctrine of God was thought to be more amenable to contemporary philosophical assumptions. The Enlightenment enthusiasm for the "God of the philosophers" created a comfortable context for, and probably helped to underwrite, a similarly monistic understanding of education — in which there is only one font and source of all knowledge (the learned professor), who dispenses this knowledge in a one-way pattern of transmission: he says "Punkt" and seven hundred pens simultaneously fall on seven hundred notebooks, echoing throughout the lecture hall.[39]

None of this is meant to discourage the laudable efforts of those who are attempting to increase the rigor and the intellectual focus of theological education. On the contrary, the academic quality of our work must be beyond question. The problem arises when we try to adopt, for use in theology, the assumptions about what constitutes rigor and intellectual relevance in *other disciplines* — such as the natural or social sciences. For centuries, the faculty of rhetoric provided an alternative set of standards — standards of equal rigor and intellectual relevance to those of logic and grammar, yet not simply replacing them. By reappropriating the rhetorical tradition in the contemporary context, we can begin to establish a standard of academic rigor that is appropriate for the kinds of questions that theology asks.

---

[38]Friedrich D. E. Schleiermacher, *The Christian Faith*, trans. H. R. Mackintosh (Edinburgh: T. & T. Clark, 1928), 738–51.

[39]I owe the example to Patrick Keifert, who reports seeing precisely this event in a lecture hall in Tübingen.

Inasmuch as our own cultural context is rediscovering trinitarian theology and its virtues, we also need to re-examine our philosophy of education — reconceiving it along communitarian lines, rather than monistic ones. This means that our understanding of "truth" must be related to what emerges out of dialogical encounters of speaker and audience, rather than the didactic delivery of self-contained nuggets of information. Our students, our colleagues, and the frequently-unheard voices of the past (and the present) must also become part of the environment in which we teach. This is not just good pedagogical practice; it is not only warranted by the longstanding insights of the rhetorical tradition; it is warranted by the Christian doctrine of God.

Chapter 12

Rhetoric and Proclamation: A Relational Paradigm for the New Millennium

Susan Karen Hedahl

In a recent book on St. Augustine,[1] Gary Wills comments with some frequency on Augustine's extraordinarily wide range of rhetorical strategies. In one homiletical description, the Cross of Christ is compared to a mousetrap: the body of Jesus is the bait, and is meant to lure Satan away from humanity. This simple yet jolting analogy concerning the meaning of Jesus' death delightfully snags the listener as well: it lures us into a deeper look at the relationship between God and humanity. It is also a superlative example of rhetorical skill, employed within one of the terminus points of good theology — public proclamation.

It is fitting that a chapter on proclamation concludes the present volume's third part, which is entitled "Re-Visioning the Theological Encyclopedia." Faithful preaching provides the consummate opportunity for public expression of theological study, and it does so amidst a "wild card" mixture of listeners with a variety of theological backgrounds and potential responses. Given the complexity of any worship assembly, our re-examination of the standard theological subdisciplines must end with a question: *How can the art of rhetoric help us to think about what it means to proclaim the Gospel publicly, particularly in the contemporary post-Christian context?*

---

[1]Gary Wills, *Saint Augustine* (New York: Lipper/Viking Press, 1999).

In the present chapter, this question will receive attention from two perspectives. I will describe the necessity of a *rhetorical homiletics*, the intention of which is based on and reflects a "rhetoric of relationality" as the *sine qua non* of preaching. The first matter — a rhetorical homiletics — concerns the historical foundations of the church's attention to proclamation, as well as the use of multiple linguistic strategies in contemporary preaching. The second aspect — a rhetoric of relationality — emerges from the first. It understands a rhetorical homiletics as something decisive in the nexus of personal and corporate relationships, both divine and human.

By addressing these two areas, I will be able to provide historical, theological and pedagogical reasons for employing the approach that I advocate here. And most importantly, I will be able to probe what is at stake in expressing and defining theology and theological anthropology in this way. I am not attempting to provide a *technē for* establishing a particular preaching pedagogy, even though the approach that I offer here is one that opens up such possibilities. Rather, I am directing most of my attention to the process of identifying the contours of a proclamation that is, paradoxically, both rhetorical and anti-rhetorical. Rhetoric has been, and will continue to be, a substantive dialogical partner with homiletics; but at the same time, it offers usefully problematic tensions, through and by which homiletics does its work. From the perspective of this sometimes antithetical relationship between homiletics and rhetoric, we may speak of a rhetorical homiletics.

A Rhetorical Homiletics

By way of preface to our first area of concern, we may ask: on the brink of a new millennium, with new theological challenges on the horizon, how is Christian proclamation faring? A number of interrelated factors bear upon the answer to our question. First, we need to take note of the emergence of new proclamatory voices — particularly those that have arisen through a greater inclusivity related to gender and ethnicity. Second, denominations have splintered and have reconfigured themselves; and at the same time, denominational alignment is itself not as stable or as predictable as it was once thought to be. Third, we are beginning to recognize and attend to varying rhetorics of proclamation — including those that pay greater attention to the role of the listener in the preaching event, and those that have begun to re-evaluate and re-envision preaching as a dialogic encounter, rather than merely a monologic address. Fourth, in the American context of biblical illiteracy, we have seen the re-emergence of instructional preaching (and not simply for introductory catechetical purposes). Yet at the same time, we find ourselves acknowledging the polysemic and polyvalent realities of the biblical texts, as interpreted by multiple and varyingly knowledgeable audiences.[2]

What does a rhetorical homiletics have to offer such a mix? In order to begin to answer this question, we need to develop a more nuanced definition of both of the relevant terms: *rhetorical* and *homiletics*. First, my use of the term *homiletics* as part of this phrase is meant to refer to the act and art of preaching, purposefully focused through a rhetorical consciousness. According to this definition, Christian proclamation ranges freely through the rhetorical options available to it — employing both ancient and contemporary sources — in order to give expression to the Gospel.[3] It can take account of these multiple strands of rhetorical reality, and it can offer constructive interaction with them.

Second, in my use of the word *rhetoric*, and especially in my use of the word *rhetorical* as a modifier for the word *homiletics*, I am attempting to invoke those strategic discourse dynamics chosen by the preacher as most effective for preaching the Gospel of Jesus Christ at a given time and place. In this sense, I am focusing (as have many contributors in this volume) on rhetoric's role as the art of *invention* or *discovery* of the available means of persuasion. Christian proclamation thus finds its roots in classical and neo-Aristotelian rhetoric; these faculties provide a starting point for proclamation, though of course it may range far beyond them in matters of invention.

In my invocation of the term *rhetorical homiletics*, then, I understand both proclamation and rhetoric(s) to provide us with free rein in making homiletical choices and constructing the event of proclamation, making use

---

[2] I use the terms *polysemous* and *polyvalent* as they are used by Ciceccarelli, who in turn draws on the work of Celeste Conduit: "polysemy is the condition where there is more than one denotational meaning for a text; polyvalence is the condition where there is shared understanding of the denotations of the text, but disagreement about the valuation of these denotions." Leah Ciceccarelli, "Polysemy: Multiple Meanings in Rhetorical Criticism," *Quarterly Journal of Speech* 84/4 (November 1998): 398.

[3] For a review of some of these resources, see especially the essays by David Cunningham and Janet Weathers, chapters 1 and 2 of the present volume.

of all the contemporary postmodern perspectives available.[4] This, in turn, means that preaching in this fashion is always significantly contextualized; hence it will inevitably be, to at least some degree, uncomfortable with generic constraints — including appointed lectionary texts, denominational guidelines, doctrinal prescriptives, and the particular worldviews of speaker and listeners.

A rhetorical homiletics must take into account both the useful and the problematic elements of the relationship between homiletics and rhetoric. The alliance can be extraordinarily productive of Christian proclamation; nevertheless, homiletics sometimes finds itself uneasy with its intersection with rhetoric. A facile combination of the two enterprises can be disastrous. Collapsing proclamation into a collection of rhetorical "understandings" or "approaches" can invalidate or obscure some of the basic truth claims of the Gospel. In this case, the medium is emphatically *not* the message — however much a naïve rhetorical perspective might seek to make it so. Conversely, collapsing rhetoric into Gospel proclamation, such that it becomes "mere rhetoric," also naïvely overlooks or undervalues the richness of language's infinite power to influence, to inspire, and to change.[5]

If the relationship between homiletics and rhetoric is so problematic, one might well ask a different sort of question: why bother with the relationship at all? First, the history of homiletics has itself been rooted deeply in rhetoric since the beginning of the common era. Augustine's *On Christian Doctrine* is one of the earliest, and probably the clearest, example of a theologian's work to understand both rhetoric and preaching together.[6] To attempt to speak of, let alone to teach, homiletics without acknowledging this interaction would violate the formative elements of historical Christian preaching.

Second, rhetoric — however eclipsed or unacknowledged at times — has served and continues to serve as a springboard for contemporary forms

---

[4]For a further elucidation of these important elements of rhetorical practice, see especially the essays by A. K. M. Adam, Wes Avram, and Don H. Compier, in chapters 3, 6, and 7 of this volume, respectively.

[5]On the power of language, see the essay by James Boyce in chapter 9.

[6]St. Augustine of Hippo, *De Doctrina Christiana*, ed. and trans. R. P. H. Green, Oxford Early Christian Texts (Oxford and New York: Oxford University Press, 1996).

of proclamation; consequently, it offers alternatives for effective preaching. The debt to rhetoric that homiletics has assumed has been little understood or acknowledged in this regard. A survey of seminary offerings in the areas of rhetoric and preaching would undoubtedly buttress such an assertion.

Third, a rhetorical homiletics is unabashed about seeking proclamatory sophistication through the multiple means available to it. Both rhetoric and proclamation exhibit the quest for the display of linguistic richness, diversity and complexity. The field of rhetoric has great potential for providing us with various means of persuasion that can direct discourse to a point of view — one that (the speaker hopes) will be adopted by the listeners. Similarly, proclamation functions persuasively towards the development of a point of view — namely, the core constructs of the Christian faith as embodied in Jesus Christ. This is not simply a matter of beating the language game on its own terms. It is, rather, an investment in Paul's strategy: choosing "the chameleon approach" if it preaches well and effects a hearing and a reception of the Gospel.

> To the Jews I became as a Jew, in order to win Jews. To those under the law I became as one under the law (though I myself am not under the law) so that I might win those under the law. To those outside the law I became as one outside the law (though I am not free from God's law but am under Christ's law) so that I might win those outside the law. To the weak I became weak, so that I might win the weak. I have become all things to all people, that I might by all means save some (1 Cor 9:20–22).

The pragmatic nature of both proclamation and rhetoric means that neither is self-contained; both point beyond themselves.

However, by asserting this, one thereby acknowledges that preaching is not simply a field of discourse in need of useful rhetorical strategies. Instead, *preaching is its own rhetoric*. Clarifying what this means — both for rhetoric and for preaching — then becomes the task for a rhetorical homiletics. We begin with rhetoric.

The Means of Rhetoric

Any attempt to explicate the relationships within a rhetorical homiletics has had the tendency, prompted by its own history, to find voice primarily through Aristotelian rhetoric and its Greek and Roman offspring. This approach focuses on the triad of speaker, message, and audience in eliciting the dynamics of persuasion appropriate to a particular group. Many of the contributors to this volume have explicated the significance of this triad. However, in developing a working rhetorical homiletics, it is not enough to employ this particular approach to persuasion as its only viable basis. Instead, the contemporary homiletician must be aware of varying *rhetorics*, each offering a different set of possible means for expressing the Gospel. Effective contemporary proclamation utilizes variations on, and alternative emphases within, the standard Aristotelian triad. It must therefore be prepared to name these differences in terms of new rhetorical developments.

What rhetorical interpretative dynamics are occurring, for example, when the contemporary televised preacher may have no "live" audience physically present, but only a television camera? Is such a preacher's audience "live" in a different sense? What is involved, rhetorically speaking, when a sermon is signed rather than spoken? How is a single sermon understood within the context of the entire preaching tradition of the Christian faith? How is it understood within a given denomination's history, or within the history of a given faith assembly? What of the multiple sermon readers and writers on the internet, allowing for a veritable explosion of multiple respondents? A rhetorical homiletics must be equipped to enter into dialogue with these emerging rhetorics, in order to be prepared to offer possible responses to the questions that will inevitably arise.

Contemporary rhetorical options have richly expanded the homiletician's persuasive choices. For example, Lloyd Bitzer's early work on the rhetorical situation adds a fourth component to the triad — that of *context*.[7] Moving beyond this earlier work, both text criticism and rhetorical criticism have developed multiple rhetorical lenses; the use of these approaches can prompt the preacher to consider the sermon in terms that extend the neo-Aristotelian approach, or that address it selectively. Foss's work in rhetorical criticism offers a working taxonomy of numerous approaches that can serve as a basis for considering the means by which one's proclamation may be enriched — including fantasy-theme analysis,

---

[7]Lloyd F. Bitzer, "The Rhetorical Situation," *Philosophy and Rhetoric* 1 (Winter 1968): 1–15.

feminist analysis, metaphoric analysis, narrative analysis, and "pentadic" analyses (based on the work of Kenneth Burke).[8]

Rodney Hart's work also offers additional possibilities for a rhetorical homiletics.[9] These are focused on only one part of the traditional rhetorical triad of speaker, message, and audience — namely, the message (or "the argument itself"). Hart's argument analysis attends to an argument's form, structure, and word choice; it provides space for role analysis and cultural analysis.

Of course, all these approaches are presented by rhetorical critics who are not themselves focusing on the significance of their work for homiletics. Hence we must now ask: what are the effects of such analyses when they are undertaken by the preacher, adopting similar methods and assumptions? This question leads us to a more detailed account of proclamation.

Proclamation's Lineage

How are these current rhetorical offerings being employed in the theory and practice of preaching? Any answer to this question must take account of the tensive alliance between rhetoric and proclamation. There are several reasons for this.

First, despite the presence of the *virs bonum*[10] tradition in rhetorical practice, rhetoric has sometimes appeared unconcerned with questions concerning the true and the good — particularly when understood as little more than a cache of persuasive strategies. Whether or not this critique can justifiably be applied to rhetoric as a whole, it undoubtedly marks the practice of some rhetoricians. Fortunately, a good deal of the anxiety about this aspect of rhetorical practice can be relieved by focusing on the first canon of rhetoric — invention.

---

[8]See Sonja K. Foss, *Rhetorical Criticism: Exploration & Practice*, 2nd ed. (Prospect Heights, Ill.: Waveland Press, 1996).

[9]Rodney Hart, *Modern Rhetorical Criticism* (Glenview, Illinois: Scott, Foresman/Little, 1990).

[10]See Susan Karen Hedahl, "The Model Preacher: Ethos and the Early American Pulpit," *dialog* 29/3: 183–88.

Homiletics is, in general, a polysemic field — not a polyvalent one.[11] Basic assertions of the Gospel — what Christians would designate as truth statements — can not be reconfigured endlessly in the interests of persuasive strategy. Doing so would destroy Christian proclamation altogether. Thus, the native rhetoric of homiletics is formed primarily by the constraints of its inventive field. Its persuasive force is determined by traditional, biblical and liturgical words and related enactments: "Jesus Christ is Lord and Savior"; "forgiveness of sins"; "eternal life"; "loving the neighbor."

A second factor that circumscribes the peculiar rhetoric of homiletics is the frequent (though not constant) use of biblically-based texts in preaching. These texts — like the over-arching constraints of the inventive field of preaching — are also deeply polysemous and only somewhat polyvalent. While there seem to be many ways to read the text, depending on the particular perspectives of the reader or the critic, the interpretative strictures are strengthened by the specific historical contexts within which these texts were formed. The circumstances of history tend to close, to some extent, the terms of their limitless contemporary use. Thus, the homiletical employment of contemporary rhetorical strategies must be played out in a way that is consonant with those presented historically by the text.

A third factor is specifically theological in nature: homiletics must concern itself with some form of a doctrine of inspiration. This issue is given more attention in some faith perspectives than in others, but it must be taken into account in all evaluations of Christian preaching. Whether this spiritual component is understood as transmitted in a mediated or unmediated sense is not the point. What it *does* say to the Christian preacher is that, within the traditional triadic rhetorical setting, the speaker must contend with a rhetorical wild card that is personal in nature and ultimately uncontrollable. The views of inspiration that audiences bring to the proclamatory event necessarily become active in and through the preacher's language — originating in points that are outside as well as inside the act of preaching. This reality, sometimes described as the agency of the Holy Spirit, is a constant in all considerations of Christian preaching and may act as a reinforcement or subversive element in the proclamation.

For example, in describing the office of preaching, Martin Luther probes its roots in the Trinity through a multi-layered example of

---

[11]For this distinction, see note 2 above.

Aristotelian rhetoric, the role of Holy Spirit, and the issue of inspiration. This is demonstrated in an excerpt from one of his sermons on the Gospel of John:

> But Christ points in particular to the distinctive person of the Holy Spirit. ... He makes the Father the Preacher and the Holy Spirit the Listener. ... Thus there are two distinct Persons: He who speaks and the Word that is spoken, that is, the Father and the Son. Here, however, we find the third person following these two, namely, the One who hears both the Speaker and the Spoken Word. For it stands to reason that there must also be a listener where a speaker and a word are found. ... All three — Speaker, Word, and Listener — must be God.[12]

This passage not only demonstrates the importance of the role of the Spirit in the event of proclamation; it also hints at a significant parallel between the doctrine of the Trinity and the rhetorical tradition.[13]

A fourth factor is concerned with what I would term "the trustworthiness of language." Augustine, and those after him, were preoccupied with the issue of eloquence, playing it off against Christian truth claims in many cases. There was more at stake, however, than the issue of linguistic aesthetics: early Christian proclamation was obviously conflicted in the arena of alternative rhetorics and their debatable truth claims. Homiletics' own rhetoric was considered sufficient for the catechetical, spiritual and missiological needs of the church.

Today, however, a consciously-chosen rhetorical homiletics must make a bid for a hearing in a global context that is far more complicated and sophisticated than anyone had previously imagined. Developments in field of language study have brought questions about language usage to a new pitch. It would seem that the earlier tools of neo-Aristotelian rhetoric have modified today, in order to be placed in the service of a form of

---

[12]Martin Luther, *Sermons on the Gospel of St. John, Chapters 14–16* Volume 24, ed. Jaroslav Pelikan (Saint Louis: Concordia Publishing House, 1961), 364–65.

[13]For a detailed discussion of this parallel, see David S. Cunningham, *These Three Are One: The Practice of Trinitarian Theology*, Challenges in Contemporary Theology (Oxford and Cambridge: Basil Blackwell, 1998), especially chapter 3; see also Cunningham's essay on rhetoric and Christian doctrine, chapter 11 of the present volume.

proclamation with a radically different look, suitable for a postmodern age. A hermeneutics of suspicion towards language's infinite play in community must be balanced with a willing submission and susceptibility to its uses in various contemporary settings.

A final factor contained in Christian proclamation marks its peculiar rhetoric with *specific,* rather than general rhetorical, intentionality. The overarching goal of Christian proclamation is the effecting of a transformation in the lives of the listeners. Preaching is not a neutral act composed of episodic rhetorical dynamics that are unrelated to the larger goal that continues to exist outside the preaching of any given sermon. It is here that a rhetorical homiletics provides the constitutive elements of what I understand to be the core intentionality of proclamation, a *rhetoric of relationality.*

Toward a Rhetoric of Relationality

What are the chief features of such an approach to rhetorical homiletics? First of all, a rhetoric of relationality is *invitational* in its attitude and its habits of discourse. Older pulpit rhetorics run the risk of sounding imperialistic, discordant, and often unheard — particularly in a complex global setting. An invitational approach is essential for the global community and intrinsic to the biblical record's own missiological efforts. What does this mean generally in terms of rhetorical strategies? Older assumptions about faith assemblies are close to useless today. An invitational proclamation is acutely aware of context and audience. Further, it urges on the proclaimer more intentional study and use of language developments available from the fields of rhetoric, linguistics, and rhetorical- and text-critical methods. For the purposes of theological education, these must be linked pedagogically in new ways in cross-curricular fashion.[14]

Secondly, a rhetoric of relationality claims its own internal consistency and tensiveness through the proclamation of a God who is simultaneously *intimate* and *alien.* In other words, a rhetoric of relationality, theologically speaking, is both personal and paradoxical in nature. A rhetorical homiletics at its best preaches an undomesticated and incarnate God —

---

[14]For an example of how the audience might come to play a central role in the seminary curriculum, see the concluding essay by Donald Juel and Patrick Keifert in the present volume.

beyond our grasp yet at home with humanity. Such preaching is topically restrained in its inventiveness but wildly unrestrained in its rhetorical play. It must grasp both these elements, because it seeks to communicate Immanuel, "God with us," who is, nevertheless, also the *deus absconditus*. The God of a single human moment is also the God of non-temporality. The God over the mighty is found in the company of the powerless. Rhetorical homiletics perceives and preserves the intrinsic link between the God of galaxies and the God of Golgotha.

Third, a pulpit rhetoric of relationality is also *institutional* in nature, though not parochial. The difference between the two is essential. A rhetorical homiletics establishes itself as a porous *rhetoric of the household*, allowing the rhythms of its own rhetorical proclamation to be consistently dismantled and reformed through the bids for justice and need from within and without the community. It is not intimidated by the revelations of its own failures or needs. Such an institutional proclamation is organic in nature, both nurturing and replicating the levels at which it is played out: *catechetical*, in terms of a growth in wisdom and knowledge as part of the Christian life; *educational*, in terms of prompting growth in the faith; and *evangelical/missiological*, insofar as it fosters a commitment to the doctrinal, ecclesiastical and communal texts of a faith community.

It is also highly political in nature (whatever metaphor might be used to describe it as such). Such a rhetoric of the faith household is not naïve in addressing the continual demands made inside and outside the worshiping assembly. It articulates a rhetoric of relationality that addresses, warns, challenges, and may stand against those forces that are anti-relational in nature. Such relational intentionality in proclamation demands great vulnerability and flexibility — even courage.

A fourth characteristic of a rhetoric of relationality is its quest for *equilibrium*. It subjects itself to constant reorientation and self-critique in order to proclaim a balance between the alien and familiar, the stranger and the friend, the text and the play of the text, the *technē* and *phronēsis* of its own activities. This rhetoric and this kind of proclamation are loyal to their own purviews as well as interactive with that of the other.

Part of this quest involves the role of listening — what Fiumara has described as "the other side of our rationality."[15] The recent works on the

---

[15]Gemma Corradi Fiumara, *The Other Side of Language: A Philosophy of Listening*, trans. Charles Lambert.(London: Routledge, 1990), 68.

role of the listener in preaching[16] are only the tip of the epistemological iceberg that is now challenging the dominance of logomachies of all types, not the least of which is preaching. Without listening as a vital component of a rhetorical homiletics, many forms of proclamation today can be characterized today as a kind of logocentricism that cannot listen and thus can not learn, remaining solipsistic and incantational.

Most importantly, a rhetoric of relationality *heard from the pulpit* is unwilling to relinquish the claims made on it by the *mystery of God*, active in human community. It values that mystery and proclaims that our relationship to it — in all its fragmentary, tragic, joyous, and demanding modes — comes to us cognitively, sensuously, and affectively. In that way, it is faithful to both the rhetorical and homiletical dynamics from which it emerges.

What then of a proposed rhetorical homiletics for theological education's reformation and renewal? What of its resultant intentionality towards proclaiming a rhetoric of relationality? Such a perspective on preaching, *by its very relational nature,* is always an ongoing search. It seeks a rhetoric that is intentional, persuasive, specific, and personal — and always in search of other rhetorics. It is a perspective that is companionable, gregarious, and communal in nature. Its own form of rhetoric invites dialogue with contraries through re-shaping encounters and engagements. Most importantly, it places ultimate value on the "I," the "You" and the "We" as its ultimate assertions — and as the ultimate test of its rhetoric and its intentions.

---

[16]Two excellent resources, although written from somewhat differing perspectives, are John S. McClure, *The Roundtable Pulpit: Where Leadership and Preaching Meet* (Nashville: Abingdon, 1995) and Leonora Tubbs Tisdale, *Preaching As Local Theology and Folk Art* (Minneapolis: Fortress Press, 1997).

CONCLUSION

THEORY IN PRACTICE

A Rhetorical Approach to Theological Education: Assessing an Attempt to Re-Vision a Curriculum

Donald Juel and Patrick Keifert

Over the superbowl weekend in January of 1991, the two of us co-authored a paper for the faculty of Luther Seminary (St. Paul, Minnesota) entitled "A Rhetorical Approach to Theological Education." The paper served as the basis of a grant proposal submitted to the Lilly Endowment in the spring of the same year requesting funding for a three-year curriculum revisioning process. The energy for the project was not generated solely by the grant. Widespread restiveness with the existing curriculum, and with the strategy for training clergy that it implied, had led to preliminary conversations among faculty groups during the previous year and a half. A committee and a director had been appointed to oversee a thorough revision of the curriculum. Our proposal represented an argument for a particular direction we were commending to the faculty. The grant provided an additional incentive for generating the tremendous energy the conversations required over the next three years.

The substance of the proposal arose from three sources: more than a decade of experience in a co-taught course, entitled "Meaning and Truth: The Uses of Scripture in Pastoral Ministry"; participation in the last stages of the ATS study of theological education;[1] and research done in mainline

---

[1] See the work of David Kelsey, *Between Athens and Berlin: The Theological Education Debate* (Grand Rapids, Mich.: William B. Eerdmans, 1993); and *To Understand God Truly: What's Theological About a Theological School?* (Louisville, Ky.: Westminster/John Knox Press, 1992).

congregations. We became convinced that the difficulties encountered in training pastors for contemporary congregations that we had experienced in our own setting were not simply local; these difficulties arise from major cultural shifts and deep intellectual traditions. Re-imagining theological education requires attention to the changes. Proposals must be faithful to normative traditions but appropriate to the new setting.

We chose to cast our proposal in terms of classical "rhetorical" categories. We did so fully aware that "rhetoric" is regarded with at least as much suspicion today as it was in ancient philosophical circles. Colleagues advised us to find a category with less baggage in a culture where "rhetorical" connotes ornament and disregard for truth. Exploring that suspicion, however, has proved to be one of the more fruitful aspects of our conversations; the essence of the present volume reinforces this discovery. The desire for something more substantial and grounded than "persuasion" reveals what Richard Bernstein calls the "Cartesian Anxiety," a yearning for a clear and distinct idea or experientially based foundation that will serve as an "Archimedean point."[2] That desire, articulated by Descartes in his *Meditations,* has driven a culture into imagining that truth is either available to us in objective fashion or that we are "awash in a sea of relativity." With Bernstein, we wanted to propose an alternative to such a view in a way that is more appropriate to the Christian tradition and offers more promise of shaping effective pastoral practice.

Rhetoric has a noble history in the educational traditions of Western culture. It was the last of the three subjects (grammar, logic, and rhetoric) necessary in the training of public *leaders.* "Leadership" had become an important term in the curricular project before we had made our proposal; at this point in our history, mainline churches seem to lack leadership that can help the church reconfigure itself for mission in a culture that is no longer favorably disposed to the public presence of the church. We proposed that rhetorical categories are precisely suited to the task of leadership preparation. "Christian rhetor" is a concept worth developing as an image for pastoral ministry.

Another reason for our choice of rhetorical categories was that rhetoric aims at persuasion, the goal of which is decision and action. A legitimate

---

[2]See Richard J. Bernstein, *Beyond Objectivism and Relativism* (Philadelphia: University of Pennsylvania Press; Oxford: Basil Blackwell, 1983), 16–20.

criticism of research-based models of education is that they do not foster the ability to decide and to act. (We will return to this matter below.)

We were further disposed toward rhetorical categories because of their usefulness in contemporary biblical studies. While much of "rhetorical criticism" is enlisted in the task of locating the literature of the Bible in some distant past, study of biblical works as "persuasive" and attention to the various genres in which that persuasion is carried out have greater possibilities. That becomes clearer when the goal of biblical studies is the use of the scriptures in the practice of ministry. Attending to Aristotle's "author/speech/audience" has proved an effective way to help pastors and teachers reflect on their own use of the scriptures with actual audiences.

The use of Scripture has provided an important entrée to the curricular discussion. The function of normative tradition within the wide variety of rhetorical activities in pastoral ministry, from preaching and teaching to pastoral care and moral deliberation, has always been a major feature within the curriculum at denominational seminaries. Not only for strategic reasons, but also out of fidelity to the tradition, "beginning with Scripture" has been an important way of initiating discussion. What is the Bible good for, and how will the scriptures be used? Dealing with *ēthos, logos,* and *pathos* is appropriate in regard to the canonical setting of the biblical works, in regard to the history of their interpretation in the church, and in regard to their present deployment in ministry. Teaching at a theological seminary with a high view of the scriptures, whose main interest is preparing pastors, we view our task as identifying and engendering those habits conducive to public leadership in which the Bible is a norm of conversations.

The initial grant proposal argued for a rhetorical approach to theological instruction. Reacting to the detailed findings of the ten-year study of theological education by the ATS and to a sense that fundamental assumptions could no longer be taken for granted, we argued that the category of persuasion would be best suited to our present situation. Appropriate to the proposal, we also argued that a rhetorical process involving the whole community was the best strategy for proceeding. Thus we began a conversation among a faculty of fifty-five with the intent of re-envisioning the curriculum and producing a new approach to pastoral education.

Learning through Failure

One of the first strategic matters was how to communicate our views to the faculty. Most of our colleagues were unaware that Lilly had funded a proposal we had composed. Communicating the proposal to the faculty for discussion, evaluation, and possible action was made more difficult by our lack of any official status and the absence of a mandate from the faculty. We were, in effect, intruding into the process; colleagues had good reasons to be uncertain and even suspicious. Though some faculty members had expressed opinions, and lists had been drawn up, the faculty had come to no agreement about what the problems were to which our revisioning was directed — much less a way of addressing those problems. Such matters had to be argued and agreed upon. Finally, the variety of audiences within the faculty of fifty-five had to be taken seriously. In the process, the character of the presenters, of the presentation, and of the audience were all very much involved.

We decided to introduce our views to the faculty by way of a short essay and a presentation/demonstration. We constructed an exercise that began with a Bible study. We had previously led the faculty in a Bible study as a way into basic hermeneutical issues. The success of that endeavor, coupled with the privileged status of Scripture in the tradition, encouraged us to use the Bible study as a way into our curricular reflections. We chose the ending of Mark's Gospel as our text — for several reasons. Engagement with the ending had consistently energized interesting and productive theological discussions in the class that we had co-taught. And most important for the argument we wanted to make, the group would have to choose what to read as "the Bible." Modern translations do not make the decision about what to read as the ending of Mark's Gospel, even though the text-critical evidence is unequivocal. That we must participate in the decision about what we will read as scripture seemed a useful way into a proposal that takes seriously the erosion of so-called foundational elements in the tradition and faces squarely the inescapable need to make arguments to one another on the basis of which we must decide and act.

The faculty was divided into groups of six persons and given a list of four questions to be answered in 30 minutes, the first of which was, "What shall we read as the ending of Mark's Gospel?" We planned to gather the groups and move into our proposal on the tide of the conversation generated in the small groups. However, we had not anticipated what occurred.

As we moved from group to group, we noted a reticence on the part of non-biblical "experts" to discuss the text-critical issues involved in answering the first question. Shame was an important factor; people did not want colleagues to know how little they recalled of the intricacies of textual criticism, so faculty were willing to leave such matters to the biblical experts. Bible professors, meanwhile, tended to rehearse all the textual evidence rather than make a quick decision for the group. This took far more time than anticipated. And when groups did begin to move toward answering the first question, someone would halt the process with a question like, "But hasn't the church traditionally read a Gospel of Mark with 20 verses in chapter 16? Doesn't tradition have some weight?" Further conversations were generated. They were interesting and enlightened, but they prevented groups from making any decisions. By the end of the thirty minutes, not one group had decided what to read as the ending of Mark's Gospel. There was no tide on which to launch the discussion of our paper and our rhetorical approach. We were unable to rescue the plenary conversation which foundered on the question of how to decide on an ending — or even the *need* to decide! The session ended with irritated faculty, confusion, and no clarity about what a "rhetorical approach" might entail.

We now recognize that our experience of that session highlights a major problem in seminary education. While pastors must have the courage to make decisions and act based on limited evidence, scholarship of the sort practiced among faculty operates under no such constraints. Text-critics amass evidence and make tentative arguments. Decisions must always be made in terms of probability. There will never be complete agreement even about how to read the evidence regarding the ending of Mark, despite the fact that it is a reasonably straightforward problem. The constraints come only with the need to publish Bibles, when deadlines are imposed by publishers and must be met.

Scholarship, in other words, operates within a radically different context from that of pastoral ministry. Pastors cannot afford the luxury of lengthy reviews of text-critical theories. Preparing Easter sermons allows only a few moments in which to evaluate alternative endings and make a decision about the most reasonable that will serve as the basis for a sermon. Seldom do they learn from their professors how to be courageous and wise in such a setting. More likely, they have learned to feel shame for not knowing enough. Rather than developing the capacity to learn from mistakes and to recuperate quickly, they may well learn to avoid making mistakes by avoiding decisions — or to rely on another authority or whim. In an environment that increasingly requires leadership and innovation from clergy, we can no longer tolerate an educational system that regularly encourages the best students to move into doctoral programs — or to live with the sense that they are second-class theologians.

We might have anticipated such results from our process with the faculty and saved everyone much grief. Had we skipped the Bible study and moved into a discussion of a traditional academic paper, we might have gotten a hearing and critique of our proposal — for which there never was another opportunity. That we did not anticipate what occurred is an indication of how little sense we had of the distance between the kind of reflection appropriate to the practice of ministry and the scholarship in which theological faculty are trained in graduate programs. The experience suggests, in technical terms, how unrealistic it is to imagine a meeting of theory and practice — and how useful it may be to understand what Aristotle called practical reasoning (*phronēsis*) and its relationship to the formation of the imagination (*poiēsis*) in a theological context.

This inauspicious beginning gave way to a lively conversation that took place over the next three years. The mind of the faculty was formed largely through task forces and reports to the faculty, with occasional plenary sessions. We participated in some of the groups and did the rest of our work behind the scenes, serving as a "research team" with the project director. The topics of these specialized studies included such matters as the utility of narrative as a way of conceiving the first year ("story") and what we mean by "mission," the theme of the last year in the curriculum.

The most difficult phase of the project was the actual laying out of a program of study, including the design of specific courses. Departure from departmental structures was difficult, and many of the imaginative moments in the discussion gave way to hard bargaining. The movement of the faculty was nevertheless impressive, particularly given the size of the group and the scope of the project.

Aristotle's Triad Revisited

Looking back on the three-year conversation, Aristotle's triad of *ēthos*, *logos*, and *pathos* provide a useful way to organize some reflection on what occurred. In this section, we offer a brief examination of each.

Pathos: The Character of the Audience

Most striking, perhaps, is what we learned about the various audiences involved in the conversation. While our seminary has a particular character, that will be true of any community. Though there will be considerable differences in other institutions, we trust that some sense of the context is necessary for any project that intends to imagine an appropriate curriculum.

Faculty Colleagues. We began the process with some assumptions about the colleagues with whom we would be working and whose minds we presumed had to be changed. We recognized that there is both a remarkable coherence within the Luther Seminary faculty and remarkable diversity. Distrust and suspicion, while not paralyzing, were real features of community life that had to be attended to. Our own character as presenters was always an issue — even if not faced squarely. Most of the faculty had been educated within feeder institutions and had been well schooled in the Lutheran tradition, though there is an increasing distance between older and younger faculty; the latter are not as clearly part of the "family" (an image regularly employed twenty years ago to speak of the Luther faculty). The faculty's deep respect for the Bible and the Lutheran Confessions is reflected in assigning pride of place to the scriptures and the confessions in the school's program, though the question of precisely how those primary documents are to be interpreted elicits a wide range of opinion. On matters such as worship, ecumenical relations, and relationship to the culture, considerable differences of opinion could be expected.

Almost all of the faculty had been educated in similar graduate programs which, if not run by universities, reflected the current construction of the theological encyclopedia — based as it is on the assumptions of a university setting. We expect from one another a high level of expertise in particular fields. We anticipated there would be considerable anxiety within the faculty regarding turf matters, and we were not incorrect; all the same, making progress toward a new vision required a willingness to compromise and take risks beyond what many might have expected.

There were a number of surprises. We had imagined that colleagues would be more susceptible to "rational" persuasion.[3] In fact, colleagues *felt* their way to conclusions as much or more often than they *thought* their way to them. Appeals to "reason" (in the more restrictive sense of that term) seldom moved the community. What moved the group were *fears* and *desires*. The anxiety on the part of the director of the project about such matters was probably justified; shame and fear are real forces. The notion that speech must attend to matters

---

[3]See Janet Weathers' remarks on the nature of rationality in chapter two of the present volume.

of the affects in order to be effective is hardly new in the history of rhetoric; but we had imagined that ideas had more power. We were naïve about the faculty *pathos*.

A significant experience of this naïveté relates to the faculty's willingness to confront major issues. Our conversations were successful in identifying issues foundational to various disciplines. It became clear, for example, how completely our respective disciplines had embraced historical strategies and how serious a critique of those strategies has developed across the whole disciplinary spectrum, from biblical studies to church history to liturgics. A major faculty seminar on the topic, "What is 'History' and What Is It Good For?" was planned — then canceled, for fear that we would discover deep disagreements that would bring the whole curriculum revisioning process to a halt. Thus, while our conversations succeeded in identifying major hermeneutical issues requiring concentrated intellectual work, in many cases we experienced a failure of nerve that was never publicly confronted.

Students. We all had assumptions about the nature of our students, but those assumptions were seldom tested. The old curriculum had been structured for young people whose most pressing need was to get some *critical distance* from the tradition in which they had been raised. We presumed, in Ricoeur's terms, a first naïveté, and sought to move quickly to a critical moment. Over a period of time the faculty began to discover how poor a job the church has done in basic catechization. Students do not know the basic story of the scriptures or of the church. We cannot presume, for example, that they know Luther's *Small Catechism*. Courses that moved quickly into critical methodology (so as to achieve some distance from the tradition) had the unintended consequences of protecting students from a tradition they did not know.

Once again, the problem is hardly new; nevertheless, experiencing its extent and depth is still a surprise. In a course introducing Old and New Testament, two professors asked students to read Potok's *The Chosen* during the first week. The book serves as an introduction to Judaism for students who have known few Jews and know little about Judaism, and it nicely highlights the tensions that exist between traditional communities and the contemporary world. As students discussed the book, a consistent pattern would develop. After a few probes to see what was safe to say, students would begin speaking negatively, even in hostile terms, about hasidic Jews: they hide from the real world behind their tradition. They spoke positively about the more liberal and worldly Jews who were willing to accommodate the real world. When this tendency was called to the attention of the class, they were genuinely surprised at their bias.

They simply took cultural values for granted and viewed with suspicion religious communities who were different.

Perhaps even more striking was our experience of recognizing that, in such a situation, most of the courses in the curriculum still presumed students who had been formed by the Lutheran tradition. One group of 36 Lutheran students, when pressed gently about their own religious background, confessed that religious rituals like regular church attendance, even grace at meals, were not part of their family life. Only two of the 36 had been raised in families that two generations ago would be recognized as religiously "traditional."

Church, Society, and Congregations. Our reflections on the faculty and student audiences opened onto the larger questions of the diversity of audiences within our present culture. We agreed that what is true of our students is increasingly true of the church. An ever-smaller group of people have been well formed in their own traditions. Congregations that thrive and grow are filled with people who were not raised in the Lutheran church — and in fact have little "church" background of the sort one might have expected two generations ago. The same is true of congregations in other mainline denominations. And as the church continues to lose the support of the dominant culture, congregations can no longer count on members to reproduce themselves. While we had some difficulty agreeing on what "mission" entails, we did agree that preparing pastors to maintain congregations in the present environment is insufficient for the needs of the church. We agreed that to prepare pastors for the changed situation, we would have to give them better skills at understanding the circumstances of the people to whom they would be sent.

Ethos: Leadership

Among the terms that describe aspects of the pastoral office, "leadership" came to occupy a central place — though not without occasioning disquiet. The reason for its prominence was a sense that the various images that had shaped pastoral identity over the last decades had focused too much on personal gifts and interpersonal skills. The privatization of religion and its concomitant elevation of various models of intimacy had made a strong impression on our seminary, with pastoral care and counseling becoming perhaps the major feature of pastoral training. Even the term "pastoral" has come to connote intimate as opposed to public settings.

Given the conviction that the church no longer enjoys the support of the culture, the ability of pastors to make public arguments for the faith and the tradition becomes increasingly important.[4] The need for new visions in a pluralistic context require precisely the sorts of gifts and training the rhetorical tradition was designed to foster to prepare people for public life.

Some were sensitive to possible abuse by strong leaders. It was important for us to spell out precisely what we do and do not mean by "leadership." Persuasion and manipulation by means of cunning and violence are inappropriate, particularly in congregational settings. Alternative patterns and models, however, are not readily available.

Our curriculum project, in short, tried to describe what we mean by "leadership in mission" and how such a pastoral identity could be shaped. Most striking, to us, was the willingness of the members of the pastoral theology department to reimagine their vocation in the new context. They seemed most clearly aware that preparing "pastoral counselors" was not the main business in which the seminary must be engaged at this point in our history.

Logos: The Received Tradition

As a denominational seminary with a confessional identity that includes a high regard for the Bible, we affirm the normative role exercised by the tradition as a central feature of the pastoral enterprise. Given our sense that students who come to the seminary have been far less thoroughly catechized than previous generations and do not know the scriptures well, a major task in the curriculum is to teach the tradition. Of particular concern is the Bible, to which considerable time is devoted, including the study of biblical languages. We became aware, however, how easily biblical courses can become captive to alienating methodologies and how difficult it can be to avoid encouraging the kind of research interests appropriate primarily in Ph.D. programs. (Of course, even drawing a sharp distinction between M.Div. and Ph.D. programs can be a problem — particularly if the seminaries hope to continue to draw their M.Div. instructors from these same Ph.D. programs.) While recognizing the importance of *critical* appropriation of the scriptures and tradition of the church, the faculty adopted a curricular strategy that seems more appropriate to the actual situation of our students. The next section of this chapter provides a broad outline of that strategy.

---

[4]See Don Compier's remarks on Public Theology, chapter 7 of the present volume.

The Construct: Story, Interpreting/Confessing, Mission

Given the nature of our students and our present situation in American culture, we determined that there would be three major moments in the educational process. We entitled them, "Story," "Interpreting and Confessing," and "Mission." We imagined the curriculum as a movement from story to mission. The narrative category "story" was chosen particularly with respect to the tradition into which most students needed to be introduced. There is a concentration of courses in biblical studies and church history in the first year of study. The abandonment of introductory courses in Old and New Testament reflects growing disenchantment with survey and methods courses and a desire to move students deeply into biblical material as soon as possible. While introductory matters cannot be avoided, the challenge is to raise such questions as they become relevant in the study of biblical literature.

The goal of the curriculum is to help form pastors who are capable of creative leadership. The last movement in the formation of a pastoral imagination focuses on practical reasoning (*phronēsis*), which presumes the ability to decide and act. As we imagined the curriculum, this is the point when students must practice making arguments shaped by the tradition for the various audiences they will encounter. Their own pastoral identity (*ēthos*) in the various activities of ministry is understood in terms of the habits they are to practice.

The considerable energy invested in clarifying what "mission" entails in the present contexts of ministry revealed both a new awareness of audience and an older cultural bias. Suspicion of those who persuade by using cunning and violence, combined with the strong sense (in the wider culture) that religion is a private matter, made it difficult for some colleagues to use such categories as "mission" and "evangelism" — and even to appreciate the use of the rhetorical paradigm itself.

If the goal of the curriculum is to move students from an appreciation of the tradition to an ability to make use of it in mission, the transition between the two becomes crucial. The scriptures and tradition must be *interpreted*; this requires a critical moment. Clearly, however, critical interpretation does not automatically lead to mission; more often, it leads to disagreement. One might argue that a major factor in the development of the dominant historical paradigm for reading the Bible is a recognition that, since people will never agree in their interpretations, one should simply avoid questions of truth and settle for assessments of meaning. Our belief that this approach was inadequate became the basis for part of the agenda for our course, "Truth and Meaning: Uses of the Biblical Narrative."

The faculty agreed that the second year of study would be the appropriate place to raise the significant hermeneutical questions. At a confessional seminary, a central issue is the significance and function of the normative tradition. Initially, the faculty spoke of the need for critical interpretation of the story as the "natural" modern answer to that question. A colleague wrote a short paper at this juncture adding a key insight into bridging story and mission: confessing.

To oversimplify his argument, he rightly observed that modern consciousness can interpret the story without ever leading to mission. Indeed, the process of interpreting scripture, for example, while an essential and delightful task, can become a cul-de-sac. Recent research on the role of the Bible in moral conversations in Lutheran congregations — initially in Southwestern Minnesota, and now in southern California and Texas — shows that pastors are not likely to use scripture in moral conversation. Indeed, if they do so, they are likely to interpret it so as to show that, due to cultural and historical differences, particular texts are irrelevant to the moral topic at hand. Interpreting does not necessarily lead to mission.

Interpreting must therefore be supplemented by *confessing*; and providing attention to this element is a key role of the leader of a Christian community. "Confessing" is a "saying together" that is, however, different from uniformity. Unless the interpreter confesses Jesus Christ as Lord, mission is not likely to result. Unless the confessing is integrated with interpreting the story, the confessing is not likely to be faithful; unless the interpreting is related to the critical insight of the gospel, not just as an idea but as an experience of witness, the interpreting will not likely serve the unique mission of the church in the Divine Economy: the world will not be changed.

Needless to say, many of the controversies of the new curriculum arose precisely on this bridge question. On some matters the faculty was able to develop the requisite consensus and political will to resolve the issues; on others it was not. Perhaps the most neuralgic aspect of this conversation concerned the role of the "critical moment" in theological education. Perduring and profound differences arise here between those who believe the "critical" moment of theological education is primarily lodged in sources external to scripture and the confessing tradition and those who — while recognizing diverse sources for reflection and criticism in interpreting and confessing — believe that the scripture and the confessing tradition themselves provide the "critical moment" of theological education.

A closely related issue is reflected in David Kelsey's most helpful books[5] on theological education, when he asks, "How theological is theological education?" His answer is, "Not very." For example, the result of the theory/practice split has been a growing dominance of social sciences in the understanding of the so-called "practical" disciplines. Depending upon where one places the discipline of history, the social sciences have also come to dominate the subdisciplines of Biblical Studies and History of Christianity. In some ways, theology has become the specialty of the systematic theologians, while the other disciplines of the theological encyclopedia arrange themselves without much attention to God. The result: theological education is not very theological.

A case in point that profoundly cripples our preparation of leaders for Christian communities is in the area of *worship*. Worship within the modern encyclopedia has too often been reduced to a practical discipline. Worship courses focus on providing a certain kind of practical competence that, indeed, no public leader of worship should be without. In Lutheran seminaries, courses teach how to lead the *Lutheran Book of Worship*. If any theory is offered in such a practical course, it is drawn from ritual theory, thus from the social sciences or history. This is not bad; but it can be profoundly truncated (and often atheological).

Problems arise when graduates are sent to congregations that have overwhelmingly voted to follow diverse forms of worship in relationship to the diverse communities they are serving. The *Lutheran Book of Worship*, as it is printed, is clearly designed for a much narrower audience. Graduates are expected to innovate alternative worship; but, being grossly unprepared for such ritual resourcefulness and innovation, they get caught in worship wars. Worship wars tend to reduce these questions to choosing between tradition and novelty. Too often, liturgical scholars lose themselves in elaborate studies of historical liturgies, presuming to find the norm of worship in some supposed *ordo* (Platonic or Archetypal) that lies behind, above, beneath the amazing diversity of Christian worship in all times and places. Practical (and often desperate) pastors grasp for the most effective resources for creating a new audience — or just holding their present audiences.

Paul Holmer, in an article published in the early 1970s, had already pointed to this flaw in the contemporary reigning models of teaching worship, including at his own institution (Yale Divinity School). He argued that the logic

---

[5]See the two books cited in note 1 of the present chapter, above.

of worship is neither in the tradition, nor in novelty, but in God. The modern encyclopedia does not typically allow for the teaching of worship in such a manner. Once "thinking God" forms the logic of a course, it becomes "systematic theology." So students learn a theological theory of worship in a "doctrine of the Church" course, and a hands-on practical introduction to denominational worship texts in a "worship" course. These various components frequently fail to cohere, and only serve to aid and abet the combatants in the worship wars.

Such neuralgic issues as these could not be fully resolved prior to the implementation of the new curriculum; but neither could the curriculum move forward pretending that these issues would go away. Somehow, the ongoing debates surrounding matters of "interpreting and confessing" needed a place within the curriculum without presuming their resolution. The traditional Enlightenment encyclopedia did not account for these topics and disciplines, so we created a new category of courses: Interpreting and Confessing.

The Interpreting and Confessing portion of the new curriculum was created precisely as a place to carry on these conversations among faculty and students, so that complex and controversial issues could be attended to in a careful and systematic manner. Courses within this portion of the curriculum include: Reading the Audience, The Lutheran Confessional Writings, and a number of required core electives. All courses in this portion of the new curriculum are team-taught by persons drawn from the traditional divisions of the seminary faculty. They place at the center of the course the challenging and perduring issues of our postmodern, post-Christendom context.

Perhaps the most important decision in the process was to commit ourselves as a faculty to tasks for which we have not been trained in our various disciplines. We tended to locate these most creative — and risky— ventures in the "Interpreting and Confessing" area. The course entitled "Reading the Audience" is taught in the first year. It seeks to raise crucial questions about the relatedness of all theological formulations to their contexts; about the particularity of audiences; and about strategies for coming to terms with the structure and assumptions of particular audiences, such as congregations. In this class, the social sciences and systems theory have been high on the list of priorities. So has been the desire to show the importance of theological assumptions about the nature of human beings and human society. That the course was the least successful in the first few years of the new curriculum only indicates how difficult is the task of re-imagining theological education. The tendency is to attempt too much; the drive to "master" disciplines must give way to "befriending" them. The collegial commitment to teach the course is one of the most promising signs that the world of theological education at Luther has changed.

The presence in the second year of courses like "Truth and Meaning" is an expression of the commitment to introduce a critical moment without abandoning questions of truth — and without paralyzing students who must finally decide and act (and persuade others to do the same).

In the third year, the challenge of such courses as "Biblical Theology" is to teach (with the use of case studies drawn from students' ministry experience) in such a way as to develop habits of pastoral reflection. In such a course, the tradition has a crucial role; at the same time, the situational character of all speech is taken seriously.

A Preliminary Assessment: Suggestions and Questions

1. One reason for the utility of the rhetorical paradigm is its focus on the three "characters" in any speech-act. It is a helpful way of thinking about pastoral identity that takes the substance of the theological heritage seriously and is at the same time aware of and respectful toward the diversity and particularly of audiences.

2. A rhetorical orientation takes seriously the importance of persuasion at every level of the tradition and life of the church. Perhaps most significantly, it prepares students for life in a pluralistic society, where first principles are open to debate, and where there are no absolute and universally agreed-upon foundations for pastoral theological reflection.

3. The rhetorical tradition has in view the practical: the value of persuasion has to do largely with argumentation that leads to action. Scholarship is important not for its own sake, but for the sake of the practices it engenders. Theory and practice must be dialogically related.

4. It remains to be seen whether Christians, and particularly those responsible for shaping the future of theology and theological education, can be persuaded that the image of pastor as "rhetor" is a promising one. The suspicion that rhetoric and the rhetorical tradition tend to provoke suggests not only a yearning for secure fundamentals — the Cartesian Anxiety once again — but also a lack of trust in the ability of conversation to change people. The alternatives, however, are no more appealing. Some form of absolutism — whether based on the Bible, the tradition, or a charismatic personality — obviously appeals to many in the present context, but it is an unlikely future for mainline Christianity. Withdrawing into a view of truth which suggests that

the most one can hope for is consensus within minority communities can fail to take with sufficient seriousness both our obligation to the neighbor whom God has given us, and the public nature of theological discourse. The obstacles to conversation are real, however, and the tendency to rely on cunning and violence in persuading one another is also real.

5. The success of a rhetorical approach to theological education depends in part on convincing colleagues of the depth of the problems facing the Church. The ability of academic communities to safeguard their way of life is impressive. Perhaps the continuing decline in the membership within mainline churches, and the consequent economic pressure, will finally be the most compelling motivation for change. But many church leaders are also aware that the assumptions and practices of the modern era, and of Christendom, are no longer serviceable. Perhaps this deficit will produce positive energy for change.

Looking back on our experience with the faculty of Luther Seminary, we have concluded that, while the process of conversation was arduous, our overall experience was very promising. After a process of almost nine years, the new curricular goals have certainly not been "achieved," if this is meant to suggest an arrival at a new plateau. In fact, it is becoming increasingly clear that the future will be a time of continuous innovation. On the other hand, this result is very much in line with most current proposals for curricular revision, recognizing (as they must) that the rate of cultural change is currently so great that no "leveling-off" period is likely. At the same time, an expectation of continuous change is also highly appropriate to the rhetorical model. Rhetoric recognizes the need to bring the tradition to bear on the contingencies of particular contexts, by a wide variety of speakers, for a wide variety of audiences. And such detailed attention to the specificity of context will be absolutely essential, if Christian theological education is to continue to be able to produce clergy and lay leaders for the Church who are able to teach, to delight, and to move.

Bibliography:

Rhetorical Resources for Theological Education

Aristotle. *Rhetoric*. Many translations are available; one of the most recent is by George A. Kennedy, *Aristotle On Rhetoric: A Theory of Civic Discourse*. Oxford: Oxford University Press, 1991.

Arnhart, Larry. *Aristotle on Political Reasoning: A Commentary on the Rhetoric*. DeKalb: Northern Illinois University Press, 1981.

Augustine of Hippo. *De Doctrina Christiana*. Ed. and trans. R. P. H. Green. Oxford Early Christian Texts Oxford and New York: Oxford University Press, 1996.

Barilli, Renato. *Rhetoric*. Translated by Giuliana Menozzi. Theory and History of Literature, vol. 63. Minneapolis: University of Minnesota Press, 1989.

Bernstein, Richard J. *Beyond Objectivism and Relativism*. Philadelphia: University of Pennsylvania Press; Oxford: Basil Blackwell, 1983.

Bitzer, Lloyd F. "The Rhetorical Situation." *Philosophy and Rhetoric* 1 (1968): 1–14.

Black, Edwin. *Rhetorical Criticism: A Study in Method*. New York: Macmillan, 1965; reprint, Madison: University of Wisconsin Press, 1978.

Brinton, Alan. "Situation in the Theory of Rhetoric." *Philosophy and Rhetoric* 14 (1981): 234–48.

Burke, Kenneth. *A Rhetoric of Motives*. New York: Prentice-Hall, 1950; reprint, Berkeley: University of California Press, 1969.

Burke, Kenneth. *The Rhetoric of Religion: Studies in Logology*. Boston: Beacon Press, 1961; reprint, Berkeley: University of California Press, 1970.

Chopp, Rebecca S. *The Power to Speak: Feminism, Language, God*. New York: Crossroad, 1989.

Cicero, Marcus Tullius. *De Inventione. De Optimo Genere Oratorum. Topica*. Trans. H. M. Hubbell. Cambridge: Harvard University Press, 1949.

Cicero, Marcus Tullius. *De Oratore. De Fato. Paradoxa Stoicurm. Partitiones Oratoriae*. 2 Vols. Trans. H. Rackham and E.W. Sutton. Cambridge: Harvard University Press, 1959–1960.

Compier, Don H. *What Is Rhetorical Theology? Textual Practice and Public Discourse*. Harrisburg, PA: Trinity Press International, 1999.

Cunningham, David S. *Faithful Persuasion: In Aid of a Rhetoric of Christian Theology*. Notre Dame, Ind.: University of Notre Dame Press, 1991.

Cunningham, David S. *These Three Are One: The Practice of Trinitarian Theology*. Challenges in Contemporary Theology. Oxford: Basil Blackwell, 1998.

De Certeau, Michel. *The Mystic Fable*. Vol. 1, *The Sixteenth and Seventeenth Centuries*. Trans. Michael B. Smith. Chicago and London: University of Chicago Press, 1992.

Derrida, Jacques. *Of Grammatology*. Translated by Gayatri Chakravorty Spivak. Baltimore: Johns Hopkins University Press, 1976.

Derrida, Jacques. *The Gift of Death*. Translated by David Wills. Chicago: University of Chicago Press, 1995.

Farley, Edward. *Theologia: The Fragmentation and Unity of Theological Education.* Philadelphia: Fortress Press, 1983.

Farrell, Thomas B. *Norms of Rhetorical Culture.* New Haven and London: Yale University Press, 1994.

Fish, Stanley. "Rhetoric." In *Doing What Comes Naturally: Change, Rhetoric, and the Practice of Theory in Literary and Legal Studies.* Durham, N.C.: Duke University Press, 1989.

Foucault, Michel. *Discipline and Punish: The Birth of the Prison.* Translated by Alan Sheridan. New York: Pantheon, 1977; reprint, New York: Random House, Vintage Books, 1979.

Foucault, Michel. *Madness and Civilization: A History of Insanity in the Age of Reason.* Translated by Richard Howard. New York: Random House, 1965; reprint, New York: Random House, Vintage Books, 1988.

Fisher, Walter R. *Human Communication as Narration: Toward a Philosophy of Reason, Value, and Action.* Columbia: University of South Carolina Press, 1987.

Fowl, Stephen E. *Engaging Scripture: A Model for Theological Interpretation.* Challenges in Contemporary Theology. Oxford: Blackwell Publishers, 1998.

Gadamer, Hans-Georg. *Truth and Method.* Trans. Joel Weinsheimer and Donald G. Marshall. New York: Continuum, 1989.

Garver, Eugene. *Aristotle's Rhetoric: An Art of Character.* Chicago and London: University of Chicago Press, 1994.

Grassi, Ernesto. *Rhetoric as Philosophy: The Humanist Tradition.* University Park: Pennsylvania State University Press, 1980.

Gregg, Richard B. *Symbolic Inducement and Knowing: A Study in the Foundations of Rhetoric.* Columbia: University of South Carolina Press, 1984.

Grimaldi, William M. A., S.J. *Aristotle, Rhetoric I: A Commentary*. New York: Fordham University Press, 1980.

Habermas, Jürgen. *The Theory of Communicative Action*. 2 vols. Trans. Thomas McCarthy. Volume 1: *Reason and the Rationalization of Society;* Volume 2: *Lifeworld and System: A Critique of Functionalist Reason*. Boston: Beacon Press, 1984–1987.

Hart, Ray L. *Unfinished Man and the Imagination: Toward an Ontology and a Rhetoric of Revelation*. With an Introduction by Mark C. Taylor. New York: Herder and Herder, 1968; reprint, Atlanta: Scholars Press, 1985.

Jasper, David. *Rhetoric, Power and Community: An Exercise in Reserve*. London: Macmillan; Louisville: Westminster/John Knox Press, 1993.

Jones, Serene. *Calvin and the Rhetoric of Piety*. Columbia Series in Reformed Theology. Louisville: Westminster/John Knox Press, 1995.

Jost, Walter. *Rhetorical Thought in John Henry Newman*. Columbia: University of South Carolina Press, 1989.

Jost, Walter, and Michael Hyde, eds. *Rhetoric and Hermeneutics in Our Time: A Reader*. New Haven, Conn.: Yale University Press, 1997.

Kennedy, George A. *Classical Rhetoric and Its Christian and Secular Tradition from Ancient to Modern Times*. Chapel Hill: University of North Carolina Press, 1980.

Kennedy, George A. *A History of Rhetoric*. 3 vols. Volume 1: *The Art of Persuasion in Greece;* Volume 2: *The Art of Rhetoric in the Roman World;* and Volume 3: *Greek Rhetoric under Christian Emperors* (Princeton: Princeton University Press, 1963, 1972, and 1983).

Kennedy, George A. *New Testament Interpretation through Rhetorical Criticism*. Chapel Hill: University of North Carolina Press, 1984.

Kinneavy, James L. *Greek Rhetorical Origins of Christian Faith*. New York: Oxford University Press, 1987.

Kuhn, Thomas. *The Structure of Scientific Revolutions*. 3rd edition. Chicago: University of Chicago Press, 1996.

Lentricchia, Frank. *Criticism and Social Change*. Chicago: University of Chicago Press, 1983.

Levinas, Emmauel. *Otherwise than Being, or Beyond Essence*. Translated by Alphonso Lingis. The Hague: Nijhoff, 1991.

Lyotard, Jean-François. *The Postmodern Condition: A Report on Knowledge*. Trans. Geoff Bennington and Brian Massumi. With a Preface by Fredric Jameson. Minneapolis: University of Minnesota Press, 1984.

MacIntyre, Alasdair. *After Virtue: A Study in Moral Theory*. 2nd edition. Notre Dame, Ind.: University of Notre Dame Press, 1984.

MacIntyre, Alasdair. *Three Rival Versions of Moral Enquiry: Encyclopaedia, Geneaology, and Tradition*. Notre Dame, Ind.: University of Notre Dame Press, 1990.

Mailloux, Steven. *Rhetorical Power*. Ithaca, N.Y.: Cornell University Press, 1989.

Milbank, John. *Theology and Social Theory: Beyond Secular Reason*. Signposts in Theology. Oxford: Basil Blackwell, 1990.

Milbank, John. *The Word Made Strange: Theology, Language, Culture*. Oxford: Basil Blackwell, 1997.

Nelson, John S., Allan McGill, and Donald N. McCloskey, eds., *The Rhetoric of the Human Sciences: Language and Argument in Scholarship and Public Affairs*. Madison: University of Wisconsin Press, 1987.

Norris, Frederick W., ed. *Faith Gives Fullness to Reasoning: The Five Theological Orations of Gregory Nazianzen*. Trans. Lionel Wickham and Frederick Williams. Supplements to Vigiliae Christianae, vol. 13. Leiden: E. J. Brill, 1991.

Nussbaum, Martha C. *The Fragility of Goodness: Luck and Ethics in Greek Tragedy and Philosophy*. Cambridge: Cambridge University Press, 1986.

Ong, Walter J., S.J. *Ramus, Method, and the Decay of Dialogue*. 1958; reprint, Cambridge: Harvard University Press, 1983.

Ong, Walter J. *Orality and Literacy: The Technologizing of the Word*. New Accents. London: Methuen, 1982.

Perelman, Chaïm, and Lucie Olbrechts-Tyteca. *The New Rhetoric: A Treatise on Argumentation*. Translated by John Wilkinson and Purcell Weaver. Notre Dame, Ind.: University of Notre Dame Press, 1969.

Pickstock, Catherine. *After Writing: On the Liturgical Consummation of Philosophy*. Challenges in Contemporary Theology. Oxford: Basil Blackwell, 1997.

Quintilian, Marcus Fabius. *The Institutio Oratoria of Quintilian*. 4 Vols. Trans. H.E. Butler. Cambridge: Harvard University Press, 1959–1963.

Robbins, Vernon K., and John H. Patton. Rhetoric and Biblical Criticism." *The Quarterly Journal of Speech* 66 (1980): 327–37.

Rorty, Amélie Oksenberg. *Essays on Aristotle's Rhetoric*. Berkeley: University of California Press, 1996.

Ruether, Rosemary Radford. *Gregory of Nazianzus: Rhetor and Philosopher*. Oxford: Clarendon Press, 1969.

Schrag, Calvin. *Communicative Praxis and the Space of Subjectivity*. Bloomington: Indiana University Press, 1986.

Schrag, Calvin. *The Resources of Rationality: A Response to the Postmodern Challenge*. Bloomington, Ind.: Indiana University Press, 1992.

Schüssler Fiorenza, Elisabeth. "The Ethics of Interpretation: De-Centering Biblical Scholarship." *Journal of Biblical Literature* 107, no. 1 (March 1988): 3-17.

Simons, Herbert W., ed. *The Rhetorical Turn: Invention and Persuasion in the Conduct of Inquiry*. Chicago: University of Chicago Press, 1990.

Toulmin, Stephen. *The Uses of Argument*. Cambridge: Cambridge University Press, 1958.

Toulmin, Stephen, Richard Rieke, and Allan Janik. *An Introduction to Reasoning*. 2nd edition. New York: Macmillan Publishing, 1984.

Tracy, David. *The Analogical Imagination: Christian Theology and the Culture of Pluralism*. New York: Crossroad, 1981.

Tracy, David. *Dialogue with the Other: The Inter-Religious Dialogue*. Louvain Theological and Pastoral Monographs, vol. 1. Leuven: Peeters Uitgeverij, 1990; reprint, Grand Rapids, Mich.: Wm. B. Eerdmans, 1991.

Tracy, David. *Plurality and Ambiguity: Hermeneutics, Religion, Hope*. San Francisco: Harper & Row, 1987.

Valesio, Paolo. *Novantiqua: Rhetorics as a Contemporary Theory*. Advances in Semiotics, ed. Thomas A. Sebeok. Bloomington: Indiana University Press, 1980.

Vickers, Brian. *In Defense of Rhetoric*. New York: Oxford University Press; Oxford: Clarendon Press, 1988.

Webb, Stephen H. *Re-Figuring Theology: The Rhetoric of Karl Barth*. SUNY Series in Rhetoric and Theology, ed. David Tracy and Stephen H. Webb. Albany: State University of New York Press, 1991.

Wittgenstein, Ludwig. *Culture and Value*. Ed. G. H. von Wright and Heikki Nyman. Trans. Peter Winch. Chicago: University of Chicago Press, 1980.

Wuellner, William. "Where is Rhetorical Criticism Taking Us?" *Catholic Biblical Quarterly* 49 (1987): 448–63.

Contributors

A. K. M. Adam is Professor of New Testament at Seabury-Western Theological Seminary. He has written extensively in the areas of New Testament theology and postmodern thought. His books include *What is Postmodern Biblical Criticism?* (Fortress, 1995) and the *Handbook of Postmodern Biblical Criticism* (Chalice, 2000).

Wes Avram is Clement-Muehl Assistant Professor of Communication at Yale Divinity School. He holds a Ph.D. in Communication Studies from Northwestern University, where he wrote on rhetoric and theology in Levinas and Bakhtin. He is the author of *Where the Light Shines Through* (Brazos, 2005) and editor of *Anxious about Empire: Theological Essays on the New Global Realities* (Brazos, 2004).

James L. Boyce is Professor of New Testament and Greek at Luther Seminary in St. Paul, Minnesota. His writing is primarily in the area of New Testament theology, including for the Proclamation series (Fortress, 1997) and various articles for Luther Seminary's journal *Word & World*.

Don H. Compier is the Dean of Community of Christ Seminary, Graceland University. He wrote his Ph.D. dissertation on rhetoric and theology under Rebecca Chopp at Emory University. His recent works include *John Calvin's Rhetorical Doctrine of Sin* (Mellen, 2001) and *What is Rhetorical Theology?* (Trinity Press International, 2001).

David S. Cunningham is Professor of Religion and Director of the CrossRoads Project at Hope College in Holland, Michigan. He has written extensively on rhetoric and theology, including *Faithful Persuasion: In Aid* of a Rhetoric of Christian Theology (Notre Dame, 1992) and *These Three Are One: The Practice of Trinitarian Theology* (Blackwell,1998). His most recent book is *Reading is Believing: The Christian Faith Through Literature and Film* (Brazos, 2002).

Susan Karen Hedahl is Professor of Homiletics at Lutheran Theological Seminary, Gettysburg, Pennsylvania. She has written a number of lectionary commentaries and other works in homiletics, including texts for the Proclamation series (Fortress, 1995, 2003). She is the co-editor of *Preaching 1 Corinthians 13* (Chalice, 2001).

Bradford Hinze is Associate Professor of Systematic Theology at Marquette University. He has written a number of scholarly articles on rhetoric and theology for *Theological Studies* and other journals. He is the author of *Narrating History, Developing Doctrine: Friedrich Schleiermacher and Johann Sebastian Drey* (Scholars, 1993) and the editor of *The Spirit in the Church and the World* (Orbis, 2004).

Donald Juel (+2003) was Professor of New Testament Theology at Princeton Theological Seminary. A widely-published author and much-loved teacher, he was the prime mover and gracious host for the gatherings out of which this volume grew. He wrote a number of books on New Testament themes, including *Master of Surprise: Mark Interpreted* (Fortress, 1994) and commentaries on Luke-Acts, 1 Thessalonians, and the Gospel of Mark.

Patrick Keifert is Professor of Systematic Theology, Luther Seminary, St. Paul, Minnesota. He has a longstanding interest in the relationship between rhetoric and theology, and is the author of *Welcoming the Stranger: A Public Theology of Worship and Evangelism* (Fortress, 1992). Along with Don Juel, he co-directed the larger Lilly-funded project from which this volume grew.

Frederick W. Norris is Professor of World Chrsitianity (Emeritus) at Emmanuel School of Religion, Johnson City, Tennesee. He wrote an extensive commentary on, and edited, the rhetorically-rich theological orations of Gregory of Nazianzus, published as *Faith Gives Fullness to Reasoning: The Five Theological Orations of Gregory Nazianzen* (Brill, 1991). He is the co-editor of three other Encyclopedias and *Festschriften* on early Christianity.

Richard R. Osmer is Thomas W. Synnott Professor of Christian Education at Princeton Theological Seminary. His recent works include *Religious Education Between Modernization and Globalization: New Perspectives on the United States and Germany* (Eerdmans, 2003) and the forthcoming *The Teaching Ministry of Congregations* (Louisville, Ky.: Westminster/John Knox Press, 2005).

Janet L. Weathers holds doctoral degrees in both Speech Communication and Theology and Personality. She taught for 25 years, serving on faculties at UCLA, USC, and most recently Princeton Theological Seminary. She co-authored *New Proclamation: Year C* (Fortress, 2001) and has published articles on biblical theology, religious education, and communication. She is currently Director of the Institute for Creative Transformation.

Stephen H. Webb is Professor of Religion at Wabash College, Crawfordsville, Indiana. He is the author of eight books, many of them related to rhetoric and theology — beginning with *Re-Figuring Theology: The Rhetoric of Karl Barth* (SUNY Press, 1991) and including, most recently, *The Divine Voice: Christian Proclamation and the Theology of Sound* (Eerdmans, 2004).

Index of Names

Adam, A. K. M., 5, 13, 74, 79, 95, 97, 107, 158, 167, 185, 270
Altieri, Charles, 155
Altizer, Thomas, 134
Anselm of Canterbury, 101
Aquinas, *see* Thomas Aquinas
Arens, Edmund, 86
Arnhart, Larry, 17, 297

Bakhtin, Mikhail, 39, 87, 91, 148
Balthasar, Hans Urs von, 87, 100, 245
Barilli, Renato, 14, 297
Barth, Karl, 32, 33, 100, 101, 163, 254,
Basil of Caesarea, 226, 232, 239
Baxter, Leslie A., 39
Bazerman, Charles, 37, 183
Becker, Mortimer, 31, 219
Berkenkotter, Carol, 183
Bernard, Robert W., 81
Bernstein, Richard J., 39, 282, 297
Berquist, Goodwin F., 14
Berry, Phillipa, 63
Betz, Hans Dieter, 66, 204–205
Bevans, Stephen B. 96
Beyer, Peter, 186
Billig, Michael, 37

Bitzer, Lloyd F., 15, 203, 272, 297
Black, Edwin, 15, 297
Blondel, Maurice, 100
Bolt, Robert, 143–44
Booth, Wayne C., 31, 131
Boyce, James L., 8, 13, 97, 270
Brandt, William J., 19
Brett, Mark, 77
Brinton, Alan, 203, 298
Brown, Harold, 180
Brown, John, 55
Browning, Don S., 157, 197
Bruns, Gerald, 79
Brunschwig, Jacques, 227
Buber, Martin, 87, 91
Burke, Kenneth, 19, 25, 29, 31, 35, 38, 47–48, 53, 57, 155–56, 160, 204, 209, 216, 273, 298
Burnham, Frederic B., 133
Burrows, Mark S., 81

Campbell, James L., 206
Carroll R., M. Daniel, 77
Carroll, David, 151
Carruthers, Mary, 132
Cartesian, *see* Descartes, René
Cavanaugh, William T., 43
Chopp, Rebecca, 33, 157, 197, 298

Ciceccarelli, Leah, 269
Clines, David J. A., 77
Clutterbuck, Richard, 96
Coleman, William E., 14
Collins, Adela Yarbro, 66
Compier, Don H., 7, 13, 33, 74, 91, 107, 185, 188, 194, 241, 279, 290, 298
Conduit, Celeste, 269
Cook, Martin L., 110
Cunningham, David S., 13, 34, 48, 74, 95, 96, 104, 131, 133, 141, 154, 160, 182, 239, 246, 250, 269, 275, 298
Curran, Jane V., 16

Dabney, D. Lyle, 104
Dalton, Stuart, 159
Daube, David, 93
Davies, Philip R., 77
De Certeau, Michel, 249, 298
Del Colle, Ralph, 96
Demosthenes, 223, 226
Descartes, René (or Cartesian), 5, 41, 43–44, 46, 130, 224, 282, 295
Douglass, Jane Dempsey, 52
Doxaprates, 226
Duke, James, 109, 174, 179
Dulles, Avery, 99

Eden, Kathy, 27, 165
Eemersen, Frans von, 189
Ellis, George, 186
Emerson, Caryl, 148
Evagrius, 241
Evans, Fred J., 74
Evans, G. R., 184

Farley, Edward, ix, 172, 173, 299
Farrell, Thomas B., 141, 299
Finucane, Daniel J., 102
Fish, Stanley, 33, 66, 67, 299
Fisher, Walter R., 5, 31, 38, 45–50, 54, 56, 57, 299
Fiumara, Gemma Corradi, 277
Florovsky, Georges, 225–26
Foss, Sonja K., 272–73
Foucault, Michel, 32, 113-115, 118, 124, 185, 241, 299
Fowl, Stephen E., 74, 77, 96, 299
Fox, Richard, 149
Frei, Hans, 65, 196
Froelich, Karlfried, 78
Funk, Robert W., 150, 207–208

Gadamer, Hans-Georg, 27, 87, 88, 91, 102, 191, 299
Galli, Barbara E., 136
Gehl, Paul, 132
Geiman, Kevin Paul, 62
Gerhard, Johann, 101
Golden, James L., 14
Gorgias, 141, 223
Grassi, Ernesto, 30, 299
Gregory Nazianzen, 32, 73, 99, 223–41, 260, 301
Gregory of Nyssa, 225, 233
Griffin, David Ray, 131, 134
Grimaldi, William, 17, 31, 227, 300
Grootendorst, Rob, 189
Gros, Jeffrey, 104
Gutiérrez, Gustavo, 56

Habermas, Jürgen, 52, 86, 157, 182, 183, 300

Index of Names ✣ 311

Hagenbach, Karl, 178
Hall, Douglas John, 162–64
Halle, William W., 148
Hart, Ray L., 88, 300
Hart, Rodney, 273
Harvey, Van A., 150, 166
Hauerwas, Stanley, 40, 121, 123, 134
Heidegger, Martin, 88, 133, 134
Hilberath, Bernd Jochen, 104
Hinze, Bradford, 6, 85, 91, 96, 104, 166
Holquist, Michael, 148
Hough, Joseph C., Jr., 131, 134
Huckin, Thomas, 183
Hunsinger, George, 65
Husserl, Edmund, 88
Hyde, Michael, 27, 88, 155, 159, 165, 300
Hymer, Sharon, 117

Iremonger, F. A., 153
Irwin, William, 78
Isocrates, 16, 223

Jackson, Jared J., 203
Jackson, Sally, 189
Jacobs, Scott, 189
Janik, Allan, 40, 182–83, 303
Jasper, David, 29, 33, 300
Jauss, Hans Robert, 87, 91
Jenson, Robert W., 248, 249
John of Sicily, 226
John of Damascus, 224
John Cassian, 241
Jones, Serene, 74, 131, 300
Jost, Walter, 27, 88, 131, 155, 159, 165, 300

Kahn, Victoria, 26, 27, 165, 167
Kay, James F., 51
Keck, Leander, 81
Kelly, J. N. D., 247
Kelsey, David, 2, 65, 281, 293
Kennedy, George A., 14, 20, 22, 23, 25, 27, 28, 156, 178, 204, 206, 226, 227, 297, 300
Kessler, Martin, 203
Kinneavy, James L., 98, 101, 300
Klemm, David, 33, 134
Kline, Stephen Jay, 186–87
Kluback, William, 19, 31, 219
Kuhn, Thomas S., 181, 199, 301

Lacey, Michael J., 150, 157
Lamadrid, Lucas, 96
Lampe, G. W. H., 78
Lash, Nicholas, 101, 247
Leary, David E., 37
Levinas, Emmanuel, 32, 87, 91, 131, 139, 301
Lindbeck, George, 112, 120
Lombard, Peter, 101
Lovering, Eugene H., 79
Luther, Martin, 30, 100, 163, 214, 274–75, 288
Lynn, Elizabeth, 150
Lynn, Robert, 178
Lyotard, Jean-François, 5, 61–64, 66–67, 73–75, 80, 82, 107, 152, 158–59, 185, 301

MacIntyre, Alasdair, 71, 173, 191, 301
Macrina, 232
Mailloux, Stephen, 159–60, 301
Martin, Josef, 20

Index of Names

Martos, Joseph, 113
Mazzo, Joseph Anthony, 81
McAdoo, H. R., 161
McCloskey, Daniel N., 33, 37, 79, 181, 301
McClure, John S., 278
McNamara, Marie Aquinas, 106
Megill, Allan, 33, 79, 181, 301
Melanchthon, Philip, 163, 191
Merleau-Ponty, Maurice, 88
Michel, Andreas, 152
Milbank, John, 63, 68, 120, 127, 245, 247, 257, 259, 260, 301
Miles, Sian, 146
Miller, Richard B., 119–22
Moltmann, Jürgen, 51–52
Monagle, John F., 106
Montgomery, Barbara M., 39
Mudge, Lewis S., 137
Muilenberg, James, 203
Murphy, James J., 28
Murphy, Nancey, 186
Murray, James S., 16

Nazianzen, *see* Gregory Nazianzen
Nelson, John S., 33, 79, 181, 301
Newlands, Carole, 28
Newman, John Henry, 30, 32, 103, 131, 300
Niebuhr, Gustav, 150
Niebuhr, H. Richard, 110, 171, 190
Niebuhr, Reinhold, 149, 166
Nietzsche, Friedrich, 30, 32, 124
Norris, Frederick W., 8–9, 30, 98, 99, 229–31, 239-241, 260, 301
Nyssa, *see* Gregory of Nyssa

Olbrechts-Tyteca, Lucie, 5, 19, 35, 38–40, 154, 182, 302
Osmer, Richard R., 8, 148, 171, 186, 264

Pauck, Wilhelm, 163
Payer, Pierre J., 114
Pelikan, Jaroslav, 191, 275
Perelman, Chaïm, 5, 19, 31, 35, 38–40, 154, 182, 204, 219, 302
Pickstock, Catherine, 247, 255, 302
Pinches, Charles, 40
Placher, William C. 65, 120, 164, 194
Plato, 15–17, 24, 30, 141, 223, 225–27
Porter, H. C., 77
Powell, J. G. F., 106

Raboteau, Albert J., 54–56
Rahner, Karl, 100, 234
Readings, Bill, 62
Reuben, Julie, xii
Ricoeur, Paul, 71, 88, 133, 136–38, 145, 288
Rieke, Richard, 40, 182–83, 303
Robbins, Vernon K., 205, 302
Roberts, Mark S., 62, 152
Robertson, Roland, 186
Rorem, Paul, 81
Rosenfield, Lawrence W., 15
Rosenzweig, Franz, 87, 136, 148
Rouse, Joseph, 185
Rousselot, Pierre, 100
Ruether, Rosemary Radford, 17, 302
Rusch, William G., 104

Scanlon, Michael J., 81
Schaff, Philip, 178
Schleiermacher, Friedrich D. E., 162, 172–80, 195, 265
Schreiter, Robert J., 96, 163
Schüssler Fiorenza, Elisabeth, 133, 157, 302
Schweitzer, Friedrich, 177
Simons, Herbert W., 37, 181, 303
Soskice, Janet Martin, 259
Stendahl, Krister, 221
Stenmark, Mikael, 180, 189
Stout, Jeffrey, 63, 76
Sturm, Johannes, 191

Tannen, Deborah, 156
Taylor, Mark C., 33, 134, 300
Temple, William, 152
Thiemann, Ronald F., 158, 162, 166
Thomas Aquinas, 65, 80–82, 100–101, 122, 184, 224, 244
Tisdale, Leonora Tubbs, 278
Toole, David, 127
Toulmin, Stephen, 5, 35, 38, 40–44, 46, 120, 182–84, 189, 303
Tracy, David, 34, 87, 130–31, 133, 151, 154–63, 182, 197, 303
Turner, Philip, 148
Tyndale, William, 77

Udoff, Alan, 136

Van Huyssteen, Wentzel, 186–87
Van der Ven, Johannes, 197
Van Den Abbeele, George, 107
Vickers, Brian, 14, 25, 32, 304

Voetius, Gisbert, 172
Volf, Miroslav, 105, 117–18

Ward, Graham, 77
Watson, Francis, 77
Watson, J. S., 25, 27, 152
Weathers, Janet, 5, 31, 51, 185, 230, 269, 287
Webb, Stephen H., 6–7, 33, 74, 131, 303
Weisheipl, James, 184
Wernick, Andrew, 63
Wheeler, Barbara G., 150
Wilder, Amos N., 204, 216, 218
Williams, Frederick, 230, 236, 238, 260, 301
Williams, Rowan, 133
Willimon, William H., 221
Wills, David, 298
Wills, Gary, 267
Wisdo, David, 124–25
Wittgenstein, Ludwig, 119, 121, 206, 236, 303
Wogaman, Philip, 150
Wood, Charles, 173
Wood, Neal, 28
Woollcombe, K. J., 78
Wuellner, William, 204, 303
Wuketits, Franz, 187
Wyman, Walter, 175–76

Young, Frances, 77
Young, Iris Marion, 182

Index of Subjects

absolution, 114, 117
action, as rhetorical goal, x, xiii, 15, 18, 22–24, 31, 37, 46, 86, 88, 91, 95, 97, 99, 101, 106, 132, 136, 146, 166, 181–83, 195, 206, 208, 212–13, 256, 261, 282, 284, 295
adherence, as rhetorical goal, 40, 50, 54, 202, 205, 209, 212–14, 218–19, 221
agonistic structures, 15, 29, 107, 156
allegory, 72, 77–81, 166; *see also* typological exegesis
anachronism, 70, 76–77, 79
anagogical interpretation, 80
apophatism, 228
apostolicity, 106, 143
argument, as rhetorical element, 7, 18–22, 28, 30, 36–41, 49–50, 55, 91–94, 98–102, 125–26, 133–44, 155–56, 163, 166, 174, 194–196, 201–22, 234–36, 241, 244–46, 255–56, 259–64, 274, 281, 284–85, 289, 291–92
argument fields, 182–83, 186, 189, 195–96

argumentation, theories of, 3, 5, 20, 38, 181–184, 192, 195, 204–206, 214, 223, 295
assent, *assensus*, 38, 97–101, 212, 220
audience, 3, 7, 15, 18, 21–30, 34, 36–41, 44–47, 90–98, 101–102, 133, 136, 141, 154–56, 162–66, 188–93, 198, 202–206, 209–16, 219–22, 227–31, 235, 240–41, 255–66, 271–76, 283–84, 286–96
authority, 7, 37, 51, 53, 63–67, 70, 90, 94–95, 105, 112–14, 127–48, 158, 202, 207, 209–11, 215, 285

baptism, 102–103, 189, 210, 236, 238
Bible, 8, 32, 49, 55–56, 66, 72, 75–77, 90, 193, 204, 221, 283–287, 290–292, 295
biblical narrative, 291
biblical studies, ix, 38, 65–66, 74, 95, 165, 172, 177, 188, 202–203, 206, 224, 283, 288, 291, 293

biblical theology, 6, 8, 74–76, 80, 206, 295

Cappadocians, 30, 231–34, 247, 259–60
Cartesian anxiety, 282, 295
case studies, 27, 37, 165–66, 295
catechesis, 4, 90, 103
catholicism, catholicity, 96, 106, 113, 116; *see also* Roman Catholicism
certainty, 15, 17, 19, 41–43, 98
character, ix, 16, 18, 21, 25, 30, 63–64, 73, 75–76, 80, 94–108, 133, 136, 138, 153–54, 202, 234, 248–50, 253, 284, 286–87
Christ, 51, 52, 54, 68, 71, 94, 102, 104, 106, 107, 109, 117, 148, 207, 232, 236–238, 243, 245, 267, 269, 271, 274–75, 292
Christian rhetor, 191, 282
christology, 94, 105, 140, 238
church practices, 52
church, x, 1–3, 5–6, 9–10, 34–36, 39, 49–59, 62, 66–67, 73–75, 81, 85–108, 110, 113–14, 117–18, 123–24, 129, 145, 150, 152, 157, 162, 167, 172–175, 177, 180, 188–89, 192–198, 216, 224–25, 229, 232, 234, 250, 254–55, 263, 275, 282–96
citizen(ship), 27, 30, 42, 69, 235
coercion, 141, 193
collegiality, 157, 264, 295
communication event, 35, 39, 51, 57–58
communication theory, 53

communication, 6, 14–16, 20, 31, 33, 35–39, 44–48, 51–53, 56–58, 85–108, 129, 131, 153, 179–182, 186–192, 197, 209, 212, 243, 255, 262–63
communicative praxis, 31, 37
communicative action, 86, 181–183
communion, 86, 88, 95–96, 103–108, 148, 152
communities, 16–17, 40, 49, 51, 53, 58, 85–86, 90–97, 105–106, 118, 123, 146–47, 160, 188–199, 219–22, 234, 236, 240, 276–77, 288–89, 293, 296
confession, 6–7, 100, 109–26, 148, 164, 217, 225, 229, 231, 236, 240, 290, 292, 294
confessor, 94, 113–14
congregational studies, 198
congregations, 49–51, 53, 152, 186–87, 193–94, 196, 282, 289, 292–294
contingency, 18, 30, 35–36, 44, 135, 147, 175, 219
contrition, 116
courtroom, as metaphor for the rhetorical situation, 29, 135, 140, 142, 145, 147, 155, 235, 255
creator, 93, 119, 127, 252, 254
cross-disciplinarity, *see* interdisciplinarity
culture, 27, 31, 51–53, 58, 62, 66, 69–72, 109–12, 113–17, 133–34, 141, 145–47, 154, 157–58, 160, 162, 164, 167,

171, 173, 183, 186, 188, 204, 241, 257, 282, 287, 289, 291

death, 92, 201, 217, 220, 239, 267
decentering, 7, 130, 133
decorum, 25–27, 141, 153–55, 161, 165–66
deliberative rhetoric, 20, 24, 29, 91, 145, 156–57, 159–60, 167, 177, 182
dialogic(al), 6, 39, 85–88, 90–93, 96–97, 100–108, 148, 160, 181, 266, 268
dialogue, 6, 57, 85–108, 157–61, 189, 194–97, 207, 219–21, 227, 272, 278
discernment, 6–7, 25, 127–34, 140–41, 148, 153–54, 162–63, 166, 173, 243
discovery, as an element of rhetoric, 18–19, 24, 26, 36, 132, 154, 203–204, 255, 257, 269; *see also* invention
diversity of viewpoints, 58, 87, 90, 96, 157–58, 161, 167, 224, 233, 271, 289, 292–93, 295
divine nature, 104, 238
divine persons, 86, 104, 246, 249
division(s): of seminary structure, ix, 65, 73, 131, 171, 188, 294; of rhetoric, 17, 19–21, 97; within the church, 52, 58,
doctrine, 79, 90, 93, 110, 117, 151, 192–93, 243–66; of God and Trinity, 104, 243–66, 275; of inspiration, 274;

development of, 95–96; reception of, 102–103,

ecclesiology, 51, 75, 104–105, 118, 133, 177, 197; *see also* church
ecumenism, 87, 106, 287
eloquence, 23–26, 92, 178, 191, 275
empiricism, 32, 64, 68, 77, 148, 175–177, 180–81, 195, 197–98, 204; empirical audience, 255–58
encomium, 29, 92, 156
encyclopedia, as method, 41, theological, 171–175, 178–88, 193–195, 198–99
Enlightenment, 2, 30–31, 35–36, 158, 162, 174, 225, 265, 294
epideictic rhetoric, 20, 24, 29, 91, 157
epistemic values, 181, 183, 185, 190, 192
epistemology, 16–17, 37, 43, 58, 122, 159, 171, 187, 227, 278
equality, 51–52, 105, 258, 260
essentialism, 120, 146
ethics, 17–18, 21, 24, 26, 30–31, 40, 65, 68, 74, 76, 79–80, 87, 91, 98, 106, 110, 120–124, 130, 133–35, 139–40, 153, 165, 174–177, 186–90, 192, 195, 202, 206, 209, 211, 241, 264
ethos, 21, 119, 143, 147, 148, 274, 289
ēthos, xi, 8, 18, 21, 36, 63, 88, 91, 94–98, 106, 134–35, 139, 141–143, 147, 149, 182, 210, 212, 242, 283, 286, 291

evangelical(ism), 103, 134, 146, 189, 278
evidence, 15, 33, 39, 42, 90, 101, 133, 137, 152, 181–83, 284–85
existentialism, 126
expertise, 50, 55, 63, 65–66, 70, 73, 115, 145, 284–85, 287

faith, 6, 54, 66, 71, 77, 80–81, 85–108, 110–114, 118, 121, 124, 128, 134, 145, 148–49, 152, 176, 198, 201–202, 212–16, 220–21, 230, 234, 240
falsification, 63, 181
fellowship, 51, 86
feminism, 33, 52, 69, 109, 121, 123, 186, 188–89, 273
festivals, 237, 240
field of discourse, 45, 272
forensic rhetoric, 20, 91, 145
formal logic, 180
formation, x, xii, 95, 96, 105, 123, 137, 151, 153, 190, 192–93, 206, 286, 291
foundational(ism), 16, 37, 41, 75, 99, 110, 130–31, 179, 185–86, 188, 224–25, 229, 282, 284, 288
fourfold division of seminary curricula, ix, 7, 65, 73, 131, 171, 175, 179, 188, 294; *see also* theological encyclopedia
Fourth Lateran Council, 113
free will, 54
friendship, 86–87, 92, 105–106; with God, 86, 105

gender, 4, 48, 51–52, 69, 142, 268

globalism, globalization, 96, 152, 184–85, 196–198, 275–76
gnostic(ism), 118, 251
God, x, 8, 11, 33, 39, 58, 65, 67, 69, 75, 80–81, 86–108, 110, 118, 124, 125–26, 127, 130–36, 139–40, 146–48, 151, 161–62, 166, 171, 175, 196, 201–202, 207, 209–222, 226, 228–231, 236–42, 243–66, 267, 275–278, 281, 293–94, 296
God's authorship, 210
"good reasons," 50, 54, 55, 181–82, 190, 192, 205, 242, 284
gospel(s), 30, 52, 54, 56, 62, 70, 90–92, 94, 97, 102–103, 106–107, 166, 201–205, 207, 210, 213–16, 218, 223–25, 236, 239, 241, 248–49, 267–72, 274–75, 284–85, 292
grand narratives, *see* metanarratives
guild, academic, 9, 188, 193, 198

Hebrew scriptures, 211
Hellenism, Hellenization, 3, 22–23, 93, 225–26, 233–41
hermeneutic(s), 27, 37, 39, 77–81, 88, 93, 95, 100, 123, 130–31, 134–36, 138–39, 154–55, 159–61, 165, 182, 241, 276, 284, 288, 292
hierarchy, 7, 51–53, 178, 259, 261
holiness, 106, 140, 253
holism, 58, 94, 99–100
Holy Spirit, 15, 76, 89, 92–99, 102–106, 128, 140, 145, 217,

221, 229, 237, 240–41, 244, 246–252 *passim*, 266, 274–75

identification (Burke), 47–49, 57, 134, 148, 149, 221
ideology, 53, 64, 66, 119, 142
imagination, xi, 34, 79–80, 86–88, 91, 94, 96, 99, 102, 105, 115, 133, 137–38, 148, 154, 157, 210, 222, 258, 286, 291
incarnation, 104, 119, 252, 276
informal logic, 40, 44–45, 50
injustice, 103, 106, 143, 151
innovation, 188, 285, 293, 296
inspiration, 54, 89, 99, 132, 136, 234, 274–75
integration, 2, 4, 12, 73, 81, 87, 114–15, 132, 166, 172, 179–80, 190, 192, 211, 243, 292
interdependence, 36, 44, 67, 146, 212, 219, 258
interdisciplinarity, 35, 73, 131, 151, 185–87, 194–196
interreligious dialogue, 106
Israel, 88, 161–62, 238

judge, 113, 135, 142–43, 235, 239
judgment, 20–27, 76, 91, 94, 97, 99, 101, 108, 117, 133–35, 138, 141–43, 145–47, 165–66, 183, 185, 202, 210, 213, 217, 236
judicial rhetoric, 20, 24, 29, 113, 155–56, 204
justice, 46, 97, 99, 103, 114, 146, 159, 277

kataphatism, 228

kingdom, *see* Reign of God; two kingdoms
knowledge of God, 136, 228–29, 253–54

law of non-contradiction, 233
lawyer(s), *see* courtroom as a metaphor for rhetoric
leadership, x, 104, 150, 174, 177, 188, 190, 193, 195, 278, 282–83, 285, 289–291
legitimacy, 45, 57, 63–64, 67–68, 71, 74, 75–77, 80–81, 120, 155, 178, 254
liberation, 52, 56, 134, 141, 148, 155, 186, 188, 232
liberty, 52–53
liturgy, 95, 140, 147–48, 189, 225, 236, 238–40, 247, 274, 288, 293
logic: formal, 180; informal, 40, 44–45, 50; universal, 144, 233, 240
logos, x, 8, 18, 21, 36, 88, 91, 95–98, 106, 133–34, 138, 140, 148, 182, 241, 283, 286, 290
Lord, 68, 92, 140, 274, 292

meaning, 37, 39, 48, 56, 95–96, 110, 120, 123, 133–34, 137–40, 142, 154, 166, 171, 205–208, 211, 213, 217, 221–22, 233, 251, 267, 269, 281, 291, 295
media, 64, 149, 163, 194, 216
medieval, 28, 30, 66, 77–78, 81, 113, 183–84, 224, 242, 249
memory, 12, 43, 94, 96, 102, 124, 128, 151, 207, 252

message, 29, 44, 46–47, 56, 104, 107, 150, 202, 206, 208–211, 213–14, 218, 221–22, 263, 270–71, 273; *see also* logos
metanarratives, 61, 63, 112, 185
Middle Ages, *see* medieval
mission, ix, 30, 58, 86, 87, 92, 103–105, 119, 151, 234, 252, 275–77, 282, 286, 289–292
moral(ity), xii, 16, 24, 30, 32, 55, 94, 105–106, 111, 113–16, 118, 161, 164, 173, 176, 178, 186, 191–92, 283, 292
multicultural(ism), 190, 241
multidisciplinarity, *see* interdisciplinarity

narrative paradigm, 46–50, 54–56, 58
New Jerusalem, 213, 235
New Testament, 7, 10, 11, 14, 20, 22, 29, 72, 75, 81, 91–92, 97–98, 201–222, 288, 291
nonverbal communication, 35, 47, 48, 51, 53, 57, 117
nouns, 228, 246, 249

objectivity, 4, 8, 14, 15, 35, 36, 44, 101, 112, 121, 122, 137, 139, 154, 206, 213–14, 282
oral(ity), 20, 35, 36, 56, 88, 205, 207–208, 210, 212, 255, 262
Orthodox, 104, 224–25, 235, 260
orthodoxy, 94–95, 103, 132, 224–226, 241
orthopraxis, 94–95, 132

panegyric, 92

particularity, 16, 161–62, 294
pathos, x, 8, 18, 21, 36, 88, 91, 94–95, 97–98, 102, 106, 133–34, 138–40, 182, 241, 283, 286, 288
peace, 140–41, 148
pedagogy, 6–8, 26, 71–72, 109–113, 125–26, 152, 161, 164–65, 167, 263, 268
penitence, 114, 118
performative speech, 124
perichōrēsis, 237, 264
Phaedrus, 16, 227
phronēsis, 177, 277, 286, 291
pistis, 98, 101
pluralism, 31, 34, 42, 120, 131, 133, 153–54, 156–57, 164, 185–86, 190–91, 193–94, 290, 295
poetry, 15, 30, 32, 231
politics, 15, 17–18, 28, 32, 119, 151, 176, 219, 222, 249, 276
polysemy, 57, 270, 275
polyvalence, 270, 275
positive science, 174–75, 179–80
post-Christian worldview, 2–4, 7, 75, 264, 267, 294; see also *postmodernism; secularism*
postmodern(ism), 3, 5–7, 9, 14–15, 32–34, 36, 62–64, 71–77, 80–82, 95, 111, 121–22, 126, 130, 133–35, 137, 155, 158, 159, 180, 185–187, 191, 194, 223, 226–27, 229–31, 233, 240–41, 264, 270, 276, 294
practical reasoning, 6–7, 35, 38, 40, 44–46, 177, 184, 285, 291; *see also* phronēsis

practical theology, x, 7–8, 81, 148, 165, 171–175, 177–180, 188, 190, 193–198
prayer, 12, 44, 54–57, 68, 89, 126, 128, 140, 148, 163, 238
preaching, 3, 11, 30, 39, 56–58, 81, 90, 93–94, 103, 166, 189, 193, 201–202, 207, 213–14, 220-21, 222, 236, 241, 250, 267–78, 283
privatization, 111, 289
probability, 15, 19, 30, 80, 203, 204, 218–19, 285
processions, divine, 243–55
proclamation, ix, 3, 11, 56, 90, 96–98, 102–103, 112, 144–45, 164, 207, 210, 212, 218–21, 238, 267–278
proofs, 21, 64, 97, 99, 133, 137, 219; *see also* evidence
prophets, 210, 216
propositional truth, 90, 93
Protestant(ism), 42–43, 104, 114, 123, 150, 162, 171, 199, 224
prudence, *prudentia*, 26, 155, 177
public affairs, 33, 131, 152, 180
public policy, 150, 166
public theology, 9, 110, 148, 150–158, 161–164, 167, 241, 290
publication, publishing, 45, 70, 163, 264, 285

rational(ity), xii, 2–4, 28, 30, 35, 41–56 *passim*, 85, 101, 110, 116, 119–21, 131, 138, 158, 161, 171–72, 179, 180–95, 197, 205, 236, 255, 277, 287

rational-world paradigm, 45–46, 55
real relations, 245–48
reasoning, 6–7, 16–17, 35, 38, 40, 41, 44–46, 66, 69, 79–80, 99, 158, 177, 181–184, 227–31, 233, 237–240, 260, 286, 291
reception of an argument, 27, 73, 93–97, 102–104, 150, 160, 165, 271
redemption, 118, 142, 148, 251
Reign of God, 92,
relations, relationality, 68, 103–106, 114, 146, 205, 242–50, 255–261, 263, 287
relativism, 39, 120, 130, 135, 139, 147, 233, 235, 240, 282
relativity, 39, 234, 282
religious discourse, 121, 132, 206, 213
religious education, 186, 195–96
religious language, 10, 206–208
religious studies, 68, 76, 119–123, 125, 150, 164
religious tolerance, 42
Renaissance humanism, 191
resurrection, 92, 119, 217
revelation, 8, 85–97, 103, 108, 110, 122, 140, 159, 161–62, 175, 215–218, 220, 243, 253
rhetor, xi, 17, 24, 26, 47, 73, 88, 108, 130, 191, 210, 260–61, 282, 295
rhetoric of relationality, 11, 267, 276–278
rhetoric of science, 179, 185, 195
rhetorical competence, 191, 194

rhetorical criticism, 10, 14, 202–206, 214, 221, 269, 272–73, 283
rhetorical elements: *see* argument; audience; character; ethos; logos; pathos
rhetorical hermeneutics, 160, 165
rhetorical homiletics, 9, 267–78
rhetorical norms, 181–84
rhetorical situation, 11, 91, 133, 147, 154, 203, 205, 272
rhetorical turn, 130, 171, 178–81, 185, 193, 197–98, 205
Roman Catholicism, 42, 100, 104, 113–15, 122, 150, 224
Roman rhetoric, 23–30, 34, 153, 156, 255
rule models, 180–81, 184

salvation, 86, 93, 100, 116
sanctification, 86, 104
science(s): as knowledge (= Gk. epistēmē, Lat. scientia),, 16, 23–24, 172–200, 233; natural, 27, 45, 115, 131, 265; modern ("objective"), 36, 37, 63, 64, 66–69, 72–82, 120–21, 171; social 2, 195–197, 265, 293–94
scripture(s), 62, 67, 72–81, 95–96, 128, 148, 191, 201–222, 229, 240, 264, 281–84, 292; *see also* Bible; New Testament
secular(ism), 14, 25, 63, 66–67, 109–27 *passim*, 178, 196, 214, 216
selfhood, 112, 115, 124–25
sermon(s), 40, 44, 46, 58, 66, 129, 204, 210, 232, 255, 267–78, 285; *see also* preaching; proclamation
sin, 76, 92, 110–14, 220, 236, 238, 274
skepticism, 26, 42, 112, 154
slavery, 54–56
social sciences, *see* science, social
soul, 115, 118, 229
speaker, 6, 18, 20–22, 25–27, 36, 39–40, 44, 89–104 *passim*, 116, 136–140, 146–47, 153–54, 202, 207, 209–211, 219, 221–22, 230, 235, 256–66 *passim*, 270–71, 273–75, 296
speech-act theory, 295; *see also* performative speech
spirit: *see* Holy Spirit; spirituality
spiritual(ity), 56, 77, 113, 153, 166, 184, 216, 230, 265, 274
stasis theory, 235
style, stylistics, 8, 14, 19–22, 25–26, 36, 108, 164, 203, 205–206, 237
substantive(s), 246–250, 258
syllogism, 19, 225, 227, 240

teacher(s), 8, 62, 94, 120, 123–26, 153, 197, 228, 283; *see also* pedagogy
teaching, 3, 6, 9–10, 39, 75, 103, 107, 109–127 *passim*, 145–46, 148, 161, 164–65, 172, 189, 193, 196–97, 206, 214, 243–44, 262–264, 283, 293–94; *see also* teachers, pedagogy
teachings (doctrines), 68, 90–93, 243–44, *see also* doctrine
technē, 15, 64, 132, 267, 277

tenure, academic, x, 163, 193
testimony, 6–7, 29, 89, 99, 102, 121, 130, 134–48, 149–67 *passim*, 201, 212, 215, 216, 218, 243
"texts of terror" (Trible), 89, 193
theological encyclopedia, , ix, 7, 65, 73, 131, 171, 175, 179, 188, 293–94; *see also* fourfold division
theories of practice, 195–98
trinitarian, Trinity, 9, 13, 67–68, 74–77, 86–91, 96, 103–106, 117, 160, 196, 228, 237, 243–66, 275
tropes, 6–7, 29, 92, 109, 112, 114, 132, 137, 140–41, 147
tropological interpretation, 79
truth, 7, 16–17, 38–44, 65, 75, 90, 93–94, 97, 100, 110–26 *passim*, 127, 130–47, 152, 154, 182, 192, 205–207, 213, 218–20, 225, 231, 233–36, 262, 266, 270, 274, 281–82, 291, 295
two kingdoms, 220
typological exegesis, 78

universal audience, 122, 154
universal logic, 144, 233, 240
universal reason, 161; *see also* rationality
universities, xii, 1–2, 131, 134, 151, 162, 171–91, 264–65, 287; of Berlin, 2, 65, 173, 264–65, 281; of Paris, 61, 65, 82

validity, 39, 64, 73, 76, 162, 197, 209, 222, 227

verb(s), 247, 258
verbal: communication, 35, 47–48, 51, 53, 57, 89; descriptions of relations, 247–249, 256, 258
violence, 24, 43, 137, 141–42, 144–47, 290–91, 296
virtue(s), 22, 24, 26, 39–40, 69, 115, 173, 191–92, 226, 234, 266

wisdom, x–xi, 21–24, 50, 52, 54, 66–68, 94, 99, 153, 163, 178, 207, 262, 277
witness, 94, 97, 102–105, 136, 140–45, 149–52, 164, 202, 211, 215, 217–219, 292; *see also* testimony
Word of God, 8, 89, 94, 201–22
word, *see* language; logos; Word of God
worship, 56–58, 86, 90, 93, 96, 103, 113, 147–48, 188, 212, 231, 235, 267, 286, 293–94

www.ingramcontent.com/pod-product-compliance
Lightning Source LLC
Chambersburg PA
CBHW031435230426
43668CB00007B/536